IPA

**Brewing Techniques,
Recipes and the
Evolution of
INDIA PALE ALE**

D0980410

MITCH STEELE

brewers
publications

A Division of the
Association of Brewers
Boulder, Colorado

Brewers Publications
A Division of the Brewers Association
PO Box 1679, Boulder, Colorado 80306-1679
BrewersAssociation.org

Printed in the United States of America.

10 9 8 7 6 5 4 3 2 1

ISBN: 978-1-938469-00-8

Library of Congress Cataloging-in-Publication Data

Steele, Mitch.
IPA : brewing techniques, recipes, and the evolution of India pale ale / by Mitch Steele.
p. cm.
Includes bibliographical references and index.
ISBN 978-1-938469-00-8 (alk. paper)
1. Ale. 2. Brewing. I. Title. II. Title: India pale ale.
TP578.S74 2012
663'.42–dc23
                    2012014552

Publisher: Kristi Switzer
Technical Editors: Steve Parkes, Matt Brynildson
Copy Editing: Daria Labinsky, Theresa van Zante
Index: Doug Easton
Production and Design Management: Stephanie Johnson Martin
Cover and Interior Design: Julie White
Cover Photography: John Edwards Photography

CONTENTS

Foreword vii

Acknowledgments xiii

Introduction 1

1. **English Beer and Ale Prior to 1700** 9

2. **The 1700s and the Birth of IPA** 15
   Beers of the 1700s 15
   Beer on Boats 19
   East India Company and Hodgson's Bow Brewery 21
   Ingredients in the 1700s 28
   The Pale Ale Brewing Process 31
   Hodgson's Bow Pale Ale Recipe 34

3. **The Burton IPA: 1800–1900** 39
   Burton's Entry into the Indian Market 42
   What's in a Name? Becoming India Pale Ale 46
   A Changing World 49

4. **Brewing the Burton IPA** 61
   Ingredients 67
   Beer Specifications 75
   Domestic IPA 78
   The Burton IPA Brewing Process 79

5. **IPA Brewing around the World: 1800–1900** 95
   England: London and Other Areas 95
   Scotland 102

United States 109

Canada 119

Australia. 120

India 121

IPA in Decline 122

6. IPA Post–World War I 123

England 123

United States 132

7. The Craft-Beer IPA Revolution 139

8. IPA Variations. 165

Double/Imperial IPA 165

Brewing Double IPA 169

Black IPA. 170

The Story of Stone Sublimely Self-Righteous Ale 175

Belgian IPA 178

Session IPA. 180

Triple IPA. 181

White IPA. 181

9. IPA Ingredients and Brewing Techniques 183

Malt 183

Specialty Malt 185

Brewing Sugars 185

Water 187

Milling Your Grain. 188

Mashing 189

Hops. 192

Hop Products 195

Developing the Hop Recipe and Calculating Bitterness . . . 202

Hopping Techniques in the Brewhouse 205

Final Thoughts on Formulating a Hop Recipe. 209

Fermenting Techniques for IPAs 210

Factors That Impact Yeast Performance
    and Flavor Development. 214

Commercial Dry-Hopping Procedures. 219

Brewing Tips by Style 224

10. IPA Recipes 229

Recipe Specifics. 229

Historical Recipes 231

Early Craft-Brewing Recipes 243

Contemporary U.S. Craft-Brewing Recipes 249

Contemporary British Recipes. 267

Double IPA Recipes 275

Black IPA Recipes 285

Appendix A: Analysis of Various IPAs

from the 1800s. 294

Appendix B: 1900s English IPA Analytical Profiles . . .298

Appendix C: Reading Historical Brewing Records . .305

Appendix D: Conducting Your Own IPA Hunt. . . . 309

Notes. 315

Bibliography 321

Recipe Index. 329

Index 331

FOREWORD

When I was a young technician in the hops lab at Kalamazoo Spice Extraction Company (now Kalsec Inc.), I read a news brief in a beer industry magazine about a craft brewer from California taking a job with Anheuser-Busch. For some reason this story intrigued me. Was this craft brewer going on a mission? Was he on a quest for greater knowledge? Or was he selling out? I myself am a curious brewer who has always been interested in visiting larger breweries to learn about cutting-edge brewing technology. I have hundreds—actually, thousands—of pictures of lauter tuns, beer pumps, gearboxes, valve sets, pipe fences, fermenters, yeast brinks, and the like, which I have captured at breweries all over the world. Hoping to glean gems of information that might lead me closer to making a better beer, at Master Brewers Association of the Americas (MBAA) or American Society of Brewing Chemists meetings I'm always keen to strike up conversations with brewers, engineers, and scientists who work in the major brewing leagues. I especially like conversing with the old guard—the brewers who have been in the industry for decades and have seen it all go down.

It's often said that one of the most difficult beers in the world to perfect is an American-style light lager, because there is nothing at all to hide potential defects. This is a beer that has evolved by losing all its fur and fangs. Everything the brewer does is left naked in the glass with nothing to cover it up except carbonation, sweetness, and light yeast character. No hop aroma, no chewy, smoky malt middle, and no bitter hop finish. It must be brewed consistently, centering on balance and drinkability, and be executed without a flaw.

In the hops lab back in Kalamazoo, we would analyze these light lager beers with gas chromatographs and high-pressure liquid chromatography machines. We were not only able to measure the IBUs of these beers, but we could break down, evaluate, and report the individual isomers of iso-alpha acid present. We looked at the hop oil profiles and reported to the brewers exactly what their hopping recipes had produced to the finest detail. Most of the time these beers were created using downstream bittering extracts, so that hop aroma wouldn't get in the way of drinkability and all hop notes could be controlled.

The brewers of these light lagers have the greatest resources and technology ever applied to beer at their disposal. They hold the technology to create any beer style imaginable. If anyone in the world could replicate a classic stout, Pilsner, or India pale ale (IPA), they could. They are the brewing equivalent of Microsoft, BMW, and NASA, but for some reason they choose not to brew New-World IPAs in their own breweries. Maybe the world of beer has changed too much since the 1800s to come full circle? Maybe something was lost in the massive brewing vats and the vast lager cellars of these breweries that pushed them to a point of no return? Maybe the majority of the world's beer drinkers are not ready to turn back time? Possibly, for the large modern breweries, acquisitions are an easier way to test the viability of new styles than brewing these risky beers themselves? Only time will tell, but for now the greater brewing world has been distracted from what beer once was. The Industrial Revolution, Prohibition, two world wars, and Depression-era economics, followed by brand consolidation, all played a part in the world's changing tastes in beer. The quest for the ultimate balance and drinkability filtered away the distinctiveness and character that once was. Light lagers took over and changed the definition of beer and ale for the average consumer.

In the mid-1990s I was fortunate to work with Greg Hall at the Goose Island Beer Company and to help formulate Goose Island IPA. Being a great beer formulator, Hall knew exactly what he wanted in an IPA. Together we traveled to the West Coast and experienced firsthand what brewers were doing with this beer style at that time. Of course, Hall had some specific requests based on his additional travels in England and his understanding of Old-World IPAs. He wanted to brew the beer with no specialty malt, only pale ale malt; Burtonized water; English ale yeast; and a sturdy hopping regime.

I helped design the hopping program and figured out how to run a beer with an excessive amount of hops through the brewery. I also insisted on adding Centennial hops from Yakima, Washington, to the recipe, thereby lending a New-World hop aroma to the beer. We experimented with dry hopping by using T90 pellets, and realized that adding the hops to green beer, just at the end of primary fermentation, greatly accentuated the hop character and afforded a bright beer that could be turned over in a reasonable amount of time. A blend of English and American hops helped us refine the flavor and create something that was very unique. From the moment Goose Island IPA was released, it drew considerable attention. Today it continues to grow in sales and in popularity at an astounding rate. We found ourselves on the leading edge of a revolution by simply re-creating a modern version of what was a popular style 150 years earlier. IPA is currently the fastest-growing style in the craft-brewing segment.

Reading this book reminds me that beer history is repeating itself. What has developed into a real craft-brewing business started when a brewer decided to market a beer with distinct flavor and character. This is hardly an original idea, but with modern technology and new raw materials, our craft-brewing movement is carving a permanent and unique mark into beer history! Two hundred years from now, someone just like Mitch Steele will retell the story from yet another perspective—one that discusses how American IPA resurfaced and stormed a nation of light lager drinkers. How does this new chapter end? We will have to wait and see.

As Mitch tells us, the raw materials that truly define craft brewing are American hops—more specifically, the "4 Cs" of hoppy brewing: Cascade, Centennial, Chinook, and Columbus. Their citrusy, fruity

American character has become one of the defining notes that differentiate American craft-brewed ales from all other beers. It is difficult to imagine modern craft brewing without them. Thanks to Charles Zimmerman, Al Haunold, Stan Brooks and their U.S. hop-breeding programs, we are able to create beers with a bold, defining character, which we can truly call our own—American style. At no time or place has this been more evident to me than in my recent travels throughout Europe, lecturing for Hop Growers of America.

Tasting American IPAs and rubbing American hops with European brewing students is an experience I wish I could share with every brewer back home. I can't tell you how many times I have heard "This is crazy," "This is not beer," or "This would never sell in Germany," as I see these brewers' eyes light up with excitement.

Each year the curiosity for these beers increases, and the demand for American aroma hops expands into new markets. Jean De Clerk, in his 1957 book, *A Textbook of Brewing*, states that "American hops are characterized by a rather fruity flavor which is unsuitable for European beers." And yet now, 55 years later, beers are surfacing throughout Europe that showcase new American hop varieties. The seeds of the revolution have taken root. What we don't know is how widespread this trend will become. Are we sure that we want it to spread throughout the world? Do we really dream of the day when large, shareholder-driven companies take hold of a style like IPA and turn it into a product for the masses? Maybe we do, maybe we don't. But at this point we can be proud that our New-World IPAs have found a serious audience, and at the same time we can hope that our hard work and passion don't meet the same fate that IPA met during its last historical run.

I owe Mitch a great deal of gratitude for introducing me to Ian Jeffery and helping me land a collaborative brewing gig at Marston's Beer Company in Burton-on-Trent, which is, as you will read, a key city in the history of IPAs. At Marston's I was able to see the last active Burton Union fermentation program left in the world and to brew hoppy American-style pale ale. The casks that we produced were served at pubs all over England.

Mitch is correct when he says that every brewer owes him- or herself a pilgrimage to Burton-on-Trent to absorb the brewing history of that place. Although it may not be a tourist destination, Burton-on-Trent is the true epicenter of modern pale ale brewing. Mitch spent some quality time in this brewing mecca, meeting with brewing historians, publicans, and brewers, so he could collect firsthand information for this book. Now he has taken what he has learned and neatly woven it into an engaging and eye-opening history of IPA blended with immensely technical brewing information. Mitch not only debunks the classic story of what the first IPAs really were and how they were made, but also chronicles the tragic account of ale's rise and fall over the last three centuries. Then he goes on to include a serious volume of recipes and techniques from classic old-world IPAs to modern craft-style double IPAs. This book should sit on every brewer's bookshelf.

I have known Mitch for more than a decade, and yet I can't exactly say when or where I first met him. Quite possibly it was at the Anheuser-Busch booth at the Great American Beer Festival® while tasting his pilot batch of IPA, or maybe it was at an MBAA meeting on the East Coast, where I listened to him lecture on brewing techniques. Even more likely it was after a session at a Craft Brewers Conference, where several of us sat at a pub and discussed the intricacies of brewing hoppy beers. (Like-minded brewers seem to always find each other and share information.) Whenever or wherever it was, since that time I have admired his noble name, his brewing knowledge, and his beers.

It was a wonderful day when I heard that Mitch was leaving Anheuser-Busch and coming back to craft brewing to head up production at Stone Brewing Co. Perhaps he is an American brewing prodigal son? For sure he is a curious brewer who took a serious walk on the other side. He has studied abroad, learned from the best, and taken some time to share his passion with us. It is an honor to say that I have brewed with Mitch and can call him a friend.

Cheers to one of the great brewers of our time and to his epic book on India pale ales.

Matt Brynildson
Brewmaster
Firestone Walker Brewing Company
Brewer of Union Jack and Double Jack IPA
Paso Robles, California

ACKNOWLEDGMENTS

I was continually amazed by the kindness and generosity I received as I requested time for interviews and discussions from people I consider experts on the subject of IPA and historical brewing. Almost without fail, the people in the business whom I contacted to ask questions for this book responded enthusiastically, and generously gave me some time and shared a lot of information. Not only was it extremely gratifying, but it cemented my belief that we all work in the very best business in the world, and that brewers, by and large, are simply just "good people."

This book wouldn't have been possible without the help and support of so many. Please accept my apologies in advance for anyone I may have inadvertently left out:

All the brewers in England who hosted me, submitted to interviews, gave me tips on where to find some great information, and in some cases, provided recipes: IPA Hunters Mark Dorber, Roger Putman, Ray Anderson, Tom Dawson, Paul Bayley, Steve Brooks, and Steve Wellington; Emma Gilliland, Des Gallagher, Paul Bradley, and Gen Upton of Marston's Beer Company; Bruce Wilkinson and Geoff Mumford of Burton Bridge Brewery; Alastair Hook, Peter Haydon, and Steve Schmidt of Meantime Brewing Company; John Keeling and Derek Prentice of Fullers; John Gilliland, Gill Turner, and William Lees-Jones of J. W. Lees Brewery; James

Watt and Martin Dickie of BrewDog; and Kelly Ryan, Stefano Cossi, Alex Buchanon, and James Harrison of Thornbridge Brewery.

The American brewers who helped me find information, submitted to interviews, and in some cases, submitted recipes: Neil Evans and George de Piro of C. H. Evans Brewing Company; Peter Egelston, J. T. Thompson, and David Yarrington of Smuttynose Brewing Company; Mark Carpenter of Anchor Brewing Company; Ken Grossman of Sierra Nevada Brewing Company; Teri Fahrendorf, Vinnie Cilurzo, Adam Avery, Tomme Arthur, Jeff Bagby, Doug Odell, and Garrett Oliver; Al Marzi and Charlie Storey of Harpoon; Tim Rastetter of Thirsty Dog; John Maier of Rogue; Larry Sidor of Deschutes; Mike Roy, Fred Scheer, Bill Pierce, Sam Calagione, and David Kammerdeiner of Dogfish Head; Matt Cole of Fat Head's Brewery; Greg Hall and Brett Porter of Goose Island; and the amazing Vermont brewers Steve Polewacyk of Vermont Pub and Brewery, John Kimmich of The Alchemist, Shaun Hill of Hill Farmstead Brewery, and Sean Lawson of Lawson's Finest Liquids.

The writers, beer bloggers, and beer historians: Pete Brown, Martyn Cornell, Ron Pattinson, James McCrorie, Roger Protz, Gregg Smith, and Ray Daniels; Bil Corcoran of *MyBeerBuzz.com*; Brad Ring of *Brew Your Own*; Don Marshall of the Oxford Brookes University Library; Alex Barlow; Philip Withers of Thunder Road Brewing Company in Australia; Nate Wiger and Corey Gray of BeerLabels.com; Dennis Robinson of Seacoast New Hampshire; Richard Adams, former president of the Portsmouth Athenaeum; and homebrewers and beer researchers Christopher Bowen and Kristen England.

I also want to thank those who, over the years, have supported me, taught me, and inspired me as a brewer. Without them, I wouldn't be where I am today to have this wonderful opportunity: Michael Lewis, my brewing professor at the University of California, Davis; Bill Millar, who gave me my first professional brewing opportunity at San Andreas Brewing Company; Judy Ashworth, who was the first publican to pour one of my beers; Marty Watz and John Serbia, who first hired me at Anheuser-Busch in 1992, and Greg Brockman and Doug Hamilton, who showed me the ropes in my first job there; Mike Meyer, Doug

Muhleman, Paul Anderson, Tom Schmidt, Dan Driscoll, Frank Vadurro, and Hans Stallman, who gave me many great opportunities and mentored me through several positions at Anheuser-Busch.

The brewing business is largely about friendship, and I want to thank those brewing friends of mine not already listed who have been there for me over the years and whom I respect for their most excellent brewing skills: Jim Krueger, Kevin Stuart, and Peter Cadoo; Anheuser-Busch "buds" George Reisch, Jim Canary, Otto Kuhn, Paul Mancuso, Dan Kahn, Rick Shippey, and John Hegger; Paul Davis, Scott Houghton, Jaime Schier, and Will Meyers; and my Brew Free or Die friends, Phil Sides, Shaun O'Sullivan, Andy Marshall, and Tod Mott.

Thanks also goes to the Brewers Association team who have supported me throughout my career, no matter whom I was brewing for: Charlie Papazian, Bob Pease, Nancy Johnson, Paul Gatza, and Chris Swersey. And to "Team Stone" for always being amazing: Michael Saklad, who carted me all over New England to learn about the origins of black IPA; Todd Colburn and Tyler Graham, who helped with all the photos in this book; our awesome Brew Crew; and photographer John Trotter.

Some very special thanks go to Kristi Switzer of Brewers Publications for giving me this opportunity and for being a never-ending source of encouragement; Ron Pattinson, Martyn Cornell, Steve Parkes, and Matt Brynildson for doing a technical fact check of the material presented here; Steve Wagner, for giving me the opportunity of a lifetime to join him and Greg Koch at Stone Brewing Co., for being my research and traveling partner for the material presented here, and for being a continual inspiration and mentor as a brewer.

Finally, I want to thank my family: my parents, Bud and Fay Steele; my in-laws, Pat and Kathy Coleman; my kids, Sean and Caleigh; and most especially my wife, Kathleen, for her love and support, and for never complaining while I spent many weekends and vacation days at work on this book.

INTRODUCTION

India pale ale (IPA) has been my favorite beer style since I first tried one back in the 1980s. I'm not sure who brewed that first one, but I do remember being completely hooked by the hop flavors in beers such as Anchor Liberty Ale, Sierra Nevada Celebration Ale, Rubicon IPA, and Triple Rock's IPA when I was first starting out as a craft brewer in the San Francisco Bay Area. And of course, the 1980s also is when I first learned the "history" of IPA—the story we've all heard, that this stronger, more highly hopped beer was invented in the 1700s and was brewed specifically to survive the six-month ocean voyage from England to India. As I have discovered in researching this book, that story is a myth, but the real history of IPA is no less fascinating.

Despite my growing love for the IPA style, I never really had the opportunity to brew IPAs until many years into my brewing career. When I was brewing at San Andreas, owner Bill Millar wanted to keep all his beers sessionable—an admirable goal and one that worked well for us in the small farming town of Hollister, California. So as much as I wanted to brew an IPA, the style didn't really fit into Millar's plans, and I was never very successful at broaching the subject with him. This was in the very early 1990s, and the IPA style hadn't really taken off yet.

Then I joined Anheuser-Busch (A-B) and learned so much about brewing lagers. But of course, IPA was not a style that was on that company's radar. Even after I moved to the New Products Group and we test-brewed one or two excellent IPAs at A-B's 15-barrel pilot brewery, the beers never really got further than our taste panel. But we once served a test batch of our IPA at the Great American Beer Festival (GABF), and what sticks out in my memory is the number of people (including Jim Koch from Boston Beer Company) who told me that it was the best beer we were serving. Out of the 15 beers we were pouring during that festival, our IPA was the one that got people talking. Still, our marketing people wouldn't even consider it. Imagine if Anheuser-Busch had released a 70 IBU, 6.5% abv IPA, dry hopped with Columbus and Cascade hops, back in 1996.

My IPA education continued as I started homebrewing again when I lived in St. Louis, and I pursued that hobby all the way through my time with Anheuser-Busch in Merrimack, New Hampshire. In the mid-1990s, I had the opportunity to travel to San Diego for several business trips and was amazed by beers such as Blind Pig IPA and Port's IPA. Roughly 75 percent of what I brewed at home was some sort of IPA— especially double IPAs later on, when I became aware of that style. As I started judging at the GABF and the World Beer Cup in the late 1990s, I always requested IPA and double IPA as my top preferences to judge in order to taste and to learn more about them. San Diego pub owner Tom Nickel (then head brewer at Oggi's Brewing Company) was on the panel at the very first judging session for double/imperial IPA in 2003, and he gave the rest of us judges an amazing primer on the new double IPA style—what to look for as positive flavor attributes and as negative attributes, and what kinds of brewing techniques were being used to produce that massive hop flavor. I still have my notes from that tasting session, and a few months later I added to them when Nickel and Vinnie Cilurzo gave an excellent presentation on the double IPA style at the 2004 Craft Brewers Conference. In this presentation, they imparted the key elements to brewing great double IPAs. Their brewing tips are well represented in this book.

From 1999 to 2006, when I lived in New Hampshire, I was in the Brew Free or Die homebrew club. My knowledge of great IPA expanded tremendously. We all were brewing IPAs, and at our meetings we sampled some that were becoming available from craft breweries such as Stone Brewing Co., Russian River, and Dogfish Head. Both Castle Spring's Lucknow IPA and Harpoon IPA became staples in my beer refrigerator, and I continued to research and explore the style at every opportunity (and yes, that meant plenty of tasting!). In 2006 we finally developed and released a short-lived IPA from Anheuser-Busch's Merrimack brewery. It was called Demon's Hopyard IPA after a popular New Hampshire hiking area, Devil's Hopyard. The test batch of this beer, for which a group of us developed the recipe, was amazing, and I couldn't wait to brew the real batches and get them released. (The original recipe is in this book.)

But at about that time, Stone Brewing Co. posted an ad on the Brewers Association Forum for a head brewer. Of course, being an IPA lover, I was already a huge fan not only of Stone's beers but also of the brewery and its business philosophy. I (semi) jokingly told my wife, Kathleen, about the ad, and we laughed about the idea of moving to San Diego, one of our favorite places. But the next day when Kathleen asked me if I had heard back from Stone, I realized she wasn't joking. Then we started talking seriously about leaving Anheuser-Busch and New Hampshire to join a brewery that made some of my favorite IPAs in the world.

I joined Stone in 2006 and never got to taste the full-sized batches of Demon's Hopyard IPA. But people back East told me it didn't have the hop character that the test batch had and was a disappointment, which I feel really bad about. I know we could have made it an excellent IPA with a little tweaking of the dry-hop process.

Regardless, I was now at Stone and had the pleasure and honor of brewing some of my all-time favorite IPAs as well as Stone's other great beers. To say I was in career heaven is an understatement. My IPA quest has continued here at Stone, with my involvement in formulating and brewing IPAs such as Stone 10th Anniversary IPA, Stone 11th Anniversary Ale, Stone 14th Anniversary Emperial IPA (a recipe that was directly inspired by the research for this book), and Stone 15th Anniversary Escondidian Imperial Black IPA. And I hope there will be many more IPAs in my brewing future.

When first approached about writing a book on IPA for Brewers Publications, I was, as you might suspect by now, very excited. I began researching IPA on the Internet, through blogs such as Martyn Cornell's *Zythophile* and Ron Pattinson's *Shut Up about Barclay Perkins*, and on Google Books. I quickly became aware that there was a ton of information on IPA brewing that hadn't really gotten out to craft-beer fans yet, and I was thrilled to be able to try and put it all together.

IPA is a beer style that has gone through many drastic changes throughout its history. There are at least three distinct versions of the beer. The first was the stock pale ale version from Hodgson, which evolved into the Burton version of the 1800s that was brewed with white malt and Goldings hops. It was brewed, and aged for a long time, to be crystal clear, very light colored, intensely hoppy, and elegant.

Then in the late 1800s, as the export business declined, domestic popularity of IPA grew. But temperance movements and taxation motivated brewers to brew lower-alcohol beers, so the IPA morphed into a lower-alcohol, less-hopped, and eventually unaged running beer, brewed with sugars, other adjuncts, and crystal malts. Finally, as craft brewers have revitalized the style, IPA has returned to its original alcohol and hopping levels, and it has become a vehicle to showcase the new American hop varieties that are being developed. The term "hop bomb" is often used to describe (in a positive way) today's craft IPA, and we brewers get as excited as any fan about trying IPAs with new hop varieties, new flavors, and style variations.

While doing research for this book, I met many passionate and knowledgeable brewers, beer writers, and beer historians who gave their time to talk with me about IPA. They generously shared what they knew in order to help make this book the best it could be. During interviews and research I discovered a lot about IPA that I didn't know. For example, no one really knows any details about the pale beer George Hodgson brewed and shipped to India. There are no records of what this beer's alcohol content was, what ingredients were used, or how it was brewed. Historians have posed what look to be very valid theories about this beer, based on known brewing practices at the time, advertisements, price lists, and tasting comments from brewers, writers, and India colonists. There is now a general consensus on the properties of Hodgson's pale beer, which was shipped to India and directly inspired the Burton brewers of the 1800s to develop their own version.

Shortly after I signed on to write this book, in the summer of 2009, I was at the White Horse Pub in London for a Stone event, where I was introduced to a homebrewer named James McCrorie. McCrorie sat down with me for almost two hours and told me everything he could about historical IPA brewing—information he had gathered while a member of the Durden Park Beer Circle in London. The Durden Park Beer Circle is a group of homebrewers who are passionate about historical English beers. They have researched old brewing logbooks to understand the recipes and procedures the brewers used. In the 1970s Dr. John Harrison and members of the Durden Park Beer Circle wrote and published *Old British Beers and How to Make Them,* an incredibly well-researched book that provides recipes and brewing procedures for historical versions of many English beer styles. McCrorie was the one who first told me about October ale and its possible link to Hodgson's IPA, the extra pale (or "white") malt used in the Burton IPA, the absence of crystal malts, and the importance of Scottish brewers in the development and the history of the 1800s IPA. To me, this was all new and fascinating information, and I wrote copious notes as he talked. We met again on a later trip, and McCrorie had samples of his homebrewed, 1800s-version IPA that were absolutely delicious, hoppy, bitter, crystal clear, and quite different from today's craft-brewed IPA.

On the same trip, I ran into Mark Dorber, the former landlord of the White Horse Pub and the current owner of the Anchor Pub in Walberswick, England. As we were chatting, I mentioned the book project to him, and he told me about the IPA symposium he had held at the White Horse Pub in the early 1990s. Several prominent brewers and historians attended, and each participant presented papers on IPA brewing, and in some cases, brought beers they had brewed. Dorber gave me a copy of the papers that were presented at the symposium, and much of that information is included here. He also invited me to look him up when I returned to Burton to do research.

When Stone co-founder and IPA research ally Steve Wagner and I started to prepare for that trip, Dorber got together with Roger Putman, former Bass brewmaster and now editor of *Brewer and Distiller*

International magazine, and together they planned a mind-blowing symposium for us. Included were Wagner and myself; Dorber and Putman; Ray Anderson, president of the Brewery History Society; Steve Wellington from Worthington's Museum Brewery; Tom Dawson, former Bass brewmaster; and Paul Bayley and Steve Brooks, former Marston's brewmasters. We were hosted at both the National Brewery Centre at Coors (formerly Bass) and the Marston's Brewery. For the better part of two days we toured Burton, looked at archived brewing books and logs, talked IPA history at length, and of course, drank a fair amount of beer! Much of what you are about to read in this book came from these discussions about Burton Union fermentations, historical and current IPA brewing, and the impact of IPA on the town of Burton-on-Trent. It was a once-in-a-lifetime experience for a beer geek like me, and I am forever indebted to Dorber and Putman for setting it up.

The IPA Hunters, gathered in front of Marston's pub. Back row, from left to right: Steve Wagner, Mark Dorber, Paul Bayley, Mitch Steele. Front row, from left to right: Steve Brooks, Ray Anderson, and Tom Dawson. Not pictured: photographer Roger Putman.

In early 2008 Wagner and I returned to England to brew an IPA for the Wetherspoon pub chain at Shepherd Neame Brewery (this recipe is available in *The Craft of Stone Brewing* [Ten Speed Press, 2011]). While at a release party for that beer in London, I met beer writer Pete Brown. He told me an amazing story about how he had just replicated the IPA journey from Burton-on-Trent all the way to India, and that he was now writing a book about his experience and the history of IPA. His book, *Hops and Glory* (Macmillan, 2009), is not only a great historical account of IPA and the East India Company but also a fantastic read and very funny. Over a few beers and an English vegetable platter we discussed IPA, and he willingly provided notes and data from his own research to help with this book.

Brown was also kind enough to introduce me to Steve Wellington. Wellington was recently retired from Miller-Coors and for many years was the Worthington's White Shield brewer at the Museum Brewery at the National Brewery Centre in Burton-on-Trent. Not only did he brew the Calcutta IPA that Brown took with him on his trip to India, but he was genuinely one of the friendliest, nicest brewers I had ever met. He provided two recipes for this book, and he spent time helping me research IPA at the Museum Brewery, the National Brewing Centre, and the Bass Archives.

People who have written books and done research on IPA—such as aforementioned writers Pete Brown, Martyn Cornell, and Ron Pattinson, as well as author Roger Protz—have all been very generous with their time and their own research. These beer historians have painstakingly gone through old newspaper advertisements found in the British Library and other archives, brewing documents and literature, 200-year-old brewers' logs, and history books to piece together their own theories on IPA, much of which is documented in this book. Both Cornell and Pattinson have done incredible research on historical beer styles, and they fact-checked the material in this book. I thank them from the bottom of my heart for helping me make sure I got it right! Their work has put to rest many of the myths and conventional wisdoms about IPA and other historical beer styles, and I encourage anyone who reads this book to also read their blogs and their books to learn more about the amazing history of many beer styles that we all *think* we know about.

Brewing logbooks on the shelves of the archives at the National Brewery Centre in Burton-on-Trent. Most logs are ornate leather-bound books with detailed and exquisite handwriting inside.

My brewer friends have also been amazingly generous and forthcoming in contributing recipes and stories for this book. The result is the most comprehensive collection of IPA recipes ever seen. These range from some of the earliest recipes ever found to some of today's best classic craft-beer recipes from both the United States and Great Britain. And for the first time ever, we have officially released the recipes for Stone IPA, Stone 10th Anniversary IPA, Stone Sublimely Self-Righteous Ale, and Stone 14th Anniversary Emperial IPA. So get your brewing boots on and have some fun.

As I conclude the three-year project of writing this book, I look back and realize I've become more of an IPA geek than I ever was. Beer writer Stan Hieronymous told me early on that one of the hardest things about writing a book like this is knowing when to stop the research and to start writing. I totally agree with him. I am still researching as I finish this manuscript and hope to continue to learn more about historical brewing. I salute those researchers who share the desire to learn the truth about historical brewing techniques, and I applaud homebrewers, such as Christopher Bowen and Kristen England, and professional brewers, such as Dan Paquette, Tom Kehoe, Alastair Hook, John Keeling, and Derek Prentice, who have worked hard to re-create historical beers in their own breweries. There is still much to learn about many historical beer styles, and it is a fascinating subject that should open the doors to many long-forgotten beer styles and brewing techniques.

1 | ENGLISH BEER AND ALE PRIOR TO 1700

Ale it is called among men, and among gods, beer.
—*Old Norse Alvisimal, one of the first known mentions of "ale,"
from the 11th century*

So laugh, lads, and quaff, lads, twill make you stout and hale; through all my days, I'll sing the praise of brown October ale.
—*Reginald De Koven, song from* Robin Hood

Brewing in England appears to have started before the time of Christ and flourished during the Roman occupation, when English brewers supplied beer to Roman troops. The taverns that existed during Roman times were often marked with a pole (called an ale-stake), to which a bundle of evergreen leaves was attached. After England was conquered by the Normans in 1066, brewing became a more organized activity that was often done at the abbeys and the monasteries built following the invasion.

For the most part, the ale from these early times had only three ingredients: malted grain (mostly barley, but often wheat and oats were used), water, and yeast.[1] Boiling was not always part of the brewhouse process, and the use of herbs and other spices wasn't commonplace until later in the Middle Ages.[2] By the 1500s and 1600s, a sharp division and debate developed between brewers in England who brewed "ales" without hops (but occasionally with herbs and spices) and brewers who brewed "beer" with hops.

The spiced, unhopped ales were flavored with ingredients such as bog myrtle, yarrow, rosemary, sage, mugwort, ground ivy, and wormwood. Unhopped and unspiced ales continued to be brewed. They were occasionally mixed with honey, herbs, and fruits and heated for holiday celebrations (e.g., wassail and buttered ale) and for medicinal purposes.[3] The following is a description of ale from 1542:

> *made of malte and water, nothing else but yest, barme, or godesgood. Must be freshes and clear, must not be ropy or smoky, must not be drunk under V days olde. Newe ale is unwholesome, sowre ale and deade ale is unwholesome.[4]*

The use of hops in beer has uncertain origins, but at some point people recognized hops had a preservative value and used them in many beverages, including mead and beer, to help keep the drinks from spoiling.[5] The first beers with hops are thought to have been brewed in Central Europe, and references exist from AD 1150 about their preservative value. Hops are believed to have first been cultivated around 1100 or 1200 in Germany and in the 1300s in Holland, although there is now evidence, through archeological research, of substantial hop material found in waterlogged sites in western Switzerland and France that suggest hop cultivation as early as the sixth to ninth centuries.[6] The first hopped beer in England was probably imported from the Flanders area in the mid-1300s, and the first mention of beer brewing was noted in 1391 in the London City Letterbooks.[7] When Flemish immigrants settled around Kent, England, in the 1500s, they started growing hops and brewing hopped beers there.

For the next two centuries debates raged over whether hops were a proper ingredient for ale, with regulations and such being passed to separate and distinguish unhopped ale from hopped beer. But the tide was turning, and hopped beers gained a foothold in English breweries. By 1655, after high taxes were placed on hops imported from Europe, hops were grown in 14 counties in England. In 1710, Parliament banned the use of hop alternatives in the brewing of beer, and by 1800 more than 35,000 acres of hops were planted across the country.[8]

When hops were first used in English brewing, most English beers and ales were brewed on estates, in taverns, and at inns, and most brewing was done by women, who were known as alewives. By the 1500s commercial breweries that sold beer to taverns and other businesses had been established, mostly in the larger cities, but the commercial brewing industry didn't really start to dominate brewing until the first wave of the Industrial Revolution in the 1700s. Prior to that time much ale and beer was brewed by innkeepers and pub owners—and by families who used ale as nourishment and refreshment for peasants, servants, and family members. Most Englanders drank ale at every meal, because water supplies were never guaranteed to be free of bacteria and other impurities. Ale was a staple of the British lifestyle at the time, and it was said that in 1695, 28 percent of the annual per capita income in England went to ale and beer.[9] Men maintained their involvement in brewing through the establishment of the town-appointed position of the aleconner, who ensured beer quality and proper pricing, and by forming brewers guilds in the cities.

A wood carving of Elinore Rummin, the famous alewife of England (1624).

During this period, malt was often kilned over straw, peat, or wood and would usually be light amber to dark brown in color.[10] Smoky flavors often resulted from the kilning process, though these flavors were not desirable in the beer. This situation helped lead to the process of aging the beer in wood for extended periods, which helped mellow some of the smoky flavors and make the beer more palatable. Barley malt was not the only grain used in brewing; oats, wheat, millet, corn, peas, beans, and other grains were also used. "Mum," a nonbarley beer that became popular in 1600s London, was a strong ale brewed with wheat and occasionally oats and beans. It was spiced and casked for up to two years (less if placed on a boat; it appears that even in the 1600s, brewers realized that an ocean voyage could hasten the aging process).[11]

One of the most important technical developments to impact the brewing industry in the 1600s was the discovery of how to produce coke from coal. Coke is made by heating coal to extreme temperatures. This

Scene from an estate brewery.

drives off sulfur, tars, other gases, and the smoke-producing compounds that made coal unsuitable for kilning malt. The process is analogous to making charcoal from wood. Using coke as a heat source allowed for much better temperature control. Maltsters started using coke in the kiln about 1643, and by employing lower kilning temperatures, they were able to develop pale malt in the late 1600s. Brewers found several advantages to using pale malt, including the production of a beer free of smoky or peated flavors and with better extract recovery (i.e., stronger beer from the same amount of grain) from the brewhouse.[12]

English brewhouse practices from the 1600s typically employed multiple mashes from a single charge of malt. This process involves mashing in the malt with water, drawing off the resulting wort (without sparging, which wouldn't be introduced for another 100 years), and fermenting it as a strong ale. When that wort was drawn off the grain, the grain was mashed again with another charge of water, typically at a slightly higher temperature than the first mash. This process was repeated three or four times to produce worts with descending gravity levels for strong ales, table beers, and small beers.[13]

Brewing also was a seasonal activity, usually starting in October and ending in March or April. It was thought that pale malt didn't ferment effectively in temperatures higher than 72° F (22° C). The lack of refrigeration made fermentation temperature control difficult in the late spring and summer months, so typically, brewing was suspended during the warmer seasons. Hops were known in this period to be a preservative, and hopping rates were increased sequentially, so that by March worts were hopped as much as two to three times higher than for beers brewed in January.[14]

The development of pale malt led directly to the development of several new beer styles, including a golden-colored ale known as pale ale. It was first seen in about 1675 and became one of the world's most popular beer styles 200 years later.

Over the next couple of centuries, the use of pale malt led to the creation of several other new and popular beer styles, including Pilsner and helles lager and the tripels of Belgium. Today pale malt has become a standard in the brewing industry; brewers now use pale malt as a base in almost all their beers and colored "specialty" malts for flavor and color.

One of the earliest English strong pale beers was known as the October beer and ale. It was brewed in October and November by using only freshly harvested hops and pale malt. October beers were well-aged beers put into barrels with dry hops for aging after a monthlong primary fermentation. During the warmer summer months, the bungs in the barrels were loosened as the fermentation restarted. The aging process was typically one year but could go as long as two years before the beer was tapped and consumed. October beers had high starting gravities of 19–25 °P (1.100 SG), were hopped at two ounces of hops per gallon, and had an alcohol content of 8–12% abv.[15]

The brewing processes for pale and October beers provided the basis for what would become India pale ale in the late 1700s. From its origins as a stock (or aged) pale ale in London to the height of its popularity in the 1800s, India pale ale was described as a moderately strong golden ale, aged for a long period of time, and often brewed only in the fall after the harvest of fresh hops and with fresh pale malts.

2 | THE 1700s AND THE BIRTH OF IPA

A glass of bitter or pale ale, taken with the principal meal of the day, does more good and less harm than any medicine the physician can prescribe.

—Dr. S. Carpenter, England, 1750

BEERS OF THE 1700s

The 1700s started a 200-year era of growth, with an eventual worldwide presence, of English beer. This period in history marks the transition from when much of England's brewing was done at pubs and on estate properties to a time when commercial breweries in cities supplied beer to multiple regions and exported much of their beer to other countries and continents. The start of the Industrial Revolution in the early part of the century helped fuel the development of the commercial brewing industry, the subsequent expansion and proliferation of porter and ale breweries, beer exportation, and technical developments in brewing science.

Several technological advances were made available to the brewing industry during the 1700s. The introduction of steam power, hydrometers, and thermometers all advanced the technology of brewing and helped improve consistency and control over brewing processes.[1] The advent of pale malt in the late 1600s was one of the technological brewing developments with the greatest impact. Instead of being kilned over wood, straw, or other fuel sources that produced an amber or brown malt and an occasional smoky flavor, pale malt was kilned over coke, which burned more cleanly at lower temperatures and produced a very light-colored malt. Using pale malt in brewing allowed for the development of several key beer styles, including pale ale, October ale, and October beer. The 1700s also saw the development or the rapid expansion of some other key historical beer styles, including a brown beer called London porter and Burton ale. But pale beers gained ground in the middle of the century and provided the basis for what eventually became India pale ale in the 1800s.

At the start of the century, pale malt was still relatively rare and expensive, so its use was limited mainly to the wealthier estate brewers away from the cities. Pale malt was developed in the North and Midlands areas of England, so the commercial breweries starting up in the South of England brewed with amber and brown malts, and the success of their brown ales and porters reflected that.[2] As the century progressed, coke-fired kilning gained prominence in the commercial breweries. Brewers realized they could obtain higher-quality beer and improved efficiency by using pale malt as a base, then blending it with amber or brown malt for color and flavor. The abundance of coke as a fuel also helped, for there was growing concern about the availability of traditional fuels such as wood. The first documentation of London brewers brewing pale beers was in 1717, but country estate brewers were brewing pale ales when the malt was first developed in the late 1600s, and pale beer was sold in London as early as 1709. By mid-century, pale ale was growing in popularity, and many commercial breweries in the London area were using pale malt to brew pale beers alongside their porters.[3]

One of the more notable strong pale ales from this period was the pale October beer. It was brewed with fresh pale malt and fresh hops from that season's harvest, and was made only from October through November. Produced from the first mash of 100 percent pale malt, it was a very high-gravity, highly hopped beer that was aged in barrels for up to two to three years before serving.[4] Because it was expensive to age and brew, October beer was favored by the wealthy and not really available to the working classes. This beer is thought by some to be the precursor to India pale ale and, as we shall see later, shares several ingredients and brewing procedures with it.

Table 2.1 October Beer Recipes

October beer 1	October beer 2
11 bushels malt/hogshead	14 bushels malt/hogshead
Aged 9 months	Kept 12 months
3.5 lb. hops, 75-min. boil	6 lb. hops

Source: October beer recipes are from Fox, The London and Country Brewer (1736).

Note: Eleven to 14 bushels per hogshead would theoretically result in a gravity of 1.140 (28.5 °P).

Table 2.2 Early 1700s Hopping Rates

Beer type	Lb. hops per hogshead	Lb. hops per bbl. (31 gal.)
Pale ale	1.25	0.81
October brown beer	3.00	1.95
October pale beer	6.00	4.86

Sources: Hopping rates for October pale beer from Pattinson, "Early 18th Century British Beer Styles," Shut Up about Barclay Perkins (blog; August 22, 2008), and Fox, The London and Country Brewer (1736), 73.

Brewing techniques in the 1700s were substantially different than those from the 1800s to the present day. For example, sparging was not invented until the late 1700s, by Scottish brewers, and did not see widespread use in England until the mid-1800s.[5] Multiple mashing was the brewing technique used by English brewers, and four types of beer could be produced from a single batch of grain that underwent four separate mashes. In order of decreasing gravity and alcohol content, strong keeping ale, stock ale, small beer, and table beer could be produced from a single charge of malt.[6] The four worts could also be blended to produce beers of varying strengths.

Table 2.3 Early 1700s Beer Data

Beer type	OG (SG)	FG (SG)	% ABV	% ADF
Amber ale	29.63 °P (1.118)	13.75 °P (1.055)	7.93	53.57
Pale ale	31.90 °P (1.127)	14.50 °P (1.058)	8.69	54.51
October strong beer	28.50 °P (1.114)	16.25 °P (1.065)	9.50	53.91

Sources: Pattinson, "Early 18th Century British Beer Styles," Shut Up about Barclay Perkins (blog; August 22, 2008), and Fox, The London and Country Brewer (1736), 42.

Note: Notice how sweet these beers are!

It's also important to note that this period pre-dated the discoveries that yeast was a living organism and that there were biological differences between ale yeast and lager yeast. Therefore the terms "ale" and "beer" meant completely different things from what they mean today. Ale was a lower-hopped malt beverage, while beer referred to the newer, more highly hopped styles that were often brewed with pale malt. Small and table beers were considered "beers" because they were normally brewed with higher hopping rates. Brewers knew that the lower alcohol content made these beers more susceptible to spoilage and increased the hopping rates to help preserve them.[7]

The separation between ale and beer was well defined through most of the century, although toward the start of the 1800s the definitions became less clear. A tax increase on malt in 1710—and beer drinkers' adaptation to the taste of hops—encouraged brewers to increase hop usage, especially in their strong keeping ales and stock ales. Also in 1710, a ban was placed on hop substitutes, further encouraging the use of hops in what were traditionally low-hopped ales. By the time the highly hopped pale "ale" styles became popular in the early 1800s, many different beers with wide ranges of hopping amounts were referred to as ales.

Another important definition in the 18th century was that of mild ale. Unlike today, where the term "mild" generally refers to a low-hopped, lower-gravity ale, in the 1700s a mild was a beer that was served fresh, without significant aging time. A mild could have significant hopping and alcohol strength, for the term "mild" referred more to the beer's age than to its strength. On the other hand, beers that were aged were known as stock, stale, or keeping beers. These beers, by definition, were brewed to be aged, which meant higher alcohol levels and, in most cases, higher hopping levels (as much as six to eight pounds per barrel). They very likely had some *Brettanomyces* yeast action, which resulted in tart flavors developing as the beer aged. The extended aging process helped smooth out the flavors, and in the case of London porter, helped reduce some of the smoky character from the kilning process used on the brown malts.[8] It's also important to note that certain beer types, such as London porter, were available in both mild and stale versions. The stale version of porter has been well documented as having high hopping rates and a characteristic tartness that developed as the beer aged in vats or casks. It was often blended with mild versions in taverns.

BEER ON BOATS

The development of beer exporting is one of the most significant factors in English beer history of the 1700s and 1800s. The presence of beer on ships was not a new development, as most British ships traditionally stowed casks for their crews as a substitute for water. Sailors were rationed a gallon of beer per day, since it was one of the best alternatives to water, which was in short supply on a ship because it went "brackish." The sailors' beer ration helped fuel the development of beer exportation to British colonies in the late 1600s and the early 1700s, as the British Empire grew toward its peak of worldwide dominance.

In the early 1700s most English beer being exported from London went to the colonies in America. Beer shipments from London, Liverpool, and Bristol were also sent to multiple destinations, including Australia and the West Indies. Beer exports to India (or the East Indies) were noted as early as the beginning 1700s.[9]

Around the same time that London brewers were shipping beer to India, Burton brewers started exporting Burton ale (described as nut brown or darker, sweet, and of very high strength) to Russia and the Baltics. Burton's entry into the export market was a direct result of the Act of 1698, which allowed for commercial shipping to take place on the River Trent from Burton to Hull. By 1712 Burton brewers were shipping beer to Hull, and from there it was shipped to London (as much as 638 barrels in 1712) or to the Baltics. Exportation helped spur the rapid growth of the brewing industry in Burton, a small town that could not support its breweries with just the local population. Records also show that Burton ale and pale beer were being drunk in Sumatra in 1716 and shipped as early as 1718 to Madras.[10]

It seems likely that the majority of the beer and ale shipped to India in the 1700s came from London breweries, especially given the accessibility to ships that sailed there. The conventional wisdom of the past was that much of the beer arrived in varying levels of quality, with reports of beer arriving flat, sour, sweet, or murky. There are even reports of bad

Table 2.4 Total Beer Exports from England in the 1700s (Bbl.)

Destination	Year			
	1697	1750	1775	1800
Europe	1,254	2,928	17,328	13,518
Africa	120	12	636	810
North America	7,130	9,186	20,202	68,164
Asia/India	696	1,482	1,680	9,162
Totals	9,200	13,608	39,846	91,654

Source: Mathias, The Brewing Industry in England, 1700–1830 (1959; as cited in Meantime Brewing Company literature).

Note: The volume shipped to North America is higher than all the other destinations combined. Shipments to India gained in volume in the 1800s.

beer being dumped into the harbor if it didn't pass inspection by the quality testers in India. But today some historians discount those stories and think it would have been used for something else if it wasn't fit to be consumed as beer. But the extent to which bad beer arrived in India is certainly not as widespread as once thought. In reality, much documentation shows that beers of all strengths and styles were successfully shipped to India in the 1700s. Shipping manifests and advertisements show that small beer, table beer, brown ale, porter, cider, and Madeira were exported in significant quantities, and there is confirmation that these beverages arrived in excellent condition, too.[11]

Although brewers did not have good knowledge of today's yeast management and sanitation practices, they knew from experience that stronger beers survived long ocean voyages better and that hops were an excellent beer preservative. This knowledge is thought to have originally come from Europe in the 1500s, when the Flemish immigrants brought hops to England and started using them in England-brewed beers. By the early 1700s it was common knowledge among brewers that adding more hops to beer brewed for keeping or exportation would help preserve it. Some of the first brewing textbooks from the 1700s recommended adding 33 percent more hops to the casks.[12] As beer exportation grew, the popularity of stock and strong beers expanded as well.

The route to India is a challenging one, and a heartier beer definitely had a better chance of surviving the voyage with good flavor and proper conditioning. For the beer, the challenges of the voyage were due not only to the temperature extremes incurred by sailing across the Equator twice, but also to the six-month duration of the voyage, the agitation caused by the rolling of the ship on the waves, and perhaps most importantly, the microbiological condition of the beer and the casks in which the beer was stored. Microbial infections were common in beer, especially stock ales that were aged in wood casks and exposed to beer spoilage bacteria and wild yeast. The flavor of stock beers in the 1700s and 1800s was often described as sour or tart, which is why they were frequently blended with fresh (or mild) beer in English taverns.

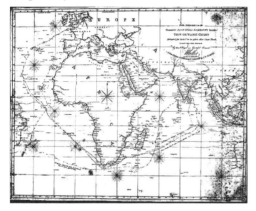

The shipping route from England to India included two equatorial crossings and could take as long as six months.

Knowing that stronger beers had a better chance of surviving, brewers got creative with what they shipped to India, even going so far as to attempt shipping beer concentrate. Sailors in the mid-1700s tried freezing beer to concentrate it, and then added water back toward the end of the voyage. This freezing concentration process was also attempted with wort, the idea being that the wort would be diluted upon arrival in India, then allowed to ferment. But indications are that these attempts all failed— either because of the heat in India, or because of microbiological problems, or because the beer simply didn't taste good.[13] Early reports from India about the beer that did arrive in decent shape included complaints that it was too strong and soporific, which is further evidence that strong beers were often chosen by brewers for exportation.

EAST INDIA COMPANY AND HODGSON'S BOW BREWERY

The East India Company was founded in 1600, and by the 1700s it was the primary force of trade between the colonies in India and England. The East India Company's business model was to bring exotic Indian goods back from the colonies to England and sell these items at great profit. The company had more than 70 ships—known as "East Indiamen" — and the officers on these ships were allowed a certain amount of freight tonnage capacity on the ships heading from England to India, since there wasn't much business for the East India Company itself to conduct on this part of the journey. This private trade allowance enabled the ships' officers to pack the holds of the ships bound for India with English consumer goods. They would then sell these goods to colonists in India, often through the India trading posts, which were called "factories." These items gave the colonists the comforts and tastes of home, and included pale beer, porter, ale, port, wine, rum, gin, cheese, ham, pickles, hardware, jewelry, perfumes, glassware, and clothing. And of course, this perk was a great private business for the East Indiamen officers, as they could take up to 50 tons of goods and were not charged for shipping or freight.

The East India Company's headquarters was located at the intersection of the Rivers Lea and Thames in East London. Just two miles upriver on the River Lea from the East India Company was the Bow Brewery, founded by George Hodgson in 1752. Hodgson started it as a porter brewery, like many other brewers in 1700s London, and he brewed an average of 11,000 barrels annually in his first 16 years

Hodgson was known for brewing both porter and October beer— the strong, aged pale beer popular with the 18th-century gentry, who were also among those who settled in India. At some point in the mid-1700s, Hodgson developed a business relationship with the officers of the East India Company and supplied them with beer to ship as part of their private trade allowance. This enterprise became very successful for both Hodgson and the company. Because of his proximity to the East India Company and his very favorable credit terms, Hodgson was able to develop a virtual monopoly on beer exportation to India. His credit terms were basically

MERCHANTS of EAST-INDIA.

The East India Company's seal.

A View of the EAST INDIA HOUSE, Leadenhall Street, London.

The East India Company's headquarters.

12–18 months, which allowed the company's officers to pay for the beer only after they had sold it all in India and returned home. Hodgson further cemented his position in the late 1700s and the early 1800s by employing price-gouging techniques. He would undercut any other brewer who attempted to gain entry to the Indian market.[14]

Table 2.5 Beer Shipments to India, in Barrels

Year	Barrels shipped
1750	1,480
1775	1,680
1800	9,000

Source: La Pensée and Protz, *Homebrew Classics: India Pale Ale* (2003).

Note: Beer shipments to India increased drastically between 1775 and 1800. Much of this beer came from Hogdson.

The actual beer that Hodgson sent to India has been the subject of much interest, discussion, and debate. Most fans of India pale ale are familiar with the story that Hodgson "invented" a special, highly hopped, high-alcohol beer brewed specifically to survive the ocean voyage to India. But research done by beer historians and brewers over the past several

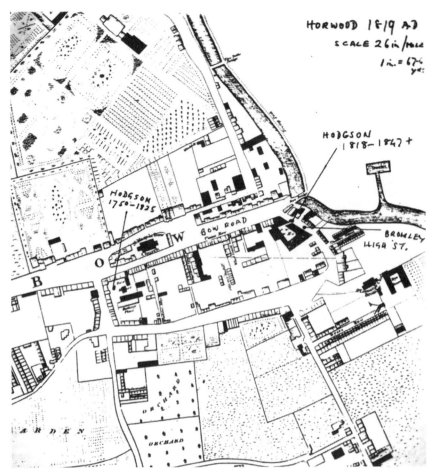

This map shows the location of both versions of Hodgson's Bow Brewery in East London. Today both sites have apartment buildings (or flats) built on them. Map from Dr. John Harrison, courtesy of Mark Dorber.

years has uncovered absolutely zero evidence to support the idea that Hodgson's beer was formulated or invented specifically for exportation to India. In fact, the information uncovered by this research upholds the current theory that the beer Hodgson shipped to India was one of his standard pale stock beers. It survived the voyage well and proved to be a thirst-quenching beer that, perhaps, suited India's hot, muggy climate better than the porters, brown, and amber beers that were also being sent. It was shipped after only a year of aging—earlier than normal for a stock pale ale—and the ocean voyage hastened its maturation. This

The apartments, or flats, now located on one of the former Bow Brewery sites. Photo courtesy of John Trotter.

serendipitous development fueled the rise of one of the most popular beer styles in the history of England and the world.

There's much evidence to substantiate the theory that Hodgson's India beer was a standard pale beer. Hodgson was primarily a porter brewer. In London in the mid-1700s, a porter brewery was considered different from a small brewery or a specialty ale brewery that brewed pale ales using all pale malt. Although the Bow Brewery did brew pale ale, its focus was clearly on porter. As late as 1812, Hodgson's son, Mark, referred to the Bow Brewery as a porter brewery.[15] In 1787 the Bow Brewery produced more than 16,000 barrels of porter (which placed it at approximately 20th in size among London porter breweries) and was exporting only about 10 percent of its overall production to India.

Hodgson did produce other beers besides porter, including pale ale, strong ale, and a mild ale that was exported to West Africa. All his beers appear to have been shipped successfully to India, but none of the research uncovers any mention of "India ale" or "India pale ale." In fact, the first known designation of the beer as "pale ale for the India market" or even "India ale" came in the 1820s, and the term "India pale ale" was not used in print until 1835. Hodgson's first ad appeared in 1793, and porter and pale ale were given equal billing. This would seemingly contradict the idea that Hodgson invented a beer specifically for India, because if he had, he almost certainly would have made note of it in his advertisements.[16]

Porter and other beer styles were successfully shipped by several brewers to India, as evidenced by the historical ads and references from the *Calcutta Gazette* and other sources.[17] The first ad for beer in the *Calcutta Gazette*, from April 8, 1784, states: "London Porter and Pale Ale, light and excellent." No mention that the pale ale was a beer designed specifically for India, or that the beer was brewed by the Bow Brewery. Ads for pale ale, porter, small ale, and strong ale appeared in the *Calcutta Gazette* through about 1790.

Hodgson successfully shipped porter to India all the way into the 1840s.[18] This evidence deflates the theory that a pale strong beer with heavy hopping was the only beer that could be successfully shipped to India. More likely, considering the hot and humid Indian climate, dark, sweet ales were simply not preferred, and beers brewed with pale malt suited the climate better. Porter, in fact, remained one of the favorite drinks of the English army members stationed in India until the late 1800s.

There is no reference in advertisements or books published in the late 1700s that refer to the popular Bow beer as anything other than a pale beer or a pale ale. The first instance of the beer being described as specifically brewed for India was seen in 1820—more than 50 years after Hodgson started exporting his beer—in an advertisement that described Hodgson's beer as "Beer as prepared for India." The first written claim of Hodgson "inventing India pale ale" comes from William Molyneaux's *Burton-on-Trent: Its Histories, Its Waters, and Its Breweries*, which was published in 1869—more than 100 years after Hodgson started shipping beers to India.[19]

In May 1809 the *Calcutta Gazette* referred to "Hodgson's Select Pale Ale," and an advertisement in the June 1822 edition read, "Hodgson's warranted prime picked Pale Ale of genuine October brewing," which was the standard time frame for brewing stock pale ales and October ales. Later ads showed no reference to the beer as "India pale ale."

Pale ale shipped to India was mentioned in Michael Combrune's *Theory and Practice of Brewing*, published in 1762. John Ashton's book, *Social Life in the Reign of Queen Anne*, published in 1882, includes an advertisement from 1715 that "Pale Ale for the East Indies" could be supplied by the Fountain Brewhouse, by the Hermitage. This is 40 years before the establishment of the Bow Brewery and is evidence that other brewers shipped pale beer to India before Hodgson ever did.

CAPE WINE, TAYLOR'S STOUT,

AND

HODGSON'S PALE ALE.

THE undersigned have remaining on hand, from the cargo of the *Leslie Ogilby*, a few pipes of superior Cape Madeira, shipped by the Wine Company, similar to that per *Leda*, so much esteemed in the Colony.

And they have now landing from the *Esther*, Taylor's Stout, and Hodgson's Pale Ale, in excellent condition.

LAMB, BUCHANAN, & CO.

Castlereagh-street, Aug. 5, 1833.

As late as 1833, Hodgson was still not advertising its export pale ale as "India pale ale." Ad courtesy of Martyn Cornell.

Despite the evidence that George Hodgson did not "invent" IPA, it is indisputable that the Bow Brewery was the most renowned brewer of pale beer or pale ale for export to India in the late 1700s and the early 1800s, and that it dominated the market. The brewery's success was due to (1) its reputation for producing excellent beer that arrived in great condition; (2) the reliability of the beer supply (enhanced by the brewery's proximity to the East India Company docks); and (3) the ruthless business practices employed by George Hodgson, his son, Mark, and later his grandson, Frederick, who took over the brewery in 1819.

Table 2.6 Hodgson's Production, in Barrels

Year	Strong	Small	Table
1786	19,099	532	57
1792	11,524	4,657	9,461

Source: Richardson, *The Philosophical Principles of the Science of Brewing* (1805).

Since the Bow Brewery no longer exists, and no brewing ledgers or other brewery records have been uncovered, researchers have looked at sources such as advertisements and historical brewing textbooks in an attempt to gain some understanding of Hodgson's pale beer, how it was brewed, and what it tasted like.

First, let's examine what we know about the ingredients and brewing processes used in the 1700s. This will help us understand the brewing process used for Hodgson's Pale Ale.

INGREDIENTS IN THE 1700s

Water

The brewing water used in London is relatively soft and low in calcium. Although this soft water was preferred by brewers and fueled the popularity of dark beers, for which it is better suited, it complicated the clarification process in pale ales and made it more difficult for brewers in London to brew pale beers that had nice clarity. Still, before the rise of Burton brewing, London brewers had a preference for soft water and would boil water to precipitate and remove calcium when seasonal differences in hardness occurred. Soft water was thought to allow for improved keeping properties in brown and dark ales.[20] Brewers tested water quality by looking at clarity, and also checked the softness by making sure it lathered with soap.

Malt

One hundred percent pale malt was used in most pale beers. The 1700s was well before the advent of crystal malts or black malt, so the choices for London brewers were amber malt, brown malt, and pale malt. Although there is one reference to keeping ale being brewed with a blend of pale and 25 percent amber malts, other recipes and references to pale beer indicate it was brewed with 100 percent pale malt.[21] The malt was primarily two-row, although there are indications that coarser four-row malt (which no longer is available for brewing) was used occasionally. The best pale malt came from north of London, from areas such as Derbyshire, Lincolnshire, and Norfolk where coke was readily available for kilning. Southern malt was dried with straw—and western malt with wood—well into the 18th century. These were not preferred for pale ales, though availability dictated at times that malt be locally sourced. As the century wore on, more malt was kilned with coke, and wood in particular was used less and less frequently for fuel.

Hops
London brewers had their pick of the hops that came from Kent, and these were the preferred hops to use in pale ale, as the presence of sea air in the growing region was thought to provide superior flavor. The hops were most likely around 3–4 percent alpha acid, and while some varieties were noted in brewing texts for their fine flavor, several undesirable hop varieties were described as coarse and nausea inducing. Hop types used in the 1700s include Kent, Farnham Pale, Canterbury Brown, Flemish, and Long While. By the 1750s, as the popularity of well-hopped beer continued to grow, several hop varieties had been identified as suitable for use in pale ale, including Farnham Goldings hops from Surrey, and hops from Herefordshire and Worcestershire. In 1840, the Bow Brewery was documented as using 100 percent Kent Goldings hops in its pale ale.

Hops were packaged tightly in hop pockets or bags for delivery to the breweries, and this packaging, as well as the lack of refrigeration, left them susceptible to rapid aging and oxidation. Although brewers did at times repack hops in tight bags, and made every effort to keep them cool, when they brewed their finest pale ales in the fall and early winter only the freshest hops were used. The practice of using only the freshest hops and brewing seasonally continued well into the 1800s. It also seems likely that Hodgson's first pale ales were not heavily hopped, as the early advertisements referenced pale "ale" not pale "beer." But as time went on, the hopping rates gradually increased. By the 1820s, the model for the Burton brewers' versions appears to have been a very highly hopped beer.

Yeast

Although the discovery of yeast as the organism that ferments wort to alcohol was still decades away, London brewers understood that yeast was an important ingredient in beer, and they recovered yeast from fermentations for repitching. Yeast was often collected as it foamed out of bungholes in the fermentation vats and casks.

Brewing had to be done regularly to maintain the brewery's yeast, and this presented quality issues, because brewers could not control fermentation temperatures in the heat of the summer months. This drove the development of different seasonal beer styles that better survived weather extremes. As the 18th century continued, some porter breweries in London developed methods to press, dehydrate, and store yeast for longer periods of time. Given the high gravities of the keeping beers, it's probable that brewer's yeast had a good alcohol tolerance. Also, because microbiology didn't exist in the 1700s, it's highly likely that yeast cultures consisted of multiple yeast strains, including *Brettanomyces*, and were possibly infected with *Pediococcus* and *Lactobacillus* bacteria, which resulted in the characteristic and well-documented tartness of stock ales and porters.

Finings

As pale beers gained in popularity, beer clarity became more important. The best pale ales were described as light, bright, delicate, and straw colored. For the most part, brewers used natural settling and time in casks to clarify pale beers, but some brewers also ran their beer through flannel material to "filter" out solids and hasten clarification. The addition of hops to casks also hastened settling and probably played a significant role in the growing popularity of dry hopping in casks.

The first documentation of isinglass as a fining agent was seen in 1700, in the book *Directions for Brewing Malt Liquors*.[22] Some brewers would add wheat or beans to the boil to clarify wort. Hartshorn (deer antler) shavings, egg shells, alum, and gelatin were also used as fining agents, but in general, fining agents appear to have received limited use during this period.

Other Ingredients

As the popularity of hops grew in the 18th century, the use of other flavoring ingredients diminished, and it is safe to assume that none were used in Hodgson's Pale Ale. Treacle was noted to have been added routinely to porter and Burton ales to increase strength, and carrot seeds, wormwood, and horehound were fairly common hop substitutes, though it appears by the 1700s, most commercial brewers were limiting their ingredients to water, malt, and hops.

THE PALE ALE BREWING PROCESS

Water Treatment

As described previously, London brewers preferred the natural soft water available in London for brewing. If the water did come in hard, the only treatment was to boil it and allow the calcium to precipitate out. Water was heated to boiling by wood or coke fuel and was deemed ready when it had cooled sufficiently to comfortably dip a finger in it, or to the point where the brewer's face could be seen as a reflection on the water's surface. By the late 1700s the thermometer gained widespread use. It was documented in Combrune's 1762 book, *The Theory and Practice of Brewing,* and temperature control improved significantly.

Mashing, Holding/Resting, and Straining

Mashing and lautering occurred in a wooden vessel, typically oak or teak. In this period, mashing was defined as the process of mixing the malt with the water. A separate rest step is listed in the recipes and brewing logs, and that's where the mash was held for enzymatic conversion of the starch to take place.

The milled malt and the water were mixed manually in the brewing vessel by brewers with paddles. The process of mixing could continue for more than an hour before the rest occurred at a single conversion temperature. Multiple mashings and rests would be conducted with a single charge of malt to get three or four beers of descending strength. The first mash occurred typically with water temperatures ranging from 150° to 170° F (66° to 77° C) and about 60 minutes of rest time. The mash water temperatures were increased with each successive mash, although they typically did not exceed 185° F (85° C). The rest times usually decreased with each successive mash.

Some brewers added more malt to the later mashes to increase gravities of the small beers. Brewers knew that a lot of extract was lost if initial mash temperatures were too high. They favored a lower temperature with the first mash, with the understanding that hotter temperatures in subsequent mashes would make up the difference if the first mash temperature was too low.

"Top mashing" is the process in which the mash tun is filled with water, then milled malt is added from the top and manually mixed in. After a holding period, the liquid is drawn off the top and subsequently boiled.

During the first mash, which could rest for as long as three hours, the brewers usually added more milled malt or even put sacks over the liquid surface to retain temperature. Also, making the initial mash fairly stiff (low water) and adding more hot water 15–30 minutes into the rest was common.[23]

"Bottom mashing," using a false bottom and draining the wort through the grain bed, became more common later in the century. In the case of October ale and other very strong pale beers, wort could be recycled back through the grain bed to increase the strength.

Multiple-batch mashing was the standard practice, which resulted in separate worts with gravities ranging from a high of 27.5 °P (1.110 SG) to a low-gravity table or small beer at about 7.25 °P (1.030 SG). Sometimes first and second worts would be blended together to make a stock ale.

Wort Boiling and Hop Addition

After the wort was separated from the grain, it was boiled. It's interesting to note that, back when ales were unhopped, the boil was not always part of the brewing process. But by the 1700s, wort boiling was standard procedure. Extra-strong worts, such as October ale worts, were often held in a vessel called an underback and allowed to settle before boiling, in a process called "blinking." This helped produce a clearer wort.[24] Normally, the boil was done in a copper vessel, with an open wood or coal fire underneath to heat the wort. Boil times could be anywhere from three to eight hours, and probably depended on the intensity of heat supplied to the kettle.

Hops were added during the boil and were often only allowed to boil for 30 minutes before being pulled out and replaced with another charge. It is cited in many brewing texts of the period that brewers believed that boiling hops for more than 30 minutes extracted rough and harsh flavors and bitterness.[25]

Because hops had seeds, they were often packed in strainer bags before being added to the kettle. This allowed for easier removal and prevented the seeds and the cones from carrying over to the hopback and whirlpool. From the kettle, the wort was transferred into another vessel—sometimes a hopback with a false bottom that could be packed with more hops. Occassionally hair sieves were used to strain the hops from the wort, and hops recovered from the first and the second mash were frequently reused in the lower-strength worts.

After the boil, wort was held in a vessel to settle out solids, then cooled in a shallow coolship, called a "cooler" in British breweries. The cooler was most often made of wood but at times was constructed from stone, and later, metal. Cool air was allowed in from the environment, sometimes with the aid of fans. Periodically the cooling pans were located in the cellars to hasten wort cooling. Later in the century, refrigeration devices that used cold water were employed to chill wort. Brewers at that point knew that wort was especially susceptible to microbiological infections and watched closely for signs of "foxing," or souring. Foxing got its name from the reddish-tinged foam that formed on top of spoiled wort or fermenting beer.

Fermenting and Aging

Next, wort was transferred to vats or casks used for primary fermentation. Yeast was added, and fermentation proceeded for several days. Fermentation temperature control was largely managed by air temperatures and seasonal brewing. However, if necessary, some brewers could cool their fermenting wort by running water through a copper pipe placed in the fermenting vessel or by adding cold wort to the fermenting batch. In the winter, if the fermenting beer got too cold, a stone bottle filled with boiling water would be dipped into the fermenting vessel to warm things up a bit.

After primary fermentation, pale ale was typically racked into casks for aging. Some ales are known to have been left in the primary fermentation cask, yeast and all, for aging. Casks were oak, and were pretreated by soaking in cold, then boiling, water. If more intense barrel cleaning was required, a lime solution would be used. When filled with beer, dry hops were added, and the beer would be aged for a long period of time. A strong October beer would be allowed to age through the winter, and then often it was debunged or vented as the beer warmed up in the spring and summer, allowing a secondary fermentation to take place. It doesn't appear that strong beer in casks was primed with sugar or wort to generate a secondary fermentation. More likely, the secondary fermentation used residual fermentable sugars in the beer, or perhaps the secondary fermentation was the result of bacterial or wild yeast activity.

Strong keeping beers were aged for two years as a standard, but if shipped to India, they were aged for closer to a year prior to the voyage. The casks were often taken to another location (a store) for aging, and a person called the "moving cooper" or the "abroad cooper" was charged with checking the clarity and secondary fermentation of the beer in the stores. If finings were used, the moving cooper would often add them himself. He was also responsible for checking quality and returning any soured beer back to the brewery, where it could be reused as a blending beer or in the preparation of finings.

HODGSON'S BOW PALE ALE RECIPE

Now that we have reviewed a bit about ingredients and processes, we can look at what we know about Hodgson's Pale Ale and develop some assumptions on how this beer was brewed.

One theory presented in the early 2000s suggested that Hodgson's Pale Beer was a descendant of the October ale that was brewed first by estate breweries shortly after the development of pale malt. Although Hodgson was primarily a porter brewer, he did brew October beer, and his pale ale shipped to India was advertised in 1822 as being "the finest October brewed ale." One argument that favors the popularity of October ale in India is that many of the colonists in 18th century India were country gentry, who were already familiar with, and fond of, October ale.[26] Recipes for October ale can be seen in *The London and Country Brewer*, published in 1736, where uses of 11–14 bushels of pale malt per hogshead (462–588 pounds per hogshead, or 265–337 pounds of malt per barrel) are reported, resulting in original gravities of 25–27.5 °P (1.100–1.110 SG).[27] Kettle hopping rates ranged from 2 to 3.5 pounds per barrel, and the beers were matured in wood for at least one to three years. By all accounts, the beers were exceedingly bitter, and the aging process helped tame the hop bitterness and bring the flavors into balance.

A similar beer, called March ale, was also brewed from the most recent crop of malt and hops. But fermentation in the warmer temperatures of spring caused some concern about off-flavor development, so brewers upped the hopping rates to as much as two and a half times that of the October ales. March ales had original gravities in the 20 °P (1.080 SG) range, and like October ales, they were dry hopped in hogsheads and allowed to age.

The advertisements published in the late 1700s reveal that the pricing of pale beer or pale ale was similar to that of stock bitters and less than that of strong ales. It would follow then that the pale ale exported to India was brewed to an original gravity and alcohol strength similar to that of a stock bitter—approximately 17.5 °P (1.070 SG) original gravity and about 6.5% abv. It is important to note that this is not a particularly strong beer for the time. These gravity and alcohol level estimates are supported by many beer researchers, including Martyn Cornell, John Keeling of Fuller's Brewery, and Dr. John Harrison of Durden Park Beer Circle, who claimed that Hodgson's IPA was 1.070 original gravity. Beer writer Roger Protz also claimed it had an original gravity of 1.070.

We can reasonably assume that Hodgson's beer was brewed with 100 percent pale malt, as it had often been described as clear and straw colored. We can also assume that Hodgson used a lot of hops in his pale ale, since that would align with the idea of a keeping/stock beer, dry hopped in the cask. This is supported by a story from 1820. The East India Company approached Samuel Allsopp with a bottle of Hodgson's beer to try to secure another supplier. When Allsopp's head brewer, Job Goodhead, tasted Hodgson's beer, he spit it out because it was so bitter. A similar review of Hodgson's beer comes from George's Brewery of Bristol, which commented on Hodgson's beer in 1828: "We neither like its thick and muddy appearance or rank bitter flavor."[28] Although these comments were documented in the 1800s, it's reasonable to assume that

Hodgson did not change the characteristics of his ale much after its initial success.

We almost certainly know that Hodgson's beer was dry hopped. Dry hopping was a standard procedure for keeping ales, and even porters and stouts. Beer historian and writer Martyn Cornell cites two references—one involving India colonists attempting to grow hops from the dregs of a hogshead, and the other involving shipwrecked sailors trying to eat the hops that were left on the bottom of a hogshead to get at the moisture held in them.

In 1847 W. H. Roberts wrote that the brewers who failed in the India trade used too low an original gravity or too low a hopping rate. Since Hodgson succeeded in India, it's safe to say that his beer had a higher original gravity and was well hopped. Hodgson's beer set the standard.

HODGSON'S PALE ALE: A SUMMARY

Here's what we believe about Hodgson's Pale Ale and beers shipped to India:

- Hodgson started shipping porter, pale ale, strong ale, and table beer to India shortly after establishing his brewery. Beers of all types were successfully shipped to India through the 1700s.

- His proximity to the East India Company helped foster a business relationship that lasted well into the 1800s, helping to make the Bow Brewery the major supplier of beer to India.

- Because Hodgson never claimed to have invented a beer for India, and because no documentation exists that claims his beer was anything other than a pale beer, it is safe to say that the pale beer Hodgson shipped to India was one of his standard beers, and it accounted for a small amount (at least initially) of his overall production.

- From pricing tables, we can see that Hodgson's Pale Ale was priced to be about the same as beers at 6.5% abv and about 17.5 °P (1.070 OG). It's reasonable to deduce that his beer was brewed to the same specs, as exceptionally strong ales would command a much higher price.

- An ad from 1822 describes the beer Hodgson shipped to India as the finest October brewed ale, indicating that fresh malt and hops were used. Since many of the colonists were fans of the October ale style, it's possible that Hodgson's was a lower-gravity version of this beer.

- Hodgson's beer was described as clear, brilliant, and straw colored, indicating that only pale malt was used.

- Because Hodgson was primarily a London porter brewer, he probably brewed with soft water. This would mean that his pale ale might not clarify well without extensive aging. (One of the reasons Burton brewers were so successful with export beer is that the hard water with high calcium levels prompted yeast flocculation.)

Research shows that pale ales were aged at least a year before shipping to India, thus allowing the beer to undergo a secondary fermentation in the warmer summer months, and were debunged in the stores until the beer was flat so the casks wouldn't explode on the ocean voyage. The beer picked up some carbonation on the way to India. It may have also been fined, since fining agents such as isinglass came into use shortly after the establishment of the Bow Brewery. There is documentation that Hodgson's beer was muddy at times, further suggesting that soft water was used without fining agents, and that some sort of fermentation activity possibly occurred during the ocean voyage.

- Hodgson's beer was most likely brewed with hops from Kent. These were the hops preferred by London brewers, and they were close enough to get first pick of Kent hops. It's likely that the initial beers he shipped were not overly hopped, as they were referenced as "pale ale," not "pale beer." It was common knowledge that hopping had to be increased for beers destined for export, and it seems likely that the hopping rates in Hodgson's beer increased as time went on. We do know his beer in the early 1800s was exceptionally bitter, as tasting has been documented.

- Hodgson's beer was dry hopped in the aging casks. This was standard practice for beers of all types, and there are historical references to the hop dregs in the casks of India beer.

- Although Hodgson was a ruthless businessman and engaged in price gouging, competitors brewed similar beers for India in the late 1700s and the early 1800s. Some records do exist from these breweries, and we can expect that they tried to emulate Hodgson's success by brewing a similar beer. Looking at their beers, we can surmise what Hodgson's beer was like.

Although there exists no definitive description of taste or brewing procedure used for Hodgson's Pale Ale, much of the research done by beer historians and brewers has given us a clearer picture of what Hodgson was brewing at the Bow Brewery. At the turn of the 19th century, other brewers started brewing competitive examples, and documentation still exists from those beers that provides very detailed information on how India pale ales were brewed at the height of their popularity in Burton-on-Trent, Edinburgh, and London.

3 | THE BURTON IPA: 1800–1900

The Burton-on-Trent Abbey was founded along the banks of the River Trent around AD 1000. As abbeys often were associated with breweries in the Middle Ages, it's only natural that a brewery was established on the site, perhaps as early as 1100. But certainly brewing was documented in Burton by the 14th century.[1]

Burton, located in central England, grew to become an important trading center, and Burton beers became well known throughout England for traveling much better than beer from other areas. As a result, Burton beers could be found in London and other parts of England as early as 1630.[2]

The water used for brewing in Burton was recognized as being special before brewers really understood why. The high levels of calcium and sulfate in the water enhanced fermentation and yeast flocculation. This meant that the beers from Burton had little in the way of fermentable sugars, a condition that promoted microbiological stability in the finished beer. So the beers from Burton were clearer and had a much lower tendency to spoil or sour than beers from other towns and regions.[3]

The export business from Burton flourished after 1698, when the passage of the Trent Canal Act allowed for water-based trade from River Trent to Hull. The act allowed Burton beers to be shipped on the River

Trent to the port city of Hull, on England's east coast, and from there the beer was easily shipped to London, the Baltics, and Russia. In 1777 the opening of the Mersey Canal from Burton to Liverpool created another export passage, and about 45 years later, it became one of the main methods of transport for Burton IPA. Since Burton had a population of only 5,000 in the late 1700s and 10,000 in the mid-1800s, there were not enough people locally to support the many breweries that operated there. But the export business thrived and supported the town's breweries for many generations.

English beers had become very popular in Russia during the time of Peter the Great (the late 1600s and the early 1700s). After the Trent Canal Act was established, Burton brewers became the major suppliers to Russia and the Baltic nations, and their best-known beer was Burton ale, a strong, sweet, dark amber beer that eventually evolved into the barley wine style. In the late 1700s, many brewers opened in Burton to take part in the trade to Russia. Brewers in Burton who exported their beers at this time included Bass, Clay, Evans, Leeson, Musgrave, Wilson (Allsopp), and Worthington.

As is the case with much of English brewing history, politics played a significant role in the successes and the failures of the export business to Russia and the Baltics. In 1766 Catherine the Great and England signed a formal commercial treaty that allowed for an increase in beer shipments to St. Petersburg. But in 1783 Russia imposed a 300 percent tax, most likely to stimulate its own brewing industry. This led the English brewers to turn their focus to Prussia and Poland. Russian trade ceased completely in 1800, and the Napoleonic wars in 1806 further prevented merchant ships from sailing from England to the Baltics. When the Napoleonic wars ended, exports to Russia were attempted again, but relations between England and Russia went south. Heavy tariffs were imposed on English goods in 1812 and again in 1822. Though some shipments continued to London, the political turmoil in Russia and the Baltics effectively left the Burton brewers without an outlet for their beer. Thus, their output in 1820 was significantly lower than it had been 40 years earlier.[4] Burton ale, like most strong English stock ales, lost popularity in the 1800s, when India pale ales and other styles came to the forefront.

But it was still brewed for domestic consumption, and in fact is still made today. Current versions include Young's Winter Warmer, Fuller's 1845, Marston's Owd Rodger, and Theakston's Old Peculier.

Table 3.1 Beer Shipped to the Baltics

Year	Barrels shipped
1740	Nil
1750	740
1775	11,025
1880	8,100

Source: Mathias, *The Brewing Industry in England, 1700–1830* (1959; as cited in Meantime Brewing Company literature).

While Burton's brewers struggled to maintain their export business to Russia, Hodgson's Bow Brewery of London continued its dominance of the export market to India. Other London brewers, such as Whitbread, W. A. Brown Imperial Brewery, and Barclay Perkins made some gains into the market, but Hodgson was an expert in manipulating supply to create artificial demand. It flooded the market in times of perceived beer shortages, effectively price gouging the other brewers out of the market. The folks at the East India Company grew weary of Hodgson's price manipulations (prices ranged from 20 to 200 rupees for its ale) and the changing of credit terms to suit the brewery's own needs.

In 1813 the East India Company started losing its monopoly on the India trade because new shipping and import companies started to provide some competition. Hodgson's unethical business practices further derailed the East India Company's domination of the Indian market, as Calcutta merchants struggled with beer supply uncertainties and wild price fluctuations of Hodgson's beer.

Free trade measures passed by the English government in 1820 allowed for even more competition, and that same year Mark and Frederick Hodgson further alienated the East India Company by attempting to form their own importing company as direct competition. Still, Hodgson's ale was held in very high esteem by the relocated English gentry in India. Hodgson remained the East India Company's major beer supplier, and officers still enjoyed 12- to 18-month credit lines. But when Hodgson changed the deal by raising prices, demanding cash payments up front, and attempting to establish themselves as retailers and merchants in India, the East India Company finally grew fed up and looked to get its beer from someone else.[5]

BURTON'S ENTRY INTO THE INDIAN MARKET

The story of Burton's entry into the Indian market is remarkably well documented, perhaps best so in John Stevenson Bushnan's 1853 book, *Burton and Its Bitter Beer.* In 1821 Burton's most prominent brewer was Allsopp, founded by Benjamin Wilson in the 1740s. East India director Campbell Marjoribanks (pronounced "Marchbanks") visited Samuel Allsopp in London to discuss the Indian market. Marjoribanks sent a sample of Hodgson's pale beer to Allsopp and asked the brewer to produce a similar beer for India. Allsopp agreed, most likely influenced by the struggles he was facing in other export markets. Allsopp's brewers and maltsters attempted to replicate the Hodgson ale, and the legend goes that the first attempt was brewed in a teapot by Allsopp brewmaster Job Goodhead. By 1823 Samuel Allsopp was shipping his early version of pale ale to Liverpool and to India, where it received mixed reviews. It was noted by some as being too dark, sweet, too strong, and in need of more aging time and more bitter character. Recipe reformulations followed, and Allsopp's maltsters developed a method for producing an extra pale or white malt, which soon became a required ingredient for the IPA style.

At about the same time, Burton brewers Bass (founded in 1771) and Salt (founded in 1771 as Joseph Clay & Son) also started brewing beers specifically for the Indian market. Hodgson responded to these first Burton shipments to India by dropping prices and increasing its own shipments—doubling its shipment to 6,181 barrels in 1822. In 1823 Hodgson's shipments had dropped back to 1,148 hogsheads, and over the next 10 years, the four brewers fought for dominance over the Indian market.[6] Given the inconsistencies in the quality of Hodgson's ale—the "rank bitterness" and the occasional "muddy" appearance—plus the endorsement of the East India Company, Allsopp's and Bass' ales began a climb to push Hodgson off the top spot. Although Hodgson's beer was still preferred by many of the East India Company's officers, the continued turmoil with pricing and supply drove the company to the Burton brewers. Hodgson further angered the East India Company by sending its beer out as "brewers, shippers/merchants, and retailers" in an effort to monopolize the entire supply chain. Soon Allsopp's beer was preferred to Hodgson's, even though Captain Chapman of the East India Company continued to urge Allsopp to increase the bitterness in its version. Allsopp's beer was described as having a bright amber color, clear as crystal, with a peculiar fine flavor.

In an 1825 letter from a J. Balton in Calcutta to Allsopp, Balton describes the maturation of Allsopp's Ale as:

> One month after bottling*: dark, turbid, and decomposed.

> Three months: Starting to clear, sparkling,
> Champagne-like appearance.

> Eight months: bright amber, crystal clear,
> very peculiar fine flavor.

After this, Balton recommended that Allsopp increase the bitterness and reduce the malt. The maturation process and the knowledge of how this beer improved with age was a key development to the success of the Burton IPA.[7]

By 1826 Allsopp's IPA was of a quality to demand the same price as Hodgson's beer in India. Hodgson's beer still had the best reputation in India as late as 1829, but there were signs that the brewery was losing the battle. In 1830 the *New Monthly Magazine* assailed Hodgson for sending "very indifferent beer, sometimes very bad beer, and sometimes no beer at all," and mentioned that Allsopp had responded by brewing and sending a wonderful beer, a "most heavenly compound."[8] By 1832 Bass had overtaken the other IPA brewers, including Allsopp, with more than 40 percent of all IPA exports to India. By 1837 Bass was shipping more than 5,000 barrels annually to India, and its IPA accounted for more than 60 percent of the brewery's production.

---

* This apparently means the cask beer was bottled in India. How widespread this practice was is uncertain, but it certainly was used.

Table 3.2 Exports to India and Costs

Year	Hogsheads	Rupees per hogshead
1813–1814	3,400	58
1816–1817	8,800	55
1819–1820	2,300	63
1823–1824	11,400	51
1826–1827	2,600	79
1827–1828	6,000	58

Source: Tizard, *The Theory and Practice of Brewing Illustrated* (1846). Courtesy of Pete Brown.

Note: The jump in barrelage in 1823–1824 is the direct result of Burton Brewers shipping IPA to India.

Bass Ale being served in India.

What's interesting about this drawing is the indication that both porter and ale are advertised on the sign next to the hotel door.

Scene involving the shipping of beer from England to India.

The ill feelings caused by Hodgson's business practices drove Indian merchants to the Burton breweries for their more ethical business practices and more consistent beer supply. As the Burton brewers perfected their recipes and brewing processes, the quality and flavor of Burton's IPAs became preferred within five to 10 years. Hodgson's beers were inconsistent, and the pale dryness, better clarity, increased bitterness, and consistency of the Burton beers helped them surpass Hodgson's for good by the 1830s. Allsopp's beer in particular was noted by brewing text author William Tizard as having a "superior lightness and brilliancy of their shipments." Hodgson reacted to the Burton infringement by shipping its beer to other countries, including Turkey, Syria, Greece, and Egypt, where it was sometimes known as "Bengal Wine."[9] The brewery started advertising its pale ale as a medicinal restorative, and began touting its use of the "finest East Kent hops." In 1836 Hodgson suffered a major blow when its beer was apparently adulterated by people filling Hodgson-labeled bottles with an inferior beer. Hodgson responded by publishing an advertisement regarding its bottled beer: "None are genuine unless labeled Hodgson and bottles are sealed and corks are branded."[10] Burton brewers had better control over their agents and their bottlers than Hodgson, and that gave them an additional competitive advantage.

Table 3.3 Barrels Exported to India in 1832

Total U.K.	Bass	Hodgson	Allsopp
12,000	5,250	3,900	1,500

Source: Gourvish and Wilson, *The British Brewing Industry, 1830–1890* (1994). Courtesy of Pete Brown.

WHAT'S IN A NAME? BECOMING INDIA PALE ALE

The actual name "India pale ale" didn't arise until several years after the Burton brewers started brewing the beer. This is an important factor to consider when researching the history and origins of the style. The legend that Hodgson "invented" the style in the 1700s is thrown into serious doubt, given the fact that Hodgson never put a name to his beer, except to call it a pale ale, until the 1830s. This would imply that the original IPA was a standard pale ale–style beer that was already being brewed. The first printed reference to this beer being anything unique or designed especially for India is subject to much debate and research.

Model of East Indiaman loaded for India, as seen at the Museum of London Docklands. Photo by John Trotter.

An advertisement published in 1817 by the W. A. Brown Imperial Brewery noted its "pale ale prepared for the East and West India Climate," and in 1822 there was an ad for "Pale Ale brewed expressly for the Indian Market." The first reference to the name India pale ale could very well have been in the Indian newspaper *Bengal Hukaru* in 1828, which referenced a "new beer, India Pale Ale." Since this is almost 50 years after Hodgson started shipping his pale ale to India, the argument can be made that it was the new Burton-brewed versions that prompted a renaming of the beer. The words "India pale ale" were thought to have been first used in English print in 1835 in the *Liverpool Mercury*, for Hodgson's "India Pale Ale," which referred to the use of the finest East Kent Hops and the beer's tonic qualities. Another early reference was seen in a June 15, 1837, ad placed by beer merchant George Shove in the London *Times* to promote Hodgson's ale. In 1838 Shove's business was taken over by Edwin Abbott, who continued to place advertisements for Hodgson's East India Pale Ale and Export Stout. This is the same Edwin Abbott who went on to buy Hodgson's brewery in the next decade. One of Abbott's early ads, from the *Kentish Gazette* on May 15, 1838, stated: "White and Abbott are the sole vendors in the ISLE OF THANET, DEAL, DOVER, CANTER-

BURY, &c. of HODGSON and Co.'s long celebrated INDIA PALE ALE; any sold as such other Houses in this district is not genuine, they being exclusive parties to whom its Sale is confided." During the 1840s the beer was known as "India Pale Ale," "Pale Ale as brewed for India," "Indian Pale Ale," and "East India Ale," until brewers and advertisers apparently settled on India pale ale, and that name was used from the 1850s on. William Molyneaux's claim that Hodgson actually invented the style, made in his 1869 book, *Burton-on-Trent: Its Histories, Its Waters, and Its Breweries,* came about 100 years after Hodgson first started shipping pale ale to India and long after the Hodgson family sold the brewery.

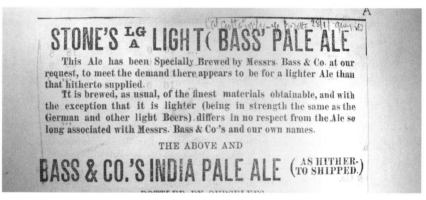

A Bass Light Pale and India Pale Ale promo. Photo by John Trotter.

The Mersey Canal (to Liverpool) in Burton-on-Trent, at Marston's. Burton brewers shipped their beer to London and Liverpool via canals where it was stored in warehouses for aging and then loaded directly onto boats bound for India and other countries.

Casks were loaded onto canal barges for shipment from the breweries to port cities.

A CHANGING WORLD

In 1839 the Birmingham and Derby Junction Railway completed the Derby-to-Birmingham rail line in Burton. This had an immediate, huge impact on the Burton IPA supply to the rest of the country. Overall IPA production increased by 50 percent within a year.[11] Bass' home trade immediately quadrupled. At the completion of this railroad, as Burton IPA began to be seen more frequently in London, Hodgson finally responded with some aggressive marketing, and an advertising war broke out in the newspapers between Hodgson, Allsopp, and Bass. These ads finally referenced the beer as India pale ale, and Hodgson's, while struggling overall, made some inroads against the mightier Burton competition. An 1838 advertisement in the London *Times* read, "Hodgson's East India Pale Ale and Stout: Abbott & Co., Wapping, have the only depot in London of the above long-celebrated beers; in the bottle for home consumption." An 1844 ad described Hodgson and Abbott's Pale Ale as "this highly celebrated beer, which has been held in such high repute in India for nearly a century."

But in general Hodgson failed to advertise as boldly as the Burton brewers, being unable or unwilling to reference its India success or the attributes of the beer as forcefully as the Burton brewers, and thus was never able to generate a comparable appreciation domestically for the Hodgson name among the up-and-coming middle classes in England.[12] This was a huge issue, because as the century progressed, domestic IPA consumption became the driver of the style's growth. Hodgson had capacity issues and was unable to expand properly, and so maintained its focus on the export business, which was slowly slipping away. In the 1840s Hodgson was either losing interest or grew tired of competing with powerful Burton brewers, and the brewery was sold to Edwin Abbott. The brewery was renamed Abbott's Bow Brewery and continued to struggle until declaring bankruptcy in 1862. It was bought and became the Bow Brewery Company Ltd., then became part of Smith, Garrett & Company in 1869. In 1927 Smith, Garrett was taken over by Taylor Walker. The Hodgson brewery was demolished in 1933, and flats were built on the site.

Table 3.4 Imports of Beer and Porter into Calcutta

Year	Butts	Hogsheads	Dozens
1831	418	5,566	2,105
1832	111	5,946	1,167
1833	252	7,916	2,293
1834	322	7,193	2,028
1835	244	6,282	2,632
1836	140	4,519	1,392
1837	404	9,544	3,241
1838	841	11,356	2,102
1839	606	8,937	719
1840	391	10,779	671
1841	824	11,808	2,989
1842	669	11,035	6,457

Source: Tizard, The Theory and Practice of Brewing Illustrated (1846). Courtesy of Pete Brown.

Note: This is the first reference of bottles being shipped to India! Dozen = case of twelve 26 oz. bottles; butt = 108–140 gallons; hogshead = 52.5 gallons. Shipping bottled beer to India was common; it was not all shipped in casks. The bottles themselves were packed in casks filled with straw.

As Hodgson was failing in the 1850s and 1860s, the IPA market became dominated by the three major Burton brewers: Allsopp, Salt, and Bass. All three started brewing the India beer at about the same time, in the early 1820s, and it is unclear whether Allsopp or Salt was the first brewery to actually ship the beer to India, but Allsopp was definitely referred to most in literature about the period. In the 1840s the Burton IPA business grew from 70,000 barrels per year to more than 300,000 barrels per year. In the period from 1850 to 1880, Burton's overall beer output increased from 300,000 barrels to more than 3 million barrels per year, establishing Burton-on-Trent as a major global brewing center.

Drawing of the Salt Brewery in Burton-on-Trent. Taken from Barnard, The Noted Breweries of Great Britain and Ireland *(1891).*

By 1855, as the National Railway's first stage was completed, Bass' beer production alone climbed to more than 300,000 barrels per year.[13] IPA became the beer of England's railroad age, and Bass had agents in all of England's major cities that the railroad serviced—and Allsopp and Salt were not far behind. Domestic and international demand for Burton IPA was exceeding supply, so the Burton brewers started expanding. In 1858 Allsopp built a four-acre brewery next to the Burton railroad station for the sole purpose of brewing IPA, and at one point it had the largest racking cellar in Burton, capable of holding more than 40,000 casks.

Table 3.5 Number of Burton Brewers

Year	Brewers
1708	1
1784	13
1793	9
1818	5
1834	9
1841	13
1851	17
1869	26

Source: The National Brewery Centre Museum, Burton-on-Trent.

Note: The peaks in Burton breweries occurred in the late 1700s, the height of shipping Burton ale to Russia and the Baltics, and in the late 1800s, the height of IPA. Some of the breweries opening in Burton had relocated there for the water.

Bass and Allsopp eventually left Salt behind and became rivals for the majority of the India pale market. They owned 70 percent of the IPA output in Burton in the late 1860s, despite the opening of 11 more breweries in the town, which took the total number of breweries to 26. IPA breweries also began to be built in other parts of England and various regions in the world. Once the chemistry of the Burton well water became understood, brewers were able to imitate it with the addition of salts and brew reasonable approximations of the Burton IPA. Even so, many brewers found it more advantageous to simply build breweries in the Burton area and take full advantage of the water there. These brewers included Ind Coope, Charrington, and Truman, Hanbury & Buxton.

Bass built two more breweries, one in 1853 (known as the Middle, or White, Brewery) and another in 1863 (known as the New, or Blue, Brewery). In 1876 Bass rebuilt its original (Old, or Red) brewery, which dated from 1777. Bass owned 37 malthouses, and its cooper's area covered three acres. The Bass name became synonymous with pale ale, to the point where there was some confusion among consumers about other brewers of the style. Bass brewed 900,000 barrels of beer in 1874. By 1882 bottled Bass Ale was available in every country where an Englishman had set foot, and by 1889, Bass had become the largest brewery in

Table 3.6 Brewers Relocating to Burton

Brewer	From	Year
Ind Coope	London	1856
Charrington & Co.	London	1872
Truman, Hanbury & Buxton	London	1874
Mann, Crossman & Paulin	London	1875
A. B. Walker & Sons	Liverpool	1877
Thomas Sykes & Co.	Liverpool	1879
James Parker & Son	Liverpool	1879
Peter Walker	Warrington	1880
Everard & Co.	Leicester	1892

Source: The National Brewery Centre Museum, Burton-on-Trent.

Note: Several brewers relocated to Burton at the height of IPA brewing to take advantage of the brewing water.

the world. In 1889 the brewery employed 2,250 people, compared to 867 men employed by all brewers in Burton in 1821.[14] Bass, Ratcliff & Gretton's Ale Stores in St. Pancras were documented as having nine acres of beer storage on three floors—an estimated 90,000 barrels of beer—and under the Midland Goods station in Burton, another 8,000 butts of beer were held exclusively for export bottling. The bottling company was the Read Brothers, "bottlers of ale and stout for exportation."[15]

Outside of Burton, most of the competition in Great Britain was provided by brewers in Edinburgh and Alloa, Scotland. Specific brewers included Barclay Perkins of London, Younger of Edinburgh (whose IPA brewing techniques are well documented in chapter 5), and Tetley's of Leeds. Originally a malthouse, Tetley's started brewing IPA in the 1850s. By 1859 it was brewing more than 36,000 barrels of IPA annually, providing some reasonably serious competition.

Until about 1840 the majority of India pale ale was still shipped to India, but by mid-century, the style had become one of the most popular in its home country as well. Several social changes were occurring in England that contributed to the growth of IPA's popularity domestically. First, England was becoming an industrialized country. This meant that workers had free time and money to spend when they got off work. Beer consumption began to skyrocket as lifestyles changed. Per capita annual beer consumption grew from 28.4 gallons in the 1820s to more than 40 gallons in 1870. Mild ale, unaged and somewhat sweet (though not necessarily low in alcohol), supplanted porter as the drink of the working class, reaching more than 100,000 barrels annually in the 1870s. IPA, with its longer aging time and higher cost, became the drink of the upper middle class.[16] Usually priced at a premium (which made sense, considering its strength), IPA became principally an urban drink and a status symbol for the middle and upper classes. As standards of living increased after 1850, IPA became more accessible and more popular. It was pale, clear, and often served chilled and in glassware, enhancing its appeal and inviting comparisons to the best French champagnes.[17]

The transition in the brewing industry from home, farm, estate, and pub brewing to commercial brewing also contributed to the widespread popularity of English beer from specific brewing centers. As the 1700s ended and the 1800s began, brewing transitioned to an industry populated by large commercial breweries staffed by hundreds of people. In 1831 only 54 percent of all beer in England was brewed by commercial breweries. But by 1900, 95 percent of the farmhouse and pub breweries had disappeared, and beer from commercial breweries all over England could be found everywhere. Bottling and improvements in transportation made beer easily shipped and widely available. Continued advances in the science of brewing resulted in stable beer and vastly improved quality and consistency.

Many English medical professionals touted the dry IPA as a restorative beverage, which only helped its popularity. Beer had been discussed as having positive health benefits since the 1700s, and in the 1800s IPA became preferred over wine and the sweeter, darker beers, with the dryness of IPA being favored by diabetics. IPA was considered by many to be a medicinal cordial.

Many factors contributed to the growing domestic popularity of IPA. But one that apparently did not was the legend of a boat carrying India pale ale that shipwrecked off the coast of Liverpool or Scotland. The shipments of IPA were supposedly recovered and drunk by the locals, who then spread the word of this wondrous new beer across the country. Beer researchers have found no written evidence of such a shipwreck.[18]

Table 3.7 Per Capita Beer Consumption: England and Wales

Year	Avg. gallons
1800	33.9
1810	30.2
1820	29.0
1830	33.8
1840	30.5
1850	29.5
1860	31.6
1870	38.2
1876	42.1
1880	33.6
1890	33.4
1900	34.3
1910	29.4

Sources: Gourvish and Wilson, *The British Brewing Industry, 1830–1890* (1994); Meantime Brewing Company, "India Pale Ale."

Note: English beer consumption peaked in 1876.

More likely, the rise of IPA popularity domestically was fueled by colonists returning from India and craving the pale beer they had enjoyed there.

In 1822 an ad appeared in the London *Times* for an auction of "139 hogsheads of India pale ale, brewed expressly for the Indian market, and suitable for warm climates OR home consumption!" In 1830 a similar auction was held for 150 hogsheads of "Pale Ale for the Indian market" from the Hope Brewery, and in 1833 a London *Times* ad read, "For Families from India, Hodgson's and Co.'s Bottled Pale Ale in England."

In 1852 Burton IPA survived a big scare when Professor Monsieur Payen of France claimed in writing that the large amounts of strychnine apparently being exported from France to England were being used as an additive to increase the bitterness in IPA. This claim was reprinted in the English medical journal *Medical Times and Gazette*, which prompted written rebuttals from both Michael Thomas Bass and Henry Allsopp.[19]

Accusations of adulteration were commonplace in the 1800s. Indeed, written documentation establishes that many brewers used illegal substances in the beers to provide flavor, color, or extra preservation. In 1830 the Burton brewers jointly filed a libel suit against the Society for Diffusing Useful Knowledge for claiming that the brewers adulterated their beers.[20] In the mid-1800s, 215 beers were analyzed and 142 of them were found to be adulterated with substances such as tobacco, *Cocculus indicus,* Quassia, saltpeter, and grains of paradise. Preservatives such as salicylic acid, hyposulfurous acid, and bisulfate of lime were described in Charles Herman Sulz's 1888 book, *A Treatise on Beverages: Or the Complete Practical Bottler.*[21] And in the 1850s both Bass and Allsopp found themselves in court, defending their breweries against adulteration charges.[22]

In 1905 a damning reference to the use of bisulfate of lime by brewers appeared in a letter from Scottish brewer Wm. Hunter to a John Bowie. The complaint was about summer beers that were going hazy, sharp, and sour, and the use of bisulfate to preserve them, which, if overdone, causes hydrogen sulfide flavors in the beer: "You need not say anything about the cause, as we do not speak of adding bi-sulfate of lime to the beer, although, of course, *all* brewers do it, and it is a wholesome, healthy addition. In cases where the smell is unbearable, take the casks back to the store, roll them about for a few days, and you will find the odor disappears."[23]

Despite the claim that all brewers used preservatives, throughout the 1800s Bass and Allsopp both vigorously defended their beers in court from any accusation of artificial preservation or adultery.

Taxes and temperance movements have affected how beer is brewed in England since the 1600s, and they certainly influenced the IPA brewing process in the 1800s and 1900s. In the late 1700s progressive taxation was introduced that established beer taxes based on the cost of ingredients. This led to the classification of beers as strong, table, and small. Strong and table beers were taxed at significantly different rates, and blending them to avoid paying higher taxes was a serious offense.

In 1830 the tax system changed again to be based on the amount of malts and hops used in the beer. In this new taxation system, strict regulations were also placed on malting practices. In 1862 William Ford, secretary of the Maltsters Association, wrote against this method of taxation: "The present immoderate duty on malt and the reduction of duty on wine has brought the price of wine to nearly that of ale. It has had a serious effect on the consumption of ale termed 'India Pale.' Thus has the government forced the sparkling ale (that beverage which was wont to be the pride, not only of the middle, but even the higher orders of society) from their tables to make room for the production of foreign countries."[24] This new tax also struck a blow to noncommercial (farmhouse and pub) brewers. They were now forced to pay the same tax rate as the larger commercial brewers who had the advantages of efficiencies due to greater technical skill and access to more sophisticated brewing equipment.

The reduction in farmhouse and estate brewing was accelerated when the Truck Amendment Act was passed in 1831. This law prevented estate owners from paying their servants with anything but cash, except in certain circumstances. But more importantly for brewers, intoxicating substances such as beer were specifically prohibited from being used as compensation. Brewing frequency on farms and estates was subsequently reduced, and beer had to be brewed strong to last through the nonbrewing periods. Low-gravity table beer production was virtually eliminated.[25] "Beer money" became the payment standard in place of the beer ration, both on estates and in the military. This scrip was used by the payees to buy beer or other consumables.

Fueled by a government desire to reduce gin consumption, the Beerhouse Act of 1830 allowed anyone to brew and sell beer, ale, or cider, whether from a public house or from their own home, upon obtaining a moderately priced license of just under two pounds for beer and ale. Hundreds of new pubs called Tom and Jerry houses quickly opened throughout England, reducing the influence of the large breweries. What this act eventually led to was an increase in really bad beer that was improperly handled in the pubs. When the laws were finally changed, the result was the creation of tied houses—pubs tied to a particular brewery—which gave the breweries increased control over the quality of their beer. Many pubs disappeared, and running beers became more popular, since they could be served soon after being brewed.

In 1840 a reduction on the glass tax promoted the use of bottles, and beer bottling companies became prevalent, especially in port cities.

Thus began the rise in popularity of buying bottled beer and consuming it at home, a practice embraced by the newly formed middle class.

In 1880 Prime Minister William Gladstone changed the beer tax laws with the Free Mash Tun Act, which based beer taxes on a Standard Original Gravity, as opposed to malt and hops usage. A "National Standard Gravity" was established, and from 1880 to 1907, the National Standard Gravity of beers in Britain dropped from 14.25 °P (1.057 SG) to 13.25 °P (1.053 SG), and to 12 °P (1.048 SG) during World War I. Brewing higher-gravity beers meant paying higher taxes. Taxation, changing tastes to lower-gravity beers, and temperance movements all contributed to a reduction in the strength of English beers over the next several decades.[26]

Though the IPA style became one of the most popular styles in the late 1800s, by World War I the Burton version had become less popular. In London particularly, it had been supplanted by lower-gravity IPA. Several factors contributed to the reduction in IPA brewing, but probably the most significant was the growing popularity of lower-gravity pale lagers—the Pilsner and the helles beer styles from Central Europe. With the development of industrial refrigeration, lagers could be produced year-round, and be released and shipped throughout the year. The clean flavor of lager appealed to many beer drinkers—especially those in hot climates. As such, lagers started to become very popular in India, Australia, and the United States. Because the Burton brewers had put so much focus on domestic IPA production, it's possible they missed this key trend and neglected to defend their turf in these faraway lands. In the 1880s and 1890s, much criticism was aimed at Burton brewers for letting the export business slip away. But with the popularity of their beers domestically, and the ease of shipping them via railroad, there may not have been much financial incentive to continue investing in distant markets, especially as increased competition reduced the profitability of exporting. In the 1880s German brewers such as Becks set up satellite lager breweries in India and Australia, and successfully utilized artificial refrigeration to lager their beers. This helped seal the doom of English IPA in those areas.

The rising popularity of lower-alcohol pale lager in England fueled interest on the part of British brewers to make something similar to compete. Some brewers, such as Allsopp and Barclay Perkins, started brewing lager beers themselves. Allsopp, a mainstay of IPA brewing, took a huge financial hit by entering the rush for tied houses late and overpaying. Allsopp was ultimately unable to compete with the marketing power of Bass, and after its production peaked in 1876, brewing quantity was reduced every year until it turned to lager brewing. After a failed merger attempt with Salt in 1907, Allsopp went into receivership in 1911 and struggled on until eventually merging with Ind Coope in 1935. Salt went into receivership in 1907 after the Allsopp merger failed and was taken over by Bass in 1927.

One of the other beers designed to compete with lagers was light pale ale, or light bitter, a lower-alcohol, lower-hopped version of IPA. It became a standard offering of many IPA brewers as early as 1850. Other brewers developed what were called "running beers," the forerunners of today's real ales or cask beers. These beers were significantly lower in alcohol content and hopping than IPA, were ready for drinking very quickly after brewing, and required virtually no aging, so the sales margins were higher. The availability of brewing sugars helped lighten the body of running ales. Their fresh character and relative lack of acetates and esters, as compared to stock beers, were embraced by British beer drinkers, who found them more similar in taste to the Central European lagers. As beer drinkers' preferences moved quickly away from the aged stock ales, running ales and light pale ales eventually overtook IPA. The younger upper- and middle-class beer drinkers embraced English bitter, and an evening of "doing bitters" became a popular activity.[27] Hopping rates and original gravity started dropping as these lower-strength beers became more popular. Averaged hopping rates in English beers dropped from 3–5 pounds per barrel in the late 1800s to 1.9 pounds per barrel by 1908.

Temperance movements worldwide also hit the IPA business hard, especially in India, as tea became the beverage of choice. Public drunkenness was no longer acceptable—especially among the wealthy, the major consumers of IPA. The rising popularity of gin and the ill effects of its overconsumption provoked a public response that targeted all types of alcohol. The temperance movement was embraced by factory owners (who wanted their workers to come to work every day without being hungover), politicians, women, and others. The movement also contributed to the growth of lagers, lighter ales, and running beers, which had a lower alcohol content than IPA and other stock ales.

Per capita beer consumption in England peaked in 1870.[28] Between 1888 and 1900, as England suffered through an economic recession, Burton saw a 33 percent reduction in breweries. Once the temperance movements gained steam and World War I impacted the supplies of ingredients and the ability to distribute beer, the town's dominance as a global brewing center was effectively over.

4 | BREWING THE BURTON IPA

This beer must come from Allsopp's vat,
It is so bright and mellow,
There's none but he can brew like that,
Oh! He's a famous fellow,
Such ale as this, wherever sought,
None other could invent sirs!
 'tis only brewed, 'tis only bought,
At Burton-Upon-Trent sirs!
O Beer! O Hodgson, Guinness, Allsopp, Bass!
Names that should be on every infant's tongue
—C. V. Calverley, English poet and parodist

The Industrial Revolution that took place in the 1700s and 1800s had a huge effect on the cultures, the lifestyles, and the economies of the countries that were involved. It started in England and resulted in periods of great economic and technological growth that changed the lives of English, European, and American citizens, as well as of those in other industrialized countries. As workers transitioned from farming and manual labor to factories, the greatest cultural impact was on living standards, with better working conditions, fewer hours, huge increases in pay, and conveniences that allowed for more comfortable living, easier travel, and additional free time.

The move to a machine-based economy impacted the brewing industry substantially. The advent or popularization of technical tools such as hydrometers, thermometers, and microscopes led to a dramatic advance in the understanding of the brewing process. The result was an increased ability to manage the brewing and fermentation process to make it more consistent, which drastically improved the quality of the beers being produced.

Some of the major industrial technologies that were developed during this period include steam power and steam heating, which allowed brewers to move away from wood- and coal-fired brewing vessels; iron making, which enabled brewers to move away from wood and stone vessels in the brewery; and the development of roadways, canals, and railways, which provided much easier transportation methods for brewers to get their beers to cities and ports.

Bass steam engine on display at the National Brewery Centre, Burton-on-Trent. Photo by John Trotter.

The "second" industrial revolution, which started about 1850, further advanced the technology available to the brewing industry. The perfection of steam engines improved the railroads and the ships, which cut the time of shipping to India by three months. Steam was used routinely by brewers to sanitize and strip flavor from wood fermenting vessels and casks. Other innovations in the brewing industry included the drum roaster, which was used for making roasted and crystal malts; the beer engine, for dispensing cask beer; cast-iron brewing vessels, which allowed for more rapid and effective heating and chilling, cleaner brewing processes, and larger brewhouses; the Steel's Masher, a grist hydration device that eliminated the need for hours of manual mash mixing by brewers with paddles; steam-powered rakes; steel heat exchangers that replaced open coolships; furnaces that eliminated the need for open fires in the brewhouses; the introduction of pumps that allowed for water, wort, and beer transfer by means other than gravity or manual pumping; and industrial refrigeration, which in the late 1800s finally enabled brewers to keep their ingredients fresh enough to brew year-round. Also, the internal combustion engine and electrical power helped breweries develop into complex technical wonders.

Another important change was the development of the chemical industry. This gave brewers the means to clean the brewing equipment and to adjust their brewing water by adding salts. The period also marked the introduction of cement, which was used in brewery construction.

Not coincidentally, several scientific brewing textbooks were introduced during this period. Some of the best include Tizard's *The Theory and Practice of Brewing Illustrated*, Roberts' *The Scottish Ale Brewer and Practical Maltster*, Mathias' *The Brewing Industry in England, 1700–1830*, and Loftus' *The Brewer*. These books provide great references for brewing researchers in all aspects of English brewing except one: yeast. The chapters these authors wrote on the science of fermentation are almost unrecognizable with today's level of knowledge. Although brewers and brewing scientists understood that the presence of yeast was critical to ensure fermentation, no one realized that yeast was a living organism, or that its metabolism was the engine of alcoholic fermentation, until the work of Louis Pasteur in the 1860s. Pasteur proved that fermentation was caused by the action of yeast, and that yeast was a living organism.

In the 1860s and 1870s, after Pasteur published his groundbreaking works, he traveled to breweries throughout Central Europe and England. He helped brewers identify their yeast and solve fermentation issues. As a result of Pasteur's travels, breweries started hiring chemists. The first noted brewery to hire a brewing chemist was Worthington's in Burton in 1866. Worthington's brought in scientist Horace Tabberer, one of the early pioneers of yeast culturing and yeast strain separation. The brewing chemist soon became the most highly esteemed and highly paid member of the brewery. He implemented many technological and scientific processes, including the introduction of new malts and sugars, the addition of brewing salt to brewing water, the improvement of malting operations, the monitoring of yeast strains and cultures, and fermentation control.[1] Consider this description from *A Glass of Pale Ale*, a Bass trade publication from the early 1900s: "[The] brewery is under the direction of gentlemen of the highest skill as scientific and practical chemists, and who are especially conversant with chemistry as bearing upon the art of brewing."

Horace Tabberer's lab at Worthington's.

The IPA that emerged during this time was one of the first beer styles that the Industrial Revolution spawned, and the beer became the symbol of bold technological innovation. It inspired many beer styles to come, including pale ale, Pilsner, and the running beers of the latter part of the century.

By all accounts, this India pale ale was unique in several ways as compared to the more common stock ales, porters, and pale ales of the day: It was crystal clear, very pale or the lightest amber, quite dry, and heavily hopped, although not overly bitter in taste. The taste of the beer was described as delicate, refined, and like a fine wine or champagne. It was a refreshing beverage—indeed, it was the first English beer type that was routinely served chilled. The Indian colonists used ice shipped from America's Great Lakes and saltpeter (potassium nitrate) to chill the beer.[5]

IPAs IN THE 1800s

There is plenty of documentation that describes the flavor of IPA throughout the 1800s, especially in medical journals, because IPA, being so dry, was thought to be a restorative beverage well suited to those suffering from diabetes—even better than the sweeter porters and stouts. Pereira, in his book *A Treatise on Food and Diet,* published in 1843, describes Burton India pale ale as "the Pale Ale prepared for the India market, and therefore known as Indian Pale Ale. Is free from these objections. (The objections being the strong, sweet, and sugary character of porters and stock ales, which weren't good for diabetics.) It is carefully fermented to be devoid of all sweetness, in other words to be dry, and it contains double the usual quantity of hops, it therefore forms a most valuable restorative beverage for invalids and convalescents. For ordinary use at the table, the weaker kinds of ale, popularly known as Table Ale, are to be preferred."

Similarly, Dr. William Prout wrote in *On the Nature and Treatment of Stomach and Urinary Diseases,* "People with stomach disorders cannot assimilate the sweeter ales. Some of the finer kinds of Burton Ales, however, are unobjectionable; particularly those prepared for the Indian Market, which are not only carefully fermented to be quite dry, or free from saccharine matter; but they also contain double the usual proportion of hops."

A *Liverpool Mercury* ad for Hodgson's ale in 1835 describes the beer as having "desirable qualities of keeping in any climate, and not bursting in the bottle, that have long enabled it to maintain the highest character it possesses, as particularly suited for exportation. Being brewed from the finest East Kent hop, it contains a particularly fine tonic quality, and is consequently much recommended by the faculty, even to invalids."

In 1840 a *Hull Packet* ad read: "Stock of both draught and bottled India Pale Ale....From great perfection to which this ale has been brought to withstand the effect of an Indian climate, it is divested of acidity, and is a most delightful summer drink, entirely superseding every other malt liquor."

In 1841, Bass published an ad in the London *Times* describing its beer as follows: "This particular style of ale varies greatly from the common malt liquors. It is more perfectly fermented, and approaches nearly the character of a dry wine; it has the light body of a wine combined with the fragrance and subdued bitter of the most delicate hop. That it is wholesome in an eminent degree is proved by its being drunk as the common beverage in India, where, from the nature of the climate, nothing which is not friendly to health can be used as an article of diet by Europeans." The ad goes on to reference Dr. Prout's statements.[2]

Allsopp followed with a similar advertisement one day later, and soon after, ads for Burton India Pale Ale appeared almost daily in the *Times*.[3] Mathias, in *The Brewing Industry in England, 1700–1830,* says: "Burton India Pale Ale has the remarkable virtue of arriving pale, clear and sparkling in Calcutta, more successfully than any other."

An 1877 ad by Read (Bass' bottler at Midland Railway and in London) provides one of the best descriptions of Bass IPA: "Bass Champagne Ale brewed from picked materials and with water naturally charged with the crystal salts peculiar to the Burton district. Hopped with the choicest growths of Kent and Surrey hops, possessing tonic bitter principles of the most refined delicacy. Carefully selected at Burton during the cold brewing weather, sent to London, kept in the Read Brothers' splendid stores until well matured, and then bottled by them. Champagne bottles are the best—they hold more than ordinary bottles, and they travel with less breakage. Messrs Bass Red Triangle label guarantees the brewing and it is endorsed by the Bull Dog label on the reverse side of the bottle. The sparkling lightness of this ale renders it the most suitable for hot climates, and with its nutritive value, ranks as 'the national beverage at its best.'"

References to the beer arriving as "ripe and sparkling," and comparisons to the finest champagne for its excellence and delicacy of flavor, are seen in many other ads.

This is from a description of Bass IPA aging in a cask: "A man inserted a screw into the side of a huge cask, and forthwith there sprang a pile-like stream of the purest amber which sparkled and shone in the dingy light of the oil lamps. Look at that! Isn't that clear? That is eighteen months old. Our better classes of ale have to be kept for a long time before sending them out, but the cheaper kinds are sent out almost as soon as we get them. The best ales need a little age on them." [4]

Also, it was not overly strong. Initial complaints that the beer was soporific influenced the brewers to reduce the strength to what were considered at the time as moderate levels.[6] The other important flavor descriptor used was the word "fresh." Despite being aged for 12–18 months or more, the India pale ale had a fresh character that differentiated it from stock ales—perhaps a lack of sourness or an intense hop character from the dry hopping. IPA was advertised as a summer beverage by many; it was highly hopped and able to stand (or keep) for a very long time.

Even negative reviews still tell us something about how these beers were brewed. Critics cited in the book *The British Brewing Industry, 1830-1980,* by T. R. Gourvish and R. G. Wilson, described poor-quality bottled IPA as having too much alcohol, too much sediment, too much hops and too little gas. Beer that was too old was described as harsh, but too young and the beer was lively, with a lot of breakage. Aging was critical, and it must have been carefully monitored by the brewers.

A careful combination of brewing ingredients and brewing techniques were used to brew this ale. Each ingredient and process contributed its own piece to the IPA puzzle and to the success of Burton in particular in brewing these beers.

INGREDIENTS

Water

Burton IPA had several unique ingredients that set it apart from Hodgson's and others' versions. One of the most important was the brewing water found in the Burton area. Burton beers already had a well-earned reputation for surviving exportation better than other English beers, and brewers felt a big part of that success was due to the mineral-rich water, which facilitated beer clarification during the aging process.

The wells differ significantly in mineral content, so as brewers in Burton gathered knowledge on the wells, they selected well water for brewing that gave the optimal characteristics for their beers.[7] Later, as the Trent occasionally got contaminated with bacteria, moving the water sources farther from the river became more important for beer stability. Salt, one of the original IPA brewers in Burton, along with Allsopp and Bass, moved its water source a quarter-mile away from the brewery very soon after it started brewing IPA, to get the right water profile. Bruce

Wilkinson at the Burton Bridge Brewery theorizes that the sterility of the water coming through tens of thousands of years of rock sedimentation also contributed to the early success of Burton beer exportation—not so much for the quality imparted on the beer itself as for the sterility of the water coming from the wells, which allowed for cask cleaning and rinsing without any risk of contributing to beer spoilage.

The Bass water tower from the old brewery still stands in Burton-on-Trent.

The high calcium in Burton water reduces wort pH, which increases enzyme activity in the mash. This allows for reduced protein, better starch conversion, and a drier beer. The extra calcium facilitates yeast flocculation and also provides better trub separation in the whirlpool and less protein haze in the beer. With high levels of calcium, there is less color development during the wort boil and a lower harshness in hops' bitter character. The high sulfate levels in the water give a full, yet dry flavor, enhance the hop bitterness, and produce a crisper, cleaner bitterness than beers brewed with softer water.

There are significant differences in the Burton-on-Trent water chemistry, depending on where the wells are located and how deep they are drilled. The earliest breweries located themselves closer to the River Trent and drilled their wells only to a depth of 30 feet. The brewers eventually moved their wells to get higher mineral content and also to reduce the chances of pulling in *E. coli* or other harmful bacteria that was making its way into the river. The later wells were drilled 100–200 feet deep.[8]

Table 4.1 Various Burton Waters (Grains per Gallon)

	Worthington deep	Worthington shallow	Allsopp	Bass
Sulfate of Lime	70.99	25.48	18.96	54.40
Carbonate of lime	9.05	18.06	15.51	9.93
Carbonate of magnesia	5.88	9.10	1.70	
Sulfate of magnesia	12.60		9.95	0.83
Sulfate of soda	13.30	7.63		
Sulfate of potassium			7.65	
Chloride of sodium	9.17	10.01	10.12	
Chloride of potassium	0.97	2.27		
Chloride of lime				13.28
Carbonate of iron	1.22	0.90	0.60	
Silica	1.12	0.84	0.79	
Total solid residue	124.29	74.29	65.28	78.44

Sources: *The Lancet*, no. 1 (1852), 474; Barnard, *The Noted Breweries of Great Britain and Ireland*, Vol. 1 (1889), 417. Courtesy of Ron Pattinson.

Note: Grains per gallon (gpg) x 14.25 = ppm or mg/L.

Table 4.2 Analysis of Various Burton Brewing Waters (Grains per Gallon)

	Burton above marl	Burton below marl	Dublin Grand Canal	Chalk water (South of England)	New River (London)	Thames Valley deep well (London)	Brewing well Lea Valley
Carbonates of lime and magnesia precipitated on boiling	11.4	15.4	11.0	14.2	11.2	4.9	12.2
Lime not precipitated on boiling	17.7	25.5	0.9	1.1	1.1		0.7
Magnesia not precipitated on boiling	4.3	10.2	0.9	0.1	0.2		1.7
Carbonates of the alkalis						13.0	
Sulfuric acid	33.9	56.8	0.5	0.6	0.9	8.4	2.4
Chlorine	3.0	2.5	1.2	0.9	1.4	8.0	1.6
Nitric acid				0.2	0.4		

Source: Southby, *A Systematic Handbook of Practical Brewing* (1885), 161–165. Courtesy of Ron Pattinson.

Note: Grains per gallon (gpg) x 14.25 = ppm or mg/L.

In 1830 the chemical nature of Burton water was revealed in the libel suit the brewers filed against the Society for Diffusing Useful Knowledge for claiming that Burton brewers adulterated their beers. This wasn't the first such claim against Burton brewers, but it did spread knowledge about the water that the brewers held in such high esteem.9 By the mid-1800s, several brewers in London and other parts of England were adding gypsum to their brewing water. The term "Burtonization" was coined in the 1882 text *The Manual of Brewing* by Egbert Hooper, who attributed the invention of the process to chemist Charles Vincent in 1878.10 Burtonizing water is still done by many IPA brewers today, although in the late 1800s, some brewers—for example, Ind Coope, Charrington, and Truman—simply built breweries in Burton to get the high mineral water at the source.

Malt

Only one malt was used in Burton IPA, and that was the extra pale or white malt (aka East India malt), which was kilned to only about 1.5 °L (3° EBC). Allsopp was the originator of this type of malt. The brewery malted its own barley using a lower kiln temperature of about 150° F (65° C) compared to the more standard 170–180° F (77–82° C). The result was a bright yellow malt that produced a beer deep golden or light amber in color.[11] After Allsopp's maltsters enhanced the malt, it was further developed by Burton brewers and Lancashire maltsters cooperatively, in order to get as pale a beer as possible. In fact, the effort to reduce color in IPA is common throughout the brewing processes used by Burton brewers.[12]

White malt is very similar to today's Pilsner malt, which, interestingly, was itself developed after an apparent industrial espionage mission by Czech brewers into England's best malthouses. The malt used to brew the very first batch of Pilsner Urquell was kilned in an English kiln that had been sent to what is today the Czech Republic.

Malt quality was of the highest importance, so brewers ran their own malthouses and developed tests to make sure the malt was well modified and would not throw a haze into the finished beer. One such test involved brewers tossing samples of malt into water; if the kernels sank, they were judged to be undermodified and of poor quality.[13] Later, as technology took hold in breweries, malting became a more exact science. With standardized analytical methods, brewers were able to take malt samples and brew wort on a small scale in the lab to measure expected color and extract recovery.

Chevalier and Goldthorpe were the preferred English barley varieties in the 1800s. Breeding programs led to the development of several new varieties in the 1900s, such as Spratt Archer and Plumage Archer.[14] In years of poor malt quality or low production, and in the late 1800s when brewing requirements exceeded English malt supply, barleys from California and the central United States, the Middle East, Austria, and Holland were used as well. Most of these foreign malts were shipped to England as raw barley and were malted at the English breweries to ensure proper germination and color.[15]

Brewing sugars and sugar-derived coloring compounds were first allowed in England in 1812, then were subsequently forbidden again in

1816 because of apparent abuse by brewers. West Indian sugar companies and other sugar suppliers complained about sugar and molasses not being allowed in beer, and in 1847 brewing sugars were again used in the brewing process. This had a huge impact on the English brewing industry, especially in London, where sugar use became frequent in the 1860s and common by the 1880s. By 1900 more than half of all English brewers were using brewing sugars.[16] Most Burton brewers resisted the use of sugars and other adjuncts in any of their beers until World War I, and kept their IPAs all malt until well into the 20th century.

Colored malts were not used in IPA in the 1800s. In fact, brewers went out of their way to avoid the amber and brown malts that were so prevalent in the early 1800s. Even after the drum roaster was developed in 1817 to allow brewers to use pale malt as a base with colored, highly roasted malts at smaller percentages, IPA was still brewed to be as light as possible, with pale malt only.[17] Crystal malt, which began to be used more frequently in the latter part of the 1800s, was not used in IPA until the 20th century, after the style evolved to a running (fresh) beer with a much lower starting gravity and alcohol content.

Today, only a few breweries, such as Marston's (above), still employ a cooper. Photo by John Trotter.

Hops

Hops in this period were named after the region in which they were grown, although varietal identification of hops gained ground in the latter part of the century. There is no doubt whatsoever that the hops used in Burton IPA for most of the 1800s were those from East Kent, later named East Kent Goldings, which were reportedly harvested for the first time in Canterbury, Kent, in the 1700s. These quickly became the most favored hops for all the brewers in England and Scotland.

Burton brewers used, to a lesser extent, the highly prized Farnham hop, the mild Worcestershire hop, and Surrey and Hereford hops. They avoided the hops from Northclay and Nottingham, which were described as rank. But without question the hop most associated with Burton IPA is East Kent Goldings.[18] When the Fuggle hop (thought to be derived from the Worcestershire hop) from Horsmonden, Kent, was introduced in 1861, it found its way into many IPA recipes. American hops from Oregon and the Northeast (Fuggle and Cluster) became available in the 1870s. When East Kent hops were not available, these hops from the other regions were used in the best IPAs. Because their flavor was not preferred by British IPA brewers, they were typically used early in the boil so that their distinct flavor contributions would be minimized.

Hops arrived at the breweries packed in bales or bags called pockets, and were not as compressed as the ones used today. In fact, some breweries would give the hops an additional pressing in order to extend their quality. Because artificial refrigeration didn't become common until the late 1800s, hops tended to lose their bitterness, aromatic, and flavor qualities much more quickly than they do today, and the additional pressing with a screw press to two-thirds of their original bulk helped to preserve them.[19] IPA, being the star of most breweries' lineups, was made with only fresh hops because of the importance of the hop to the flavor of the beer.

Breweries had huge hop stores, or warehouses, that were often located below ground to keep the hops cool. They staffed the hop stores with trained firefighters to deal with any threat to the highly combustible hops.[20] The staff would weigh out the hops for each of the following day's brews.

Hopping rates used for IPA were typically listed in brewing texts on a pounds-per-quarter basis. A quarter of malt is eight bushels, or 336 pounds. For Burton IPA, hops were added at anywhere from 8 to 22 pounds per quarter of malt, which at a gravity of 1.070 (17.5 °P), equates to 5–6 pounds per barrel of beer. About two-thirds of the hops were added at the start of the boil, and the rest were added in the hopback. Although the alpha acid content at the time was probably 25–30 percent of the hops used in today's American IPAs, it equates to using 1.5–3 pounds of American high alpha hops per barrel, which is a staggering amount, especially since the dry hops used in the casks (1–2 pounds of fresh hops per cask) aren't included in the totals! IPAs from other brewing areas, and those produced for domestic consumption, were apparently hopped at about 50 percent of the export versions by later in the century.

Yeast

Bass brewing log from October 1875. It notes that an 1875 crop of East Kent hops were used. Photo by John Trotter.

The Burton brewers maintained their own stores of yeast and sometimes shared them from brewery to brewery. Based on the yeast research work done in the late 1800s and the early 1900s, these yeast cultures are thought by most researchers to have been mixed cultures containing anywhere from seven to 14 strains. But at the time when IPA brewing started in Burton, the knowledge that yeast was a microorganism responsible for metabolizing sugars into alcohol and carbon dioxide was not understood. For this reason, there is little documentation regarding the yeast used or yeast management practices employed by the Burton brewers who were making IPAs. There was considerable scientific debate in the early 1800s concerning what role yeast really played in the fermentation process, and there were plenty of scientists who believed that alcohol fermentation was a chemical process. But brewers knew that without yeast, you would not get beer, so yeast management played a critical role in brewing.

Most English brewing yeast strains were vigorous top-cropping ones, so systems evolved to collect the yeast from the top. This, in turn, further enhanced the tendency of the yeast to gather at the top of the fermentation vessel. Today's top-fermenting yeasts are usually collected from the bottom of the fermentation vessel. Yeast settling is often promoted by the chilling of beer in the tank, a technology that was not available to English brewers at the time.

Secondary strains identified in Bass cultures in the late 1800s and the early 1900s confirmed the presence of *Brettanomyces* and Torula strains that did not survive well in wort but functioned well in lower-oxygen beer. Today's brewers in Burton believe that the Burton Union system's cleansing and collection process kept all the strains in the house cultures in proper balance.[21] The yeast cultures were so hearty that Fuller's was able to repitch yeast that had been collected from a six-month-old beer and successfully referment it.[22] For that reason, brewers in Burton sought to make the beer as bright (free of yeast) as possible prior to shipment to India; otherwise, the yeast would be able to restart the fermentation, and the casks or bottles would be subject to exploding.

BEER SPECIFICATIONS

By most written accounts, the first Burton IPAs were brewed to an original gravity of 17.5 °P (1.070 SG) and about 70 IBUs, and as pale as possible in color. Alcohol content probably ranged from 6–7% abv, which would indicate low terminal gravities of about 3 °P (1.012 SG). The first IPAs made by Allsopp, Bass, and Salt were brewed to replicate Hodgson's Bow ale, which most beer historians now believe was a stock (aged) pale ale. Over time, after receiving complaints of these being too soporific, gravities appeared to drop a bit, and specific gravities dropped to 15–16.5 °P (1.060–1.068 SG). Later, in the 1840s, new analytical techniques to calculate alcohol and starting gravities were implemented, and it appears that most IPAs brewed in Scotland and parts of England averaged 15 °P (1.060 SG) and 6.5% abv. Most references cite the Burton IPA as having been a little higher, 16 °P (1.064 SG) and 6.5–7% abv.

Table 4.3 **Burton Ale Analysis**

Burton ale	OG (°P)	OG (SG)	Brewers days (SP)
1st sort	27.75–30.00	1.111–1.120	40–43
2nd sort	24.25–27.75	1.097–1.111	34–44
3rd sort	19.25–23.00	1.077–1.092	28–33

Source: Pereira, *A Treatise on Food and Diet* (1843).

Note: The original Burton ale was much stronger than IPA.

Table 4.4 Allsopp Beers: 1870–1948

Year	Beer	Style	Acidity	
1870	Old Burton Ale	Strong ale	0.32	
1870	Old Burton Ale	Strong ale	0.25	
1870	Burton Ale	Strong ale	0.56	
1870	Mild	Mild	0.22	
1879	Burton Ale	Pale ale	0.23	
1896	Burton Light Dinner Ale	Dinner ale	0.20	
1896	Luncheon Stout	Stout		
1901	Red Hand India Pale Ale	IPA	0.14	
1921	IPA	IPA		
1922	PA	Pale ale		
1922	Extra Stout	Stout		
1926	Stout	Stout		
1928	Stout	Stout		
1932	Lager	Lager		
1934	Brown Ale	Brown ale		
1935	Milk Stout	Stout	0.06	
1937	Milk Stout	Stout	0.06	
1937	Milk Stout	Stout	0.05	
1937	Lager	Lager	0.05	
1948	Burton Pale Ale (bottled in Brussels)	Pale ale	0.08	
1948	John Bull Ale	Pale ale	0.05	
1948	Burton Pale Ale Export (bottled in Brussels)	Pale ale	0.07	

Sources: British Medical Journal (January 15, 1870); *Whitbread Gravity Book; Truman Gravity Book.* Courtesy of Ron Pattinson.

Note: A lot can be learned from this data. First, look at the Burton Ale, how strong it was and how sweet it was. There is a lot of residual sugar left in those beers. Second, the IPA is medium strength and very dry. It's not as strong as the Burton Pale Ale from the same period. The IPA final gravity numbers are very low, perhaps lower than regular brewer's yeast can get to. Third, note the lower acidities in the beers starting in the 1930s. This would suggest the elimination of acid-forming microbes from the fermentation process of aging in wood cooperage containing *Brettanomyces* or *Lactobacillus.*

FG (SG)	FG (°P)	OG (SG)	OG (°P)	ABV	Attenuation
1040.38	10.10	1121.63	30.41	10.64	66.80
1030.11	7.53	1111.45	27.86	10.69	72.98
1008.61	2.15	1086.40	21.60	10.30	90.03
1014.78	3.70	1057.33	14.33	5.53	74.22
1013.99	3.50	1069.51	17.34	7.88	78.79
1007.72	1.93	1053.92	13.48	5.81	85.02
1011.51	2.89	1063.47	15.89	6.69	80.94
1008.62	2.16	1061.57	15.38	6.80	85.27
1004.40	1.10	1054.40	13.60	6.56	91.91
1009.50	2.38	1045.70	11.43	4.71	79.21
1014.70	3.68	1053.70	13.43	5.06	72.63
		1048.40	12.10		
		1049.30	12.33		
1009.40	2.35	1041.00	10.25	4.10	77.07
		1035.90	8.98		
1013.80	3.45	1049.30	12.33	4.61	72.01
1015.10	3.78	1050.60	12.65	4.60	70.16
1014.50	3.63	1050.30	12.58	4.64	71.17
1011.80	2.95	1045.20	11.30	4.33	73.69
1008.90	2.23	1062.80	15.70	6.73	83.14
1008.20	2.05	1038.20	9.55	3.9	78.53
1007.10	1.78	1052.60	13.15	5.95	86.50

Most of the IPA shipped to India was actually consumed by agents of the East India Company and other merchants and wealthy colonists. English and Scottish soldiers stationed in India preferred porter but also drank brandy, the Indian liquor Arak, and later, gin and rum. Since the 1820s, officials in the military had been concerned about the effect of these spirits on their troops and encouraged the consumption of beer as an alternative. In 1878 the military issued the following specifications for the IPA they would purchase, which tells much about how a quality IPA was brewed:[23]

- IPA had to be brewed with 100 percent malt.
- OG had to be 15 °P (1.060 SG) minimum.
- Hops had to be used at 20 pounds per quarter minimum (about 4–5 pounds per barrel), plus 11 pounds new hops in the dry hop in barrels.
- Beer had to be casked not more than 21 days after brewing.
- Casks were required to be made from well-seasoned Baltic or Bosnian oak staves, free from sap, strong, stout, and well made. Casks had to be steamed at a temperature of not less than 230° F (110° C), and the staves were required to be one inch thick.
- Beer had to be brewed between November 1 and May.
- Beer for bottling was to be kept on hand for 9–12 months before bottling and to have one summer and one autumn fermentation before bottling.

DOMESTIC IPA

Although IPA originally appears to have been brewed as a stock pale ale, with no special recipe considerations for the ocean voyage, IPA brewed for consumption in England eventually evolved into a lower-gravity and lighter-hopped version. All beers destined for India in the mid-1800s, including pale ales, stouts, and porters (all of which were successfully shipped) were typically brewed to be more alcoholic and 10–15 percent more bitter than the domestic versions. Tizard wrote in 1843 that the domestic version of IPA is less spirituous and bitter, and this was echoed by Loftus in 1856.[24] In fact, eventually several IPA styles were brewed for different countries, including an Australian version, an American version, and the original Indian version. George Amsinck documents that domestic IPAs were brewed with 3.5 pounds of hops per barrel, while the export versions were brewed using 6 pounds per barrel. As the century wore on, IPA gravities and hop usage dropped, and followed the pattern established by the entire English brewing industry, as taxation, temperance movements, and general tastes evolved to favor lower-alcohol beers.

Table 4.5 Bass Price List: 1879–1880

	Per tun of 4 hogsheads	Per tun of 6 barrels	Per tun of 12 kilderkins (British pounds)
Pale Export Ale	20	21	23
No. 1 Export Burton Ale	25	26	28
No. 2 Export Burton Ale	23	24	26
No. 3 Export Burton Ale	21	22	24
No. 4 Export Burton Ale	19	20	22
No. 2 Imperial Stout	23	24	26
No. 3 Extra	20	21	23
No. 4 Double	19	20	22

Source: Bass, *A Glass of Pale Ale* (1884).

Note: Much can be determined from price lists. Note here that Bass No. 1 Export Burton Ale commands the highest price. Pale Export Ale falls in line with a couple of other brands and, therefore, is probably about the same OG.

THE BURTON IPA BREWING PROCESS

Malting

As described earlier, the malting process for the pale malt used low kilning temperatures of approximately 150° F (66° C) to get a low-color malt, about 1.5 °L, with high levels of available extract. The malt was germinated sufficiently to be well modified (meaning that the enzymes were fully developed), and as such, it could be used effectively in single-temperature infusion mashes (the English brewing industry's standard mash profile) without requiring any complex temperature rests or decoctions.

Most commercial breweries in Burton had their own malting facilities and employed maltsters as an important part of their staff. Independent malting facilities could also be found throughout England, primarily

Table 4.6 Truman (Burton) 1883 Hopping Rates

Date	Year	Beer	Style	OG (SG)	FG (SG)	ABV
Jan. 16	1883	6	Mild	1067.0	1018.6	6.41
Feb. 16	1883	7	Mild	1062.3	1013.9	6.41
Feb. 16	1883	8	Mild	1054.0	1015.0	5.17
Jan. 17	1883	A	Ale	1056.2	1015.5	5.39
Jan. 22	1883	C5 R	Ale	1075.6	1024.4	6.78
Jan. 23	1883	C5 S	Ale	1076.7	1027.7	6.49
Jan. 16	1883	L 5 S	Ale	1075.3	1023.8	6.82
Jan. 23	1883	L4	Ale	1080.9	1023.8	7.55
Jan. 19	1883	L4 S	Ale	1078.9	1028.3	6.71
Feb. 8	1883	P1	Pale ale	1066.5	1018.3	6.38
Jan. 19	1883	P1 B	Pale ale	1067.9	1022.2	6.05
Apr. 9	1883	P1 export	Pale ale	1068.7	1022.2	6.16
Jan. 15	1883	P1 S	Pale ale	1067.3	1018.3	6.49
Jan. 22	1883	P2	Pale ale	1061.5	1017.7	5.79
Jan. 18	1883	P2 B	Pale ale	1063.2	1020.8	5.61
Mar. 6	1883	P2 S	Pale ale	1062.6	1017.7	5.94
Jan. 22	1883	PA	Pale ale	1057.6	1016.6	5.42
Mar. 6	1883	S4	Ale	1075.9	1026.6	6.52
Feb. 14	1883	S4 x	Ale	1077.6	1027.7	6.60

Sources: Truman brewing records; Pattinson, "Late 19th Century Pale Ales," *Shut Up about Barclay Perkins* (blog; November 8, 2010).

Note: The Export Pale Ale has the highest hopping rate. Its gravity is right in the middle of the pack.

in the Lancashire region, and could be used as a supplemental or a sole source of malt by the brewers. Alfred Barnard's *The Noted Breweries of Great Britain and Ireland* describes in detail the malting facilities at Allsopp, Bass, and Salt breweries.

The Brewing Season

The IPA brewing season typically took place in the fall, following the tradition of October ale. This allowed for the use of the freshest hops and malt in the IPA brew, and for an extended aging period in wood casks over the winter and spring. Then, as weather warmed, the casks in which the beer was stored were debunged, and aging and secondary

App. attenuation	Hops lb./qtr.	Hops lb./bbl.
72.31%	5.56	1.51
77.78%	5.77	1.50
72.31%	5.77	1.30
72.41%	2.50	0.49
67.77%	5.74	1.78
63.90%	9.15	2.87
68.38%	8.57	2.75
70.55%	5.00	1.93
64.21%	9.83	3.47
72.50%	16.95	4.62
67.35%	16.56	4.75
67.74%	17.44	5.17
72.84%	16.95	4.62
71.17%	11.89	3.02
67.11%	16.11	4.37
71.68%	18.00	4.65
71.15%	11.89	2.83
64.96%	9.60	3.15
64.29%	10.04	3.45

fermentation was allowed to take place over the following nine to 12 months. At the end of the aging period, the casks were either transferred to fresh barrels to separate the yeast, or simply bunged and put on a boat to India, where another fermentation apparently took place, as evidenced by the description of IPA arriving in India in "sparkling" condition.[25]

As the century progressed, and as brewing techniques evolved and advanced, brewing season was extended through May, but summer IPA brewing was avoided by many brewers until industrial refrigeration allowed for year-round brewing. IPA continued to be known as an October beer or a March beer throughout the 1800s, and marketing material signified that only the finest, freshest ingredients were used, and fermentation took place only when the temperatures were mild.

The Brewhouse Process

The British brewers continued to use the multiple mash process until the mid-1800s, when the Scottish practice of sparging became popular. Parti-gyling was the norm, and blending of worts made from multiple mashes from a single grain charge to achieve a target specific gravity level was used. Typically for IPA brewing, the first two worts from a mash were combined to obtain a target original gravity of about 1.070 (17.5 °P).[26] Mash tuns were constructed from wood (usually oak or teak), and later in the century from steel, iron, or copper. Mashing occurred by placing hot water in the mash tun and adding the milled malt while brewers stirred the mash with paddles or oars. This was the method used until steam power was implemented to turn the mash mixers.

Mashing typically took up to 90 minutes in the bigger breweries. It is important to note that "mashing" in brewing logs and literature from this period referred to the process of mixing the milled grain with water. The conversion rest was another step altogether. In the middle of the century, the Steel's Masher was introduced. It was essentially a wort hydrater that combined the milled malt and the water prior to their going into the mash tun—thus eliminating the need for manual mixing.

After mashing and rest, the wort was drained through the false bottom and placed in a kettle for boiling. Kettles (or coppers) were direct fired with coal or wood as fuel. Fresh hops for IPA wort were added, and the boil proceeded for a specific amount of time—usually several hours. The Burton practice was unique in that low-intensity boils were used. In fact, the wort kettles were deliberately undersized to prevent a boil so intense that it foamed out of the kettle.[27] This long, low-intensity boil, more a simmer than the intense boils we look for today, was used to minimize any color development through Maillard reactions. The goal was to make the wort as light in color as possible, and that meant using low-color malt and low-intensity boils.

Hops were typically added in two stages: one addition at the start of the boil, and one addition midway through or toward the end. About two-thirds of the total hop bill was added to the first wort boil, and the wort was then passed through a hopback to remove the hops. The hops from the first wort were left in the hopback. The remaining one-third hop charge was added to the second wort boil, and when that boil completed, the wort was transferred into the hopback on top of the hops from the first wort boil. After the boils, the used hops were often recovered and pressed to remove any entrapped wort so they could be reused in subsequent lower-gravity worts. Hop pressing was apparently widespread and was standard practice for both Bass and Allsopp.[28]

Hopping quantities were high—especially by today's standards—even with the lower alpha acid content of the hops used in the 1800s. From the brewing texts of the time, Tizard cites that IPA was hopped at 22 pounds per quarter, or 5 pounds per barrel, and that the dry hop was 2 pounds of new hops added to each barrel. (Assuming a 54-gallon hogshead, that equates to more than 1 pound of hops per barrel in the dry hop.) Roberts, in his 1847 book *The Scottish Ale Brewer and Practical Maltster*, also refers to 22 pounds of hops per quarter, and given the range of gravities of 11–17.5 °P (1.044–1.070 SG), that equates to 4–7 pounds per barrel of hopping. Hopping rates were heavier when beers were brewed in spring and summer, and in general, decreased toward the latter part of the 1800s.

Fermentation/Burton Union System

After trub separation in the hopback, wort was transferred to a cooling vessel. Physical wort chillers did not appear on the scene until the late 1800s, so the most common method was to transfer the hot wort to a cooler (what we today call a coolship)—a flat, open-topped shallow vessel that allowed for atmospheric cooling. This cooling process risked spoilage by bacterial and wild yeast infection, but brewers were aware of this and took precautions to avoid it. They brewed only in seasons where the nights were cool, which made for reasonably quick wort cooling and allowed for quick yeast pitching to minimize spoilage risk. Late summer and early fall during the harvest season was the time frame when most bacteria were present, so brewers avoided producing wort until the weather cooled, microbial activity diminished, and wort could be chilled and yeasted quickly.[29] Later in the century, brewers used iron coolships and other cooling vessels, such as the "Morton refrigerator" that had water pipes running through them.[30] Well water was pumped through the vessel to hasten the cooling of the wort, or the wort was partially cooled in a coolship (which also helped settle out trub), then run over refrigeration systems cooled with water to get it to pitching temperature.

Prior to the development of the Burton Union system, wort sometimes was fermented and sold as beer in one single barrel. The barrels required frequent topping to clear them of yeast, which resulted in high beer losses.

The famous Burton Union fermentation system was developed around 1838 by Liverpool brewer Peter Walker, who patented the process.[31] By the middle of the century, all the prominent Burton IPA brewers were using this method for fermentation. The process involved a primary fermentation in a round vat or a stone or wood square. Wort was chilled to a relatively cool temperature of 59–60° F (15–16° C) prior to fermentation, then during primary fermentation, the wort temperature rose by approximately 7–8° F to about 67–68° F (19–20° C). At that point, anywhere from 12 to 36 hours, or until high kraeusen was reached, the beer was dropped from the primary vessel into the Burton Union system—a series of large casks—and the fermentation continued. Each row of casks had a large, flat pan or trough placed on top and each cask was equipped with a swan-neck pipe that rose from the top of the cask to the trough. This setup allowed the top-fermenting yeast to travel from the cask into the swan neck and be deposited into the trough, where it was then collected and either pressed and stored or used immediately for repitching.

The transfer of the fermenting beer into the Burton Union system was gentle to avoid excessive foaming. It could take as long as two or three hours to fill the casks to the level maintained for the rest of the fermentation. At some point, after much of the yeast had been collected, the casks could be topped up from one or two casks in the system.

The Burton Union process accomplished several things: First, the drop from the primary vessel to the Union system, despite being a gentle process, agitated and aerated the fermenting beer. This reinvigorated the yeast and helped complete fermentation, which contributed to the characteristic dryness for which IPA became known. Second, the yeast removal process in the Union system, referred to as cleansing, not only removed yeast from the beer but also helped get rid of protein and other undesirable compounds. This resulted in a very clear and clean beer when it was moved from the Union system into aging casks. At the end of fermentation, the beer had a cell count of only 1–1.5 million yeast cells per milliliter of beer, which is about the same level as a beer going into a cask of real ale today. This lower yeast content allowed for a more controlled secondary fermentation in the cask during the warmer summer months.

The Burton Union system also allowed for fermentation temperature control, as the casks were equipped with interior coils in which cool water could be pumped to maintain proper fermentation temperature. In addition, the Union system provided an effective and easy way to re-collect the top-cropping yeast. After the discovery that the Burton yeasts consisted of several strains, the brewers thought the Union system allowed for natural selection and collection of the most desirable strains, and that contributed to the enduring success of the Burton beers and their reputation for high quality. Yeast collected from other vessels did not provide the same fermentation results and flavor as yeast gathered from the unions.

The costs of operating and maintaining a Burton Union system became prohibitive in the mid-1900s, and even though brewers such as Bass struggled with developing similar fermentation characteristics and flavors using conical fermenters, most of the Burton Union systems had been pulled out of the big Burton breweries by the 1970s. Today the only Burton brewery that still uses the Burton Union system is Marston's, although Firestone Walker in Paso Robles, California, uses a modified version to ferment its beers.

Filtering

The Burton water and the Burton Union fermentation system resulted in a naturally clear IPA, especially after extended cask aging. Yet documentation exists that suggests some brewers filtered their beer. Straining through flannel or other porous cloth was one method,[32] and several textbooks suggest filtering through alternating layers of sand and charcoal.[33] But it's doubtful these methods were widely practiced, because the technology didn't exist to perform the process in a way that didn't oxidize the beer.

The Burton Union system's swan necks deposit yeast into the troughs.

Marston's Burton Union systems are the only ones left in Burton. Photo by John Trotter.

Barrels

One of the most important facets of IPA brewing was the aging process. In fact, beer historians have made the point that long aging was the most important step in the brewing of a proper IPA. After the Burton Union fermentation process was complete, the beer was transferred out of the union casks into hogsheads (oak barrels) for aging. Brewing records show that the beer in these casks was tasted periodically by the brewers to ensure proper flavor and microbiological stability. Hops, sometimes boiled for a short time, were placed in the cask to help with stability, beer clarification, and flavor. It is unknown when, and if, fining agents—such as egg whites or isinglass—were routinely added to these casks. But the argument is often made that the mineral content of the Burton brewing water and the Burton Union fermenting process helped cleanse and clarify the beer down to 1–1.5 million yeast cells per milliliter of beer prior to aging. So perhaps in Burton, fining agents weren't needed or used.

Dry hopping in the cask was not limited to IPAs and export beers but was a normal part of the brewing process. Plenty of documentation indicates that porters, stouts, and many other beers were dry hopped, typically at a rate of a quarter-pound to 1 pound per cask, with IPA being substantially more.[34]

At some point during the aging process, many of the Burton casks were shipped to stores (warehouses) in Liverpool, Hull, and London, where they were aged further before being shipped to India or prepared for domestic consumption. It is important to realize that in the 1800s very few breweries bottled their own beer. Bass did not have its own bottling line until 1950. The brewers used independent or semi-independent bottling companies to bottle their beer from casks that were kept in the stores. Bottling companies took their business as seriously as brewers and competed aggressively. Labels from the 1800s show that several different bottlers in both London and Liverpool could be used to bottle the same beer. The "Bulldog Mark" on the bottles was considered an indication of the very highest quality.

Casks were shipped from the breweries on narrow boats via the canals from Burton to Hull and to Liverpool. There was always a risk that the barge operators (aka Gainesboro Captains) would pilfer some of the delicious beer from the casks and replace it with water. This theft became commonly referred to as "sucking the monkey," and was prevented by packing the casks in another, larger cask.[35] Casks on this trip, if not equipped with theft-prevention measures, could be cooled by pouring canal water over their surface.

One of the largest cask stores in London was located in what is now the St. Pancras train station. The lower level still has the brick arches under which the casks of Salt and Bass IPA were stored. Another large store was the Younger's store, located by the London Bridge.

It took two people to transport full barrels of beer. Drawing courtesy of the National Brewery Centre, Burton-on-Trent.

The Cooper and the Cask

In a shopping mall in central Burton, called the Cooper's Square Shopping Centre, there is a life-sized statue of the Burton cooper. The plaque reads:

The Burton Cooper

Created in 1977 by James Butler RA,

this bronze statue depicts a cooper,

a traditional local craftsman

hammering down the trusses on the cask

so that iron hoops can be fitted

it celebrates the historic cask making

and repairing skills

which have been associated

with Burton upon Trent

since the brewing industry was first founded

Since its unveiling in 1994, the image of the cooper portrayed in this statue has become a symbol of Burton.

Although today only a handful of breweries still employ a cooper, the importance of the cooper to 19th-century brewers cannot be underestimated. Almost all beers produced spent some time in wood, and that wood had to be maintained. The cooper was responsible for selecting and purchasing the wood used for vats, Union systems, and hogsheads. The cooper was in charge of aging the wood, treating the wood, and building and maintaining the barrels and vats. When staves returned from India, the cooper's team rebuilt the barrels for subsequent trips. The coopers' yards in the Burton breweries were huge, taking up as much acreage as the breweries themselves. Drawings depict stacks of barrels, staves, and uncut wood. It was said that "armies of coopers" existed in Burton.[36]

A cooper's shop. Photo courtesy of the National Brewery Centre, Burton-on-Trent.

Mountains of barrels at Bass.

The Bass barrel yard.

The wood used for casks themselves was slow-growth oak from Northern Europe. It was specifically selected because of its very tight grain pattern, which meant that it would contribute little, if any, flavor or tannic astringency to the beer that was aged in it. Although brewers tested American and French oak, the overwhelming choice for brewers' casks was slow-growth oak from the Baltic and Poland.

When the wood arrived at the brewery it was cut, boiled to remove all sap, and aged for about a year before being built into casks. The casks were filled with boiling hot water for two to three hours prior to use (presumably to sanitize and remove any remaining oils or other flavor compounds). If any sourness was reported, the casks were steam treated to remove any flavor. After each use, the barrels were cleaned with boiling water or steam treated. Casks were reused for up to eight to 10 years.

Aging and Shipping

IPA was aged in wood casks at least nine months before it was shipped to India or prepared for domestic consumption. The aging process allowed secondary fermentation to complete, flavors to develop, the beer to settle crystal clear, and it to be completely flat when shipped to India. That the beer be flat was a prime requirement, as early shipments to India were plagued by exploding barrels and bottles. During the summer months, as secondary fermentation got under way, the bungs were often removed from the tops of the barrels to release pressure and prevent them from exploding. Tizard's 1846 book, *The Theory and Practice of Brewing Illustrated,* states, "All extraneous matter which forms the yeast, lees, etc., be removed, because agitation during the voyage would otherwise produce extreme fretting, leakages, and premature acidity." This may imply that some acidity was expected. But the aging process also refined the flavor of the hops, softened the bitterness, and made IPA a very drinkable beer. Young IPA, prior to aging, was said to have been so bitter that it was undrinkable.

As mentioned previously, aging took place in large stores that were often located away from the breweries in the shipping towns of London, Hull, and Liverpool. Interestingly, much of Bass' beer was barrel aged on site, outside. Trained staff from the breweries checked the beer's quality as it aged.

IPA was either bottled or kept in its original aging cask for shipment to India. Shipments took place from November through March, so the beer would arrive in India before the monsoon season. This means that the IPA was aged in England for at least a year in casks before being shipped! Later, when the trip was shortened due to the availability of steamships, the shipping season was expanded to November through June. But summer shipping was still avoided.

When IPA arrived in India, it developed a character that was often referred to as "sparkling." Despite having already undergone a secondary fermentation in England over the summer, apparently the beer underwent some additional fermentation during the voyage. Most resources indicate that the beer was not primed prior to shipping, which makes sense, given that the casks were not located close enough to the breweries for any sort of priming operation. Some of the beer was aged further in India or removed from the barrels and bottled there. Originally the six-month ocean voyage was a major factor in the resulting IPA flavor. But by the 1830s—the start of the heyday of Burton IPA—shippers began using steamships, which cut the voyage down to three months. At the height of IPA exportation to India, the opening of the Suez Canal in 1868 shortened the trip to only three weeks.

Author Pete Brown, who replicated the six-month voyage from England to Calcutta for his book *Hops and Glory,* feels strongly that the IPA aging process on early voyages was similar to that of Madeira sherry. In fact, the earliest boats carried Madeira alongside IPA, and the aging process may have resulted in some similar cooked flavor development, especially since in Brown's experience, the hold where the casks would have been stored is the hottest and most stifling area on the boat. There is no air circulation in the hold, and the air remains stale and hot, no matter what the outside temperature is.

After the beer arrived in India and was consumed, the oak barrels were often broken down to staves and used as ballast on the returning ships. Once in England, the staves were returned to the coopers in Burton and reassembled into casks to make the journey again.

It is apparent from period advertisements that bottles were shipped with increasing frequency to India in the 1800s. Especially after 1840, when glass taxes were reduced, bottled beer became less expensive to produce. Also, technology improved to allow for easier and better manufacture of bottles. Bottle labels can be found in brewing archives dating back to 1836, labeling the beer as India Ale, or as India Pale Bitter Ale. Bottles shipped to India were usually packed in barrels, with plenty of cushioning (straw, wood shavings, sea salt) to avoid excessive agitation.

The case for *Brettanomyces*

The secondary fermentation of IPA that occurred in the barrels during the summer months of aging in England and during the boat trip to India remains the subject of much interest and speculation. From the flavor descriptions of IPA in India that we have seen and the documented arrival of the beer in sparkling condition, the secondary fermentation undoubtedly is the source of much of this beer's unique character.

The one theory that seems to make the most sense is that the secondary fermentation in the IPA barrels was the result of *Brettanomyces* yeast activity. This theory has much substantiating evidence, including the fact that *Brettanomyces* yeast was first isolated and identified in a Burton secondary yeast culture in 1904 by N. Hjelte Claussen of Carlsberg. The yeast was named *Brettanomyces claussenii*, and Claussen described it as follows:

> Brettanomyces *produces a slow fermentation in wort or beer fermented with ordinary brewers yeast. The carbonic acid developed by its actions is retained very firmly . . . forms a copious and lasting foam. In the course of the fermentation rather a considerable amount of acid is formed . . . the taste and flavor of which cannot fail to attract the attention of any connoisseur by their striking resemblance to the flavor of stored English beers.*

> *In English breweries as well as anywhere else, the primary fermentation is carried on by the* Saccharomyces, *whereas the secondary fermentation of the typical English beers, as being due to* Brettanomyces, *essentially differs from those secondary fermentations on the Continent. In other words, the action of* Brettanomyces *is absolutely necessary to bring English stock beers into proper cask and bottle condition, and to impart to them that peculiar and remarkably fine flavor which in a great measure*

> *determines their values. . . . Hence it is evident that the secondary*
> *fermentation effected by* Brettanomyces *is indispensable for the*
> *production of the real type of English beers.*[37]

Brettanomyces is resilient, thrives in wood, and can actually consume the carbohydrates in wood when other food sources are not available. This helps explain how *Brettanomyces* might adapt well to the IPA aging process. It has the ability to entrench itself deeply (up to 0.3 inches) into the wood of a barrel, where it could survive on wood carbohydrates during the return journey from India and then also survive the steam sanitation process at the brewery before the barrels were reassembled.

The flavor and analytical characteristics of IPA detailed in this chapter and in chapter 5 also support the theory of *Brettanomyces* action in the 1800s IPA. For example, IPA is repeatedly described as being exceptionally dry. Analysis backs this up, with final gravities recorded in the 1–2.5 °P (1.004–1.010 SG) range, which is lower than one would expect standard brewer's yeast to ferment out. Add to this the fact that brewers took great care to brew and ferment a very dry beer—and then made great efforts to remove yeast before the beer was transferred into the barrel to avoid barrel explosions during shipping. Furthermore, during aging, the barrels were debunged to ensure reasonably flat beer at the time of shipping (again, this was done to avoid barrel explosions), yet the beer arrived in "sparkling" condition, which means that some secondary fermentation must have occurred during the voyage! Only *Brettanomyces*, other wild yeast, or bacteria could have consumed whatever complex carbohydrates were left in the beer prior to shipping. But wild yeast and bacteria can be ruled out because sourness and diacetyl were not used to describe the flavor of IPA.

5 | IPA BREWING AROUND THE WORLD: 1800–1900

Hurrah for Jones' brewery, may it never fail
Brew us beer and porter and beautiful stock ale,
That's the stuff for me, my boys, it drives away all pain,
Whenever I can get a glass of it I'll have it just the same.
—*Frank Jones Brewery Song*

Though Burton-on-Trent was undoubtedly the center of IPA brewing in the 1800s, there were several other brewing regions where IPA also became a major style. As the popularity of IPA grew, and as scientific research advanced the understanding of brewing water chemistry and yeast, IPA brewers sprang up all over the world. Some of the most notable IPA brewers of the 1800s were located in Scotland, London, Australia, and the United States. Most brewers in these areas patterned their India pale ales after the Burton-on-Trent versions from Bass and Allsopp, but there are some differences in brewing techniques and ingredients that are worth exploring.

ENGLAND: LONDON AND OTHER AREAS

Hodgson's Bow Brewery, Barclay Perkins, Whitbread, and other breweries continued to make beer for export throughout the 1800s. Because of Hodgson's success, most of the brewers initially patterned their IPAs after the Bow ale. Later, as Burton brewers gained the majority of the market, these other regions modeled their IPAs after the Burton ones, especially with regard to the brewing water profile. The IPA, along with several other beer styles, grew from a niche style to a major style in England in the middle of the century.

Although IPA production in London expanded, brewers still continued to make their traditional styles during the first half of the century. IPA was important but not necessarily the largest volume beer these brewers produced.

One of these traditional beers was stock ale (keeping ale, or old ale), a high-alcohol beer aged in vats and casks, thus exposing it to a variety of yeast and bacteria. The biochemistry of the aging process and bacterial action was not understood by the brewers of the time. But the aging and the eventual souring of stock ales were very important to the flavor of these beers. Keeping beers were often blended with young beers when served or packaged. For example, a Prize Old Ale was described as an 18-month beer blended with a two-month beer, while a Brewers Reserve was described as an 18-month beer blended with a six-week beer.[1] Stock ales continued to be brewed by many brewers until the late 1800s.

Porter remained a heavy hitter for many brewers; in fact, Hodgson's Bow Brewery continued to refer to itself as a porter brewer as late as the early 1800s. Porters and stouts were heavily exported to India in the 1800s.[2] But as the century wore on, many brewers moved away from the heavier, sweeter, aged styles, and increased their focus on brewing pale, sparkling, bitter, and lower-alcohol beers. Porter remained a staple with London brewers until the middle of the 20th century, but in other regions, it had virtually disappeared from the breweries' lineups after World War I.[3]

Mild ale was the other beer type, besides IPA, that became incredibly popular in the 1800s. Since it wasn't aged, this young, sweeter beer was often brewed with less hops than other styles. Strengths and dryness could vary, and some milds were quite high in alcohol. The key factor with mild ale was that it was consumed young, and because it lacked long aging times, it was less expensive than the vatted, aged beers and could be purchased by all classes. It became the drink of the working class of the Industrial Revolution. The definition of mild ale has changed significantly over time. What most people think of as a mild ale today (dark and low in alcohol) was first brewed after World War I. In the 1800s mild was young but could have varying hopping rates and strengths.

Pale ale (bitter), stout, brown ale, Burton ale, and other beer types were brewed as well. In the late 1800s, as the demand for less alcohol and fresher beers increased, some traditional English brewers, such as Barclay Perkins, turned to brewing pale lagers. Others opted for brewing running ale—the young beer made with the newer crystal malts and aged for just a short period of time before being sold. The development of lagers and running ales had a significant impact on IPA popularity in the last part of the century.

But IPA was the beer that generated the most excitement in the early 1800s, and by the mid-1800s, it was not just a beer to be exported. In England the demand for IPA was significant, and domestic consumption continued to grow until it peaked in the 1880s. The increasing popularity of IPA in England coincided with the rise of overall beer consumption and the transition from estate brewing to commercial breweries. Also, as pale malt became more readily available, pale, bitter beers increased in popularity. Praised by doctors for its health-enhancing qualities, IPA became the status drink of the upper middle classes.

IPA was generally priced higher than porter or mild ale, so it's no surprise that London—given the financial status of its residents, its abundance of shipping ports, and its many stores that were used for aging Burton (and Scottish) IPA—became a center for domestic IPA consumption. But it's quite possible that there were brewers who started applying the "IPA" tag to domestic pale beers that were less alcoholic and less hoppy than the original IPAs, just to take advantage of the demand.[4]

In the early 1800s, as Hodgson's India ale continued to thrive and Burton brewers worked on perfecting their own IPA recipes, brewers from other areas of England increased their production of similar beers. One of the earliest was George's Brewery in Bristol, a porter brewer, which began brewing a West India small ale in 1815. George's provided the famous quote in a conversation with a Calcutta merchant about Hodgson's ale: "We neither like its thick and muddy appearance or rank bitter flavor."[5] This comment is striking evidence, even if only partly true, of the difficulty of getting good beer clarity in a pale beer when brewing with the soft London brewing water. In 1828 George's Brewery produced a Burton-style IPA that was higher hopped and more bitter for export to Calcutta, but it eventually failed.

As Hodgson's brewery faded into obscurity in the mid- to late 1800s, London brewers Barclay Perkins, Charrington, Whitbread, and the brewery that became Fuller's picked up the slack with their IPAs. Ridge Street Brewery in Oxfordshire and Tetley's in Leeds were also substantial IPA brewers. Some of these IPAs were brewed exclusively for domestic use; they weren't even exported![6]

These other English IPA brewers employed ingredients similar to those used in Burton. Like the Burton brewers, they placed great value on extremely pale malt and wanted a very high attenuation rate. Malt supplies were not restricted to English malt; German and American malt were used as well. These malts were shipped to England as barley and malted in English malthouses.[7]

London brewers, because of their proximity to the region, had the first pick of the hops from Kent and, like Burton brewers, preferred the Farnham and the Goldings hops for their IPAs. London brewers did use a lot of hops, not only in their IPAs but in their porters and strong ales as well. For example, Barclay Perkins' minimum hop usage early in the century was 2.5 pounds per barrel of beer.[8] Not all the hops came from Kent, and in the latter 1800s, European and American hops were used routinely in IPA, especially in years of poor harvest quality of English hops. New York hops were used until the late 1800s, when evidence of California and Oregon hop usage is also seen in brewing records.

There were some substantial differences in the IPAs brewed in London versus those brewed in Burton. London water was softer than Burton water and resulted, according to historical documents, in a beer that had a softer hop character and less clarity than the Burton IPAs. The other major difference was the wort boil. Burton brewers preferred a long, less intense boil to minimize color pickup, while London brewers tended to use a shorter, more intense boil. Also, London IPAs were documented as having a very fast fermentation process, with a higher temperature pitch in the upper 50s to low 60s° F (14–18° C), and 48 hours in primary, followed by racking into barrels.[9] This may have resulted in a fruitier, more complex beer character, which again would lessen the perception of hops in the resulting beer. Later records do show most pitch temperatures being slightly lower, in the mid- to upper 50s° F (12.5—15° C).

Fermentation typically occurred in a large vessel, with possible racking to a secondary tank before casking. The Burton Union system of fermenting was not generally used in London breweries. Aging took place in either tanks or casks, and beer was then shipped to stores, to complete the aging process. Finings were more common in London IPAs than in Burton IPAs, and more common in domestic versions than in exported versions.

Table 5.1 London IPA OG and Hopping Data

Date	Brewery	Location	OG (SG)	Hop rate oz./gal. (lb./bbl.)
1832	Truman (IPA)	London	20.00 °P (1.080)	2.2 (5.1)
1832	Truman (XXK March Beer)	London	22.25 °P (1.089)	2.2 (5.1)
1834	Barclay Perkins	London	16.00 °P (1.064)	2.7 (6.1)
1838	Reid	London	14.50 °P (1.058)	2.6 (5.8)
1864	Whitbread	London	17.50 °P (1.070)	3.1 (7.0)
1868	Amsinck	London	16.25 °P (1.065)	3.2 (7.2)
1876	Fremlins	Kent	18.75 °P (1.065)	2.1 (4.7)
1878	Simonds	Reading	18.25 °P (1.073)	2.2 (5.1)

Source: Data from Harrison, "London as the Birthplace of India Pale Ale" (1994).

Note: Specifications are from London IPA brewers in the 1800s. Although the brewers' specifications vary considerably, their model was Hodgson's IPA, so we can assume Hodgson's was somewhere in this range. Also note the similarity in hopping and OG between Truman's IPA and Truman's XXK March Beer.

London IPAs were also noted as being slightly darker than the Burton versions, possibly due to the use of colored malts, the more intense kettle boils, and again, the influence of the softer water on beer clarity (or lack thereof).[10] IPA became very popular in England by the second half of the 1800s, and the domestic versions were typically brewed to a slightly lower gravity (e.g., 15.5 °P versus 17 °P, 1.062 versus 1.068 SG). Sugar usage in brewing was deemed legal in 1847 and appeared to have caught on more quickly in London than in Burton. By the late 1800s sugar was a common ingredient in London-brewed IPAs. But some Burton brewers resisted the use of adjuncts until World War II. Another common adjunct was flaked maize, which was used in Fuller's IPAs in the late 1800s, and more frequently by other brewers in the early 1900s.

As the scientific understanding of the benefits of brewing with hard water became better known, English brewers such as Ind Coope from Essex and London porter brewers Charrington (in 1872) and Truman, Hanbury & Buxton (in 1873) moved to Burton or set up satellite breweries there to be part of the IPA revolution. Ind Coope became the most successful of the transplanted breweries. It survived well into the 1900s before being swallowed up in the brewing industry conglomeration of the late 20th century.

English brewing techniques improved at a pace similar to that of other brewing regions. As the Industrial Revolution took hold, brewers moved away from wood vessels for brewhouses and fermentation, and started using steam power. Later in the century, they used refrigeration.

Although brewers had been adding gypsum to their water for decades, the process of Burtonizing brewing water to replicate the well water in Burton became a well-documented and common brewing practice.[11]

Barclay Perkins' Anchor Brewery in 1840. Drawing courtesy of Ron Pattinson.

IPA demand and production started to decline in the late 1800s. The development of crystal malts and the increasing knowledge in science that allowed for better yeast management and brewing techniques led to the brewing of a new style of beer, the "running ales," in the late 1800s. These were lower-alcohol and younger versions of traditional styles that were served with live yeast in the cask just weeks after being brewed. Running ales grew in favor as a response to the rising popularity of pale lagers in the latter part of the century. Although lager was becoming popular all over the world, in England, it was derided as a "ladies' drink." Despite this, lager brewing helped influence the popularity of the lower-alcohol, younger running ales.

The temperance movement and a change in the way beer was taxed favored running ales, as did a drinkers' preference for beer that was lower in alcohol and fresher on the palate. In 1880 Prime Minister William Gladstone changed the law so that beer was taxed on its original gravity instead of on the quantity of malts and hops used in brewing. The original gravity of English ales fell steadily thereafter. Running ales—unaged low- to medium-strength ales—remained the prominent ale in most parts of England.

In the late 1800s, steam was pumped through coils in the interior of the kettle, or copper, to heat the wort. Photo courtesy of J. W. Lees.

SCOTLAND

Scotland already had a rich brewing tradition dating back to the 1100s. Edinburgh was a brewing center, and the dark, sweet, and strong Scotch ales were the hallmark of Scottish brewing. Much of this beer was exported, going to France and the Baltics, as well as to expatriates in the United States.[12] In the case of the United States, the ships used to transport ale were loaded with American tobacco for the return voyage to Scotland.[13] This strong Scotch ale, brewed to a gravity of more than 1.100, was also referred to as "Scotch Burgundy." Scottish brewers excelled at brewing strong ales, and were well versed in the benefits of aging their strong beers for long periods of time to improve flavor and clarity. In fact, one beer type brewed on estates was called "maturity ale." It was brewed shortly after the birth of an heir to a gravity of 28.5 °P (1.140 SG) and aged until that heir reached maturity (21 years).[14]

Although Scottish brewers were exporting beer to India as early as 1800, pale ale brewing wasn't introduced to Edinburgh until the 1820s, by brewer Robert Disher, who had purchased the Edinburgh and Leith Brewery in 1821. At the time there were 25 brewers in Edinburgh, where the brewing water, similar to that of Burton-on-Trent, was high in calcium and sulfate, which favored brewing with pale malts and getting great beer clarity when aged.[15]

Twenty years later, IPA was being brewed by many Scottish brewers, including Younger and Campbell. It was first called pale India ale, then East India ale, before brewers finally settled on India pale ale, like the brewers in England. These IPAs were not only shipped to India but also to Australia and the Far East. Scottish IPA proved to be very popular in India, perhaps because many of the troops stationed there were from Scotland.[16] Later in the century, when these soldiers returned home, they wanted the same beer, and that fueled the demand for a domestic version of IPA that was slightly lower in gravity and hopping. The domestic IPA was well received, and its popularity and growth was assisted by the installation of railroads across Scotland.

In the 1800s the brewers of Edinburgh were second only to those in Burton-on-Trent in brewing IPA for export. By 1890 fully one-third of all the British beer being exported was from Scotland, with the largest exporters being Younger and McEwan's.[17] By the late 1800s Scottish brewers were providing most of the beer shipped to British armed forces around the world.[18]

Edinburgh was known by the nickname "Aulde Reekie" because of the wafting aromas from all the brewhouses in the city. Technology—including steam, refrigeration, and electricity, as well as the development of brewing science in the latter part of the century—also positively impacted the Scottish brewers and the quality of their beer. By 1900 Scotland exported 123,000 barrels annually, and brewers were moving in droves to Edinburgh to take advantage of the hard water there.[19]

The biggest brewer in Scotland was Younger, and fortunately, their brewing logs and archives have been well preserved. In addition, one of the best technical books about brewing in the 1800s is *The Scottish Ale Brewer and Practical Maltster* by W. H. Roberts, which includes a chemical analysis of dozens of IPAs from the mid-1840s. From these and other sources, we have a pretty good understanding of how Scottish IPAs were brewed.

The Younger Brewery in Edinburgh was one of the largest IPA brewers outside of Burton-on-Trent. Drawing courtesy of Ron Pattinson.

Scottish brewers had differing opinions on whether soft or hard water was best for brewing. Softer water increased extraction from malt and improved fermentation, while harder water was better for preserving ale. As the century progressed, more brewers moved to the Edinburgh area, where the water was noted to have a profile similar to that of Burton-on-Trent's. By the 1870s water treatment in areas with soft water grew more common.

For IPA the base malt had to be very pale and of the highest quality. Scottish brewers looked for at least 65–75 percent extract recovery from their malt, and insisted that it be kilned at the lowest possible temperatures to maintain high extract levels and delicacy of color and flavor. Scottish malt varieties used included the distinctly flavored Bere, Bigg, Scotch Common, and Chevalier. IPA and export ales from Younger were described as having a bright, golden color, and by the 1870s Younger was sourcing its malt from all over the world, including Europe and the United States. Charles McMaster, beer historian at the Edinburgh Brewing Heritage Society, notes that amber malt was used in some Scottish IPAs as well, and he opines that Scottish IPAs had a darker color than their Burton counterparts. After 1850 sugars also found their way into the grain bills of Scottish ales.

Scotland's climate is not very conducive to growing hops, so most came from other locales. In the mid-1800s, 90 percent of the hops used in Scottish ales came from Kent, and brewers felt the same way as their English counterparts did about the varieties. Farnham and Goldings were considered the best, and other varieties, such as Nottingham, were described as coarse and best suited for strong keeping ales. Brewers believed that 25–35 percent of the hop quality was lost after the first year, so fresh hops were used routinely in IPA brewing.

Scottish brewer's yeast ferments well at lower temperatures, and brewers routinely fermented Scottish IPAs and other ales in the mid-50s to 60s° F (12.5–18.5° C). Fermentations subsequently took a few days longer than the five days seen by the brewers in Burton-on-Trent. Some brewers would rotate yeast and use different yeast cultures at different times of the year. They also practiced trading yeast cultures with other brewers. The theory was that rotating yeast helped keep things "fresh" in the brewery, similar to rotating crops in fields. One of the advantages of Scotland's colder climate is that the brewers could maintain optimal fermentation temperatures throughout the year and thus were not limited to seasonal brewing.

Generally, Scottish brewing practices employed higher mashing temperatures than those in England, and the beers therefore finished a little sweeter with a higher terminal gravity. Prior to the middle of the century, mashing was typically done by putting all the brewing water in the mash tun first then adding the milled malt. Mashing (mixing the malt with the water) took just under an hour, then the mash tun would be covered and the mash allowed to rest for two to three hours for conversion. Steel's Masher was invented in 1853 and was used in many Scottish breweries by the 1860s—thus eliminating the need for manual mixing. After mashing, lautering took place. The Scottish invented the practice of sparging in the late 1700s, and its use was widespread in Scotland by the 1800s.

Wort boils were 60–90 minutes, considerably shorter than the Burton IPA boils. Brewers were concerned that hop flavors would become coarse if boils were longer. They watched closely for the "breaking of the wort," the point at which trub formation becomes optimum. Hop usage was 4–8 pounds per quarter of malt (1.25–3 pounds per barrel)—quite a wide range. Like the English, the Scottish tended to use more hops in spring beers when the weather started to warm. The hopping level in Scottish IPA was thought to be about two-thirds the level of hopping used in Burton IPA, especially after 1870. Hopbacks were introduced later to Scottish brewers, so most brewers used a haircloth sieve to remove hops from the wort as the wort was cast out of the kettle. The resulting wort was a little cloudy but not a concern to the brewers, who assumed that the hop carryover would help keep the wort-chilling process more sanitary.

Table 5.2 Scottish IPA Hopping Rates

No. hops/qtr.	Add at SOB*	Add at 60 min.	OG (°P)	OG (SG)
10	4	6	23.75–25	1.095–1.100
8	4	4	21.25–22.5	1.085–1.090
7	2	5	17.5–20	1.070–1.080

Source: Roberts, *The Scottish Ale Brewer and Practical Maltster* (1847).

*SOB = start of boil.

Table 5.3 Younger's and Others' IPA OG and Hopping Rates

Year	Brewer	Beer	OG (°P)	OG (SG)	Hop rate (lb./bbl.)	Hop rate (oz./gal.)
1835	Wm. Younger	'I' Ale	20	1.080	3.5	1.7
1848	Wm. Younger	Export Ale	15	1.060	5.2	2.3
1850	Alexander Berwick	Export Ale	16	1.064	4.5	2.0
1866	Wm. Younger	Export Ale	16	1.064	4.7	2.1
1885	Ushers	IPA	15	1.060	3.4	1.5
1896	Wm. Younger	No. 3 Pale	19	1.073	3.4	1.5

Source: McMaster, "Edinburgh as a Centre of IPA" (1994).

Wort chilling took place in coolships. Later in the century, the first chillers were put into use, with simply a tube of circulating cold water in the cooling vessel.

Fermentation typically was started in the mid-50s° F and allowed to rise to about 58–67° F (14–19° C). Although Younger used a Burton Union system of fermentation, in many breweries fermentation occurred in open-top wood vats. During high kraeusen, the foam was beat back into the fermenting beer, not skimmed or otherwise removed.

After fermentation, beer was run into a square tun (receiving vessel) or vat and allowed to settle for one to two days; then it would be run into a cask. This practice not only helped ensure fermentation was almost complete when the beer was put in casks, but also helped improve the clarity of the beer in the cask. As brewers in Scotland did not routinely use finings at the time, this settling process was an important contributor to clarification. Hops were added to the cask at this point as well, which assisted in clarifying the beer.

Younger was required to age its beer at least a year, and the beer was flat when shipped. Until the advent of steam-powered ships and refrigeration, Younger shipped its beer only from November through June, which indicates the beer was already quite well aged by the time it was shipped. It may have been discovered by accident that shipping flat beer helped prevent casks from exploding during the voyage.[20]

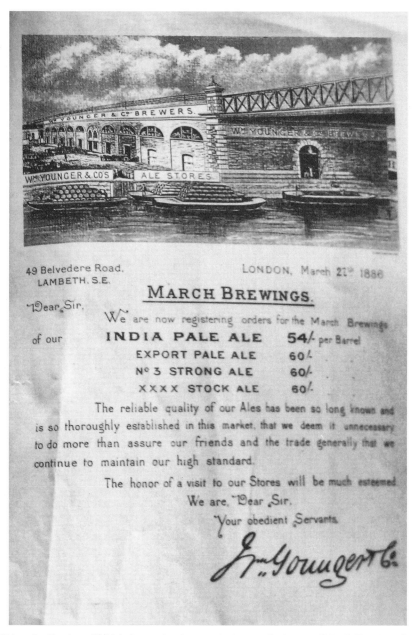

This price list from 1886 is interesting because it denotes the beer as "March Brewings," as opposed to October brewings (not shown). The artwork at the top depicts a large Younger store in London, complete with canal boats carrying barrels. Price list courtesy of James McCrorie.

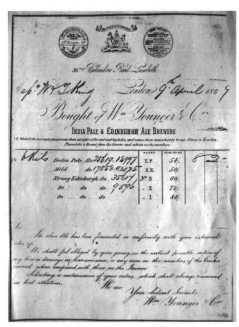

WM. YOUNGER & CO's
PRICES FOR EXPORTATION.
(Continent of Europe excepted.)

FREE ON BOARD AT LONDON OR LIVERPOOL.

(At Glasgow 6d. per Doz. Quarts, and 3d. per Doz Pints less.)

IN BOTTLE.

Packed in Casks of **4** Dozen Quarts and **8** Dozen Pints.	Glass, Wired and Capsuled.		Stone, Wired and Capsuled.	
In Cases, 3d. per Dozen Quarts, and 2d. per Dozen Pints extra.	Quarts.	Pints.	Quarts.	Pints.
INDIA PALE ALE, per doz.	7/9	5/4	8/3	5/4
DOUBLE STRONG ALE ,,	8/2	5/9	8/6	5/9
EXTRA STOUT ,,	7/9	5/4	8/3	5/4

IN BULK.

	Per Hogshead.	Per Barrel.	Per Kilderkin.
	£ s. d.	£ s. d.	£ s. d.
PALE EXPORT ALE, including Casks	4 15 0	3 8 6	2 2 6
No. 4 do. do.	5 0 0	3 12 0	2 4 2
No. 3 do. do.	5 5 0	3 15 0	2 6 0
DOUBLE BROWN STOUT do.	4 15 0	3 8 6	2 2 6

Younger's price lists. Note how the price of IPA compares to the Export Pale Ale and the strong Edinburgh Ale (aka Scotch Ale). Price lists courtesy of Ron Pattinson and James McCrorie.

Domestic Scottish IPA averaged 15.5 °P OG (1.062 SG), while the exported versions averaged 17 °P OG (1.068 SG). Taken from Roberts' *The Scottish Ale Brewer and Practical Maltster*, the data in appendix A, "Analysis of Various IPAs from the 1800s," show that some IPAs sent to India were as low as 11.16 °P OG (1.044 SG), which further adds to the argument that low-gravity beers certainly survived the trip. Scottish ale was documented as being sweeter than English IPA, and in 1858 one Calcutta agent wrote to Younger: "Your beer is well known for its body. This is an obstacle to it becoming a favorite brand, as it takes so long to ripen. The few casks of your last lot were fully 18 months before sufficiently ripe to drink." The beer was described as golden, highly impregnated with the finest hops, refreshing, and an excellent stomachic.[21]

To collect the data, Roberts uses state-of-the-art analytical technology of the time, including temperature-corrected saccharometers. Roberts focused on final gravities and attenuation levels to determine alcohol contents, and his book was the first to really research the strength of ales across England. It was initially released in 1837, although two other editions were published in 1846 and 1847.

UNITED STATES

For the first part of the 1800s, brewing was concentrated in the northeastern United States. Brewing practices mirrored those of England, with Philadelphia, New York, and parts of New England having the biggest breweries. Philadelphia and New York City were major brewing centers at the start of the 1800s, and porter breweries were ubiquitous throughout the region. Philadelphia was a major export center, and beers from American breweries were exported to many locations, including India and China. Beers from England were imported heavily into the United States as well, and up until the late 1800s, the United States was the highest volume recipient of English beer.

Given the continuing influence of England on the former colonies, the breweries in the northeastern United States predominantly brewed English types of beers. Later in the century, as immigrants from Central Europe began to inhabit the mideastern and midwestern parts of the United States, lager brewing gained a foothold and later became the dominant brewing type in the country. Ale brewers maintained their grasp on the Northeast, however, and as Burton brewers in England perfected the IPA style, these brewing techniques found their way to several breweries in the mid-Atlantic and New England regions.

Before the introduction of IPA, American ale brewers were brewing stock ales and imperial pale ales. These were aged a long time and were described as having sour or tart flavors. The "imperial" tag denoted quality and luxury. When the popularity of IPAs from England became known, American brewers started brewing their own versions of these beers. They were very similar to stock ales, with starting gravities of 16–17.5 °P (1.064–1.070 SG) and fermenting dry to 1–3 °P (1.004–1.012 SG).[22] Two to three pounds of hops per barrel were used prior to dry hopping, and this resulted in estimated IBUs of perhaps as high as 70. Sugar was routinely added to increase gravity, alcohol, and quaffability. These brewers were also known for brewing porters, Burton ales, and other English beer styles.

Malt was grown in the Chesapeake region and in New England in the early part of the century. It frequently suffered from weather damage and poor growing conditions, so American brewers were not reluctant to use adjuncts in their beers. Common adjuncts included honey, molasses, corn, and later, sugar and rice.[23] Malted wheat and rye were frequently used as barley malt substitutes. Hops were in better abundance and were cultivated in New York State, Western Pennsylvania, and Ohio. Later in the century, malt was grown in the Midwest and California, and hop farms were established in California and Oregon. These American malts and hops were not only popular with American brewers but also with English brewers, who regularly imported them to use in their beers, especially when weather conditions negatively impacted the English crops.

C. H. Evans, Frank Jones, Christian Feigenspan, Ballantine, and Matthew Vassar were some of the predominant IPA brewers in the 1800s. They followed the Burton process, using pale malt, high hopping rates, and extended aging time in wood. Many of these American IPA brewers used wood vats instead of hogsheads for aging but otherwise followed many English processes, including malting their own barley and shipping casks to local bottling plants. They often used barley grown in the United States or Canada and American hops—some grown in Ohio and Pennsylvania and much grown in New York State.

At this time, many of the U.S. hops were the Cluster variety, which had been discovered growing naturally in North America. Later in the century, Goldings and Fuggle cuttings made their way to the United States and were grown there.

The C. H. Evans brewery was started by Benjamin Faulkins in 1786 in Hudson, New York. Robert Evans and James Phipps purchased the brewery in 1856, and it became the C. H. Evans Brewing Company in 1873, eight years after Cornelius Evans entered the partnership. Family owned for its entire existence, it made its name by brewing authentic English-style beers using 100 percent American ingredients. The water profile in the Hudson Valley was hard, similar to that of Burton, which is why the founders chose that location. The brewery malted its own barley on site and had its own yeast strain. It brewed English beer types, including IPA, a 10 percent Burton ale, and stout.

C. H. Evans in the 1800s.

Like most large commercial breweries in the 1800s, C. H. Evans did their own malting.

The C. H. Evans IPA was aged so long that the beer was crystal clear in the bottles.

The flagship beer of C. H. Evans was the IPA, which was brewed with American malt and hops to 7% abv. The IPA was aged in hogsheads for at least a year, and this aging allowed the beer to be crystal clear and virtually free of any sediment when bottled at the main bottling plant in New York City. In fact, advertisements from the late 1800s show this absence of sediment as a major selling point for the beer. Another selling point was the supposed medicinal benefits of both the IPA and the stout. One ad reads: "Turn it upside down, no dregs, rich as cream, without sediment, free from false ferments, allowed 2 years to ripen in wood before bottling."

C. H. Evans brewery's biggest year was in 1910, when it brewed more than 70,000 barrels, making it one of the largest ale brewers in the United States. At its peak, the brewery site had 12 buildings, including a malthouse and a small bottling facility, and its beer was shipped as far away as Arizona and California.

Neil Evans, who started a new version of the C. H. Evans Brewing Company as a brewpub in Albany, New York, tells the story of the end of the brewery. The brewery had always been run by a pair of brothers, and when Prohibition started, Neil's grandfather made the unilateral decision to close it, causing a family rift that was never mended. The brewery buildings were sold to the Peter Barmann Brewing Company of Kingston, New York, in 1924, dismantled in 1928, and burned mysteriously to the ground in 1930. No brewing records or logs exist, and what Neil relates about brewing at C. H. Evans came from discussions with his grandfather and other family members.

FRANK JONES' BREWERY & MALT HOUSES.
PORTSMOUTH N.H.
DEPOT 82 & 84 WASHINGTON ST. BOSTON.

Drawing of the Frank Jones Brewery. Courtesy of Scott Houghton.

Because of Prohibition and the tumultuous end of the C. H. Evans brewery, very little in the way of records or recipes has been found. Neil Evans thinks that the traditional Genesee 12 Horse Ale may have a flavor profile similar to the old C. H. Evans IPA.

Another popular U.S. brewery was the Frank Jones Brewery. It was opened in 1858 in Portsmouth, New Hampshire, by Frank Jones, a businessman and New Hampshire native and John Swindell, from England. Within a few months, Jones took 100 percent ownership of the brewery, and by the 1880s was brewing 150,000 barrels per year, making him the largest ale brewer in the United States at the time. As the Jones Brewery grew, it continued building, adding malthouses, barrel rooms, and a bottle shop in the 1890s. It also bought the Henry Souther & Company Brewery in Boston, and operated it as the Bay State Brewery until 1905. Bay State was capable of brewing 650 barrels per day. Frank Jones employed more than 500 people in Portsmouth and was a major fixture in the town.[24]

According to an article in the *Portsmouth Chronicle,* the Jones Brewery used Canada barley and brewed stock ale, amber ale, cream ale, and IPA. It aged these beers in barrels after primary fermentation. Also notable was the presence of Quassia in the brewery. Quassia is a tropical fruit that some English brewers used as a low-cost substitute for hops.

Frank Jones was not only a businessman, he also ventured into politics, becoming the mayor of Portsmouth and subsequently a two-term U.S. Congressman in the 1870s before returning to full-time brewery duties. Like many American brewers in the late 1880s, Jones sold his brewery to British investors, but he remained in control of the brewing operation and sat on the board of directors. The brewery never re-opened after Prohibition and eventually was sold to its rival Portsmouth brewery, the Eldridge Brewing Company, which continued to release Frank Jones Ales and Lagers until closing in 1950.

Descendant Don Jones started the brewery again as a craft brewery in the late 1980s before closing and selling the equipment to Portsmouth craft brewers Smuttynose Brewing Company. Relics of Frank Jones can be seen throughout present-day Portsmouth, including the original brewery buildings at Jewell Court and Islington Street, the Odd Fellows Building at the intersection of Fleet and Congress Streets, the nearby Wentworth by the Sea Hotel, and the Rockingham Hotel. Peter Jones, Don Jones' brother, has opened the Frank Jones Restaurant in Barrington, New Hampshire, and is trying to have the original Frank Jones Ale brewed again.

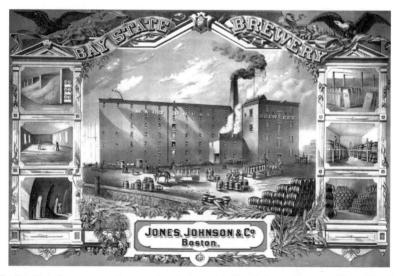

The Bay State Brewery was also owned and operated by Frank Jones. Courtesy of Scott Houghton.

The Christian Feigenspan Brewery was founded in Newark, New Jersey, in 1866 or 1870 (reports vary). Its Pride of Newark brewery brewed "dark beer," "brown stout," porter, imperial pale ale, amber ale, and IPA. Feigenspan gained notoriety for having 30 two-story fermenters, 9,800 barrels of fermentation capacity, and a "Monks Cellar," which contained 100-barrel oak vats for aging the IPA. Its IPA was considered its best beer. It was aged in wood for two years, "longer than any other," and was stated as being for "sipping."

Christian Feigenspan.
Photo courtesy of Bil Corcoran.

Feigenspan was a prominent brewery prior to Prohibition and had just bought the Dobler Brewery of Albany when Prohibition hit.[25] Possibly because of World War I–era restrictions on the allowable alcohol level of beer (set at a mere 2.75 percent), Feigenspan entered into Prohibition with 4,000 barrels of aging ale in its cellar. The brewery tried in vain to sell it for use in foods such as malt vinegar, but ended up dumping it. At the start of Prohibition, "medicinal beer" was allowed to be brewed by four companies, and Feigenspan was one of them. But when the "Anti-Beer Law" was passed in 1922, that beer was dumped as well. Feigenspan failed to completely recover after the repeal of Prohibition and ended up being purchased by Ballantine during World War II. In its brochure from a period between the end of Prohibition and World War II, one interesting statement is that the discovery of India pale ale was "an accident. It was discovered that English ales developed a new, heartier flavor through the longer aging en route."

The Feigenspan Brewery. Photo courtesy of Bil Corcoran.

The "Monks Cellar," containing the oak aging vats where IPA was reportedly aged for two years. Photo courtesy of Bil Corcoran.

Peter Ballantine immigrated to the United States from Scotland in 1830 and founded his brewery in Albany, New York, in 1833. In 1840 he moved brewing operations to Newark, New Jersey, where they remained until 1971.[26] Ballantine was famous for its ales, including its IPA and its Burton ale, which was reportedly aged in oak vats for up to 20 years, then bottled and given as gifts to preferred customers. One of the few ale breweries to survive Prohibition, Ballantine has some good records of its brewing processes and recipes. These will be explored in chapter 6.

Vassar Brewery was established near Poughkeepsie, New York, in 1797 by Englishman James Vassar. The abundance of wild hops in the area, and Vassar's intention to grow barley on his property, led to the establishment of a small commercial brewery on his farm, which sold casks of beer alongside the dairy products Vassar brought to market. In 1801 the family partnered with Oliver Holden and founded a brewery in Poughkeepsie. Vassar sold beer in casks and in bottles as far away as New York City.

In 1810 James Vassar's sons, Matthew and John Guy, took over the brewery from their father, and in 1811 John Guy was killed when he entered the brewery after a fire had destroyed it. Matthew Vassar rebuilt the brewery, and it continued growing. John Guy's sons, Matthew Jr. and John Jr., came into the business in 1832. Matthew Vassar Sr. left the company to found Vassar College, and Matthew Jr. joined him in the 1860s.

The brewery thrived until the late 1890s, with two fully functional breweries peaking at about 20,000 barrels per year. Malt was produced at the brewery itself or was sourced from a few local maltsters. The hops used were locally grown as well, and both hops and malt suffered from seasonal variation and the poor kilning technique used by U.S. hop growers (who generally kilned too hot) in the first part of the 19th century. Vassar's average use of malt was 3.5 bushels per barrel and 2.5 pounds of hops per barrel when it brewed porter, brown ale, single pale ale, and IPA. In 1866 Vassar's nephew Oliver Booth purchased the brewery and specialized in exporting beers to the Caribbean. He refused to brew lagers and developed other businesses until the brewery finally closed in 1899. A remnant of the Vassar Brewery can be found at Vassar College, where one might hear the following song:

And so you see, for old V.C.
Our love shall never fail.
Full well we know
That all we owe
To Matthew Vassar's ale!

In the 1890s the United States went through an economic depression, and breweries had already started to consolidate. British businessmen invested in breweries in common areas and consolidated them in an effort to corner regional markets. Some victims of these consolidations were the IPA brewers. This, coupled with Prohibition in the early 1900s, ensured the demise of most of the American IPA brewers. Unfortunately, records are scarce for these IPA brewers.

Thomas Ryan's Consumers Brewing Company in Syracuse, New York, founded in 1880, was a noted brewer of ales, porters, and India pale ale.

The Robert Smith India Pale Ale Brewery was originally founded in 1784 by Joseph Potts in Philadelphia. Potts sold the brewery to Henry Pepper in 1786, after the Revolutionary War, and the brewery was run by his son George. Robert Smith, who had apprenticed at Bass Brewery, came to the United States in 1837 and purchased Pepper's brewery in 1845. Advertised as America's oldest brewery, the company was incorporated in 1887 and moved locations. In 1893, after Smith's death, the brewery was run by Schmidt's and produced approximately 60,000 barrels per year until Prohibition.[27]

The brewery that became the John Betz Brewery was started in Philadelphia by Robert Hare prior to the Revolutionary War. Its claim to fame was as one of the first of two breweries to introduce porter to the United States. George Washington was a noted fan of Hare's porter, which was shipped to Calcutta in the early 1800s. After changing hands and becoming the Gaul Brewery in 1804, it was later purchased in 1880 by John Betz, who had trained in New York as a brewer and had come to Philadelphia 13 years earlier and worked at the Gaul Brewery. Betz introduced lager brewing to his brewery but also brewed a 6.5 percent IPA and a 7.5 percent East India pale ale. Betz's half-and-half was a mixture of two-year-old ale and stout, and Betz's Best was a lager that was said to rival Bavarian imports. The Betz brewery reopened after Prohibition and remained in business until 1939.

Table 5.4 U.S. Beer ABWs and ABVs

Beer/brewery	ABW	ABV
Peninsular Brewery (Detroit)	4.81	6.01
Bass Ale	5.61	7.01
Bass Stout	7.24	9.05
Schlitz Milwaukee Lager	4.00	5.00
Niagara Beer	8.87	11.09
Toledo Brewing and Malting Company	4.81	6.01
Farrell's East India Ale	4.81	6.01
Farrell's East India Porter	5.61	7.01
Best's Milwaukee Export Beer	4.81	6.01
Carling's Porter	7.42	9.28
Tennent's Pale Ale	5.61	7.01
Tennent's Stout	6.43	8.04

Source: University of Michigan, *Contributions from the Chemical Laboratory* (1882).

Note: It is interesting that Farrell produced an East India Porter alongside its IPA.

CANADA

Canada's biggest breweries were founded by immigrants from England and Scotland who brought traditional English brewing techniques with them. Molson Brewery, founded by English colonialist John Molson, in 1786 in Montreal, is North America's oldest brewery. Molson traveled back to England to get brewing equipment and barley seeds to grow the malt for his beer. Before electrical refrigeration became available, Molson was confined to a 20-week operating season, because the company had to rely on ice from the St. Lawrence River. Nevertheless, production grew throughout the 1800s as the Montreal brewery steadily added more land and equipment. Population growth and increasingly sophisticated bottling and packaging techniques also contributed to Molson's profitability in the early days. It brewed an IPA, and its ale, called Molson Export, is still Canada's largest volume ale.

Labatt Brewing Company was founded in 1847 by John Kinder Labatt and brewer Samuel Eccles in London, Ontario. By 1853 Labatt was the sole owner and was brewing 4,000 barrels per year. Labatt's started to grow rapidly after the Great Western Railway expanded to include London, thus allowing the brewer to ship his beer to Montreal and Toronto. Labatt's son, John Labatt II, apprenticed at a brewery in Wheeling, West Virginia, and while there he learned how to brew IPA. At age 26 he assumed the role of brewmaster at Labatt's, and by 1878, Labatt's IPA had won awards all over the world. The company continued to grow until Canada implemented its own Prohibition, which allowed breweries in some provinces to continue brewing for export. By the end of Canadian Prohibition, only 15 of the country's 65 breweries had survived.

The Alexander Keith Brewery's IPA survives to this day. Founded by Scottish Brewer Alexander Keith in 1820 in Halifax, Nova Scotia, the brewery made its name in the mid-1800s by brewing a nationally renowned IPA. Now a subsidiary of Labatt, its current IPA is 5% abv.

AUSTRALIA

In Australia, a colony of England at the time, the first brewery opened in 1795, and by the late 1800s, there were several hundred breweries producing mostly ale and porter. Commonly referred to as colonial ale, the Australian ale was typically a high-alcohol beer brewed with a percentage of rice, corn and/or sugar, and other flavorings. At the peak in the late 1800s, hundreds of thousands of gallons of ale were brewed annually in Australia. About 10 percent of the beer that was consumed in Australia was imported from England—mostly IPA, pale ales, and a beer called 3P, an imperial porter. These beers were typically shipped in large hogsheads and were often bottled upon arrival.

Australian brewers were heavily influenced by British beers, and there existed somewhat of an inferiority complex associated with colonial beer. Many of the beers were awful—and quite possibly hazardous. No one wanted to drink them unless real English beers weren't available.

Australian beers were sometimes named after famous British brewing regions or breweries; others would have labels printed with the name of a popular English beer and add a small "a la" to the label. By the 1880s quality was improving due to advances made in science and technology. The brewers started listing themselves on the stock market, and in the 1890s many breweries went under during an economic collapse.[28]

In 1888 the Foster brothers from New York City moved to Australia and started a brewery that utilized refrigeration and brewed bottled lagers. After the Australian economic collapse, lagers took off and became the dominant style brewed. Consolidation played an influential role in the early 1900s, with Carlton United Brewers being a major company. With consolidation came a lack of variety, and IPA virtually disappeared from the Australian beer scene.

INDIA

Interestingly, one area of the world where IPAs were brewed was India itself! There were several breweries established in India in the 1800s. Many of them were located in the foothills of the Himalayas and in the Punjab region, but not in Bombay. The Murree Brewery Company, the largest brewery in India, had four breweries in the Punjab region. The largest of these, the Gora Gully Brewery, brewed with Punjab-grown barley and hops imported from England, California, and Bavaria. The Mohan Meakin Brewery (known as "the Bass of India") used a Burton Union system to ferment its beers.[29]

MacKinnon's was another major brewer. Established in 1834 in Mussoorie, it had a Burton-trained brewer who produced an IPA that was filtered into casks from aging vats by using a German-style beer filter. At an elevation of 6,000 feet, the brewery had crystal-clear mountain water that was used not only as an ingredient in its beer but also as a power source (the brewery had no steam engines). Crown Brewing Company and A. B. Crichton also established breweries in Mussoorie.

There were other breweries as well, and their beer was drunk mostly by the colonists and the soldiers; the Indians had not yet acquired a taste for beer. These local beers were in competition with imported IPAs, and Indian brewers' output matched what was brought in from England. In the late 1870s, Indian brewers were able to procure contracts for the majority of the army's northern garrisons and stations.

By 1901 there were 27 breweries in India brewing IPA, porter, and ale. Fourteen of these brewers were located at high elevations with a good supply of clean water. Half of the beer produced by these high-altitude breweries was purchased by the English Army.[30]

IPA IN DECLINE

As the 1800s drew to a close, several movements and occurrences contributed to a rapid decline in the brewing of IPA. Temperance movements gained steam in America, England, and Australia, and appearing intoxicated in public was becoming less and less acceptable. As a result, drinkers switched to lower-alcohol beers, such as the running beers of England and the lagers from Germany, America, and Australia. Beer gravities all over the world dropped, and nowhere was this seen more than in England. As World War I became a reality, rationing and increased taxation perpetuated the drop in original gravity and the reduction in alcohol of the beers being brewed. In India, German lager breweries were built, and the pale lager style quickly overtook IPA as the favorite of the colonists. In the United States, Prohibition resulted in the loss of most of the ale breweries, and it took 50 years for small ale breweries to make a comeback.

Nevertheless, IPA, despite dramatically changing in flavor, brewing process, and alcohol content, continued to be brewed in England throughout the 1900s and later became the most popular craft beer style in the United States—100 years after its popularity peaked in England.

6 | IPA POST-WORLD WAR I

The government will fall that raises the price of beer
—*Czech Proverb*

ENGLAND

In 1900 the average specific gravity of all beer brewed in England was
13.75 °P (1.055 SG), a slight drop from the 14.25 °P (1.057 SG) seen
when this data was first recorded and used for tax purposes in 1880.
Beer gravities had started to drop steadily after the peak of IPA popularity in the 1880s. This decrease was partly a result of the increasing presence of running ales, which were brewed with the new crystal malts and
possessed a fresher flavor similar to the pale lagers that were becoming
popular in Europe, the United States, and Australia. Today's "real ale"
descended from running ales, which in turn descended from original
pale ales and IPAs. Running ales—fairly low-alcohol beers with minimal
aging—were made possible by science and by improvements in brewing
technology. For example, the ability to replicate Burton water with salt
additions resulted in quicker clarification in a pub cask.[1]

The temperance movement that started in the late 1800s continued
to gain strength in the 1900s. Although it never reached the heights of
the disaster that was Prohibition in the United States, the temperance
movement and the disfavor bestowed on public drunkenness produced
significant changes in the drinking culture of England. The economic

Table 6.1 Allsopp's IPA: 1901–1922

Year	Brewer	Beer	Package	OG (°P)	OG (SG)	FG (°P)	FG (SG)
1901	Allsopp	IPA	Bottle	15.14	1061.57	2.23	1008.62
1921	Allsopp	IPA	Bottle	13.46	1054.40	1.14	1004.40

Sources: Wahl and Henius, *American Handy-book of the Brewing, Malting and Auxiliary Trades* (1902), 823–830; *Whitbread Gravity Book*. Courtesy of Pattinson, "Allsopp Beers 1870–1948," *Shut Up about Barclay Perkins* (blog; December 25, 2010).

Note: The Allsopp IPA from the 1900s is incredibly well attenuated.

Table 6.2 Analysis of British Beer Styles in 1905

Beer	OG (°P)	OG (SG)	Lb. hops/ bbl. wort	oz. hops/ gal.
Mild ale	12.5–14.5	1.050–1.058	.75–1.5	0.38–0.77
Pale ale	12.00–13.75	1.048–1.055	2.0–3.0	1.03–1.55
India pale ale	13.75–16	1.055–1.064	3.0–4.0	1.55–2.06
Strong ale	16.25–20.75	1.065–1.083	3.0–4.0	1.55–2.06
Porter	12.5–14	1.050–1.056	.75–1.5	0.38–0.77
Single stout	15.75–17.5	1.063–1.070	2.0–3.0	1.03–1.55
Double stout	18.75–20.75	1.075–1.083	2.5–3.5	1.29–1.81
Imperial stout	21.25–24.5	1.085–1.098	3.0–4.0	1.55–2.06
Export stout	15–24.5	1.060–1.098	3.0–5.0	1.55–2.58

Source: Baker, *The Brewing Industry* (1905). Courtesy of Pattinson, "What Is Authentic IPA?" *Shut Up about Barclay Perkins* (blog; December 15, 2010).

Note: This table shows the wide range of IPA gravities in 1905. Hopping was still relatively strong at about three to four pounds per barrel.

and political situation in England in the early 1900s further influenced the proliferation of lower-alcohol beers.

Whitbread's IPA in the early 1900s had an original gravity of 12.5 °P (1.050 SG), a terminal gravity of 3.25 °P (1.013 SG), just under a 5% abv, and a 74% apparent degree of fermentation.[2] Fuller's IPA from the same time frame was 13.25 °P OG (1.053 SG), down from the 15 °P (1.060 SG) recipe used in 1890. It was brewed with a variety of malts from England, California, and Chile, and English and Oregon hops.[3]

Attenuation	Real FG	ABV	ABW	Real atten.
85.27%	4.70	6.80	5.44	68.96%
91.91%	3.37	6.56	5.25	74.96%

During the the two world wars, when rationing was implemented and ingredient shipments from other countries became risky, beer original gravity dropped even further—hitting low points of 7.75 °P (1.031 SG) in 1919 and 9.25 °P (1.037 SG) in 1947.[4] Prime Minister David Lloyd George, when discussing the seven tax increases made on beer during World War I, blamed the lack of English munitions availability on "the lure of the drink." The average IPA original gravity followed suit, dropping from 17.5 °P (1.070 SG) to 12.5 °P (1.050 SG) before and during World War I. Such difficulties for IPA brewers continued through the 20th century, and resulted not only in many brewers dropping the IPA style altogether, but also in a fair amount of consolidation, including the purchase of Salt and Worthington by Bass, the purchase of Allsopp by Ind Coope, and the major consolidation in the 1990s and 2000s, when several traditional English brewers were swallowed up by international brewing conglomerates, with many of their brands disappearing completely.

Coincident with the drop in gravities, hop rates were also reduced—and for the same reasons. Hop rates across the United Kingdom dropped to 1.9 pounds per barrel by 1908. By 1935 hopping rates had dropped all the way to 1.29 pounds per barrel.[5]

In the early 1900s mild ale was the favored beer style in England. Porter, the beer of the working class from the 1700s to the mid-to-late 1800s, had seen steady declines in popularity for many of the same reasons as IPA, and it had virtually disappeared outside of London. During this period, mild ale wasn't the low-gravity beer that most in the latter part of the 20th century referred to as the mild style. It was brewed to a healthy gravity of 13.75 °P (1.055 SG). But mild ale was served fresh, not aged, so it cost less than the long-aged IPAs and porters—thus making it popular with laborers and others who couldn't afford the luxury of higher-priced beers. The April 1908 Licensing Bill describes the situation perfectly:

> The finest kinds of beer, usually called India pale ale or double stout, are comparatively expensive, and the price at which they are sold enables them to be sent long distances for consumption by people who can afford such luxuries. The great mass of working classes, however, drink what are known as mild beer, porter, or light bitter ale, costing fourpence a quart or a penny a glass. These beers are the staple of the local brewer's trade.[6]

Table 6.3 British Beer Standard Gravities

Year	Avg. gravity (°P)	Avg. gravity (SG)
1880	14.25	1.057
1900	13.75	1.055
1905	13.25	1.053
1915	13.00	1.052
1917	12.25	1.049
1918	10.00	1.040
1919	7.75	1.031
1920	9.75	1.039
1921	10.75	1.043
1932	10.25	1.041
1941	9.75	1.039
1942	9.00	1.036
1943	8.50	1.034
1944	8.75	1.035
1947	8.25	1.033
1950	8.50	1.034
1951	9.25	1.037

Source: From Bass, A Glass of Pale Ale (1950s).

Note: Notice the influence war had on the gravities of beers brewed in England.

The Defense of the Realm Act (DORA), established by the British government during World War I, set age restrictions on drinking, limited hours of pub operations, and so forth. It drastically impacted drinking habits in England at the time. This furthered the reduction in popularity of IPA and other higher-alcohol beers.[7]

While IPA consumption declined steadily in England, by 1900 the export business had also almost completely dried up. India was now home to several German-style lager breweries. Australia, while still importing substantial amounts of IPA from Scotland's Younger Brewery, was moving quickly toward a lager culture, with the growing popularity of Foster's and other big Australian lager breweries. U.S. brewers were struggling unsuccessfully to defeat the Prohibition movement.

Due to variable malt- and hop-growing conditions, and as shipping became easier and less expensive, it was common for English brewers to use malt and hops sourced from several different countries throughout the 1900s. Plumage Archer and Spratt Archer were the two major English malt varieties in the early 1900s. Most prominent in the 1940s and 1950s was Proctor, and the Maris Otter variety came in the 1960s.

Most barley fell into three categories: European two-row, six-row of Manchurian origin, and Mediterranean six-row, grown in California, Chile, and Australia. Manchurian six-row malt was popular with American brewers and was grown in the midwestern United States. Typically English brewers used two-row malt and Mediterranean six-row. Malt sourced from other countries often was shipped as unmalted barley and was malted on the brewery premises or in malthouses contracted by the brewers. Six-row malt was popular with both English and American brewers because of its lower cost, high nitrogen (enzyme) content, and increased ratio of husk to endosperm in the kernels, which allowed for higher uses of adjuncts such as corn.[8] It's uncertain whether the prevalence of maize/corn resulted from the increase in six-row malt usage (corn would dilute the higher nitrogen content and allow for better beer clarification), or whether the six-row malt usage increased because adjuncts such as corn, which has no enzyme, would benefit from the increased enzyme breakdown from six-row malt.

The East Kent Goldings hop variety remained the most popular hop for English IPA, but the Fuggle variety, introduced in 1875, was also used by many brewers. English brewers imported hops from Germany, California, Oregon, and New York, too. Brewing records from the early 1900s don't designate particular hop varieties, but in reviewing growing records from that period, it appears that the majority of hops from California, Oregon, and New York were the American Cluster variety and the English Fuggle, which was a major hop in Oregon and California at that time. By the middle of the century, hop sources included New Zealand and the Yakima Valley in Washington State. These hop-growing regions were preferred because their dry climate promoted excellent hop quality, with hops free of mildew, diseases, and pests. Hopping rates dropped as original gravities dropped and as alpha acid percentages increased. In fact, one source claims dry-hop rates of about one pound per barrel—down significantly from the mid-1800s.[9] But hops were still important flavor components and also assisted with beer clarification.

Adjunct usage became commonplace, even in IPA. Flaked maize and brewing sugars were as much as 10–15 percent of the sugar source in IPA. By most accounts, this was driven by a desire to keep the beer dry and the color light. Sugar use was more prevalent with the London brewers; most Burton brewers kept their IPAs all malt, at least until about World War II.

Crystal malts also made their way into English IPA recipes sometime in the 1900s. Although the original IPA was necessarily pale, 1900s English IPA developed a reputation for often being more amber than the American craft-brewed versions and had a profile more similar to a best bitter than the original IPAs of the 1800s.

Adding salts to water was common, as the benefits of calcium on yeast health and beer clarity became better understood.

By 1940 most IPA gravities had dropped to about 10 °P (1.040 SG), and World War II resulted in the virtual elimination of the style from most English breweries. Bass continued to brew IPA, in the form of its Continental Ale, which was brewed to an original gravity of 15.75

°P (1.063 SG), finished fairly dry at 4.25 °P (1.017 SG), and used 1.75 pounds per barrel in the dry hop.[10] This beer was popular in Europe in the late 1950s and the early 1960s but disappeared soon after that. Ind Coope's Double Diamond survived until the 1990s, when Ind Coope was purchased by Carlsberg Tetley. Other notable IPAs that survive to the present day include the 9 °P (1.036 SG) Greene King IPA; Wadworth's 3.6% abv Henry's IPA (originally a pale ale); and White Shield from Worthington, one of the few English breweries that maintained 5–6% abv on its IPA throughout the 1900s.

Despite the drop in gravities and hop usage, brewers such as Barclay Perkins, Whitbread, and Worthington continued to brew IPA until the latter half of the century, when the style finally succumbed to the drive toward homogenization of the beer business and lower gravities. From that time until the craft-beer revolution in the 1980s and 1990s, only a few IPAs were still produced in England, and they were certainly different beers from those brewed at the start of the century. For a more detailed look at English IPA profiles from this time, see appendix B, "1900s English IPA Analytical Profiles."

Table 6.4 British Beer Gravities by Style

Years	Stout	Porter	Mild	IPA	Average
1805–1899	1077.8	1057.5	1068.6	1058.6	1065.6
1901–1917	1074.5	1053.8	1050.3	1058.9	1059.4
1919–1929	1055.5	1037.8	1041.9	1046.7	1045.5
1930–1939	1048.9	1035.8	1036.2	1046.7	1041.4
1940–1949	1042.0		1030.2	1037.0	1036.4
1950–1959	1043.3		1032.4	1038.8	1038.2
1960–1968	1046.8		1032.5	1040.7	1040.0
2002–2005	1047.8	1046.7	1037.8	1041.7	1043.5

Sources: Data from Protz, *Good Beer Guide 2002* (2001) and *Good Beer Guide 2005* (2004); *Whitbread Gravity Book; Truman Gravity Book;* Whitbread, Barclay Perkins, and Truman brewing logs. Courtesy of Pattinson, "British Beer Gravities 1805-2005," *Shut Up about Barclay Perkins* (blog; August 10, 2008).

Note: Prior to the 1900s, mild ale was stronger, on average, than IPA. Porter was not really brewed in England after the 1930s for the rest of the century. IPA gravities are starting to climb again!

Label courtesy of Ron Pattinson.

BOTTLED BEERS

Barclay's Ales & Stouts — NETT.

	Per doz. Large Wh'sale	Retail	Per doz. Small Wh'sale	Retail	Per crt. 4 Flagons Wh'sale	Retail
Pale Ale	10/11	13/-	—	—	7/1	8/4
Farmer Ale (S. & W.)	—	—	6/-	7/6	7/1	8/4
India Pale Ale ...	—	—	6/-	7/6	—	—
"Doctor" Brown Ale	11/9	14/-	6/-	7/6	7/7	9/-
No. 1 Southwarke Ale	—	—	9/11	13/-	—	—
Stout	11/9	14/-	6/-	7/6	7/7	9/-
Best Stout	—	—	7/8	9/6	—	—
Victory Stout... ...	13/11	16/6	7/6	9/6	—	—
Russian Stout (Nips)	—	—	12/3	16/-	—	—

Barclay's Lager

	Per doz. Small Wh'sale	Retail
Light	8/6	11/6
De Luxe (Dark)	10/-	12/6

Barclay's price list. Courtesy of Ron Pattinson.

The National Brewery Centre Museum has an "N-gauge" model of the town of Burton, circa 1920. Just about every building in the model, except for the churches, is associated with the breweries. Photo courtesy of John Trotter.

Scottish brewers had a little more success in maintaining the export business for their IPA, but their dependence on exportation backfired as British colonialism withered away in the 1940s and 1950s. In 1945 Maclay of Edinburgh reintroduced its Wallace IPA. But it didn't survive for long, even though an ad stated, "IPA makes a welcome return to Maclay's Thistle Brewery after an absence of 50 years. India pale ales were originally brewed for exportation to the far outposts of the Empire. Wallace is typical of the IPA style in colour, strength, and superb hop flavor."[11]

In the early 1990s, Scottish beer historian Charles McMaster theorized that McEwan's Export Ale probably bears the closest resemblance to the original Edinburgh IPA. At 3.8% abv, Deuchars IPA, brewed by the Caledonian Brewery in Edinburgh, is certainly lighter in strength, a bit lighter in color, and perhaps more hop forward than the original Edinburgh IPA of the 1800s.

Table 6.5 Analysis of Younger's and McEwan's Scottish IPAs

Year	Brewer	Beer	Package	OG (°P)
1949	McEwan's	Export IPA	Half-pint bottle	11.7
1950	McEwan's	Export IPA	Half-pint bottle	12.2
1954	McEwan's	IPA	Bottle	12.1
1955	Younger	IPA	Half-pint bottle	7.5
1957	McEwan's	Export IPA	16 oz. can	11.6
1972	Younger	IPA	Draught	10.9

Sources: *Whitbread Gravity Book*; Daily Mirror (July 10, 1972), 15. Courtesy of Pattinson, "Scottish IPA 1947–2004," *Shut Up about Barclay Perkins* (blog; December 25, 2011).

Note: With the exception of the 1955 Younger's example, Scottish IPAs appear to be stronger than English IPAs from the same time frame. Scottish IPA was still exported in the mid-1900s.

UNITED STATES

Only one beer brewed in the United States after Prohibition successfully continued the tradition of the 1800s IPA, and that was Ballantine IPA. Despite its being virtually extinct by the 1970s, this beer provided the inspiration for the very first craft-brewed IPAs. Ballantine was well known for its three-ring symbol: "Purity, Body, Flavor." First used in 1879, the symbol was said to be inspired by condensation rings on a table.[12]

Peter Ballantine emigrated from Scotland and started brewing in upstate New York in the 1820s. In the 1840s he moved to Newark, New Jersey, and built a brewery there. By 1870 Ballantine's was the fifth-largest brewery in the United States. As described in chapter 5, Ballantine modeled its beers after the best beers of Burton-on-Trent. These included the Ballantine XXX Ale, the 20-year-aged Burton Ale, and the IPA, which was aged in wood vats for up to a year.[13]

The brewery survived Prohibition by making malt syrup and diversifying into insurance and real estate. Upon the repeal of Prohibition in 1933, Ballantine was purchased by Carl and Otto Badenhausen, who brought in Scottish brewmaster Archibald MacKechnie. They grew the business on the East Coast by buying rival Feigenspan in 1943 and becoming a mainstay sponsor of baseball broadcasts for the New York Yankees and the Philadelphia Phillies. By the 1950s Ballantine had grown into the third-largest brewer in the United States, behind Schlitz and Anheuser-Busch, and all their beer was sold in the eastern half of the United States.[14]

OG (SG)	FG (SG)	ABV	Attenuation
1046.8	1.009	4.79	81.84%
1048.8	1.013	4.52	74.18%
1048.6	1.008	5.05	63.13%
1030.2	1.007	2.91	77.15%
1046.4	1.011	4.46	76.94%
1043.5	1.008	4.60	81.15%

Unlike Great Britain, where taxes, wars, and ingredient rationing had driven gravities down to the point where the IPA was a clearly different beer style than it had been in the 1800s, the Ballantine IPA remained true to history, with gravity, alcohol content, and hopping rates similar to the 1800s IPA of Burton. Ballantine IPA was an anomaly in the lager-driven U.S. beer industry of the mid-1900s. Prohibition had successfully driven many of the smaller regional ale brewers in the Northeast out of business, thus paving the way for the lager brewing giants of the Midwest to gain total domination of the U.S. beer industry. Fourteen years without legal access to beer during Prohibition resulted in a lost taste for beer by Americans—especially for the heavier, more bitter beers—and that allowed the mild American lagers to grab a foothold as the industry re-established itself in the 1930s and 1940s. Yet somehow Ballantine IPA survived, and even flourished, until the 1960s.

The Ballantine Brewery. Photo courtesy of Brew Your Own *magazine. Used by permission.*

BALLANTINE'S ALE

America's great leader among ales, adapted to the American palate through almost 100 years' experience.

The House of P. Ballantine. & Sons is the oldest brewing firm in America. Behind every drop of Ballantine's brews there.is a golden treasure of experience dating back to 1840; yes, it takes experience to create brews as fine as these.

Today this good old name is a recognized hallmark of quality. When you order Ballantine's you are sure of getting the finest brew human skill can produce.

In 12-oz. bottles and on draught

Ballantine's XXX Ale

America's great leader among ales, adapted to American palates through almost 100 years' experience. It is a light amber, sparkling and creamy ale , delicious and thirst-quenching. It is distinguished by a high head similar to beer, and where it is served on draught, ordinary beer-drawing equipment is used. It is full-flavored and fully aged, and at its best when served at about 55 degrees F. It contains certain health properties that are helpful in creating energy and vigor. In 12. oz. bottles and on draught.

Ballantine's India Pale Ale

Aged in the wood for one year. This fullbodied amber ale is widely used in place of wine at dinner. Connoisseurs say it is "As smooth and mellow as old wine." It is especially delicious with seafood. It is a real "stock ale," in that it is not only fully and carefully aged but is, in addition, "dry hopped"—that is, extra hops are added in the keg to heighten the bouquet and flavor. Served at either room or cellar temperature, according to individual taste. In half or quarter-barrels and 6 oz. or 12 oz. bottles.

Ballantine's Extra Porter

A true brewed porter made of the finest black malt without artificial coloring or syrup additions. It is a very dark brown, with a rich brown head. It has a delightful bitter-sweet flavor, and is delicious with roasts, steaks, chops, etc. Not as strong as stout, but has similar tonic qualities and is essentially beneficial to the blood and nerves. May be served alone or in conjunction with ale or beer. It is at its best at about 55 degrees F. In 12 oz. bottles or on draught.

Ballantine's Brown Stout

Aged in the wood for one year. A very dark brown in color, with a rich brown, lasting head and distinctive bitter-sweet flavor. One of the strongest of brewed beverages, especially good with steaks, roasts, baked potatoes, etc. It has valuable nourishing and tonic properties, and is advised for enriching the blood, for athletes, for nursing mothers, for all who need a wholesome, energy-building food drink. Serve at room or cellar temperature. In 6 or 12 oz. bottles.

Descriptions of various Ballantine beers. Photo courtesy of Bil Corcoran.

Post-Prohibition Ballantine IPA was brewed to 18 °P (1.074 SG), resulting in an abv of 7.4%. It was hopped in the brewhouse to achieve 60 IBUs and after fermentation was aged in oak vats for a year, adding depth and maturity to the flavor.

Ballantine's dry-hopping process was totally unique. It used Bullion hops, a variety very hard to find now, and ground them into a powder, added water, and cooked them in a vacuum process that effectively distilled the oils from the hop material. The oils were collected and added to the beer, which gave it an intense, distinct hop presence, unlike any-thing else available in the United States at that time.[15] Ballantine's house yeast strain is widely rumored to be the same yeast Sierra Nevada Brewing Company selected as its house strain in 1979, and is now a very popular ale yeast sold by White Labs as WLP001 and by Wyeast as WY1056. One of the attributes of this strain is the neutral, clean character it imparts to ales, which makes it a great yeast for brewing hop-forward beers such as IPA. If indeed this strain is the original Ballantine's strain, it's easy to see how the beer became well known for its hop flavor. It was described by enthusiasts who remember it as being a dark amber color, with a big malt presence, massive hops and bitterness, and a big oak character.

By the mid-1960s, Ballantine was beginning to lose ground to the marketing giants Schlitz, Pabst, Anheuser-Busch, and Miller, and it fell

Ballantine IPA label, with the "story" of IPA. Courtesy Bil Corcoran.

IMPORTANT NOTICE — The process used to brew Ballantine's India Pale Ale a century ago is still employed. After bottling it continues to *age* and *mellow*. With age a slight cloudiness and precipitation develop, *which in no way affect the quality of the ale*. Connoisseurs know this to be a condition characteristic of India Pale Ale brewed according to old-time methods.

Apparently Ballantine's IPA threw a chill haze when aged. Courtesy of Bil Corcoran.

Ballantine delivery truck. Photo courtesy of Brew Your Own *magazine. Used by permission.*

Table 6.6 Analysis of Ballantine Beers: 1939

Year	Beer	Style	Package	Acidity	FG (SG)	OG (SG)	Color (SRM)	ABV	Attenuation
1939	IPA	IPA	Bottled	0.07	1018.6	1075.2	16	7.39	75.27%
1939	XXX Ale	Ale	Bottled	0.07	1014.9	1056.0	9	5.34	73.39%
1939	XXX Ale	Ale	Canned	0.07	1014.5	1056.2	11	5.42	74.20%
1939	XXX Porter	Porter	Bottled	0.08	1018.8	1059.6		5.29	68.46%
1939	Brown Stout	Stout	Bottled	0.10	1021.9	1074.6		6.86	70.64%

Source: Whitbread Gravity Book. Courtesy of Pattinson, "Ale and Porter Brewing in Philadelphia in 1859," *Shut Up about Barclay Perkins* (blog; August 23, 2010).

to ninth place overall among American beer companies. In 1969 Ballantine was sold to investors, who in the early 1970s sold all the brands to Falstaff Brewing Company. Falstaff relocated the production of Ballantine Ales to the Narragansett Brewery in Cranston, Rhode Island. It retooled the recipes, including eliminating the hop distillation process and replacing it with dry hopping, and reducing gravities, alcohol, and bitterness levels. The bitterness was reduced to 45, and the aging process was reduced from 12 months to 9 months, and eventually to 5 months. Bullion hops were replaced with Brewer's Gold and Yakima Goldings. In 1979 production was moved to Fort Wayne, Indiana. Falstaff merged with Pabst in 1985, and Pabst moved the brewing of Ballantine beers and the aging tanks to Milwaukee in 1990. In 1996 the Pabst brewery closed, and that was the end of Ballantine IPA.[16]

Nevertheless, Ballantine's IPA influenced many craft-brewing pioneers, including Fritz Maytag of San Francisco's Anchor Brewery and Ken Grossman of Sierra Nevada Brewing Company, both of whom introduced seasonal IPAs inspired by the original Ballantine IPA.

In the 1990s, Alan Kornhauser, then with Portland Brewing Company, attempted to rebrew the original Ballantine's recipe. He developed a hop distillation method and called the beer Woodstock IPA. Several Ballantine clone recipes are available on the Internet, and perhaps Pabst, which still owns the brand, will rebrew Ballantine's IPA to the original recipe someday.

7 | THE CRAFT-BEER IPA REVOLUTION

All other nations are drinking Ray Charles beer, and we're drinking
Barry Manilow.
—*Dave Barry*

If you want to taste a good British beer, go to the GABF!
—*Unknown*

By the late 1970s beers from both the United States and England had
lost much of their variety. In the United States, the large lager brewers continued their massive, marketing-based growth by squashing or
swallowing up smaller regional breweries. The result was that the top
10 brewing companies controlled 69 percent of the market in the late
1950s. The large brewers continued to grow through the 1960s and the
1970s, to the point where, in 1980, the top 10 brewers produced 93 percent of all the beer brewed in the United States.

These brewers—Pabst, Schlitz, Anheuser-Busch, Miller, Stroh,
Coors, and others—all produced the same kind of beer, American
lager, brewed with high percentages of adjuncts and hopped to levels
below 15–20 IBUs. This crisp, light lager had become symbolic of the
American brewing industry, and other beer styles were able to maintain no more than small niche positions in the market. In particular, ale
brewing in the United States was very rare, and many of the "ales"
brewed by regional and larger brewers were simply higher-strength
lagers fermented at ale fermentation temperatures, which resulted in
an estery and sulfur-laden beer.

One remaining holdout was Ballantine IPA, which still maintained its
high strength and hopping levels. But it too had been sold by the late

1960s, when production moved from New Jersey to Rhode Island. The gradual adjustments to the recipe—aging for less time, lowering abv and hopping, changing the dry-hopping process, and eventually eliminating dry hopping and wood aging altogether—had begun, so that by the late 1970s, it bore little resemblance to the big, hoppy, bitter beer that it had been in the 1950s and the 1960s.

In England, cask ale production was dropping significantly—perhaps due to the uncertain quality of pub cellarmanship in the middle of the 20th century—and kegged draft ale and bottles took the leading

Table 7.1 Top 10 American Brewers by Year

	1950		1960		
	Brewery	Barrelage	Brewery	Barrelage	
1	Joseph Schlitz Brewing Co.	5,096,840	Anheuser-Busch, Inc.	8,477,099	
2	Anheuser-Busch, Inc.	4,928,000	Joseph Schlitz Brewing Co.	5,694,000	
3	Ballantine, Inc.	4,375,000	Falstaff Brewing Corp.	4,915,000	
4	Pabst Brewing Co.	3,418,677	Carling Brewing Co.	4,822,075	
5	F. & M. Schaefer Brewing Co.	2,772,000	Pabst Brewing Co.	4,738,000	
6	Liebmann Bros.	2,695,522	P. Ballantine & Sons	4,408,895	
7	Falstaff Brewing Corp.	2,286,707	Theodore Hamm Brewing Corp.	3,907,040	
8	Miller Brewing Co.	2,105,706	F. & M. Schaefer Brewing Co.	3,202,500	
9	Blatz Brewing Co.	1,756,000	Liebmann Breweries	2,950,268	
10	Pfeiffer Brewing Co.	1,618,077	Miller Brewing Co.	2,376,543	
	Total U.S. beer barrelage	82,830,137	Total U.S. beer barrelage	87,912,847	
	Top 10% of total barrelage	38%	Top 10% of total barrelage	52%	

Source: BeerHistory.com, "Shakeout in the Brewing Industry" (2011).

Note: This data perfectly illustrates the consolidation and homogenization of the American beer industry before craft brewing.

positions in U.K. brewing packages. Bass had stopped producing Continental IPA. Although it still brewed Worthington's White Shield, production fell, as Bass put more focus on the kegged version of Bass Ale. IPA brewing was still done, and Greene King IPA and other versions of the lower-alcohol IPAs that came about around the turn of the century were available. But the traditional IPA—best represented at that time by Worthington's White Shield and Felinfoel Double Diamond in England and Ballantine IPA in the United States—was well on its way out as a viable beer style.

	1970		1980	
	Brewery	Barrelage	Brewery	Barrelage
	Anheuser-Busch, Inc.	22,201,811	Anheuser-Busch, Inc.	50,200,000
	Joseph Schlitz Brewing Co.	15,129,000	Miller Brewing Co.	37,300,000
	Pabst Brewing Co.	10,517,000	Pabst Brewing Co.	15,091,000
	Adolph Coors Co.	7,277,076	Joseph Schlitz Brewing Co.	14,900,000
	F. & M. Schaefer Brewing Co.	5,749,000	Adolph Coors Co.	13,800,000
	Falstaff Brewing Corp.	5,386,133	G. Heileman Brewing Co.	13,270,000
	Miller Brewing Co.	5,150,000	Stroh Brewing Co.	6,161,255
	Carling Brewing Co.	4,819,000	Olympia Brewing Co.	6,091,000
	Theodore Hamm Brewing Corp.	4,470,000	Falstaff Brewing Co.	3,901,000
	Associated Brewing Co.	3,750,000	C. Schmidt & Sons	3,625,000
	Total U.S. beer barrelage	121,861,000	Total U.S. beer barrelage	176,311,699
	Top 10% of total barrelage	69%	Top 10% of total barrelage	93%

At the start of the 1960s mild was the most popular beer style in England. But as the decade progressed, pasteurized, bottled, and kegged bitters increased in popularity. Canned beers became much more common in the 1970s, and as these packages increased in popularity, alcoholic strength and bitterness decreased in these beers, similar to what was happening in the United States and Canada. By the end of the 1960s, lagers had a strong foothold in the British beer market too, with brands like Carlsberg, Carling, and Harp making major inroads to eventually become 20 percent of the beer market by the mid-1970s.

As the homogenization of the beer industry took hold in both England and the United States, a few significant events signaled the start of a beer revolution and the eventual movement toward a return to variety and flavor.

In England the Campaign for Real Ale (CAMRA) was formed in 1971 as a response to the overwhelming success of kegged bitters and lagers—and to the resulting threat of losing the traditional cask brands that were so important to English brewing history and culture. CAMRA's strength and clout increased, as did lager brewing. Now kegged bitter has virtually disappeared from the British beer scene, although cask ale continues to struggle against the consolidation of English brewers and the continued strength of lagers such as Carling and Foster's.

In the United States in 1965, Fritz Maytag, a graduate student at Stanford University, bought the failing Anchor Brewing in San Francisco with family money. Anchor was the last remaining brewer of the once ubiquitous steam beer—an amber-colored lager with substantial hop bitterness that was fermented at ambient temperatures. Steam breweries were common in California before Prohibition, as German-trained brewers settled in the San Francisco Bay Area during and after the gold rush of the mid-1800s. Ice was not available to these brewers, but they found that they could make a flavorful lager beer by using the cool coastal nights and the foggy days to maintain fermentation temperatures.

When Maytag bought Anchor Brewing it was literally on the verge of going out of business. Anchor Steam Beer had limited sales in San Francisco and was plagued by microbiological issues and consistency problems. Over the next several years, Maytag attempted to clean up the brewery, and the beer, and to remake the Anchor brand. By 1973 he had stopped adding coloring to make a dark version of Steam Beer, and had formulated a traditional porter to take its place.

Maytag went to prep school in New England, and while there, he developed an appreciation for traditional ales such as Ballantine. He was fascinated by historical and traditional brewing procedures and did extensive research in Europe—especially focusing on beer styles that were no longer popular. For example, when he formulated Anchor Porter, it is quite possible that there were no porters still being brewed in England. And when he decided to brew Old Foghorn Barleywine Style Ale, barley wine was a style that had become an old lady's drink in England. Packaged in small bottles called "nips," it was the subject of some derision among beer enthusiasts there.

The original bottle of Anchor Liberty Ale, and (right) today's Liberty Ale. Courtesy of Mark Carpenter.

In 1973 Maytag and Jack McDermott traveled to England to research real ales with the intent of brewing an ale at Anchor. There were no ales being brewed on the West Coast at the time (save Seattle's Rainier Ale), so in traveling to England they hoped to find some authentic ales to research. They wound up being disappointed with the uninteresting beers that were being brewed in England, but they were able to learn about the use of sugars in brewing and the technique of dry hopping.

The first version of Anchor Liberty Ale was brewed in early 1975 to commemorate the bicentennial of Paul Revere's ride. The first 50-barrel batch was infusion mashed and brewed with sugars like the English ales they had tasted on their trip two years prior. It was heavily hopped with Hallertau hops and fermented with an ale yeast—a first for Anchor, which used a lager strain in its other beers. The resulting beer was roundly criticized for being too bitter. Undaunted, the team at Anchor reformulated the beer to be released as the 1975 Christmas Ale, the brewery's first-ever seasonal beer. The brewers pulled the brewing sugars out of the recipe, making the beer all malt, and for the first time, used the relatively new Cascade hops for bittering, flavor, and dry hopping. Anchor kept the beer massively bittered (for the time) at more than 40 IBUs. The new Liberty Ale was released every holiday season until 1984, when it became a full-time beer for Anchor.

Anchor Liberty Ale was the first beer to feature the Cascade hop, with its pronounced citrusy and grapefruity flavor, as a primary aroma and dry hop. Although Anchor never officially called Liberty Ale an IPA, it was the first American IPA in every sense since Ballantine IPA, which by 1975 was a shell of its former self. In fact, Mark Carpenter, longtime brewmaster at Anchor Brewing Company, says that Liberty Ale was definitely influenced by Fritz Maytag's love of the original Ballantine IPA.

The next American IPA brewed was also inspired by the old Ballantine IPA. This was Celebration Ale, first brewed by Sierra Nevada Brewing Company in 1981. Ken Grossman, the owner of Sierra Nevada, had brewed beer since the late 1960s, when he owned a home winemaking shop in Southern California. His fascination with hops started at that time, when he began selling whole hops out of the shop. Grossman would make an annual pilgrimage to the Yakima Valley to purchase any and all hops he could lay his hands on, including the leftover, one-pound rectangular "brewers cuts" from each lot that were routinely sent to professional brewers for evaluation and selection. Because of his willingness to buy whatever was available, Grossman brewed with many, if not all, of the American hop varieties available at that time, including Cluster, Bullion, Brewer's Gold, and the brand-new Cascade.

Like Maytag, Grossman found the new, citrusy, and grapefruity Cascade hop much to his liking, and when he and Paul Camusi were starting the Sierra Nevada brewery, they used Cascade and other American aroma hops in their beers. Sierra Nevada Pale Ale was flavor hopped with Cascade by using the traditional British hopback process in which hop cones are placed over a hop screen and wort from the kettle is transferred over and through the hops on the way to the whirlpool.

In the fall of 1981, as Sierra Nevada was beginning to formulate its first Christmas beer, Grossman came across a field of baby (new) Cascade hops on his annual trip to Yakima and decided to use them in the new beer. He remembered drinking and enjoying Ballantine IPA in the late 1960s and was inspired to brew an IPA reminiscent of it. Not coincidentally, many people believe that Sierra Nevada's yeast strain came from the old Ballantine strain. The yeast produces a low ester profile, which allows hop and malt character to really shine, a definite trait of Sierra Nevada's beers. For the first time, Sierra Nevada decided to dry hop a beer. The brewers used the baby Cascade hops in the dry-hop process, which involved placing mesh bags full of hops in the bright beer tanks prior to transferring in the beer. Sierra Nevada Celebration Ale was the result. A deep amber, intensely hop-forward, and bitter beer, Celebration has remained a favorite annual holiday release since the first time it was brewed in 1981.

Like Maytag, Grossman recalls taking a trip to England to research the ales, the brewing history, and the traditions, and coming away disappointed with the sameness of the beers being brewed. He went with beer writer Michael Jackson in the 1980s and returned to the United States even more convinced of the potential of American hop varieties that had such distinctive and intense flavors.

Although Anchor Liberty Ale and Sierra Nevada Celebration Ale can be considered the first two American craft-brewed IPAs, the first

American craft brewer to actually use "IPA" in the name of his beer was Bert Grant, whose Grant's IPA was first brewed in Yakima, Washington, in 1983.

Bert Grant was born in Scotland, and his family moved to Canada when he was a toddler. A chemistry whiz in high school near Toronto, he was hired as a chemist by Canadian Breweries at the age of 16. He continued working in the brewing industry for the rest of his life, serving in roles at Canadian Breweries and then being hired by Labatt as director of brewing research and innovation. Eventually frustrated by the "dumbing down" of beer during the 1960s, Grant joined hop supplier S. S. Steiner and moved to Yakima, where he worked on developing hop pelletizing procedures and researched new hop varieties.

While in Yakima, Grant built a pilot brewery in his basement and brewed beers that he liked to drink—hoppy, bitter, and based on traditional ale styles. He maintained his own yeast culture and brewed beers that people liked so much that he was talked into opening his own brewery in Yakima in 1982. His first beer was a Scotch ale. It was hoppier than the generally regarded style guidelines, but in Grant's own words, "All beers should be hoppier." In 1983 he started brewing Grant's IPA, which deserves recognition for being the first bottled IPA since Ballantine's.

Two versions of Grant's IPA six-pack logo. Courtesy of BeerLabels.com.

Grant's IPA was brewed with 100 percent pale ale malt and hopped with Galena and Cascade. The original gravity was 12 °P (1.048 SG), with a low terminal gravity of 2.8 °P (1.011 SG), making the beer fairly dry, with an abv of 5%. Heavily hopped to 50–60 IBUs, it was by far one of the hoppiest beers of its time. Grant's yeast strain also added some spiciness to the flavor profile. Writing for Grant's biography, beer writer Michael Jackson recalled the first time he tasted Grant's IPA: "I was just stunned by the bitterness of it. I just loved the bitterness of it. I thought, 'Christ, he's really going to do this. Bert really expects people to buy this?'"

Bert Grant was one of the first craft brewers in the United States to demonstrate what has become a model of success for many brewers to follow: Brew what you like to drink, and the people will come. Grant was not afraid to be controversial; he made friends and some detractors by traveling around with a vial of hop oil and adding a dose of hops to any beer he deemed not hoppy enough (which in the 1980s was most of them). A true pioneer of the U.S. craft-brewing industry, Grant passed in 2003 at the age of 74, but his legacy of brewing lives on with the popularity of the IPA style, which has arguably become the most frequently brewed craft-beer style in the United States.

THE STORY OF THE CASCADE HOP

In the 1930s George Segal, a cheese merchant from New York City, noticed hop flowers being sold in candy shops during Prohibition. His interest in hop farming was piqued, and in the 1940s, after the Repeal of Prohibition, he bought land in the Franklin Lakes area of Upstate New York and started growing hops there. Seeing some success in growing and selling varieties such as Cluster, Northern Brewer, and Bullion, he expanded his farming operation to Sonoma County, California, where he eventually established the Sonoma County Cluster Growers Cooperative.

In the 1950s Segal bought 60 acres of farmland in Grandview, Washington, near Yakima, and started growing hops there as well. This move was fortuitous because in the 1950s the New York State hop industry was virtually wiped out by blue mold. To make matters worse, a heptachlor fungicide was used to clear the hops of the mold, but the fungicide sterilized the land, in effect making it unusable for future plantings.

George's son John Segal abandoned New York in 1960 and moved the entire family farming operation to Grandview. He also got involved with hop research programs conducted by the U.S. Department of Agriculture in both Oregon and Washington.

In 1968, the first planting of an experimental hop variety (numbered 56013) was harvested at the Mission Bottom Farms near Salem, Oregon. Working with USDA hop researcher Al Haunold, farm owners Carl and Don Weathers were paid a flat fee by the U.S. Brewers Association Subcommittee of Hop Research to grow small quantities of this new hop variety on a two-acre plot for three years. Research was conducted to gauge brewer interest, as well as to further study the growing and varietal characteristics of this new hop, which was originally bred in the late 1950s by Oregon-based USDA hop breeder Stan Brooks. Despite receiving positive reviews in rub evaluations (i.e., qualitative aroma evaluations made by rubbing the hops between one's hands to burst the lupulin glands), the variety—initially bred as a downy, mildew-resistant potential replacement for the lower-yielding, but very popular, Hallertau Mittelfruh hops grown in Germany—received little interest from large brewers.

In 1970, Chuck Zimmermann, who worked for the USDA Hop Research Group in Prosser, Washington, gave John Segal the hop and encouraged him to plant a small plot. Segal started trials with the hop on three acres of land, and showed the hop to Willard Hayes at Coors and other brewers to try to develop some interest in what he thought was a very special new variety.

Segal remained loyal to the 56013 hop. He planted it every year and was optimistic that some brewer would finally recognize its value and start using it. But big brewers remained reluctant to use the hop until Verticillium wilt hit the German noble hops (Hallertau, Tettnang) hard in the late 1960s and the early 1970s, thus driving hop prices upward.

Then in 1972 the 56013 hop, renamed Cascade as a tribute to the Pacific Northwest mountain range, was released to the public. Coors committed to buying some at one dollar per pound—about double the price of other American-grown hops such as Cluster and Fuggle. Segal also developed a relationship with Fritz Maytag of Anchor Brewing Company, and Maytag ended up using Cascade hops in his Liberty Ale. As head of the Washington State Hop Growers Association, Segal willingly sold rhizomes of the Cascade hop to other growers as the popularity of this unique hop grew rapidly in the 1970s. The citrusy, grapefruity Cascade became synonymous with craft-beer hop character in the 1980s. Pale ales not brewed with Cascade were the exception rather than the rule, and it became the favored hop in craft-brewed IPAs when they became more popular in the 1990s. To this day, the Cascade hop remains one of the most popular craft-brewing hop varieties.

Imagine the current brewing world without the influence of the Cascade hop and a very different scenario emerges. The success of Cascade led directly to the popularity of other American hop varieties with pronounced citrusy aromas (e.g., Centennial and Chinook) and encouraged breeders and farmers to take a chance on newer, highly aromatic varieties.

Many potential new hop varieties are developed every year, but most never make it to commercial production—either because of poor growing characteristics or because no one believes in the potential of the hop to make a positive impact to brewers. Cascade very nearly suffered the same fate, and we should acknowledge the forward-thinking efforts of Stan Brooks, Alfred Haunold, Chuck Zimmermann, and the Segal family for believing in the Cascade hop.

```
USDA ACCESSION NO.:56013
SELECTION:        Seedling selection 55187 made in 1956
                  at Corvallis, Oregon
GENUS:            Humulus
SPECIES:          lupulus
CULTIVAR:         Cascade
PEDIGREE:         OP seed collected on USDA 19124 in 1955
                  [Fuggle x (Serebrianka Fuggle S)] x OP
PRIMARY SITE:     USDA World Hop Variety Collection, OSU East Farm
ORIGIN:           Open pollinated seed collected in 1955, seedling
                  selected in 1956 by S. N. Brooks.
DATE RECEIVED:    Selected in 1956
METHOD RECEIVED:  Seedling selection
AVAILABILITY:     Commercial cultivar, no restrictions.
```

REFERENCES:
Brooks, S. N., C. E. Homer, S. T. Likens, and C. E. Zimmermann. Registration of Cascade hop (Registration No. 1). Crop Sci. 12:394.1972.
Homer, T. E., S. T. Likens, C. E. Zimmermann, and A.Haunold. Cascade, a new continental type hop variety for the U.S. Brewer's Digest 47:56 62. 1972.
Romanko, R. R. In: Steiner's Guide to American Hops, 2nd. ed. 1986.

```
MATURITY:          Medium to medium late
LEAF COLOR:        Medium green to dark green
SEX:               Female, occasionally produces a few sterile male
DISEASES:          Downy Mildew:  resistant in the crown, moderately
                   susceptible in shoots and cones flowers
                   Verticillium wilt:  moderately resistant
                   Viruses: initially infected with all hop viruses
                   but cleaned up by meristem tip culture and heat
                   treatment and re-released under the new Accession
                   No. USDA 21092.
VIGOR:             Very good
YIELD:             Very good, 1800 2200 lbs/acre
SIDE ARM LENGTH:   24 30 inches
ALPHA ACIDS:       6.2% (ten year range: 5.1 to 8.5%)
BETA ACIDS:        5.0% (ten year range: 4.0 to 6.6%)
COHUMULONE:        33 36%
STORAGE STABILITY: Poor
OIL:               1.27 ml/100 g (10 year range:0.62 to 1.8
MAJOR TRAITS:      Crown resistance to Downy Mildew, ratio of alpha/
                   beta similar to European aroma hops.

OTHER INFORMATION: Used as an aroma hop in certain brewery blends. In
                   1986, 2256 acres produced 4.43 mill. lbs, 9.0% of
                   U.S. production; adapted to Oregon, Washington and
                   Idaho. 1997 production: 2,003 million lbs on 1,037
                   acres, all in Washington.
```

Sierra Nevada Brewing Company, Anchor Brewing Company, and Grants Yakima Brewing and Malting Company began to see success in the mid-1980s. The craft-brewing industry in the United States started its first stage of real growth, with small breweries and brewpubs opening in various places around the country. Many of the brewery openings were concentrated in the San Francisco Bay Area of California; in Boulder, Colorado; and in Portland, Oregon, and Seattle, Washington, in the Pacific Northwest. These small microbreweries and brewpubs offered niche beers with a lot of flavor, which was very unusual in the mid-1980s, when the beer market was almost exclusively the realm of the huge American lager brewers. Experiencing varying degrees of success, these first microbreweries were plagued by quality and consistency issues, and some didn't survive. Nevertheless, the seeds of change had been planted. In the late 1980s, a wave of pub and microbrewery openings spread across the country, and craft brewing took hold for good.

Most craft brewers in the 1980s started out using traditional English brewing procedures, brewing on small systems equipped with a combination mash/lauter tun and a combination kettle and whirlpool or with an English-style hopback. Infusion mashing was the standard procedure, and many brewers brewed all-malt English-inspired beers—usually a pale, an amber, and a dark porter or a stout. Many of these new craft brewers had started as homebrewers (homebrewing was legalized in the 1970s by President Jimmy Carter). Until *The Complete Joy of Homebrewing* was published by Charlie Papazian, homebrewing texts were only available by British writers. Perhaps this explains the predominance of English brewing techniques when the craft-brewing industry began.

As homebrewing gained in popularity and homebrew shops opened across the country, talented brewers looked for opportunities to make their hobby a profession. Many of the brewers took inspiration from Sierra Nevada Celebration Ale and Anchor Liberty Ale, and looked to brew IPA-style beers, both at home and in the brewpubs, where customers were enjoying having their palates challenged by hop-forward beers.

THE ORIGINS OF AMERICAN IPA:
A CRAFT-BREWING PIONEER'S PERSPECTIVE
By Teri Fahrendorf

The first IPA I ever tasted, I didn't know it was an IPA. I was a homebrewer in the San Francisco Bay Area in the mid-1980s, working as a COBOL programmer. Having made wine in college in Wisconsin, I had turned to homebrewing after relocating to California, because good wine was so cheap there, and I needed something to ferment.

The San Andreas Malts was my local homebrew club, and many of us not only became fast friends, but about 10 of us went pro in the late 1980s. I remember drinking Anchor Liberty with my future-pro homebrew buddies Grant Johnston, Ed Tringali, Alec Moss, Phil Moeller, and others. We didn't know Anchor Liberty was an IPA. It didn't say so on the label. It was just a darn tasty beer. So please forgive me later when I innocently and honestly tell you that the first commercial IPA I ever tasted was my own.

There was no such thing as American IPA, although in hindsight Anchor Liberty was the proto-renaissance American IPA. The holy grail of American IPA then was Ballantine IPA, but Ballantine had stopped brewing it nearly 20 years before, so we read about it when we could. We devoured technical and historical beer information wherever we found it: Michael Jackson's *1977 World Guide to Beer* was our style bible. Charlie Papazian's and Byron Burch's homebrew books were our procedural technical manuals. Just one thing was missing: help to replicate a historical IPA beer recipe.

Why were we after a historical replication of the style? Because not only was there no American version of the style available to taste, but there was no modern British version, either. Due to Britain's punitive excise tax laws that penalized alcohol levels, IPAs had been watered down to the strength and bitterness of an American industrial lager.

There was no Internet to search for information or contacts, yet somehow my friend Grant Johnston scared up a rare copy of the Durden Park Beer Club's beer recipe booklet. The Durden Park Beer Club was a group of British homebrewer historians who had been meticulously researching the ancient brew logs of the bastions of British brewing, such as Bass, Whitbread, and Marston's. These men carefully tested and replicated the storied recipes and published them sized for homebrew systems. We began to homebrew British IPAs with British ingredients, but we still had never tasted a commercial example of the style.

Before I left to attend the Siebel Institute in Chicago, I went to the Great American Beer Festival (GABF) in 1988. In fact, I made my decision to become a professional brewer at that GABF. While there, I met Fred Eckhardt, who was selling Xeroxed copies of his forthcoming book, *The Essentials of Beer Style*. His book became my recipe design bible, and it included not only a list of commercially available beers for each style, but also a list of the traditional malts and hops that were used. In his original edition, I remember reading that Munich malt and Kent and Styrian Goldings were traditionally used in IPA.

After Siebel and job hunting, I briefly worked at one brewery, then went on to Triple Rock Brewing Company in Berkeley, California, where I was hired as head brewer. By this time I had experienced having my employer shut down and bounce my paychecks (my first brewing job), and I was very conscious that the ingredient decisions I made could affect a brewpub's ability to stay afloat. So one of the first professional decisions I made was to embrace my philosophy that "I am an American brewer, brewing American beers, with American ingredients." It may sound lofty, but it helped me stay in paychecks for my entire brewing career.

At Triple Rock I began to think about brewing an IPA, so naturally I wanted to replicate the flavors of imported British and German malts and imported hops. I also like to shock people, and brewing an IPA with American ingredients was extremely unorthodox then. It was also shocking to use bittering hops for aroma, so I picked Chinook as one of my aroma hops and as my sole dry hop.

Triple Rock already had an IPA called Gandhi's Grog IPA and it was 35 IBUs. I redesigned it to avoid crystal and caramel malts, which I believed were not traditional, and increased the IBUs to 40. Yes, I wanted to shock my brewing friends, but I also wanted the customers to drink my beer, and 40 IBUs was a lot in 1989!

Then I moved to Eugene, Oregon, to become the brewmaster for Steelhead Brewing Company. On January 22, 1991, Steelhead opened with an IPA on draft as the seasonal beer and never took it off tap. I believe Bombay Bomber was the first IPA served continuously as a standard flagship beer at any brewpub in the United States and it quickly developed a cult following. Locals still ask for a pint of "Bomber." The bitterness level was 57 IBU. My calculations showed it to be 45, but when I had the IBU tested, it was 57. That was quite high in 1991!

As the U.S. craft-brewing movement continued to grow in the 1990s, brewers became more comfortable with challenging their customers' palates with hop-forward beers, and IPA became a mainstay year-round offering for many brewers, as opposed to being a seasonal or special-release beer. This development was helped along by several new American hop varieties, including Centennial (first dubbed a "Super-Cascade"), Chinook, and Columbus. Collectively, along with the Cascade hop, these hop varieties became known as the "4 C's" and were featured prominently

Table 7.2 Analysis of Various IPAs in 2002

Brand	Brewery	OG (°P)	OG (SG)	TG (°P)	TG (SG)
Bridgeport IPA	Bridgeport Brewing Co.	13.55	1.054	2.93	1.012
India Ale	Samuel Smith Old Brewery	12.16	1.049	2.98	1.012
Greene King IPA	Greene King	9.42	1.038	2.66	1.011
Deuchars IPA	Caledonian Brewery	10.58	1.042	2.46	1.010
Indian Pale Ale	Harveys	7.78	1.031	2.24	1.009
James Squire IPA	Malt Shovel Brewery	13.21	1.053	3.54	1.014
Imperial Pale Ale	Maritime Pacific Brewing Co.	17.11	1.068	2.59	1.010
Indica IPA	Lost Coast Brewing	15.87	1.063	2.26	1.009
Full Sail IPA	Full Sail Brewing Co.	14.91	1.060	3.00	1.012
Woodstock IPA	MacTarnahan's Brewing Co.	14.91	1.060	3.02	1.012
ImPaled Ale (IPA)	Middle Ages Brewing Co.	13.77	1.055	3.38	1.013
Quail Springs IPA	Deschutes Brewery	14.35	1.057	3.00	1.012
Hop Ottin' IPA	Anderson Valley Brewing Co.	15.42	1.062	3.41	1.014
Pyramid India Pale Ale	Pyramid Breweries, Inc.	16.27	1.065	4.12	1.016
Wolaver's India Pale Ale	Panorama Beer Co.	15.09	1.060	2.98	1.012
Rogue XS Imperial Ale	Rogue Brewing	20.35	1.081	3.49	1.014
India Pale Ale	Cascade Lakes Brewing Co.	13.20	1.053	1.85	1.007

Source: Jurado, "A Pale Reflection on Ale Perfection," The Brewer International 2 (2002).

AE	ABV	ABW	RE	RDF	Calories	pH	IBU	Color (SRM)	Color (EBC)
3.00	5.56	4.45	5.00	64.8	180.6	4.16	50.0	10.2	20.09
3.04	4.75	3.80	4.79	62.1	161.7	3.87	33.2	14.7	28.96
2.72	3.43	2.74	4.02	58.2	124.2	3.99	28.4	15.0	29.55
2.52	4.15	3.32	4.09	62.6	139.3	3.98	24.3	6.7	13.20
2.29	2.82	2.26	3.31	58.4	101.6	3.97	26.4	10.1	19.90
3.62	5.05	4.04	5.44	60.5	177.5	4.08	26.9	13.6	26.79
2.65	7.74	6.19	5.44	70.2	229.9	4.39	66.6	12.3	24.23
2.32	7.20	5.76	4.94	70.7	211.8	4.48	66.1	26.0	51.22
3.07	6.24	4.99	5.39	65.7	199.7	4.33	58.8	9.3	18.32
3.09	6.24	4.99	5.39	65.7	199.7	4.45	48.4	14.9	29.35
3.45	5.43	4.34	5.43	62.3	184.6	3.96	52.1	15.2	29.94
3.07	5.94	4.75	5.26	65.1	191.9	4.23	41.9	8.8	17.34
3.48	6.33	5.06	5.80	64.3	207.5	4.43	78.6	17.6	34.67
4.19	6.44	5.15	6.51	62.1	220.8	4.14	63.3	11.0	21.67
3.05	6.36	5.09	5.39	66.1	202.2	4.51	42.9	11.0	21.67
3.55	9.08	7.26	6.92	68.5	278.5	4.32	67.3	14.9	29.35
1.89	5.93	4.74	4.04	70.8	174.0	4.74	26.4	13.0	25.61

in many of the IPAs being brewed in the 1990s. Brewers such as Steelhead in Eugene, Oregon; Rubicon in Sacramento; Harpoon in Boston; Pizza Port in the San Diego area; Blind Pig in Temecula, California; Brooklyn Brewing Company in New York; Bridgeport Brewing Company in Portland, Oregon; and Lucknow in New Hampshire became known primarily for their flagship IPAs.

By the late 1990s most ale brewers in the United States were brewing at least one version of an IPA, and the category grew as brewers produced bigger and more intense versions in an informal and friendly game of one-upmanship. The style was evolving from its craft-beer origins as an extra-hoppy pale ale brewed with crystal malts to a beer brewed with minimal coloring malts and ever-increasing hop bitterness and hop flavors. As new hop varieties were developed, brewers would look for opportunities to use them in IPAs, which resulted in the popularity of hops such as Amarillo and Simcoe. The growing popularity of American IPA inspired many brewers to brew even bigger versions—hop bombs that became known as the double or imperial IPA, and variations such as Belgian IPA (an IPA fermented with Belgian yeast), brown IPA, and black IPA. American craft brewers such as Port Brewing Company, Russian River Brewing Company, Stone Brewing Co., Dogfish Head, Bell's, and Three Floyds became known for being IPA brewers, and for having several variations of the style in their portfolios.

The English craft-brewing movement also began in the late 1970s, when several small breweries started producing real ales that were cask conditioned, had no artificial carbonation, and followed the guidelines set forth by CAMRA. In 1982 former Ind Coope employees Geoff Mumford and Bruce Wilkinson started brewing traditional ales at their 15-barrel Burton Bridge Brewery, in Burton-on-Trent. One of their bottled beers, the 7.5% abv Empire Pale Ale, is modeled after the Burton IPAs of the late 1800s and the early 1900s. It is brewed with Maris Otter malt and Challenger and Styrian Goldings hops, and is aged for an extended period in oak barrels.

Brewmaster Alastair Hook of Meantime Brewing Company in Greenwich, England, also brews a historical version of an English IPA, with Goldings and Fuggle hops at 7.4% abv and 75 IBUs. More recently, brewers at Thornbridge, Dark Star, and BrewDog have brewed IPAs using American and New Zealand hops that have more in common with their American craft-brewed counterparts than with traditional English versions.

Although it was established in the early 1800s in Burton-on-Trent, Marston's never brewed an IPA until recently. Photo courtesy of John Trotter.

Low-alcohol IPAs are still common in England. Growing in popularity are beers such as Caledonian's Deuchars IPA—3.8% abv draft, 4.5% abv bottled, 28 IBUs, brewed with British pale malt, Fuggle, Styrian Goldings, and Willamette hops. Greene King IPA, one of the most popular cask beers in England, is 3.6% abv and 30 IBUs, and it is brewed with First Gold and Challenger hops. These beers bear little, if any, resemblance to the historical IPAs from the 1800s versions. Beers such as Samuel Smith's India Ale (5% abv), Marston's Old Empire (despite using Cascade hops), Worthington's White Shield, and Freeminer Trafalgar IPA are certainly a bit closer to the IPAs of the 1800s. But little, if any, IPA was being brewed in the latter part of the 20th century that was heavily dry hopped and aged extensively in the 1800s Burton tradition. One of the issues facing the English brewing tradition is the current temperance movement, which has been successful in assigning beers "alcohol units" and promoting abstinence by attacking binge drinking.

Perhaps a good way to understand the growing popularity of IPA brewing in the United States is to review the professional beer competition at the annual Great American Beer Festival (GABF), held every fall in Denver, Colorado. The GABF has become the largest beer festival in the United States, and the professional competition uses a blind tasting panel of well over 100 professional beer judges that includes brewers from breweries of all sizes, professional beer writers, and others with exemplary beer-judging skills.

In 1982 the first GABF was attended by 22 breweries pouring 40 beers for about 800 attendees. Judging started in 1983, and until 1987, the judging was done by festival attendees, the so-called "consumer preference poll." In 1987 the Professional Blind Tasting Panel was implemented with very basic style guidelines that included only ales, alts, and lagers. In 1988 pale ale was made into a separate category, and the gold medal went to Anchor Liberty Ale. In 1989, as the style grew to sufficient size, a separate IPA category was created, and Liberty Ale again medaled, finishing with a silver, while Rubicon IPA, brewed by Phil Moeller in Sacramento, California, won the gold medal (a feat he repeated in 1990).

As craft brewing matured in the early 1990s, IPA became the flagship of several breweries, including Steelhead, Harpoon, and Rubicon. The IPA category also grew to become one of the most heavily entered and highly contested at the annual GABF competition. In fact, since records started being maintained in 1999, IPA has been the most entered category in every year except 2000 and 2001, when "American" IPA was second only to American Pale Ale in number of entries. But the argument can be made that if English IPA, made a separate category in 2000, is included in the totals, IPA finished first in entries every year since 1999.

Today the GABF is a three-day event attended by close to 50,000 beer fans and nearly 500 breweries. IPA remains the largest category and one of the most anticipated announcements of the awards ceremony.

Table 7.3 Great American Beer Festival: American IPA Winners, 1989–2011

Year	Gold	Silver	Bronze	# of entries
1989	Rubicon IPA, Sacramento, CA	Anchor Liberty Ale, San Francisco, CA		
1990	Rubicon IPA, Sacramento, CA			
1991	Seabright Barking Rooster, Santa Cruz, CA	Breckenridge IPA, Colorado	Mendocino Blue Heron, Hopland, CA	
1992	Hubcap IPA, Dallas, TX	Seabright Barking Rooster, Santa Cruz, CA	Great Lakes Commodore Perry, Cleveland, OH	
1993	Estes Park Renegade Red, Estes Park, CO	Anchor Liberty Ale, San Francisco, CA	Coopersmith Punjabi, Fort Collins, CO	

Year	Gold	Silver	Bronze	# of entries
1994	Hubcap Vail Pale Ale, Dallas, TX	Sierra Nevada Celebration Ale, Chico, CA		
1995	Hubcap Big D's Vail Pale Ale, Dallas, TX	Pacific Coast Columbus IPA, Oakland, CA	Il Vicino Wet Mountain IPA, Albuquerque, NM	
1996	Prescott Ponderosa IPA, Prescott, AZ	Blind Pig IPA, Temecula, CA	Pacific Brewing Co. IndiaPendence IPA, San Rafael, CA	
1997	Marin IPA, Larkspur, CA	Castle Springs Lucknow IPA, Moultonborough, NH	Brew Works Back Bay IPA, Boston, MA	
1998	Pike 5280 Roadhouse IPA, Seattle, WA	Bells Two-Hearted Ale, Kalamazoo, MI	Big Time Scarlet Fire IPA, Seattle, WA	
1999	Bear Republic Racer 5 IPA, Healdsburg, CA	Marin IPA, Larkspur, CA	Castle Springs Lucknow IPA, Moultonborough, NH	118
2000	SLO IPA, San Luis Obispo, CA	Stuft Pizza & Brewing Torrey Pines IPA, San Diego, CA	Hoptown IPA, Pleasanton, CA	89
2001	Sleeping Giant Tumbleweed IPA, Billings, MT	Pizza Port Wipeout IPA, Carlsbad, CA	Pelican Pub and Brewing India Pelican Ale, Pacific City, OR	98
2002	Drake's IPA, San Leandro, CA	Prescott Ponderosa IPA, Prescott, AZ	Big Time Scarlet Fire IPA, Seattle, WA	94
2003	Hoptown IPA, Pleasanton, CA	Two Rows Hopzilla IPA, Dallas, TX	On Tap Hop Maniac IPA, San Diego, CA	94
2004	Pelican Pub and Brewing India Pelican Ale, Pacific City, OR	Pizza Port Wipeout IPA, Carlsbad, CA	Schooner's Grille and Brewery IPA, Antioch, CA	93
2005	Santa Barbara Castle Rock IPA, Santa Barbara, CA	Oggi's Torrey Pines IPA, San Diego, CA	Alesmith IPA, San Diego, CA	102
2006	Bend Brewing Hophead Imperial IPA, Bend, OR	Bear Republic Apex IPA, Healdsburg, CA	Ram Restaurant and Big Horn Brewery Taildragger IPA, Boise, ID	94

Table 7.3 (*continued*)

Year	Gold	Silver	Bronze	# of entries
2007	Odell IPA, Fort Collins, CO	Russian River Blind Pig IPA, Santa Rosa, CA	Mission El Camino IPA, San Diego, CA	120
2008	Firestone Walker Union Jack IPA, Paso Robles, CA	Russian River Blind Pig IPA, Santa Rosa, CA	Bend Brewing Hophead Imperial IPA, Bend, OR	104
2009	Firestone Walker Union Jack IPA, Paso Robles, CA	Ballast Point Sculpin IPA, San Diego, CA	Russian River Blind Pig IPA, Santa Rosa, CA	134
2010	Pizza Port Pseudo IPA, Carlsbad, CA	Fat Head's Head Hunter IPA, North Olmsted, OH	Lumberyard Extra IPA, Flagstaff, AZ	142
2011	La Cumbre Elevated IPA, Albuquerque, NM	Oskar Blues Deviant Dale's, Longmont, CO	Fat Head's Head Hunter IPA, North Olmsted, OH	176

IPA and its variations (double IPA, black IPA, English IPA, and Belgian IPA) continue to be among the most popular American craft-beer styles. American-style IPAs are now being successfully brewed in England, Japan, Australia, Denmark, and many other countries. Although Cascade remains the most popular craft-brewing hop for IPA, other newer hop varieties are being used with increasing frequency. Varieties such as Centennial, Chinook, Columbus, Amarillo, and Simcoe are being added on a regular basis. Also, craft brewers continue to use their IPAs as a vehicle to showcase new and excitingly different hop varieties, such as New Zealand hops Nelson Sauvin and Motueka, English Target, Japanese Sorachi Ace, and newer American varieties like Citra and Calypso. Every year or two, a new hop variety is introduced, and an IPA-style beer is considered by many brewers to be the best way to exhibit the qualities of the new hops.

Table 7.4 Great American Beer Festival: English IPA Winners, 2000–2011

Year	Gold	Silver	Bronze	# of entries
2000	Goose Island IPA, Chicago, IL	Main Street Hop Daddy IPA, Corona, CA	Buckhead Brewery and Grill Renegade IPA, Stockbridge, GA	27
2001	SLO Progress, San Luis Obispo, CA	Mash House Hoppy Hour IPA, Fayetteville, NC	Goose Island IPA, Chicago, IL	24
2002	Firestone Walker IPA, Paso Robles, CA	SLO Progress, San Luis Obispo, CA	McCoy's New-comb's IPA, Springfield, MO	25
2003	E. J. Phair IPA, Concord, CA	Bull & Bush Man Beer, Denver, CO	Utah Brewers Co-op Squatters IPA, Salt Lake City, UT	23
2004	Utah Brewers Co-op Squatters IPA, Salt Lake City, UT	Goose Island IPA, Chicago, IL	McCoy's New-comb's IPA, Springfield, MO	26
2005	Sierra Nevada IPA, Chico, CA	Utah Brewers Co-op Squatters IPA, Salt Lake City, UT	Minneapolis Town Hall Brewery 1800, Minneapolis, MN	32
2006	Carolina Brewery IPA, Chapel Hill, NC	Pizza Port Beech Street Bitter, Carlsbad, CA	Triumph Bengal Gold IPA, New Hope, PA	26
2007	Utah Brewers Co-op Squatters IPA, Salt Lake City, UT	Goose Island IPA, Chicago, IL	Pizza Port Beech Street Bitter, Carlsbad, CA	38
2008	None	None	Main Street Hop Daddy IPA, Corona, CA	28
2009	Pizza Port Beech Street Bitter, Carlsbad, CA	Goose Island IPA, Chicago, IL	Brewers Alley India Pale Ale, Frederick, MD	40
2010	Pizza Port Beech Street Bitter, Carlsbad, CA	Mountain Sun Illusion Dweller, Boulder, CO	Samuel Adams Latitude 48, Boston, MA	32
2011	Sam Adams Latitude 48 Haller-tau Mittlefrueh, Boston, MA	Napa Smith Organic IPA, Napa, CA	Deschutes Down 'n' Dirty IPA, Bend, OR	46

Table 7.5 Analysis of Various Craft-Brewed IPAs by Region

Region	Brewery	IPA Name	ABV	Color (SRM)
California	Russian River	Blind Pig	6.65	7.3
California	Bear Republic	Racer 5	7.44	8.7
California	Port Brewing	Wipeout IPA	7.99	10.8
California	Alesmith	IPA	7.25	7.7
California	Green Flash	West Coast IPA	7.53	15.9
California	Rogue	Brutal IPA	6.70	14.1
California	Mission	IPA	7.66	10.6
California	Lagunitas	IPA	6.50	8.7
California	Firestone Walker	Union Jack IPA	7.82	7.9
California	Stone Brewing Co.	IPA	6.90	9.0
West Coast	Maui Brewing	Big Swell IPA	6.25	8.6
Pacific Northwest	Alaskan	IPA	6.04	7.1
Pacific Northwest	Deschutes	Quail Springs IPA	6.00	10.0
Pacific Northwest	Deschutes	Inversion IPA	6.80	12.0
Rocky Mountain	New Belgium	Ranger IPA	6.71	7.9
Rocky Mountain	Great Divide	Titan IPA	7.50	12.1
Rocky Mountain	Avery Brewing	Avery IPA	6.81	7.1
Rocky Mountain	Odell	IPA	7.00	9.5
Midwest	Fat Head's	Headhunter IPA	7.50	8.5
Midwest	Goose Island	IPA	5.95	10.0
East Coast	Brooklyn	East India IPA	7.30	10.0
Northeast	Harpoon	IPA	5.90	8.6
Northeast	Smuttynose	IPA	6.74	8.4
Northeast	Southern Tier	IPA	6.65	10.9
Northeast	Gritty McDuff's	21 IPA	6.84	17.3
Northeast	Sebago	Frye's Leap	7.30	10.0
Northeast	Shipyard	IPA	5.73	10.3
Northeast	Blue Point	Hoptical Illusion	6.87	7.4
Northeast	Anheuser-Busch	Demon's Hopyard	7.00	14.0
England	Meantime	Meantime IPA	7.40	7.0
England	Fuller's	Bengal Lancer IPA	5.30	10.7
England	Worthington's	White Shield	5.60	13.2
England	St. Peter's	IPA	5.59	13.9
England	Samuel Smith	India Ale	5.31	10.7

Note: Available retail samples were analyzed independently for reference purposes. Results were used

FG (SG)	FG (°P)	OG (SG)	OG (°P)	ADF	IBU
1.009	2.4	1.060	15.0	83.92	60.5
1.014	3.7	1.071	17.7	78.68	61.8
1.007	1.9	1.068	17.0	88.50	68.1
1.009	2.2	1.064	15.9	85.81	75.3
1.012	3.0	1.059	14.7	82.07	78.1
1.011	2.9	1.062	15.6	81.10	45.6
1.008	2.1	1.066	16.5	87.21	65.9
1.012	3.0	1.061	15.4	79.76	48.6
1.010	2.6	1.069	17.4	84.41	65.5
1.012	2.9	1.064	16.0	81.88	75.0
1.010	2.6	1.058	14.5	81.78	60.5
1.010	2.7	1.057	14.2	80.54	45.6
1.017	4.2	1.061	15.3	72.40	50.0
1.018	4.4	1.067	16.8	73.80	80.0
1.009	2.2	1.060	14.9	84.89	63.4
1.012	3.2	1.069	17.3	81.21	60.4
1.005	1.4	1.057	14.4	89.82	65.6
1.013	3.2	1.066	16.5	80.50	60.0
1.014	2.5	1.068	17.0	80.00	87.0
1.018	4.6	1.062	15.5	70.30	55.0
1.010	2.7	1.066	16.5	83.60	48.0
1.012	2.9	1.062	15.5	81.29	42.0
1.011	2.8	1.062	15.6	81.64	69.4
1.013	3.4	1.064	16.0	78.03	57.3
1.013	3.3	1.065	16.2	79.32	47.3
1.008	2.1	1.064	15.9	86.32	70.7
1.008	2.1	1.052	13.1	83.49	49.1
1.011	2.9	1.064	16.0	81.05	53.9
1.014	3.5	1.065	16.2	78.40	70.0
1.012	3.0	1.067	16.8	82.00	75.0
1.012	3.0	1.053	13.3	77.40	50.0
1.009	2.2	1.052	13.1	82.90	40.0
1.011	2.8	1.054	13.5	78.86	59.6
1.010	2.5	1.051	12.7	79.74	46.2

to research any potential regional similarities.

8 | IPA VARIATIONS

When in doubt, add more hops.
—Unknown origin; repeated frequently by many craft brewers in the
United States

Hoppiness is Happiness
—On the label of Victory's Hop Wallop

DOUBLE/IMPERIAL IPA

There are currently two schools of thought on the origin of double or imperial IPA, the higher-alcohol, intensely hopped version of American IPA that took the craft-brewing world by storm in the early 2000s. In the early 1990s Rogue Brewing Company's John Maier, at the prompting of one of his brewers, brewed a half batch of a very strong, hoppy pale beer called IIPA, or as California publican Judy Ashworth dubbed it, "I squared PA." IIPA has been a mainstay of Rogue's portfolio ever since. It's brewed with 100 percent Maris Otter malt, and though the dry-hopping rate has stayed consistent at one pound of hops per barrel, the varieties have changed over the years.

In 1994 Vinnie Cilurzo brewed his first double IPA. It was also the first beer he made at Blind Pig Brewery in Temecula, California. About brewing Blind Pig Inaugural Ale, Cilurzo says, "Our equipment was pretty antique and crude, so I wanted to start out with something that was big and, frankly, could cover up any off-flavors." He calculated the bitterness at the time of brewing at 100 IBUs. It was aged on oak for nine months and was served on the brewery's first anniversary in 1995. According to Maier, he and Cilurzo have discussed their roles in the origin of the double IPA style, and neither one is sure which beer came first—and both don't really seem to worry about it too much.

Another early version, first brewed in 1996, came from veteran midwestern brewer Tim Rastetter while brewing at the Party Source (formerly in Covington, Kentucky, near Cincinnati). This beer, like so many great beers, was a happy accident. While brewing his first beer in his new brewhouse, Tim got much better efficiency (and higher gravity) than he expected, so he compensated for the extra strength in the same way most of us would—by adding more hops to the brew! He dubbed this beer VIP Ale (or Very India Pale Ale).

Steve Wagner at Stone Brewing Co. took inspiration directly from Cilurzo when brewing Stone's first through fifth Anniversary IPAs from 1997 through 2001: "Vinnie was getting some incredible-tasting beers, and I found myself picking his brain, figuring out how he was getting those complex flavors and aromas. He was very open about sharing information and techniques, and due in part to his influence, I couldn't help but want to make bigger IPAs each year, both as a gift to ourselves and to our fans, and as an homage to the envelope that Vinnie had been pushing."

Stone 1st Anniversary Ale was released as Stone IPA in 1997 and has become the company's best-selling beer. Stone doubled the hops in the IPA for the 2nd Anniversary Ale and increased the hopping rates again for the 3rd Anniversary Ale. With the 4th Anniversary IPA in 2000, Wagner bumped the alcohol up to 8.5 percent to make Stone's very first double IPA. Then with the 5th Anniversary IPA he increased the hops up even more. The resulting beer had approximately four times the hops of the regular Stone IPA, and it is now available as the slightly less alcoholic Stone Ruination IPA. Released in June 2002, it is the first regularly bottled imperial or double IPA in the world.

Port Brewing in San Diego, California, also started brewing some very big, hoppy IPAs. The individual Pizza Port Breweries in San Diego and Orange County have been awarded many medals at the Great American Beer Festival over the years for several of their double IPAs, including Hop 15 (brewed with 15 different hop varieties), Poor Man's IPA, Frank, and Doheny. It can be argued that they have set the standard for brewing award-winning double IPAs over the last several years.

One of the best-known double IPAs is Cilurzo's Russian River Pliny the Elder, which for most beer fans sets the standard for the double IPA style. Cilurzo tells how it came about:

Pliny the Elder logo.
Courtesy of Vinnie Cilurzo.

Russian River Brewing Company first brewed Pliny the Elder in 2001 as one of only 12 entries in the first Double IPA Festival at Vic and Cynthia Kralj's The Bistro [in Hayward, California]. As compared to the double IPAs I made at Blind Pig Brewing Company, I wanted Pliny the Elder to be bigger in alcohol, which meant more malt and dextrose sugar. In naming the beer, we were first looking for something relating to something big in stature; we had several names but nothing really inspired us. Finally, Natalie [Cilurzo's wife and Russian River co-owner] was looking through a brewing dictionary and looked up hops, which led us to Humulus lupulus *in the dictionary. This led us to* Lupus salictarius, *which [the book claimed] was the original botanical name for hops, which roughly translates to "wolf among scrubs," as hops growing wild among willows was likened to wolves roaming wild in the forest. This entry pointed us to Pliny the Elder, the Roman naturalist (among other things) who came up with that botanical name for hops.*

Other pioneering examples of the imperial or double IPA include Dogfish Head's 90 Minute IPA (first released in 2001, it features continuous hopping throughout the 90-minute boil); Bell's Hopslam; Lagunita's Maximus; Moylan's Hopsickle; Weyerbacher's Simcoe Double IPA; and Three Floyd's Dreadnaught.

As double IPA's popularity grew in the early 2000s, much credit was given to San Diego–area brewers for really growing the style, with some beer enthusiasts proposing the style be renamed "San Diego Pale Ale." Along with Stone and Pizza Port, Oggi's, Alesmith, and Ballast Point all brewed great examples of the double IPA style, and San Diego became the epicenter for big, hoppy IPAs. The double IPA was recognized as a separate beer style category at the 2003 Great American Beer Festival.

It has only grown in popularity since, with the majority of the awards going to California brewers. The concept of "imperializing" a standard beer style such as IPA has inspired brewers to brew similar offshoots from other styles, including imperial Pilsners, imperial porters (similar to the historical Baltic porter), and imperial Oktoberfests.

Table 8.1 Great American Beer Festival: Imperial IPA Winners, 2003–2011

Year	Gold	Silver	Bronze	# of Entries
2003	Pizza Port Frank Double IPA, Carlsbad, CA	Pizza Port Hop 15, Solana Beach, CA	Four Peaks Kiltlifter, Tempe, AZ	39
2004	Pizza Port Doheny Double IPA, San Clemente, CA	Pizza Port Frank Double IPA, Carlsbad, CA	Russian River Pliny the Elder, Santa Rosa, CA	48
2005	Russian River Pliny the Elder, Santa Rosa, CA	Pizza Port Hop 15, Solana Beach, CA	Marin Brewing Co. Eldridge Grade White Knuckle Double IPA, Larkspur, CA	59
2006	Russian River Pliny the Elder, Santa Rosa, CA	Pizza Port Poor Man's IPA, Carlsbad, CA	Oggi's Pizza Left Coast Hop Juice, San Clemente, CA	57
2007	Moylan's Brewing Co. Hopsickle, Novato, CA	Moylan's Brewing Co. Moylander, Novato, CA	21st Amendment Double Trouble Imperial IPA, San Francisco, CA	72
2008	San Diego Hopnotic 2X IPA, San Diego, CA	Hollister Brewing Co. Hip-Hop Double IPA, Goleta, CA	Port Brewing and Lost Abbey Hop 15, San Marcos, CA	50
2009	Hopworks Urban Brewery Organic Ace of Spades Imperial IPA, Portland, OR	Drake's Brewing Co. Denogginizer, San Leandro, CA	Hollister Brewing Co. Hip-Hop Double IPA, Goleta, CA	77
2010	Pizza Port Doheny Double IPA, San Clemente, CA	21st Amendment Hop Crisis! San Francisco, CA	Trinity Brewhouse Decadence Imperial IPA, Providence, RI	97
2011	Kern River Citra Double IPA, Kernville, CA	Firestone Walker Double Jack, Paso Robles, CA	Epic Brewing Co. Imperial IPA, Salt Lake City, Utah	102

As the popularity of these extreme and hoppy beer styles grew, Cilurzo coined the phrase "Lupulin Threshold Shift," defined as

> 1. *When a once-extraordinarily hoppy beer now seems pedestrian.*
> 2. *The phenomenon a person has when craving more bitterness in beer.*
> 3. *The long-term exposure to extremely hoppy beers; if excessive or prolonged, a habitual dependence on hops will occur.*
> 4. *When a "Double IPA" just is not enough.*[2]

BREWING DOUBLE IPA

When brewing a double IPA, most brewers agree that the key is to use ingredients and processes that allow the hops to really shine. This means limiting or eliminating any crystal or colored malts, using low conversion-rest temperatures and long rest times in the brewhouse to minimize any beer sweetness, and keeping the alcohol content between 8 percent and 10 percent. It's important to realize that alcohol adds body and a perception of fullness or sweetness that can detract from the hop character if much over 10% abv.

The malt bill should be kept simple, and brewing sugars like dextrose are championed by both Cilurzo and Tomme Arthur at Port. The key is to formulate the recipe so that the malt character takes a backseat to the hops. Crystal malts quickly develop raisin- and dried fruit-type flavors that can cover up hop flavors as beers age. Thus, crystal malts are not recommended for use in double IPA. Both Cilurzo and Tom Nickel (former head brewer at Oggi's) recommend using a base of English pale malt as an alternative to using crystal malts or Munich malt. This is a technique designed to get more malt character in the beer without conflicting with the hops.

The most important consideration in brewing a double IPA is, of course, the hopping. Target 80–100 IBUs in the finished beer, use a clean and powerful bittering hop, and enlist hops with powerful aromatic intensity for the flavor additions and the dry-hop process. Any of the 4 C's (Chinook, Centennial, Cascade, and Columbus), Amarillo, Simcoe, Citra, and Nelson Sauvin have all been successfully used in many double IPAs. Hop at twice the rate or more of a standard American

Table 8.2 2012 Double/Imperial IPA Analysis

Region	Brewery	IPA Name	ABV	Color (SRM)
California	Russian River	Pliny the Elder	8.54	8.8
California	Coronado	Idiot IPA	8.73	11.5
California	Firestone Walker	Double Jack	9.32	9.0
California	Port Brewing	Mongo IPA	8.37	10.0
California	Port Brewing	Hop 15	10.00	10.0
California	Stone Brewing Co.	Ruination IPA	7.80	10.0
Pacific NW	Deschutes	Hop Henge IPA	8.59	11.9
Rocky Mountain	Great Divide	Hercules IPA	10.05	16.0
Rocky Mountain	Oskar Blues	GUBNA	11.38	8.2
Rocky Mountain	Avery	DuganA	8.50	8.2
Northeast	Harpoon	Leviathan	10.14	11.2
Northeast	Smuttynose	Big A IPA	9.88	11.0

Note: Available retail samples were analyzed independently for reference purposes.
Results were used to research any potential regional similarities.

IPA, and consider hopping schedules that include mash hopping, first-wort hopping, and multiple dry hopping. Double IPA is the one style in which some craft brewers haven't been shy about using alternative hop products such as hop extract to increase the bitterness and hop oils to enhance hop flavor intensity.

Yeast selection is critical, and it's important to choose a yeast strain and fermentation profile that minimizes both ester and diacetyl production, as these will interfere with the hop flavor.

BLACK IPA

Strong and extraordinarily hoppy dark ales have been brewed since at least the 1800s. Dry-hopped strong porters (known as export porters or East India porters) were exported on a regular basis from England to India and other locations. Some examples of these were brewed by Bass, Whitbread, J. W. Lees, and Barclay Perkins. These beers were brewed to original gravities of 16–18 °P (1.064–1.072 SG) and hopped at three to five pounds per barrel, then further dry hopped in the cask.

In 1865 Barclay Perkins brewed an export porter that was 65 IBUs, and in 1880 J. W. Lees produced its hoppy and black Manchester Star. Author

FG (SG)	FG (°P)	OG (SG)	OG (°P)	ADF	IBU
1.008	2.1	1.073	18.2	88.03	68.3
1.007	1.8	1.073	18.2	89.71	83.2
1.011	2.9	1.081	20.3	85.40	65.6
1.009	2.3	1.072	18.0	86.98	87.8
1.012	3.0	1.088	22.0	86.40	71.0
1.012	2.9	1.071	17.8	83.71	105.0
1.021	5.5	1.086	21.6	73.54	59.0
1.011	2.8	1.086	21.5	86.46	80.3
1.012	3.0	1.096	24.1	87.03	94.6
1.011	2.7	1.072	18.0	84.70	60.0
1.012	3.0	1.088	21.9	85.64	72.1
1.015	3.8	1.089	22.2	82.09	92.0

Frank Faulkner, in his 1888 book, *The Theory and Practice of Modern Brewing*, describes Bass' black pale ale, which was brewed with hard water: "The palate reminds one very strongly of the pale ales produced by the Burton firms."[3] Interestingly, this coincides with today's version of a black IPA, which is similarly formulated to look black but to taste like an American IPA. Some of these historical dark hoppy beers have recently been resurrected by craft brewers. Pretty Things in Massachusetts brewed a 6% abv version of an East India porter from a recipe that was originally brewed in London in 1855. Also, Garrett Oliver of Brooklyn Brewery traveled to Manchester, England, to rebrew a batch of the original Manchester Star at J. W. Lees, which the brewery now produces as an annual release.

The American craft-brewed black IPA appears to have originated in 1989 or 1990, when Greg Noonan of the Vermont Pub and Brewery in Burlington brewed a batch of beer called Tartan IPA (perhaps inspired by a hoppy dark red ale from Tetford's brewery in Vermont) as a strong, roasty, winter IPA. A few years later, Noonan's head brewer, Glenn Walter, brewed a darker batch while going through a divorce. Inspired by "Buffalo" Bill Owen's Alimony Ale (touted as "the bitterest brew in as an annual seasonal release.

An export porter recipe log. Courtesy of Ron Pattinson.

The Manchester Star, brewed by J. W. Lees with guest brewer Garrett Oliver of Brooklyn Brewery.

The American craft-brewed black IPA appears to have originated in America"), Walter labeled his as "Black and Bitter," and finally named it Blackwatch. Blackwatch had a calculated bitterness of 100 IBUs. Then in 1995 John Kimmich, a brewer at Vermont Pub and Brewery, found the Blackwatch recipe in some files and asked Noonan if he could rebrew it. Kimmich changed the recipe a bit, however, because he had learned of Carafa dehusked black malt from well-traveled New England brewer

Tod Mott, who had been using the malt in an imperial stout. Kimmich used this dehusked Carafa malt to reduce the roasted character of the beer, adjusted the mash profile to reduce the sweetness, and upped the bitterness to 90–100 IBUs. The Vermont Pub and Brewery still brews Blackwatch on a seasonal basis.

When Kimmich started his own brewery, The Alchemist, in Waterbury, Vermont, in 2003, he decided to brew another dark IPA. Naming the beer El Jefe, after his big black cat, Kimmich modified the recipe again, reducing the Carafa malt to about 3.5 percent, which results in a brown, not black, IPA. He also changed the hopping to 100 percent Simcoe.

One brewer who took early inspiration from Noonan and Kimmich is Shaun Hill, who now owns his own brewery, called the Hill Farmstead Brewery, in Greensboro Bend, Vermont. In 2005, while working at The Shed, a brewery restaurant in Stowe, Vermont, Hill was inspired by Noonan's Blackwatch and Kimmich's El Jefe to produce his own black IPA. Hill brewed his first Black IPA in December 2005 and called it Darkside. With this formulation Hill tried to achieve a deep resinous hop character he describes as "hop saturation." The beer itself was black in color, very complex, and aggressively hopped. After a brewing stint in Denmark, Hill is now back in Vermont and is brewing more black IPA. His Hill Farmstead James, named after his grandfather, is a robust black IPA brewed with a blend of Carafa black malt and Sinamar black malt

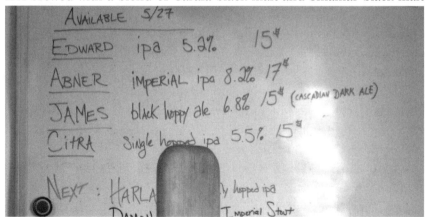

The Hill Farmstead tasting room, where "James" can be purchased.

extract, which Hill thinks allows even more of the hop profile to come through. Hill adds Warrior and Simcoe hops and uses hop extract in the kettle, which allows for a very high bitterness without a harsh character.

In the Pacific Northwest, brewers began producing dark, hoppy ales in the early 2000s. Early examples of the dark, hoppy ale that brewing aficionados in the Pacific Northwest have named "Cascadian dark ale" include Rogue Brewery's Black Brutal Bitter (aka Skullsplitter), first brewed in the early 2000s; Phillips Brewing's Skookum Cascadian Dark (brewed in 2004 in British Columbia); and Laughing Dog's Dogzilla (brewed in Idaho in the mid-2000s).

The story of Rogue's Black Brutal Bitter starts with the brewery's Imperial Bitter, which began as a 24th anniversary beer for Don Younger's Horse Brass Pub in Portland, Oregon, in 1999. It became very popular and was later released as Brutal Bitter. Rogue owner Jack Joyce apparently hated the name, but it stuck, and it has been one of Rogue's most popular beers ever since (it has now been renamed Brutal IPA).

In 2000 brewmaster John Maier decided to brew two sibling beers to the Brutal Bitter. The first was Brutal Pils, brewed with Weyermann Pils malt and Sterling hops (now grown on Rogue's own farm and processed by Indie Hops). The second was the black version, brewed with Carafa II, Munich malts, Carawheat MFB, and melanoidin malt. Originally at 15 °P (1.060 SG) and 60–70 IBU, the first test versions were brewed on a 20-gallon More Beer pilot system. In 2003 Rogue brewed Skullsplitter, a higher-gravity version of the Brutal Black Bitter, at 18.4 °P (1.074 SG). It features the same malts, with Summit hops for bittering and later additions of Simcoe and Amarillo. The beer was not filtered, and it also wasn't dry hopped, despite the overwhelming hop presence.

Maier thinks the lower-gravity version is a great example of a Cascadian dark ale, though when the brewers first made it, they "didn't know what the hell to call it." Skullsplitter is very awkward when fresh, says Maier, but mellows and tastes great with about three months of age.

One of the more popular dark IPAs today is Deschutes Brewing Company's Hop in the Dark Cascadian Dark Ale. Former Deschutes brewmaster Larry Sidor's goal when making Hop in the Dark was to brew a black beer—not a hoppy porter. He decided to use Carafa malt instead of chocolate malt or black malt. Deschutes prefers the name Cascadian dark ale for the style. Sidor explained that people in the Pacific Northwest, where Deschutes is located, know what to expect when ordering one: a dark beer with ingredients from Cascadia (or the Pacific Northwest). He thinks that the Cascadia label is an appropriate homage to the homebrewing roots of craft brewing in the region.

THE STORY OF STONE SUBLIMELY SELF-RIGHTEOUS ALE

In February 2006, a few months before I joined Stone Brewing Co., I attended the Extreme Beer Fest in Boston and tasted the first black IPA I had ever seen—Hill's Darkside Black IPA from The Shed. The style immediately intrigued me. I had previously tasted hoppy porters and Dogfish Head's Indian Brown IPA (that beer was first brewed in 1999 and is billed as a hybrid between an American IPA, an American brown ale, and a Scotch ale), but a black IPA? That was new. I liked Hill's beer, and I thought the concept of a black IPA was really a great fit for Stone. So shortly after I started there, I suggested we brew one ourselves. We proceeded to start making pilot brews on our 20-gallon system in the fall of 2006. The first couple of batches were brewed with a blend of black and chocolate malts. When done, the beer tasted like a bitter porter, which is neither what I wanted nor something that would be suitable for a Stone Anniversary Ale. I wanted a beer that tasted like a double IPA with a subdued roasted malt character that didn't interfere with the hops.

After being disappointed with the first couple of batches, I decided to go back to the drawing board. Perusing malt catalogs, I saw the listing for Weyermann's Dehusked Carafa Special III Malt. The husk on this malt is removed prior to roasting. It is known for contributing color but not the harsh astringency that results from brewing with traditional black malts. I remembered that I had used a version of this malt to homebrew a schwarzbier several years earlier, and I thought, "Bingo! This is the malt to use!" Another test batch ensued, and unfortunately, the fermentation hung a bit, the beer was sweet, and the hop character was subdued. I was frustrated, but I was still confident that if we brewed this beer in our 120-barrel, we could get the proper blend of flavors and proper fermentability to make a beer that matched what I envisioned it should be.

After some selling on my part, I was allowed to brew a half batch in our brewhouse. We changed the hopping a bit—going with a blend of Amarillo and Simcoe in the flavor hops and dry hops to give us more piney and tropical fruit flavors as opposed to the citrusy hop notes we had been aiming for in previous batches. When I tasted the beer, I knew we had nailed it, and I was ecstatic. We ended up brewing it for our 11th Anniversary Ale. It was very popular, right up there with our 10th Anniversary IPA, and a few years later, using the exact same recipe, we re-released the beer as Stone Sublimely Self-Righteous Ale. It won a bronze medal in the new American India Black Ale category at the GABF in 2010.

Stone Sublimely Self-Righteous Ale is made using a similar approach to brewing a double IPA. Gravity, alcohol, and hopping rates are very similar, and very little crystal malt is used. The only real difference is the addition of 5 percent Weyermann Carafa Special III Malt to the grain bill. I've been wondering what this beer would taste like without the addition of the black malt, and maybe someday we'll see. I think Stone Brewing Co. deserves some credit for popularizing the style by making the first black IPA to be available on a widespread, national basis, but we certainly don't claim to be the first brewers to brew this style!

Another early pioneer in black IPA brewing was Jeff Bagby at Pizza Port Carlsbad in California. At the same time we were developing Stone 11th Anniversary Ale (in fact, it pains me to say he just beat us to it), Bagby was developing the beer that would become Black Lie, brewed for the Liar's Club in San Diego (see the sidebar "Black Lie, Black IPA, and Cascadian Dark Ale").

BLACK LIE, BLACK IPA, AND CASCADIAN DARK ALE

Back when the Liar's Club in San Diego was still around, we used to sell Louis Mello quite a bit of beer for his bar. He especially liked getting casks from us. The fastest I've ever seen casks blow in a nonfestival atmosphere was on Friday nights, at the Liar's Club.

Louis called me up one day and asked if I would like to do an anniversary beer for the Liar's Club. I, of course, said yes and asked him what he had in mind. He asked if I could make a black IPA. I thought about it and said sure.

I drew up a brand-new IPA recipe with a standard malt bill and hop schedule and brewed away. Before I whirlpooled the beer, I added a bunch of Sinamar to the kettle. Fermenting away we had black IPA. I also added a little more Sinamar into the bright tank, because I didn't feel that the beer was black enough. The result was a black beer with no dark malt aroma or flavors. It had a huge hop aroma and flavor.

The beer sold like crazy at the Liar's Club and here in Carlsbad. This was back in 2007. We have made the beer about once a year ever since.

A few thoughts on black IPA—especially after a recent trip to Oregon. I now believe that Cascadian dark ale and black IPA are two different styles. I've had black IPA from several breweries, and when I was in Oregon I had what they call CDA, or Cascadian dark ale. My original thought was that brewers from Oregon were calling their black IPAs CDAs. After tasting several of them, they are different. They aren't nearly as IPA-ish. They are darker brown in color, have some dark malt flavors, and have a hoppy character. They do not have huge hop aromas, nor are they really that bitter or fully black. They are also around 5.5–7% abv. Most black IPAs that I've had are stronger, more bitter, have striking hop aromas, and are pretty absent of dark malt character altogether. CDA seems to be a combination of brown and robust porter, American strong pale ale, and American brown ale. Black IPA is just that: American IPA that is black.

Is there a difference between a black IPA and a Cascadian dark ale? Both Maier and Bagby think so. The differences may not be very distinct right now, but these beers may evolve further into two separate beer styles at some point. The Brewers Association in 2010 called the styleAmerican India Black Ale, and in 2011 changed the name to American Strong Black Ale, acknowledging the oxymoronic quality of the name Black IPA. East Coast fans of black IPA think that the Cascadian dark ale name doesn't pay proper respect to the current version's origins in Vermont, and fans of the Cascadian dark ale name think that it is a better descriptor for the style, which focuses on the flavors of Pacific Northwest (Cascadian) hops. Fans of the name Black IPA think it is the

Table 8.3 2012 Black IPA Analysis

Region	Brewery	IPA Name	ABV	Color (SRM)
California	Stone Brewing Co.	Sublimely Self-Righteous Ale	8.7	110.0
California	Pizza Port Carlsbad	Black Lie	6.9	85.0
Pacific Northwest	Deschutes	Hop in the Dark	6.5	90.0
East Coast	Victory	Yakima Glory	7.9	45.4
Vermont	Hill Farmstead Brewery	James	7.2	87.0
Vermont	Vermont Pub and Brewery	Blackwatch	6.2	n/a
Vermont	The Alchemist	El Jefe	7.0	16.0
Vermont	Otter Creek	Black IPA	5.8	63.2

Note: Available retail samples were analyzed independently for reference purposes. Results were used to research any potential regional similarities.

best descriptor for the category. Their argument is based on not only the fact that it is an IPA that is black in color, but also the theory that IPA has come to mean much more than a type of pale ale.

From a brewing standpoint, what makes black IPA unique is that it drinks like an IPA with hints of roast malt character. It's not a porter or a stout; the dark malt flavors are subtle and allow the hop character to be quite forward in the aroma and palate, just like an IPA. The brewers of the best versions avoid using large amounts of chocolate or black malts, and use the dehusked Carafa malt at 3–6 percent for color and hints of roast flavor that don't interfere with the hop flavors. All other brewing parameters are very similar to the American IPA or double IPA process.

BELGIAN IPA

Hoppy Belgian beers are normally the exception rather than the rule. Most Belgian styles are hopped at lower levels than just about any beer, with the exception being the American lager style. But there are a few hoppy Belgian beers that are close stylistically to the double IPA recipe. One early example of a hoppy strong Belgian ale is the Piraat Tripel IPA. Commonly advertised as a historical IPA, it is a 10.5% abv aggressively hopped Belgian strong pale ale from Browerij Van Steenberge N.V.

FG (SG)	FG (°P)	OG (SG)	OG (°P)	ADF	IBU
1.014	3.5	1.080	20.0	82.5	85
1.013	3.2	1.074	18.5	82.4	80
1.012	4.0	1.064	16.0	75.0	65
1.021	5.4	1.081	20.4	72.2	76
1.020	5.0	1.072	18.0	72.0	100
1.010	2.5	1.058	14.5	83.0	60
1.016	4.0	1.070	17.5	77.0	90
1.018	4.5	1.062	15.6	70.3	47

The hoppy Belgian IPA, as we currently know the style, appears to have been first brewed in 2005, when Hildegarde van Ostaden, brewer at Brouwerij De Leyerth, returned from a visit to the United States. Inspired by the American IPA, she brewed Urthel Hop-It, a strong Belgian pale ale brewed with Pilsner malt and intensely hopped with European noble hop varieties.

Another early version was Achouffe Brewery's Houblon Chouffe Dobbelen IPA Tripel. First brewed in 2006, it is described as an "Indian pale ale" that has a starting gravity of 18 °P (1.072 SG), is 9% abv, and is aggressively hopped with three different hop varieties. Duvel Moortgat, the parent company of Achouffe, was inspired by the Houblon Chouffe beer to brew its own version, Duvel Tripel Hop, in 2007. Duvel Tripel Hop is a 9.5% abv version of Duvel that is aggressively hopped with Saaz, Styrian Goldings, and Amarillo. It is now being brewed on a regular basis. Other Belgian versions include De Ranke XX Bitter, an aggressively hopped 6% abv Belgian ale, and Poperings Hommel Ale.

American versions of the Belgian IPA style include the following: Flying Dog's 8.3% abv, 60 IBU Raging Bitch; Port's Big Wednesday; Green Flash's 9.2% abv Le Freak; Victory's Wild Devil; and Allagash's 7.8% Hugh Malone.

There are two approaches brewers typically take when brewing a Belgian IPA. The first is to take a Belgian tripel recipe and hop it more like an IPA, by using either American or European hop varieties. The second approach is to take an American IPA or a double IPA recipe and ferment it with a Belgian yeast strain. Stone Brewing Co. did both versions in 2008, when it released 08.08.08 Vertical Epic Ale as a Belgian tripel hopped like an American IPA (inspired by Duvel Tripel Hop) and Stone Cali-Belgique IPA, which is standard Stone IPA wort fermented with Belgian yeast. The versions that start as tripels tend to be a bit more traditional in their flavor profile, with a characteristic lightness of color and dry flavor. The versions brewed as American IPAs fermented with Belgian yeast tend to be, as one would expect, a little fuller with aggressive bittering.

The real challenge in brewing a Belgian IPA is getting the hop flavors to marry well with the intense phenolic, spicy, and fruity character of Belgian yeast strains. Certain hop varieties, such as the intense but tropical, fruit-heavy Amarillo hop, seem to work better with the Belgian yeast flavors than hops such as the piney Simcoe or resiny Columbus. Similarly, less phenolic yeast strains seem to combine better with the American hop flavors than do strains that produce excessive amounts of clove flavors.

SESSION IPA

One of the more recent trends in American brewing is to brew a beer at less than 5% abv and hop it like an American IPA. The risk or challenge in brewing this kind of beer is avoiding excessively grassy and vegetal hop character, as the reduced alcohol in the beer changes the way the hop flavors are carried. For hop lovers, this is an exciting new trend, as some of these beers, such as Ballast Point's Even Keel, have amazing hop character and yet are sessionable, with an alcohol content more similar to a British bitter. Blending many varieties of hops in the dry hop is an effective brewing technique that adds levels of complexity that might not be found by using only one variety in a lower-alcohol ale.

TRIPLE IPA

This style has had a couple of false starts as far as style definitions, but the latest specs appear to be 10–12% abv and less than 8 °L (16° EBC) color—and intensely hoppy. Vic and Cynthia Kralj, at The Bistro, in Hayward, California, held the first-ever Triple IPA fest in February 2012. Among the best current examples of this style are Russian River's Pliny the Younger, which goes through four dry-hopping processes; Founder's Devil Dancer; and Alpine Brewing Company's Exponential Hoppiness.

WHITE IPA

The latest IPA variation comes to us from Larry Sidor, formerly of Deschutes Brewery in Bend, Oregon, and Steven Pauwels of Boulevard Brewing Company in Kansas City, Missouri. These brewers collaborated on two versions of a White IPA—effectively a blend of the Belgian Wit style and the American IPA—in the spring and summer of 2011. The Deschutes version, dubbed Conflux No. 2, and the Boulevard version, titled Collaboration #2, were brewed as a higher-alcohol 7.4% abv Belgian wit beer. They were flavored with coriander and orange peel, following the traditional style, but also assertively hopped like an American IPA with Bravo, Cascade, Centennial, and Citra hops, and spiced with additional sage and lemongrass.

Since that joint venture, several brewers have released White IPAs, including some more traditionally spiced versions, such as Knee Deep and Triple Voodoo's Northern California collaboration and Saranac's White IPA, brewed with Citra hops, wheat malt, oats, coriander, and orange peel. Deschutes released their full-time Chainbreaker White IPA in April 2012. It is brewed with Pilsner malt, wheat malt, and unmalted wheat, and hopped with Bravo, Cascade, and Centennial hops to 55 IBUs.

Other brewers choose a more exotic direction. For example, Anchorage Brewing makes its version with Australian Galaxy hops, coriander, black peppercorns, and fresh kumquats, and includes a *Brettanomyces* fermentation in French oak foudres.

Brewers formulating this developing style appear to favor citrusy and fruity hop varieties like Cascade, Centennial, Citra, and Galaxy, which combine exceptionally well with the banana esters of the yeast fermentation and the spices used for flavoring.

9 | IPA INGREDIENTS AND BREWING TECHNIQUES

Let a neat housewife . . . have the handling of good ingredients—
sweet malt and good water—and you shall see and will say there is
an art in brewing.
—*Dr. Cyril Folkingham, 1623*

MALT

Malt is often referred to as the "soul of beer," since it provides the body, sweetness, color, and perhaps most importantly, the starches that are broken down into fermentable sugars in the brewhouse process. These sugars provide the food for the yeast to metabolize and produce alcohol and carbon dioxide.

The malting process changes the raw grain to a kernel that has a modified endosperm with active enzymes, a developed flavor and aroma, and a low moisture content, which makes it suitable for long-term storage. Barley is the preferred grain used for malt and brewing beer, primarily because of flavor and because it has a husk, which facilitates separating the sweet liquid wort from the rest of the spent grain. Other grains, such as wheat, oats, and rye can also be malted and are used in brewing beer, but the dominant malt used in brewing is barley malt.

The barley kernel is made up of the following parts:

- The outer layers, including the husk, pericarp, and testa that protect the kernel.
- The endosperm, where all the starch is located. This starch, if the kernel (or seed) is planted, provides nutrients to the growing barley plant.

- The aleurone layer, a thin (three-cell) layer that surrounds the endosperm and produces the enzymes needed to break down endosperm cell walls and starches.
- The embryo, or the start of the new plant, located at one end of the kernel.
- The scutellum and epithelium, which separate the embryo from the endosperm.

The malting process to convert barley to malt involves three steps: steeping, germination, and kilning.

Steeping

This involves taking dried barley kernels and steeping them in water with agitation and forced air, under tightly controlled conditions, to increase the moisture content from about 12 percent to more than 40 percent. This effectively prepares the barley kernels for germination.

Pale malt. Photo by Tyler Graham.

Germination

This process starts the growth of the new barley plant, again under tightly controlled environmental conditions. Modern germination chambers are equipped with high-flow, temperature-controlled, sterile air and automatic turners to rotate the kernels to ensure consistency in environmental conditions. Floor malting means that the germinating malt is placed on a floor and turned by hand by workers with rakes to ensure uniform exposure to air.

Several biochemical processes involving enzymes occur in the kernel during germination. As the grain starts to grow, hormones in the grains are activated, which in turn stimulate the formation and the release of enzymes from the aleurone layer and the scutellum. Some of these enzymes break down the cell walls in the endosperm area, which frees up the starch for enzymatic breakdown into sugars. Under normal planting circumstances, this would be used to feed the new plant. Some of these enzymes will be used later in the brewing process to help break down the starches in the mash tun. Other enzymes will break down proteins, resulting in the formation of amino acids that will be used by the yeast in fermentation. During the germination process, the rootlets and acrospires start to grow. The maltsters monitor this and remove the malt from the germination chamber when the proper level of modification is reached (measured by the cell wall breakdown in the endosperm and by the acrospire length, when it reaches about three-fourths the length of the kernel).

Kilning

At a prescribed point, usually when most of the starch has been freed up, and the acrospires reach their proper length, the germinating malt is transferred to a kiln and dried with hot forced air. This process takes anywhere from one to two days. This step reduces the moisture content to about 4 percent, stops the enzymatic activity, and halts the growth process. The resulting malt kernel is friable (easily broken apart), and the endosperm tastes slightly sweet. This is pale malt, which forms the backbone of all beer styles.

SPECIALTY MALTS

When IPA was in its heyday in the mid-1800s, most of the large commercial breweries operated malthouses as part of their brewing operations, and malted their own barley. The Burton brewers perfected the production of extra pale, or white, malt, which was kilned at 150° F (65° C) to produce a malt color of 1.5 °L. Today, only a handful of breweries malt any of their own barley, and most brewers purchase ready-made malt from commercial suppliers.

Specialty malts, such as Munich, crystal, and black malts, are more heavily roasted, higher-colored malts that brewers add in small proportions to the base malt to enhance color, flavor, and malt complexity in beer. Although specialty malts are standard ingredients in many beer styles, including darker beers such as amber ales, porters, and stouts, they have only limited use in the production of standard IPA.

Crystal malts were developed in the early to mid-1800s and started to become popular in British beer styles in the late 1800s and the early 1900s. Crystal malts are taken directly from the germination chambers, then roasted in high-temperature roasting drums while still moist. Some caramel malts are produced in traditional kilns as well. This stewing process caramelizes and crystalizes the sugars in the malt, and the resulting malt has a distinctive caramelly, toffeelike flavor. Roasting to different levels of darkness changes the flavors that crystal malts provide. Darker crystal malts have more of a molasses/burnt sugar character. Colors from 10 °L to 150 °L are produced by most malt suppliers, though nothing more than 60 °L crystal is normally used in IPA recipes. Most IPA brewers choose the lightest grades of crystal malt to use, in small percentages. One of the big detriments to using crystal malt in an IPA is that, as beer ages, the flavors from crystal malt can oxidize into heavy dried fruit, raisin, and prunelike flavors that completely overwhelm the hop flavors in the beer. Crystal malt also tends to add a sweetness that can put the beer out of balance.

Munich-style malts come off the germination chamber with slightly higher levels of moisture and modification. Like pale malts, they are roasted in the kiln, but at higher temperatures to develop color and flavor. The flavor Munich malt provides is best described as toasted and nutty. Unlike crystal malts, most Munich malts retain some enzymatic activity, and the lightest grades can be used at 100 percent of the malt recipe in a brew. Some English and American brewers have used light Munich malts effectively in their IPA recipes to add some extra malt complexity.

Dark malts are not typically used in IPAs, but they are made by taking malt from the germination chamber and roasting it at extremely high temperatures to char it. Some brewers will use dark malts at 0.5–1 percent or so of the malt recipe to give their beer a reddish brown hue.

BREWING SUGARS

Although IPA is brewed by most brewers as an all-malt beer, English brewers outside of Burton-on-Trent started using sugars in IPA in the late 1800s, presumably as a way to get a drier and lighter-colored beer.

Today's craft brewers occasionally use sugars for the same reason in double or imperial IPA.

Sucrose is a disaccharide composed of a glucose and a fructose molecule that is chemically bonded. Usually derived from sugar cane or sugar beets, sucrose is a common sugar used in brewing. British brewers often use invert sugar, a hydrolyzed version of sucrose, which breaks apart the glucose and the fructose molecules. Invert sugar also provides high fermentability as well as additional flavors and complexity due to the acid treatment it undergoes during the hydrolysis process.

In the United States, powdered dextrose sugar (glucose derived from enzymatically hydrolyzed cornstarch) is a popular ingredient in many double IPAs.

WATER

Brewing water must be clean, potable, and as neutral in flavor as possible. For most homebrewers and craft brewers, municipal water is the most reliable and consistent source. Craft brewers can use carbon filters to strip chlorine treatment and other flavors from municipal water. Homebrewers can effectively remove residual chlorine either by using cartridge-type carbon filters or by boiling their water before brewing with it. Boiling volatilizes the chlorine compounds and precipitates out temporary hardness.

Water hardness, alkalinity, and mineral content are important considerations when brewing an IPA. The IPAs brewed in Burton-on-Trent in the early 1800s overtook the London-brewed IPAs in popularity, in part, because the extremely hard, high-sulfate Burton water allowed for a more intense, bitter character from the hops, better beer clarity, and enhanced shipping capability.

Your local water supplier should be able to provide a typical analysis of your water. Use this as a starting point for your brewing water.

Calcium plays an important role in brewing, because it stabilizes malt enzymes and, therefore, enhances enzymatic breakdown of starches to sugars. In addition, calcium (and to some extent, magnesium) reacts with phosphate ions in the mash, which lowers mash pH and increases enzymatic activity. Higher levels of calcium enhance beer clarity and stability. Calcium precipitates oxalate, which then prevents gushing in

Table 9.1 Water Analysis, by Brewing Regions

	Pilsen	Munich	Dublin	Dortmund	London	
Calcium	7	75	117	260	90	
Sulfate	3	10	54	283	58	
Magnesium	2	19	4	23	4	
Sodium	32	10	12	69	24	
Chloride	5	2	19	106	18	
Hardness	28	266	309	745	241	
Alkalinity	23	253		300		

packaged beer. When adding mineral salts to water, calcium sulfate (gypsum) will enhance hop bitterness and dryness, and calcium chloride will mellow the beer character a bit and add palate fullness.

High levels of sulfate enhance hop bitterness and add a perception of crispness to the bitter character from the hops. Higher levels can also form hydrogen sulfide and sulfur dioxide, which can result in a perceptible sulfate bite, often called the "Burton Snatch." This flavor can be a bit intrusive in some beers but tends to fade over time.

MILLING YOUR GRAIN

In order to prepare malt for brewing, it needs to be milled. Milling breaks open the malt husk and exposes the starch material contained in the endosperm. The natural enzymes present in the malt will become active once hydrated (mixed with water) and heated during the mashing process. Then the enzymes will attack the starches in the endosperm and break them down into sugars that can be fermented by brewer's yeast. The most important consideration when milling grain is to ensure that the husk material stays as intact as possible—not only to help with the lautering process but also to prevent the extraction of excessive tannins into the wort, which can result in an astringent or harsh flavor in the beer.

Most small brewers and homebrewers use two-roller mills. A single pass through these two corrugated steel rolls breaks open the malt kernels and crushes some of the interior endosperm, thereby exposing the starch for enzymatic breakdown into sugars. Larger brewers use four-roller and six-roller mills, which have the added advantage of separat-

Burton-on-Trent	Milwaukee	St. Louis	Stone
300	35	26	22
640	18	80	16
60	11	8	9
54		19	38
36	5	23	
997	133	98	92
236		21	43

ing out the intact malt husk and then allowing the starchy endosperm to pass through tighter sets of rolls. This finer grind increases extract recovery out of the brewhouse but keeps the husk particles intact, thus allowing for efficient lautering and optimal malt flavor.

Malt grind profiles can be measured and adjusted by brewers to either produce more extract or faster lauter tun runoffs. A coarser grind results in a faster runoff at the expense of extract recovery, while a finer grind results in a slower lauter tun runoff but with increased brewhouse extract recovery. As with many parameters in the brewing process, the brewer must balance one versus the other by taking into account brewhouse cycle times, economics, and desired beer flavor.

MASHING

The first step in the brewhouse process is mashing—that is, mixing the milled grain with water and holding it at prescribed temperatures and lengths of time to control the enzymatic breakdown of starch and the resulting sugar content.

It's important to get good mixing at mash-in. The malt endosperm material needs to be thoroughly wetted in order for the enzymatic breakdown of starches to sugars to properly occur. But excessive or violent agitation can result in damage to the malt husks, which can then create tannic flavors in the wort and beer, and can cause poor lauter tun runoff.

Most IPA brewers will mash in at close to their conversion rest temperature and use what is called an infusion mash. Infusion mashing is the traditional British practice of adjusting water volume and temperature so that when the water is mixed with the milled malt, the brewer achieves the proper temperature for conversion rest (starch breakdown to sugars). Infusion mashing requires either a well-insulated mashing vessel or a heating system to maintain temperature.

Brewers with more advanced temperature control systems can adjust the temperature during the mashing process. Most malts available for brewing are well modified, and using well-modified malt means that multi-temperature protein rests and other complex mashing schemes aren't needed. But if possible, it is good practice to raise the mash temperature to 163–165° F (73–74° C) at the end of the mash cycle before lautering. This accomplishes two things: (1) The high temperature deactivates the malt enzymes, stopping the conversion process and allowing for better control of resulting wort fermentability; and (2) it makes the wort less viscous, which facilitates lautering in the next step.

Brewers control wort fermentability—the ratio of fermentable sugars to nonfermentable sugars and dextrins (the remnants of the starch molecules)—by monitoring temperature and time during the conversion rest in the mash. There are two primary malt enzymes at work during the conversion process: beta amylase, which has an optimum activity at 130–140° F (54–60° C), and alpha amylase, which has optimum activity at 150–160° F (66–71° C). Beta amylase acts upon the nonreducing ends of the sugar chains in a starch molecule, cleaving off the two-sugar molecule called maltose, the most common sugar in wort. Alpha amylase has a more random action, cleaving varying sizes of sugar chains off the starch molecule. While some of these sugar chains may be fermentable by brewer's yeast, others may not be. An added benefit of alpha amylase activity is that it provides more reducing ends for beta amylase activity, so that alpha amylase activity indirectly results in more maltose being formed.

Because of the different optimal temperatures for these two enzymes, brewers can adjust the fermentability of the wort and the sweetness and alcohol content of the resulting beer by adjusting mash conversion temperature and time. For example, a conversion rest between 145° F (63° C) and 148° F (64° C) is thought to provide the best compromise for optimizing both beta and alpha amylase activity—and resulting in a highly fermentable wort, with maltose being the dominant form of sugar. The resulting beer will be drier and have a higher alcohol content than a beer that was mashed at a higher temperature. A low-temperature, long (two- to three- hour) conversion rest is used by many double IPA brewers because the resulting beer is very dry and doesn't have a lot of residual sugar to interfere with the flavor of the hops.

Using a higher-temperature conversion rest for a shorter time will result in a beer with higher residual sweetness after fermentation because beta amylase activity is reduced, less maltose is formed, and more unfermentable sugars and dextrins are left in the wort. Temperatures up to 158° F (70° C) can result in a beer with more body. Some IPA brewers prefer this because the beer has a more balanced malt character, but in a double IPA, lower mash temperatures are generally used, so the drier, less malty beer that results will accentuate hop flavors.

There is a fairly small temperature window in which the brewer can get satisfactory action of both beta amylase and alpha amylase. Using a mash temperature below 145° F (63° C) is not recommended because alpha amylase activity will be negatively affected and fermentability of the resulting wort will go down. Similarly, a conversion temperature above 158° F (70° C) will result in rapid degradation of beta amylase, thus causing lower fermentability. Therefore, most mash rest temperatures used by professional brewers fall between 148° F (64° C) and 156° F (69° C), although an alternative is to have two mash rest temperatures—one at 144–146° F (62–63° C) and another rest in the mid-150s° F (66° C)—to take advantage of alpha amylase activity.

Another thing that can impact fermentability is the water-to-grain ratio used in mashing. Typically, most brewers use about 1.3 quarts of water per pound of grain. Professional brewers often use a weight-basis water-to-grain ratio by calculating the weight of water from the volume (1 gallon of water = 8.33 pounds). A 3:1 water-to-grain ratio is considered optimal by most brewers, with ranges from 2.7:1 to 3.3:1. Although a higher water-to-grain ratio can increase enzymatic activity in the mash, it can also result in more rapid enzyme degradation, especially when the mash is being heated. Furthermore, high water-to-grain ratio will produce a more dilute wort, which can make hitting the target original gravity difficult. A lower water-to-grain ratio will increase extract recovery but may make proper hydration of the malt endosperm challenging.

HOPS

Certainly, no discussion of IPA brewing techniques would be complete without a lengthy review of the hop varieties, hop products, and hopping techniques that can be used to obtain the prominent hop bitterness, flavors, and aromas that characterize the IPA style.

Since it originated, dry hopping has become requisite for brewing IPA. But over the years, brewers have become more and more creative in how they supplement dry hopping with other techniques and alternative hop products. As such, innovative brewers are constantly pushing the boundaries regarding how much bitterness and hop intensity can be obtained in their beer.

The hop plant is a perennial vine, of which the female plant is the only one that produces the flowers used in brewing. The hop flower, or hop cone, is anywhere from one to four inches long and resembles a small green pine cone, with overlapping petals. Hidden at the interior base of each leaf or petal is a cluster of yellow, sticky material. These are the lupulin glands, which contain the hop resins (alpha acids and essential oils), the primary contributors to hop flavor, aroma, and bitterness in beer.

Hop cone on the vine. Photo by Tyler Graham.

Table 9.2 lists the typical composition of a hop cone. Of these components, the alpha acid content, the essential oils, and to a lesser extent, the beta acids and the polyphenols are the most important to the brewer. Most of these components are found in the lupulin glands. This is why, if using whole hops in a brew, a thorough inspection of them is required. The lupulin glands are attached loosely to the cone and can easily become knocked off if the hops are handled roughly. It is common when using baled hops to see a pile of yellow powder at the bottom

Table 9.2 Chemical Composition of Hops

Constituent	Percentage by weight
Water	6–12
Soft resins	
Alpha acids	1.5–18
Beta acids	1–10
Essential oils	0.5–2.5
Hard resins	
Polyphenols (tannins)	
Amino acids	0.1
Simple sugars	2
Pectin	2
Oils and fatty acids (higher in hops with seeds)	0–2.5
Protein and carbohydrates	15
Ash (minerals)	8–10
Cellulose	40–50

of the bale after removing all the compressed cones. This indicates that much of the bittering and aromatic power of the hops has been knocked out of the cones, which can result in inconsistent bitterness or hop flavor in the beer. At the very least, when brewing with whole hops, an inspection of the cones and a look for the presence of intact lupulin glands is a very important step.

Alpha Acids

Alpha acids are the hop component that most IPA brewers look at first when formulating their recipes. Alpha acids contribute directly to the bitterness in the beer; therefore, hops with higher alpha acid content can contribute much more bitterness to the beer (at the same addition rates) than hops with lower alpha acid content. Noble hop varieties from Central Europe and the United Kingdom, such as Hallertau, Saaz, and Goldings, typically have lower levels, ranging from 1.5–5 percent alpha acids. The newer American varieties are usually higher, with some of the "super alpha" varieties such as Warrior, Summit, and Apollo reaching levels of 17–18 percent alpha acids. These high-alpha hops were originally bred to provide a less expensive bittering source for large brewers. But as an added benefit, many varieties also have interesting and intense flavor attributes that have proved popular for IPA brewers. Because of their increased bittering power, the newer varieties, have become highly desirable for use in very bitter beers such as IPA and double IPA. The argument can be made that the development of these hop varieties contributed significantly to the rise of American IPA and double IPA as styles.

The three major alpha acids in hops are humulone, cohumulone and adhumulone. The ratio of the these three alpha acids varies with each hop variety, and some brewers look closely at the cohumulone level in hop varieties as levels higher than 30 percent are thought to contribute a harsher bitterness. Noble hop varieties originating from Central Europe (Saaz, Hallertau, etc.) typically have lower cohumulone values.

Table 9.3 Hop Alpha Acids

Alpha acid	Percentage of alpha acids
Humulone	40–80
Cohumulone	14–50
Adhumulone	5–15

In order to contribute bitterness to beer, alpha acids need to be boiled. The wort kettle boil, the step during which hops are typically added in the brewhouse, transforms the alpha acids into an isomerized form, called the iso-alpha acid. The iso-alpha acid is the compound that contributes bitterness to beer. The isomerization reaction occurs at temperatures higher than 185° F (85° C). The rate and completeness of the isomerization reaction is dependent on temperature and boiling time. Therefore, the longer one boils hops, the more bitterness is extracted.

The solubility of iso-alpha acids (the ability to dissolve in wort) is much higher than the un-isomerized alpha acids. Iso-alpha acids are much more bitter than alpha acids. In addition to imparting bitterness, iso-alpha acids also contribute significantly to foam retention and foam stability in beer, which explains why highly hopped beers typically have much thicker, denser foam than lower hopped beers. It is interesting to note that iso-humulone is the iso-alpha acid in beer that reacts with sunlight to produce skunkiness in beers packaged in green or clear bottles.

Essential Oils

Also of primary importance to IPA brewers is the essential oil content of hops. Essential oils contribute hop aroma and flavor to beer. Hop oils can contain thousands of different compounds, but the primary three are myrcene, humulene, and caryophyllene. Myrcene is the most abundant hop oil, at 30–60 percent of the total, and is lost quickly to evaporation as hops are boiled. Myrcene is the oil that many brewers believe is of prime importance for late hop addition flavor and aroma contributions. Many hop oils undergo chemical or oxidative transformation during the kettle boil and during fermentation. Different hop aromas and flavors are obtained depending on when in the process the hops are added and how long they are exposed to boiling wort or yeast fermentation. This is why many IPA brewers widely employ the technique of adding hops during different stages of the brewing process.

Each hop variety has its own unique composition of alpha acids and hop oils. Therefore, hop selection and blending is particularly important to the IPA brewer who strives to achieve the perfect combination of hop bitterness, flavor, and aroma. Table 9.4 lists some hops that are widely used by IPA brewers. It is by no means complete—there are new hop varieties being developed every year and adventurous brewers use "nontraditional" IPA hops to brew amazing IPAs.

HOP PRODUCTS

Another important consideration for the IPA brewer is which form of hops to use in the beer. Over the past 40 years, several different types of hop products have been made available to commercial and home brewers, and each offers its own advantages and challenges.

Hop Cones

Hop cones, or whole hops, are the traditional hop product. Hop cones are dried, compressed, and baled hop flowers, typically available in 150- to 200-pound bales (United States), hop pockets (United Kingdom), or ballots (Germany). Obviously, a 200-pound bale of whole hops is bulky and difficult for homebrewers or small craft brewers to consider using, as the bale is close to 5 feet by 2.5 feet by 2 feet in dimension. Several hop suppliers will break down bales into more manageable 10- to 20-pound packages for smaller brewers.

Table 9.4 Commonly Used IPA Hop Varieties

Variety	Typical alpha acid content (%)	Cohumulone (% of alpha acids)	Oils (mL/100 g)	
Amarillo	8–11	22	1.5–2	
Apollo	15–19	24–28	1.5–2.5	
Bullion	7–10	35–40	2–3	
Bravo	14–17	29–34	1.6–2.4	
Calypso	12–14	40–42	1.6–2.5	
Cascade	5–8	37	.8–1.5	
Centennial	9–11.5	30	1.5–2.5	
Challenger	5–9	20–25	1–1.7	
Chinook	12–14	39–34	1.5–2.5	
Citra	11–13	22–24	2.2–2.8	
Columbus (aka Tomahawk, Zeus, or CTZ)	13–16	32	1.5–2.5	
Delta	5.5–7.0	22–24	0.5–1.1	
East Kent Goldings	4.5–7	28–32	0.5–1.0	
Fuggle	3.5–5	26	0.7–1.5	
Galaxy	13.5–15	35	2.4–2.7	
Magnum	12–14	22–26	1.9–2.3	
Nelson Sauvin	12–13	24	1.0–1.5	
Northdown	7–8	24–29	1.5–2.5	
Nugget	12–14	26–30	1.7–2.3	
Simcoe	12–14	15–20	2–2.5	
Sorachi Ace	10–16	23	2.0–2.8	
Summit	16–18	26–33	1.5–2.5	
Target	10–12	29–37	1.6–2.6	
Warrior	15–17	25	1.0–2.0	
Willamette	4–7	32	1–1.5	

Flavor and aroma description	Typical uses and other comments
Floral, citrus, mango/tropical fruit	Popular bittering and aroma hop. May be too intense if not used with other varieties
Grapefruit, spicy	Newer variety, very intense; can get sulfury
Intense American hop aroma; black currant and catty	Hard to find, used in Ballantine IPA
Floral and fruity	Newer variety
Pear, berry, apple	Newer aromatic variety
Spicy, floral, citrus, grapefruit	Classic American aroma and dry hop; one of the "4 C's"
Floral, citrus (lemon rind), piney	Originally developed as Super Cascade, used for flavor, aroma, dry hopping; one of the "4 C's"
Spicy, clean bitter	Primarily a British bittering hop, good flavor characteristics, can be used effectively for flavor/aroma
Intense spice, pine, and apricot flavors, grapefruit	Dual-purpose hop; one of the "4 C's"
Strong citrus and tropical, grapefruit, lime, melon, passion fruit	Newer variety
Intense, pungent, herbal, floral	Good bittering hop, used frequently in dry hops; can get sulfury; one of the "4 C's"
Citrusy and spicy, with hints of tea, berry, melon	Newer aromatic variety
Spicy, earthy, herbal, marmalade	Classic British variety
Mild, grassy, floral, herbal	Flavor, aroma, and dry-hopping British ales
Citrus, passion fruit, stone fruit	Australian variety
Clean bitter	German origin, excellent bittering hop
White wine, berries	Unique New Zealand variety
Clean bitter, mild flavor	Good dual-purpose hop
Strong bitter; light herbal	Bittering, primarily
Strong resinous/piney	Bittering and aroma; nice dry hop
Herbal, dill, tangerine	Developed in Japan; unique flavor
Citrusy and herbal	Bittering and flavor; can get oniony/sulfury at high levels
Intense; herbal, floral, some citrus/tangerine	Good bittering hop, good for flavor
Mild, clean	Primarily a bittering hop
Herbal, grassy, mild	American version of Fuggle

The advantage of using hop cones is primarily one of perceived flavor. There are several craft brewers in the United States who use only whole hop cones in their beers, because they think that the compressed whole hop cone gives the best flavor. In addition, whole hops can be used in a vessel called a hopback, after the boil, to add additional flavor and assist in filtering out trub (the proteinaceous material that forms in the kettle boil). Many brewers think that whole hops give a superior flavor in the dry-hop process, and while they may use other hop products for bittering and flavoring in the brewhouse, they will limit themselves to only whole hops for dry hopping. Whole hops are much easier to inspect for quality than other types of hop products.

The disadvantages of using whole hop cones are primarily related to storage, stability, and efficiency. Hop bales are large, bulky, and difficult to maneuver. Because hop bales are not impervious to oxygen penetration, whole hops tend to oxidize and age more rapidly than other hop products. Once opened, whole hops are susceptible to oxidation and flavor degradation, so be careful when buying small amounts of whole hops that have been taken from larger packages or bales. As mentioned previously, lupulin glands can become dislodged from the cone, resulting in inconsistent bittering and flavor contributions. In addition, for the craft brewer, whole hops are more difficult to weigh out and require the use of a hop separation device (a hopback or other type of hop strainer) to remove the leaf material from the wort after the boil. Using whole hops for dry hopping requires the use of a bag or some other perforated container, so the hop leaves can be easily removed from the beer when the dry-hopping process is complete.

One variation of whole hops is the 15-gram hop plug, which has gained popularity in the United Kingdom. These compressed hops are shaped into the form of a plug, similar in shape to a hockey puck. As such they are easier to store, weigh, and use, and are popular for dry hopping cask beer.

Hop Pellets

By far the most common form of hops available and used by craft brewers and homebrewers is the hop pellet. Developed in 1972, hop pellets are made by taking the compressed bale of whole hops, shredding them, and running the hop material through a hammer mill to reduce them to a fine powder. The hop powder is then pressed through a die to form a 4- to 6-millimeter diameter pellet. Hop pellets, unlike other hop products, still retain the hop leaf material, which many brewers think is an important component of hop flavor. If desired, some hop suppliers can remove portions of the vegetative material during pelletizing to concentrate the lupulin glands. A standard hop pellet is often called a Type 90 pellet, because 90 percent of the original whole hop weight is retained in the pellet. A Type 45 pellet is one that has the same bittering potential in only 45 percent of the weight.

Using hop pellets offers many advantages. They are vacuum packed or packaged with a blanket of inert gas (nitrogen) and stored in 44-pound (25 kg) or 11-pound (5 kg) boxes that make them easy to handle, weigh out, and add to a brew. Unlike baled hop cones, which must be separated from the bale and broken down into small pieces (fist size or smaller) in order to get good extraction, hop pellets normally flow freely and thus are easy to weight out. If unopened, the vacuum-packed or nitrogen-blanketed hop pellets will remain fresh for several years. This allows brewers to hold them for long periods before using. In addition, the pelletizing process captures all the lupulin in the compressed pellets, which makes the hops more consistent with respect to bittering potential and flavor contributions. Hop utilization (the amount of bitterness captured from the hops during the brewing process) is typically 5–10 percent higher when using pellets versus whole hops.

One disadvantage of using hop pellets is that the hops will oxidize rapidly once exposed to oxygen. Because the lupulin glands have been somewhat ruptured in the pelletizing process, they will form oxidation products (resulting in harsher bittering compounds) and lose aromatic characteristics after the vacuum pack is opened. Additionally, hop pellets disintegrate rapidly into wort and beer and form a large amount of solid sludge material during the kettle boil and the whirlpool that must be separated from the wort. This can result in lower overall brewhouse efficiency, because much of the wort is left behind in the hop/trub sludge. Dry hopping with pellets can also be challenging; it can be hard to get the hops into a tank of beer, and the sludge can also be difficult to remove. Pellets, because they fall apart into their powder form rapidly when put into liquid, won't be retained in a bag or strainer basket like whole hops will. Some brewers also feel that, because the milling process generates a substantial amount of heat, hop pellets provide a grassier, more vegetative flavor when used for a dry hop, as opposed to the citrusy fruitiness provided by whole hops of the same variety. My experience has been that suppliers now have a very good grasp of optimal temperatures and control them during the pelletizing process—thus making this argument somewhat moot.

Carbon Dioxide Hop Extracts

Hop extracts are highly concentrated forms of hop resins that are, extracted with liquid carbon dioxide from pellet hops into a usable syrup form. Although traditionally used by larger brewers, hop extracts are finding their way into the world of the craft brewer. When brewing extremely bitter double IPAs, several brewers have found that hop extracts are a good alternative for maximizing bitterness without overloading the brewhouse with leafy hop material or sludgy hop pellet residue. As such, some brewers are using combinations of hop extracts in the bittering portion of their hop recipes.

The advantage of using a hop extract is that high levels of bitterness can be obtained without adding a large amount of solid material to the wort. Hop extracts are highly concentrated and contain up to 40–50 percent alpha acids. The hop utilization (efficiency at extracting bitterness) increases somewhat, and brewhouse efficiency also increases, because wort is not lost in hop leaves and the trub piles are smaller in the whirlpool. Hop extracts are quite easy to transport and store, and they remain stable for indefinite periods of time.

One of the disadvantages of using hop extract is that it is messy and difficult to use. It is challenging to remove all the thick, sticky syrup from the can it is packaged in. Freezing the canned extract, removing both the top and bottom of the can, and pushing the frozen extract into the wort is one way to maximize extract removal from the can. Another common method is to dump most of the extract from the can, then place the open can into the boiling wort or a separate container of hot wort and allow the wort to remove the remainder of the

Whole cones, pellets, and CO_2 extract are all used effectively by IPA brewers.
Photo by Tyler Graham.

extract from the can. Be careful, however, because spilling the extract on a stainless steel kettle top will result in a stain that is difficult, if not impossible, to remove.

Some brewers think that hop extracts do not provide the same flavor or aromatic quality as can be obtained by using whole hops or pellets. This can be overcome by some IPA and double IPA brewers by using extracts only for bittering, and by enlisting whole or pellet hops for flavor hopping and dry hopping.

Distilled Hop Oils

Hop oils can be steam distilled from hops and used to augment dry-hop character in beer. Most taste trials have shown that the flavor is not quite the same as using whole hops or pelletized hops, but oils can be used effectively in combination with other hop products to augment and intensify hop flavor and aroma.

Other Hop Products

Hop suppliers have developed several other products from carbon dioxide extract. Pre-isomerized extracts require no boiling to provide bitterness. Pre-isomerized hop pellets allow for higher IBU levels in beer and have found homes in some double IPAs. Pure iso-alpha acids are added by many large brewers to finished beer (post-brewhouse and post-fermentation) to adjust bitterness levels and enhance foam. Chemically reduced hop extracts that won't react with sunlight are used to prevent lightstruck character in beers packaged in green or clear glass. Other products can also adjust bitterness in beer and craft brewers are increasingly exploring the use of these types of post-fermentation hop products to increase bitterness.

Fresh Hops

Fresh hops—hops that are sent to brewers immediately after harvesting and stem and leaf removal (without drying and baling)—are becoming very popular. They add a distinctly different hop character to beer and can be used in every part of the brewing process.

Using fresh hops requires careful planning on the part of the hop supplier and the brewer, since the fresh hops must be shipped quickly in cold temperatures and used right away to avoid spoilage. Usage rates need to be five to six times that of standard dried and compressed or pelletized hops, because the hops contain five to six times the moisture (water content) of a typical dried and compressed hop cone.

DEVELOPING THE HOP RECIPE AND CALCULATING BITTERNESS

Brewers must consider the following when creating a hop recipe for their IPA:

- Hop varieties to be used and their alpha acid content
- Desired hop flavor and aroma characteristics
- Desired bitterness level
- Kettle hop utilization
- Impact of late hop additions on flavor and bitterness level

A brewer cannot develop a recipe with a target IBU level without knowing the hop utilization rate. Hop utilization is defined as the amount of alpha acids added to the kettle versus the amount of iso-alpha acids in the resulting wort. It can be expressed with the following formula:

$$\text{Hop utilization \%} = \frac{\text{Iso-alpha acids in wort x 100}}{\text{Alpha acids added to the brew}}$$

Hop utilization is best calculated once the brewer has the bitterness content in the wort analyzed. But analyzing IBU levels involves adding a strong acid and iso-octane to the wort, creating and separating an extract, and measuring the absorbance of the extraction with a spectrophotometer at 275 nanometers. This expensive and time-consuming process is beyond the abilities of most homebrewers and craft brewers, so instead, an estimate is usually used.

Hop utilization generally falls into the range of 20–40 percent. Table 9.5 shows how different processes can affect the hop utilization.

Table 9.5 Factors Affecting Hop Utilization in Kettle Boil

Change	Typical hop utilization, impact on bitterness obtained
Hop cones, 12 °P wort, 90-minute boil	20–30% utilization
Hop pellets	Increase, 25–35% utilization
Hop extract	Increase, 30–40% utilization
Increase boil time	Increase
Increase wort pH	Increase
Decrease gravity	Increase
Increase hopping rate	Decrease; bitterness will increase, but not linearly

It's also important to note that utilization numbers are for wort, and a significant drop in IBUs (as much as 33 percent) occurs during fermentation, because a drop in pH as the wort is fermented to beer causes a reduction in the solubility of isomerized alpha acids.

Bitterness extraction is highly dependent on when you add hops in the boil. Different levels of bitterness will be obtained based on when you add hops to the boiling wort and how long they are boiled. There are some published tables that approximate the bitterness or utilization obtained by adding hops at different times during the wort boil, but at best, those tables are an approximation, because every brewer has slightly different hop supplies, heat exchange, boil properties, evaporation rates, and kettle design, all of which will impact utilization and recovered bitterness.

Utilization is highly dependent on wort gravity. An increase in wort gravity will result in a decrease of hop utilization and recovered bitterness. Adding more hops will increase bitterness, but utilization will decrease. The bitterness increase is not linear, and eventually the brewer will hit a point where diminishing returns are obtained. In other words, adding 50 percent more hops will not always result in a 50 percent increase in bitterness.

For most brewers, a critical balance is necessary to obtain the proper amount of hop flavor and aroma from the kettle hops, versus extracting hop bitterness. The essential oils that are responsible for hop flavor and aroma are highly volatile compounds that will be evaporated almost completely with early hop additions. Later hop additions will retain more hop flavor and aroma at the expense of hop utilization and extracting bitterness. Part of the brewer's art is balancing these additions to get a wort with proper bitterness levels and the proper amount of hop flavor and aroma.

A typical way to determine the bitterness in wort is to calculate the alpha acid units (AAUs) from your hop addition in a 10-gallon batch:

For example, 8 oz. of Chinook at 13% alpha acids = 8 x13 = 104 AAU

IBU = AAU x U x 75/V where U = utilization and V = wort volume

= 104 x .2 x 75/10 = 156

But the utilization number is, at best, an estimate. There is research available that provides utilization values for different-gravity worts and different boil times, but these numbers cannot account for different kettle designs, mixing parameters, and other variables that can affect extracting hop bitterness.

An IBU value of 156 is probably not possible. There is a limit as to how much iso-alpha acid can be extracted in wort. As wort gravity increases, the maximum amount of iso-alpha acids that can be extracted will also increase, but at a much lower utilization rate.

It is a common misconception that IBU and iso-alpha acid content (in ppm) are the same thing (i.e., that the numbers are interchangeable). This is not true. A 1 ppm addition of pure iso-alpha acids might only increase IBU by only 0.6–1, depending on other conditions and variables. Excessive age of, and warm storage conditions for, the hops can cause additions with no measurable iso-alpha acid increase but significant IBU increase, due to oxidation of beta acids during storage.

Brewers who use their wort calculation to publish the IBUs of their beer are often not accounting for the fact that 25–35 percent of their IBUs will drop out of their beer during fermentation. Yeast will absorb some iso-alpha acids. (Yeast recovered from a fermentation often has three to four times the bitterness level of the beer it came from.) In addition, the pH reduction (typically from pH 5.3 to pH 4.5) reduces the solubility of the iso-alpha acids, and some will precipitate or solidify during the fermentation. This solid hop bittering material is often seen deposited at the sides or at the top of the fermenter after fermentation. The maximum level of IBUs in a 12–14 °P (1.048–1.056 SG) beer at pH 4.5 is probably about 80 IBUs.

So what's the answer? Unfortunately, the best way to know what wort IBUs and beer IBUs are in a given IPA is to measure them analytically! Then you can make adjustments by using simple algebra to get to your desired level. But as I said before, this analysis is beyond the means of most small brewers, so for many an estimate remains the best way to determine IBUs. There are several brewing calculation programs available that do a nice job of estimating IBU values. Suffice it to say that someone who is using a half-pound of Chinook hops for bittering a 10-gallon batch of IPA is going to have a fantastically bitter beer!

HOPPING TECHNIQUES IN THE BREWHOUSE

Although almost all brewers continue to utilize the wort kettle for adding their hops and extracting bitterness, flavor, and aroma, hops can be used in other brewhouse vessels as well.

Mash Hopping
A technique in which whole hops or hop pellets are added directly to the mash, mash hopping apparently was a common practice in the early 20th century. The theory is that the higher pH in the mash and the presence of oxygen allow the volatile compounds in the hops to form oxidation products with components in the malt. The resulting compounds are not volatile and remain in the wort throughout the lautering and

kettle boil process, and lend a "more rounded" depth of hop flavor to the beer.

There is a fair amount of discussion as to whether anything is really gained from this technique, and it would be interesting to explore this more with American craft beer. Unfortunately, most brews that are mash-hopped involve recipes with high amounts of hopping elsewhere in the process, so any flavor gain would be hard to detect through sensory analysis. But for an IPA brewer—especially a double IPA brewer— it's cool to say you do it!

Whole hops would be the best choice for mash hopping because the leaves may help in lautering, but pellet hops would work also. Given the limited flavor and aromatic qualities of extracts, adding them to the mash is not recommended.

First-Wort Hopping

First-wort hopping is similar in theory to mash hopping. Hops are added to the first wort in the kettle, and during the time it takes to fill the kettle, the volatile flavor components are bound to the malt components in the wort. In addition, the hops' longer contact time with the wort at the higher pH increases utilization, which results in higher bitterness levels. This technique also has the advantage of helping reduce foaming during the start of boil. As with mash hopping, the desired hop product to use here is usually whole hops or pellets. A good-quality, high-alpha hop with desired flavor and aromatic properties is best for this stage.

Kettle Hopping

Almost every brewer adds hops during the kettle boil (the exception being those large breweries that use no hops in the brewhouse and use pre-isomerized extracts post-fermentation to add bitterness to their beers). As discussed previously, hopping regimens during the kettle boil differ among all brewers, but they typically involve one to three additions at different stages of the kettle process.

Invariably, brewers will add a significant portion of their hops at the start of the wort boil. This so-called "bittering hop addition" is considered by most brewers to contribute very little in the way of flavor and aroma, as most of the volatile oils and other flavor compounds are boiled off during the remaining 60–120 minutes of wort boiling. Many

IPA brewers use a high-alpha bittering hop, such as Warrior, Magnum, Summit, or Apollo, for this addition. This would also be the place to use a hop extract, if so desired.

Subsequent hop charges later in the boil are often termed "flavor" and/or "aroma" hop additions, with the later additions thought to retain those volatile essential oil compounds contributing mostly to aroma. It should be noted that bitterness is also obtained by these additions, though not at such a high utilization rate as that first addition. Brewers select single hop varieties or combinations of hop varieties to get the desired flavor, aroma, and bittering contributions from these additions. Typically, when brewing an IPA, more aromatic high-alpha hop varieties such as Centennial, Cascade, Simcoe, and Amarillo can be used for these additions. Using low-flavor hops such as Nugget, Magnum, or Perle is not recommended.

Hopback Hopping

For brewers who use whole hops, a hopback is an important vessel for facilitating the removal of leaf hop material from the wort after the kettle boil. Other straining devices, such as the "hopjack" used by Anheuser-Busch, are also available, but the hopback provides the advantage of being able to hold an additional amount of whole hops. Brewers can fill the hopback with hops, and as they run the wort through the hopback, these additional hops not only help filter the wort of spent hops and trub but also contribute a significant amount of hop flavor and aroma.

Typically, a brewer would use only the highest-quality aromatic hops for this step, as bitterness extraction is of secondary importance here. With wort temperatures falling below boiling levels, recovery of aromatic and flavorful essential oils will be maximized. So pick a hop that has the desired flavor and aromatic characteristics.

Whirlpool Hopping

Many brewers, regardless of whether they whirlpool in a separate vessel or in their kettle, use this trub separation step for adding more flavor and aroma hops. Like hopback hopping, this hop addition contributes mostly to flavor and aroma, so a good-quality hop with desired flavor components should be used. It may surprise some that a significant amount of bitterness (as much as 20–30 percent of the total) will also be obtained with this hop addition. Remember that isomerization of hop alpha acids to iso-alpha acids will occur at temperatures above 185° F (85° C).

As with the hopback, only good-quality hops with the desired aromatic characteristics should be used in the whirlpool. Hop pellets are the hop product of choice in the whirlpool, because whole hops would require the use of a porous bag or other container, and extracts would not have the desired aromatic qualities.

Post-Fermentation Hopping

Dry hopping is what sets apart the IPA from most other beer styles. Dry hopping is the practice of adding hops to the aging tank, serving vessel, or cask and allowing the hops to steep in the beer to get significant fresh hop flavors without imparting additional bitterness.

Most craft brewers and homebrewers will dry hop their beer after the primary fermentation is complete. This technique allows brewers to maximize the flavors obtained from hops and to remove the hops prior to packaging the beer.

Most brewers avoid adding hops during fermentation, because much of the hop character can be absorbed by the actively fermenting yeast, thereby reducing the efficiency of the dry hop. In addition, waiting to dry hop allows for repitching of the primary fermentation yeast, if so desired. When using conical fermenters, yeast can be collected in the cone and removed prior to adding the dry hops. When fermenting in carboys, racking the beer off the settled yeast is recommended prior to dry hopping.

There is a considerable amount of debate over whether pellet hops or whole hops should be used for dry hopping. As discussed in the section on hop products, many brewers believe that whole hops give a better "fresh hop" character to their beers. My experience has been that with the technical improvements in controlling temperature during pelletizing, the dry-hop character obtained from pellet hops is comparable, and in some cases superior, to that achieved from using whole hops.

From a practical standpoint, adding pellets is convenient for most brewers, since they are easy to weigh out and somewhat easier to get into the tank. Hop pellets will settle out to the cone or the bottom of the tank, and after the dry-hopping process either they can be removed prior to filtration and packaging or the beer can be decanted off them. Whole hops require being bagged or placed in other types of perforated containers, and they get very wet and heavy—thus making it challenging to remove them from the tank. When using whole hops, brewers typically transfer the beer to be dry hopped into another tank in which the bagged whole hops have already been added. Frequently, several circulations are set up on the dry-hopped tanks to maximize flavor extraction by keeping the hop material suspended.

Allowing hops to steep in beer for an excessive amount of time can result in stemmy and vegetative flavors in the beer, which can mask the more pleasant essential oil flavors. Most brewers limit dry-hop contact time to 5–15 days, but recent research indicates that maximum flavor extraction from the hops happens in just a few days.

Some brewers further maximize hop flavor by using multistage dry-hopping techniques. They remove the first charge of dry hops and add a second or even third charge prior to packaging. Another technique is to dry hop both in the secondary and in the finished/bright beer tank.

FINAL THOUGHTS ON FORMULATING A HOP RECIPE

Single-Stage Additions versus Multiple Additions

Excellent IPAs and double IPAs are brewed using one or two hop additions in the brewhouse, and others may use more frequent additions. At one extreme is Stone Brewing Co., which uses one bittering hop addition and one flavor hop addition in the whirlpool for Stone IPA and Stone Ruination IPA. At the other extreme are beers such as Dogfish Head IPAs and the Port Hop 15, for which the hops are added continually or in many stages. Both techniques produce exceptional IPA. Practicality plays a role in the decision to use multiple additions, as does flavor.

Blending Hops

Several breweries make excellent IPAs by using single hop varieties. These are great beers for gauging the flavors a particular hop variety will add to a beer. Weyerbacher's Double Simcoe IPA is a good example of this.

Port's Hop 15 is a great example of using many hop varieties to get great IPA flavor. The goal for most brewers who employ this technique is to get hop flavor depth and complexity. One advantage of blending hops—especially the flavor hops and the dry hops—is that if you can't obtain a specific variety, reasonable substitutions can be made to approximate the desired flavor.

Overhopping

There is a limit to how much iso-alpha acids can be extracted into wort. Maximum bitterness levels can be obtained, and they are dependent on wort gravity (higher-gravity worts can be more bitter). Brewers of extreme beers often will add more hops than can possibly contribute to additional bitterness. In times of high hop prices and limited hop availability, this practice may seem foolhardy on the surface, but important hop flavors are extracted from these hops, even if bitterness is not, and flavor can suffer if they are removed for the sake of cost. Too many hops can result in excessive vegetative flavors, so be careful—more is not always better!

FERMENTING TECHNIQUES FOR IPAS

Yeast and Yeast Growth

Yeast, being a living organism, has two primary focuses: (1) to feed and sustain itself, and (2) to procreate and further the species. As brewers, our goal is to get the yeast to produce the desired flavors and alcohol content in our beer, and also to generate enough new yeast that the yeast can be pitched to subsequent batches of beer. This requires that we manage yeast cells carefully, manage the fermentation environment, manage the amount of growth that occurs, and manage the yeast health before, during, and after the fermentation. It can be challenging to control the metabolism of a living organism so it only produces the flavors we want it to produce, in the desired quantities, and stays healthy enough to do this again and again.

Yeast reproduces by budding—that is, forming a new cell from the mother cell. When brewers discuss yeast growth, they are discussing the process of yeast cell budding, or of new cells being created. They are not referring to growth in the size of the original cells. Yeast growth requires the uptake of certain nutrients present in the wort. In general, ale brewers are looking for a three- to fivefold growth in the total number of cells during the course of the fermentation. So if 20 million cells per milliliter are present at the start of the fermentation, there would be a point where there are 60–100 million cells at the height of the fermentation process. After that, some cells will start to die, and some will simply settle out of the wort. Managing yeast growth is the most critical component of maintaining overall yeast health, fermentation, and flavor development. Too much growth can result in stressed cells, decreased ester production, increased fusel alcohol production, increased diacetyl production, and subsequent difficulties in reducing diacetyl or acetaldehyde. Too little growth results in slow fermentations, increased ester production, and potential difficulties in completing the fermentation and in reducing diacetyl and acetaldehyde.

In general, an all-malt wort has all the nutrients that yeast will need to grow and ferment successfully (fermentable carbohydrates, nitrogen, minerals, vitamins) with the exception of oxygen. Oxygen is the most critical yeast nutrient for the homebrewer and craft brewer to add to wort. Dissolved oxygen in wort is required for yeast cells to synthesize bonds between unsaturated fatty acids and sterols for new yeast cell walls. These compounds play an important role in the transport of nutrients into the yeast cell and the excretion of metabolites out of the cell. Most brewers attempt to target 9–15 ppm dissolved oxygen in wort at the time of yeast pitching. This can be achieved by saturating the wort with (sterile) air. Using pure oxygen, as some brewers do, can be risky, as the saturation point in wort is much higher. When wort dissolved O_2 levels reach 20–30 ppm, excessive yeast growth can occur, and the resulting new yeast cells are stressed because the other nutrients required may not be plentiful enough to support that level of growth. There is such a thing as "too much of a good thing." Compare this situation to a human being gorging on a huge meal. What happens? The person quickly becomes tired, and sluggish, and wants to do nothing but sleep! When this occurs with yeast, fermentations may hang up, and excessive levels of sulfur and acetaldehyde may be released into the beer.

Other factors that can affect yeast growth include trub carryover (excessive trub results in increased wort levels of zinc and fatty acid, which can increase yeast growth), pitching rate (the initial amount of yeast added to the wort), fermenter design, protein content (and the ratio of amino acids versus protein), carbohydrate content, and temperature (higher = more growth). As such, all these items are important to monitor and control to maintain consistent fermentations and flavor development in the beer.

Yeast strain selection is also critically important to the IPA brewer. First, you have to start with an ale yeast. Usually the yeast selected should be a minimal producer of excessive esters, diacetyl, or sulfur. Certain levels of sulfur are acceptable, and perhaps even desired, in an English IPA. But any yeast flavor compound that overwhelms or interferes with the fresh hop character in an IPA, especially an American IPA or a double IPA, should be avoided. The exception to this guideline is the brewing of a Belgian IPA, which requires a Belgian yeast to get the proper Belgian yeast flavor profile. The trick with this style is to get an appropriate balance of yeast and hop character so the beer remains distinctively Belgian—and also distinctively an IPA.

Commercial suppliers have a wide range of yeast strains available to ale brewers. One of the most popular is the California Ale yeast strain, supposedly descended from the original Ballantine Ale strain. It produces a clean beer with minimal ester and diacetyl production, and it settles out fairly well after fermentation is complete. As such, it is an ideal yeast for making an American IPA or a double IPA. Other great yeast strains are available, but search out strains that have high attenuation rates, low diacetyl production, and good flocculation (settling) characteristics.

Yeast is available in several forms—most commonly in liquid tubes or "smack packs." Dry yeast has gotten a (perhaps deservedly) bad rap over the years, but recently there have been several new suppliers and strains available that ferment well and make great beers.

Pitch Rates

The pitch rate is defined as the initial yeast cell count in the wort after pitching (adding) the yeast. For ales, conventional wisdom is to pitch 1 million cells/milliliter wort/°P of wort. For example, a 12 °P (1.048 SG) wort should be pitched at 12 million cells per milliliter of wort; a 16

°P (1.064 SG) wort should be pitched at 16 million cells per milliliter; and a 20 °P (1.080 SG) wort should be pitched at 20 million cells per milliliter.

In reality, this standard should be used as a guideline, as every yeast strain will react differently to different wort strengths and different pitch rates. But this is a good starting point for most conventional ale yeasts.

The consequences of pitching lower or higher than the desired pitch rate are primarily related to changing the growth pattern during the fermentation. However, since we are talking about IPAs, it is likely that any resulting flavor differences will be minimized by the beer's extreme hoppiness. That said, it's still important from a flavor and fermentation consistency perspective to hit your pitch rate target, whatever it is. There's never a good excuse for sloppy brewing practice!

Starters

A tube or pack of liquid yeast from a commercial supplier is likely to provide about 100 billion cells of yeast. These are typically geared toward a five-gallon batch of a standard-strength brew and will only provide about 5 million cells per milliliter in that brew, though the yeast itself has been grown on oxygen-rich media and fed on glucose, which gives the cells an enhanced capacity for growth. If the brew is larger than five gallons, or higher than a 17 °P (1.068 SG) wort, making a starter is recommended.

A "starter" can be any volume of wort that you add yeast to before using it to make your beer. The yeast get active in this smaller volume, usually for one or two days, and then are added to five gallons of beer, or 10 gallons, or whatever size you're brewing. This can be a good way to "proof" the yeast, and when making high-gravity beers, to ensure an appropriate amount of yeast is pitched.

Measuring Cell Counts

By far the easiest way to measure yeast growth in fermentation is by measuring the cell count during the growth phase and fermentation. This is a fairly inexpensive and simple process. It requires the use of a hemocytometer (a counting chamber) and a microscope with a 10x and 45x objective (lens).

This method involves taking a sample of wort/beer, diluting the sample 9:1 with distilled water, and pipetting a small amount of the wort/water mixture into the chamber of a hemocytometer. Count the yeast cells on five of the larger grids, multiply by 5, multiply by 10 to account for the dilution, then divide by 10,000 to get the number of cells per milliliter.

The hemocytometer can also be used to measure another important factor in yeast: yeast health/viability. A viability measurement is made by taking a slurry of yeast and adding methylene blue indicator to it. After a short rest period, the yeast slurry is added to the hemocytometer. When counting the cells, count both the total number of cells and the cells that have taken up the blue dye (these are "dead" cells). Percent viability is defined as the total percentage of live (nonstained cells) in the slurry. Typically, for ale yeast, a viability of 90 percent or greater will help ensure a successful fermentation.

FACTORS THAT IMPACT YEAST PERFORMANCE AND FLAVOR DEVELOPMENT

The Fermentation Process

The fermentation process consists of three phases: The first, the lag and growth phase, is when the yeast accimilate to their new environment (the lag phase), start taking up nutrients like oxygen and amino acids, and begin their growth phase. Typically, the lag period should last no more than 12–24 hours, otherwise the sweet, sugary wort becomes a prime candidate for bacterial spoilage.

During the anaerobic/fermentation phase, all the wort oxygen is taken up by the yeast, and the yeast adjust their metabolism to a steady rate of fermentation. A constant population of yeast in the fermenting wort is maintained. This is the primary fermentation stage, and will last anywhere from three to five days in a healthy ale fermentation.

As the fermentable sugars are consumed during the final slowdown phase, the yeast metabolism reduces (or slows) and the yeast settle out of solution (flocculate). This is a key phase, especially in a high-gravity wort, as lack of alcohol tolerance could result in yeast inability to completely ferment the wort before settling out. Rousing to resuspend yeast is a practice sometimes used to keep the active yeast in contact with the beer. In addition, as the yeast cells start to die due to lack of nutrients, there is the ever-present danger of acetaldehyde formation if the cells themselves start to lyse (burst open) and release fatty acids that, when oxidized to aldehydes, result in stale flavors.

Fermentation temperature, while perhaps not as critical in a well-hopped beer, is important to control in order to maintain proper flavor development and fermentation completeness. Too cold, and the resulting beer may be underattenuated and lack complexity. Too warm, and the resulting beer may have increased levels of sulfur, esters, and off-flavors from yeast stress (elevated diacetyl, acetaldehyde).

Yeast Nutrients

In general, adding yeast nutrients should not be necessary when brewing all-malt beer and when using healthy, active yeast. Yeast nutrients are often created from dead yeast cells and have high levels of amino acids and zinc, which can help ensure a complete fermentation. But yeast nutrients can impact yeast growth and fermentation flavor development.

One important consideration for yeast nutrition is the use of candi sugar or dextrose when brewing a double IPA. At 5–10 percent of the total extract, a sugar adjunct should not cause a problem with fermentation. But at higher levels of usage, or for higher-alcohol beers, fermentation can be affected.

When yeast start fermentation, they will preferentially metabolize the simple sugar molecules (glucose, fructose) found in candi sugar or dextrose. Once these sugars have been metabolized, the yeast must synthesize an enzyme to cleave the maltose sugars formed during mashing into two glucose molecules. This enzyme synthesis can be difficult for yeast if they have moved out of the growth phase and into the fermentation phase. Often, a brewer will see an apparent lag in the middle of the fermentation as the yeast adjusts to its new sugar source. To combat this, brewers may add their sugar at the end of fermentation (in the form of a krausen) so the simple sugars are fermented after the maltose molecules have already been consumed.

Also, at very high levels of sugar usage, yeast nutrients can be diluted to the point where fermentation falters toward the end. Again, this is probably not a concern for double IPA brewers who use 10–15 percent sugar in their beer, but a high-gravity wort with more than 30 percent sugar may have trouble fermenting completely.

Diacetyl Production

Diacetyl produces a buttery or butterscotch flavor with a slick sensation in the mouth. In general, diacetyl is not desired in high levels in any beer style, but it is highly undesirable in an IPA because it will mask the fresh hop character.

Diacetyl is produced as a byproduct of yeast metabolism. Specifically, it is formed from alpha-acetolactate in the synthesis of the amino acid valine. Eventually, yeast cells will remetabolize the diacetyl to form acetoin and eventually 2, 3-butanediol—neither of which are flavor active. Diacetyl levels in beer typically max out during fermentation, then diminish as the beer ages. Only healthy yeast can remove diacetyl, so it is important that the precursor is converted to diacetyl and is transformed by the yeast before chilling and/or filtration takes place; otherwise, diacetyl can form from the precursors after packaging.

Diacetyl production is highly influenced by the yeast strain used and by the initial nitrogen content in the wort. Perhaps counterintuitively, diacetyl production is higher when amino acid levels are higher. This is because yeast will take up certain amino acids in preference to valine and will have to synthesize valine to compensate.

The rate of reduction of diacetyl to acetoin and 2, 3-butanediol is increased when (1) beer pH is lower, (2) beer temperature is higher (the popular "diacetyl rest"), and (3) the concentration of yeast cells remaining in suspension is higher.

Acetaldehyde Production

Acetaldehyde has a flavor that some refer to as "green apple," "bready," or "pumpkin seed." Acetaldehyde is often difficult for beer tasters to identify, because the flavor changes as the concentration increases. At low levels, it can be easily confused with normal fermentation esters.

Acetaldehyde is formed from pyruvate during the fermentation metabolic pathway. From there, acetaldehyde is normally converted by the yeast cell to ethanol. During fermentation, some acetaldehyde makes its way out of the yeast cell wall and into the beer, but during aging it will be reabsorbed and metabolized into ethanol. By far, the most important source of acetaldehyde in beer is related to excessive yeast contact with beer after fermentation is complete. The lack of nutrients and fermentable sugars in the beer creates a stress situation for the yeast, and eventually some yeast cells will lyse (referred to as autolysis) and release acetaldehyde, among other flavors, into the beer.

Acetaldehyde production is stimulated when there is increased aeration and yeast growth. During the latter stages of fermentation and aging, air inclusion can result in a spike of acetaldehyde concentration. The rate of reduction of acetaldehyde to ethanol during aging can be accelerated by raising beer temperatures and increasing the number of yeast cells in suspension. The risk of yeast autolysis can be reduced by racking the beer off the yeast quickly after primary fermentation is complete—thus ensuring that settled yeast in the fermenter are not subject to temperature extremes—and by using healthy yeast to start with.

Fusel Alcohol Production

Fusel alcohols are important, as they can provide some complexity to beer flavor. But in high amounts they can be harsh and boozy.

Fusel alcohols are formed as an intermediate of amino acid metabolism. Yeast cannot uptake fusel alcohols later to break them down into other compounds, so once they are formed, they are in the beer for good.

Excessive fusel alcohol production is directly related to excessive yeast growth. Being conservative with sugar additions and reducing aeration and fermentation temperatures are effective ways to keep fusel alcohol at desired levels. In addition, maintaining a healthy yeast culture helps ensure less fusel alcohol production.

Ester Formation

Esters are a major part of the yeast flavor provided to beer. Most often described as fruity, esters sometimes are also perceived as floral, perfumy, and solvently, depending on the yeast strain, the metabolic functions during growth and fermentation, and other factors. Esters are important for creating "beeriness" in the flavor profile of any beer, but excessive ester formation can result in masked hop character or an unbalanced flavor profile.

Esters are formed as a result of yeast growth. Many brewers think that increasing yeast growth will increase ester formation, but in reality a lack of yeast growth can also increase ester formation. Esters are formed from acetyl-CoA, an intermediate in the metabolic pathway of both yeast growth and ester formation. When acetyl-CoA is used for growth, less esters are formed. When there is less growth, there is more acetyl-CoA available for ester formation.

Other factors that influence ester formation include
- Higher pitch rate = lower growth = possible increase in esters
- Higher-gravity wort = higher esters
- Tall fermenters, more pressure = lower esters
- Higher temperature = lower esters if early, higher esters if late; pitch low if you have no temperature control
- Higher trub in fermentation vessel = higher growth = lower esters
- Decreased aeration = lower growth = higher esters
- All malt = higher esters

The Primary Fermentation Process

Primary fermentation is the process in which most of the sugars are consumed by the yeast and converted into alcohol and carbon dioxide. During this period, as fermentation progresses, the pH of the liquid will drop from about 5.0–5.4 to about 4.5, due to the formation of carbonic acid and other fermentation compounds. Because of this pH drop, the iso-alpha acids become less soluble, and a 20–30 percent drop in measured bitterness will be observed. The hop compounds that are lost are either (1) absorbed by the yeast cell walls or (2) solidified and deposited with the yeast slurry or on the sides of the tanks.

Temperature control is critical during primary fermentation. Excessively high temperatures can result in too much yeast growth, sulfur, and fusel alcohol production by the yeast. If temperatures are too cool, yeast performance can be stifled, and incomplete fermentations can result.

Some brewers allow their yeast to warm a few degrees after primary fermentation for a diacetyl rest. Whether to use this step or not depends primarily on the yeast strain itself, and whether the strain does an adequate job of reducing diacetyl without the warming step.

Dry hopping is typically done after primary fermentation is complete and the majority of yeast is removed from the fermenter. This allows hop flavors to be extracted without interference or absorption by the yeast. Most brewers will chill a bit after primary fermentation to encourage yeast settling and removal. Although some brewers wait until bright beer to add hops, most add during the aging process, at a warmer temperature, to maximize flavor extraction.

Aging time on dry hops is dependent on brewer preferences, but some research demonstrates that maximum hop flavor is extracted surprisingly fast, and that extended time on the hops is of little to no benefit—and perhaps even detrimental—to maximizing hop flavor in the beer.

COMMERCIAL DRY-HOPPING PROCEDURES

As craft brewing has grown and dry hopping has become more popular, many different techniques have been developed to dry hop beers.

Whole Hops

Whole hops must be added in some sort of container, otherwise it is impossible to separate the beer from the hops after the aging process. The most common technique is to use a mesh bag. One way to do this is to hang a mesh bag full of hops in an empty tank, transfer the beer into the tank, and age. The bag will have to be weighed down or tied off at the bottom of the tank so the hops remain submerged through the aging process. Care must be taken to ensure the hop bag doesn't rest against the outlet of the tank; otherwise, it may plug the outlet and it will be impossible to get the beer from the tank! After aging is complete, transfer the beer from the tank to the bright tank, then remove the bag and dispose of the hops.

Another way is to stuff a weighted mesh bag full of hops into the tank from the top. This is an impractical method for most brewers, because it requires opening the top of the tank and punching the hops back down into the beer until the bag sinks.

If using a stationary container for the hops, such as a perforated or mesh stainless steel box, place the hops in the container, place the container in an empty tank, and transfer the beer into the tank. The container full of wet hops can be pretty heavy and difficult to remove after the aging is complete.

Or try a method similar to what Sierra Nevada does with their Torpedo IPA: Pack whole hops into a mesh container situated in a housing outside the fermentation vessel. Then pump beer from the fermenting tank through the housing to extract hop flavor and then back into the fermenter.

Brewers using whole hops can also hang or secure a bag full of hops in a bright tank and transfer the finished beer on top of it. This is a fairly common method. The disadvantages are that the beer at this point is normally held at 32–33° F (0° C), so hop flavor extraction may take longer.

Pelletized Hops

Pelletized hops are generally easier to dry hop with, and several methods are used by brewers. The most common and easiest for small brewers is to dump pelletized hops in the top manway of the tank. Brewers do need to watch for gushing and foamovers when the hop pellets are added to fermenting beer. As breweries have grown and installed larger fermenting vessels, this method becomes impractical, given the sheer volume of hops that must be taken to the top of the tanks. Ladders can quickly become unsafe when using this method.

Another practice many brewers use is to pump a hop slurry into the tank. In a separate tank, they add the hops and use either an agitator or a circulation pump to mix the hops into the beer or the hot water. Then the slurry is pumped into the tank. To keep the pellet material suspended, many brewers continue to circulate the tank periodically by using either a pump and hoses or carbon dioxide gas. Oxidation control and sanitation are critical, and good sanitation practices and CO_2 purging of all vessels is required.

Another method, the hop cannon, was developed by Lagunitas Brewing and is also used by Russian River and some others. It involves adding hop pellets to a small vessel and pressurizing the vessel with CO_2. To do this, attach the outlet of the vessel to the downtube on a fermenter and open the pathway. The hops are then pressure transferred into the top of the primary beer vessel.

Finally, some brewers use a shear pump to add hops into the bottom of a vessel. The hops are ground and fed into a circulating beer stream and pumped into the tank.

Critical Steps

The most important thing when dry hopping is to mix well so hops are completely exposed to the beer. Also, hops will swell as they absorb beer, and if they are packed too tightly in the bag, the hops in the interior may not get wet at all.

Hop bags should be weighed down (a stainless-steel fitting works well) or tied off at the bottom of the aging vessel to ensure they remain completely submerged during the aging process.

If using pellets in the dry-hopping process be aware that adding too much at once can result in clumping, poor mixing, and reduced exposure of hops to the beer. To avoid rapid settling, especially in conical vessels, mix either mechanically with a pump and circulation loop from the bottom of the fermenter to the racking port, or by blowing CO_2 into the bottom of the vessel. Both techniques keep the pellet material in suspension.

After the beer has aged the proper amount of time on the hops, hop removal can be accomplished either by racking the beer off the hops or by dumping the settled hops from the bottom of a fermenter.

During the dry-hopping and finishing process (preparing the beer for packaging), avoid exposure to oxygen and unwanted microbes. This means that brewers need to carefully sanitize their process equipment and remove all air with CO_2 or hot, sterile water prior to starting the process. Pelletized hops themselves have some microbial presence; take care not to add any more through careless brewing practices.

Filtering too tightly strips hop flavors. Sterile filtration in particular results in a loss of hop flavor, so hopping adjustments should be made upstream to retain the proper amount of flavor. If injecting CO_2 to carbonate, do so gently to avoid forming large bubbles that strip hop flavor from the beer. Oxidation flavors mask hop character. Brewers comment frequently that the first flavor to go in an aged IPA is hop.

Table 9.6 IPA: Recipe Guidelines

		Historical Burton IPA	Scottish IPA	Early 1900s English IPA
Malts	Pale malt	100%	100%	85–95%
	Crystal malts	None	None	None
	Typical crystal	n/a	n/a	n/a
	Adjuncts	None	None	Maize, sugar 5–15%
	Roasted malts	None	None	None
Mashing	Mash conversion temperature	148–150° F (64–66° C)	150–154° F (66–68° C)	152–154° F (66.7–67.8° C)
	Mash conversion time	120 min.	120–180 min.	90 min.
	OG °P (SG)	15.0–18.75 °P (1.060–1.075)	14.0–17.5 °P (1.056–1.070)	12.5–15 °P (1.050–1.060)
	Fermentability	High!	High!	High!
	Target TG (SG)	0.75–5 °P (1.003–1.020)	0.75–3.0 °P (1.003–1.012)	2.5–4.0 °P (1.010–1.016)
	ABV target	5–7%	5–7%	4–6.5%
Hopping (typical rates)	Pounds per barrel	5.0–6.0	1.25–3.0	1.0–2.0
	Ounces per gallon	2.6–3.2	0.65–1.6	0.5–1.1
	Recommended hop varieties	East Kent Goldings	East Kent Goldings	East Kent Goldings, Fuggle
	Dry hop amount (lb./bbl.)	1	1	.25–.5
	Multiple dry hops	Occasionally in casks	Not typical	Not typical
	IBUs in finished beer	~70	~70	~50
Comments		Long, low-intensity wort boil, 2–3 hours	Ferment cool!	Most gravities dropped to 10-12 °P after WWI, below 10 °P after WWII
		Age 12 months or more		

	Contemporary English IPA	American IPA	Double IPA	Black IPA
	85–100%	85–97%	95–100%	88–95%
	15–40 °L	10–60 °L	10–20 °L	10–20 °L
	0–10%	3–15%	0–5%	5–10%
	Maize, sugar 0–15%	None	dextrose, candi sugar 0–10%	None typically
	Munich 0–10%	Munich 0–10%	None	Dehusked black malt, black malt extract 3–7%
	150–155° F (66–68.3° C)	148–153° F (64–67.2° C)	148–150° F (64–66° C)	148–153° F (64–67.2° C)
	15–30 min.	15–60 min.	60–120 min.	15–120 min.
	12.5–18.75 (1.050–1.075)	12.5–18.75 (1.050–1.075)	18.75–22.5 (1.075–1.090)	14.0–18.0 (1.056–1.072)
	70–80%	75–82%	80–86%	75–82%
	3.0–4.5 °P (1.012–1.018)	2.5–4.0 °P (1.010–1.016)	2.0–3.75 °P (1.008–1.015)	3.0–4.5 °P (1.012–1.018)
	5–7%	6.3–7.5%	7.5–10.5%	6–7.5%
	.75–2.5	.75–2	3.5–8	1.5–4
	.4–1.3	.4–1.1	1.8–4.2	0.8–2.1
	EKG, Fuggle, Target, Sovereign, Styrian Goldings	The 4 C's, Citra, Simcoe, Amarillo, Sterling	The 4 C's, Citra, Simcoe, Amarillo, Sterling, Nelson Sauvin	The 4 C's, Citra, Simcoe, Amarillo
	1	.4–1	.75–3	1–2
	Not typical	Not typical	Common	TBD
	40–60	50–80	70–100+	50–90
	Based on GABF guidelines; real examples are all over the map	More recent versions moving to less crystal malt		

BREWING TIPS BY STYLE

Over the past 20 years, IPA has diverged into several subcategories, each requiring different quantities and types of ingredients, and different brewing techniques. The following are guidelines for each IPA style.

English IPA

- Use good-quality, floor-malted British pale ale malt for the base malt.
- Use British crystal malts at a very low percentage.
- Use higher mash temperatures to provide increased malt flavors.
- Consider using some Munich malt in the grist to provide complexity.
- Note that British hops provide a more authentic flavor and aroma. There are several new varieties that provide a very intense, yet still very British, flavor.

American IPA

- Use a maximum of 10 percent crystal malts, none above 60 °L (120° EBC).
- Use a low-to-medium range of mash conversion rest temperatures, 149–153° F (65–67° C), to obtain some residual body and sweetness. Keep terminal gravity at 4 °P (1.016 SG) or below.
- Consider using a very small percentage of dark malt to enhance red color as an alternative to adding highly colored crystal malts.
- Use Munich malts for additional malt complexity.
- Drink fresh!

Double IPA*

- Minimize crystal/dextrin malts to 5 percent maximum to allow showcasing of hops.
- Consider using adjuncts (dextrose, light candi sugar) to drive the alcohol without increasing the sweetness.
- Use some English pale ale malt to get more malt character, if desired.
- Have a maximum 1.095 OG (23.75 °P) or the beer will be too malty, sweet, or alcoholic.
- Add hops to every part of the brewing process!
- Use hop extract in the kettle to maximize bitterness.
- Drink young!

* Thanks to Tom Nickel and Vinnie Cilurzo

Black IPA
- Limit crystal malts and dark malts. Dark malts conflict with hop flavor.
- Keep in mind that dehusked black malt contributes more color without adding too much astringency or burnt character, which in turn provides maximum hop flavor. Target 4–5 percent of total grain bill.
- Use double IPA hopping techniques, regardless of gravity and alcohol content.
- Consider using adjuncts to maximize dryness and accentuate hop flavors.

GREAT AMERICAN BEER FESTIVAL IPA STYLE GUIDELINES

English-Style India Pale Ale

Most traditional interpretations of English-style India pale ales are characterized by medium-high hop bitterness with a medium to medium-high alcohol content. Hops from a variety of origins may be used to contribute to a high hopping rate. Earthy and herbal English-variety hop character is the perceived end, but may be a result of the skillful use of hops of other national origins. The use of water with high mineral content results in a crisp, dry beer, sometimes with subtle and balanced character of sulfur compounds. This pale gold to deep copper-colored ale has a medium to high, flowery hop aroma and may have a medium to strong hop flavor (in addition to the hop bitterness). English-style India pale ales possess medium maltiness and body. Fruity-ester flavors and aromas are moderate to very strong. Diacetyl can be absent or may be perceived at very low levels. Chill haze is allowable at cold temperatures. Hops of other origins may be used for bitterness or approximating traditional English character.

Original Gravity (°P): 1.050–1.064 (12.5–15.7 °P) • Apparent Extract/Final Gravity (°P): 1.012–1.018 (3–4.5 °P) • Alcohol by Weight (Volume): 4–5.6% (5–7%) • Bitterness (IBU): 35–63 • Color SRM (EBC): 6–14 (12–28 EBC)

American-Style India Pale Ale

American-style India pale ales are perceived to have medium-high to intense hop bitterness, flavor, and aroma with medium-high alcohol content. The style is further characterized by fruity, floral, and citruslike American-variety hop character. Note that fruity, floral, and citruslike American-variety hop character is the perceived end, but may be a result of the skillful use of hops of other national origins. The use of water with high mineral content results in a crisp, dry beer. This pale gold to deep copper-colored ale has a full, flowery hop aroma and may have a strong hop flavor (in addition to the perception of hop bitterness). India pale ales possess medium maltiness, which contributes to a medium body. Fruity-ester flavors and aromas are moderate to very strong. Diacetyl can be absent or may be perceived at very low levels. Chill and/or hop haze is allowable at cold temperatures.

Original Gravity (°P): 1.060–1.075 (14.7–18.2 °P) • Apparent Extract/Final Gravity (°P): 1.012–1.018 (3–4.5 °P) • Alcohol by Weight (Volume): 5–6% (6.3–7.5%) • Bitterness (IBU): 50–70 • Color SRM (EBC): 6–14 (12–28 EBC)

Imperial India Pale Ale

Imperial or double India pale ales have intense hop bitterness, flavor, and aroma. Alcohol content is medium-high to high and notably evident. They range from deep golden to medium copper in color. The style may use any variety of hops. Though the hop character is intense, it's balanced with complex alcohol flavors, moderate to high fruity esters, and medium to high malt character. Hop character should be fresh and lively and should not be harsh in quality. The use of large amounts of hops may cause a degree of appropriate hop haze. Imperial or double India pale ales have medium-high to full body. Diacetyl should not be perceived. The intention of this style of beer is to exhibit the fresh and bright character of hops. Oxidative character and aged character should not be present.

Original Gravity (°P): 1.075–1.100 (18.2–23.7 °P) • Apparent Extract/Final Gravity (°P): 1.012–1.020 (3–5 °P) • Alcohol by Weight (Volume): 6.0–8.4% (7.5–10.5%) • Bitterness (IBU): 65–100 • Color SRM (EBC): 5–13 (10–26 EBC)

American-Style Black Ale

American-style black ale is perceived to have medium high to high hop bitterness, flavor, and aroma with medium-high alcohol content, balanced with a medium body. Fruity, floral, and herbal character from hops of all origins may contribute character. The style is further characterized by a moderate degree of caramel malt character and dark roasted malt flavor and aroma. High astringency and high degree of burnt roast malt character should be absent.

Original Gravity (°P): 1.056–1.075 (14–18.2 °P) • Apparent Extract/Final Gravity (°P): 1.012–1.018 (3–4.5 °P) • Alcohol by Weight (Volume): 5–6% (6–7.5%) • Bitterness (IBU): 50–70 • Color SRM (EBC): 35+ (70+ EBC)

10 | IPA RECIPES

Here's to the man who drinks strong ale,
and goes to bed quite mellow.
Lives as he ought to live,
and dies a jolly good fellow.
—*Old English folk song*

This chapter contains recipes from IPAs brewed throughout history. In all cases, I have tried to provide as much information as possible to help replicate these brews. That said, the old recipes are incomplete by today's standards. In addition, brewing measurements from the 1700s and the 1800s are quite different from those used today, so I have included conversion factors here and in appendix C. These will come in handy if you ever have the opportunity to peruse historical brewing texts and ledgers.

For the recipes, I opted not to give specific weights for brewing five- or 10-gallon batches. Instead, I provide percentages and weights on a per-gallon basis, so you can construct the recipe based on your own brewhouse size and efficiencies. I am confident that both homebrewers and craft brewers will have success re-creating these beers.

RECIPE SPECIFICS

Liquor Targets
These recipes come from a variety of sources, and not everyone supplied liquor targets. But I provide analytical levels (in ppm) or treatment guidelines whenever possible.

Malt Bills

These are expressed in percentages for each malt type. The original gravity of the wort is also given. From there, a calculation can be made to develop a malt bill for the specific brewing system and size. The name of the malt supplier, if available, is also listed.

Mashing and Lautering

Water-to-grain ratios are provided in pounds water/pounds grain (which also equals liters water/kilograms grain). Quarts water/pound grain measurements are provided. All water temperatures and rest temperatures are provided in degrees Fahrenheit (degrees Celsius).

Kettle Boil and Hopping

Where possible, kettle boil time is provided in minutes. Any other known additions (gypsum or Irish moss, for example) are included. Kettle and whirlpool (or hopback) hop additions are listed by hop variety, alpha acids (if available), and form of hop (e.g., whole hop, Type 90 [T90] pellet, etc.). Percentages are based on the total weight. Remember, however, that this number is a starting point—thus, you will have to calculate the utilization for your equipment. Target IBUs are included so you can more accurately calculate the amount of hops for your brewing system based on that known utilization.

Fermentation and Aging

Fermentation temperature is provided in degrees Fahrenheit (degrees Celsius). Yeast strain is included if available, as well as pitch rate in million cells/milliliter. Times are included as available. In some recipes, weight of yeast is provided, and it is uncertain whether this is pressed yeast or yeast slurry, as both are used by brewers. Dry-hopping varieties and amounts will be provided in ounces/gallon (pound/barrel, grams/liter).

Analytical Targets

Beer analytical targets are provided, and they are crucial for developing these recipes. One of the analytical targets included is the apparent degree of fermentation (ADF). In essence, this is a measure of the sweetness or dryness of the beer. Defined as (OG-TG)/OG, and expressed as a percentage, ADF values in the 80s indicate a dry beer, with very little residual sugars, while values in the 70s indicate a sweeter, maltier beer.

OG: Provided in °P (SG)

TG: Provided in °P (SG)

ADF: Provided as percentage of TG compared to OG

IBU: International bittering units

ABV: Alcohol by volume

HISTORICAL RECIPES

AMSINCK'S INDIA PALE ALE

George Amsinck, a London-based brewing scientist in the mid-1800s, traveled around England and made detailed notes on how brewers brewed their beers. In 1868 he published his studies in the book *Practical Brewings*—a great reference for all brewing historians. A special thanks goes to Ray Daniels, who sent me these recipes from Amsinck's book.

Brewing liquor:
Use hard Burton water. Boil in the kettle for 15 minutes, then allow to cool to strike temperature (for removing carbonates).

Malt bill:
Pale malt 100%

Mashing and lautering:
Double-mash system. No sparging. *First mash:* Use a water-to-grain ratio of 2.7/1 (1.3 qt./lb.) and a strike temperature of 165–168° F (74–76° C). Hold for 2 hours. Tap (wort) temperature should be 148–150° F (64–66° C) at the end of conversion. *Second mash:* Use a water-to-grain ratio of 2.7/1 (1.3 qt./lb.) and a strike temperature of 180° F (82° C). Hold for 60 minutes. Tap temperature should be 165° F (74° C).

Kettle boil and hopping:
Use East Kent or Mid-Kent Goldings (100%). Twenty-four pounds hops per quarter malt equals approximately 4.5 oz./gal. (9lb./bbl., 33.7 g/L) split evenly between the two boils. *First wort:* Boil in the kettle for 2 hours with half the hops. After straining, leave these hops in the hopback. *Second wort:* Boil for 2 hours with the other half of hops. Run over the first half of hops in the hopback.

Fermentation and aging:
Combine worts. Pitch with 2.5 ounces fresh yeast per gallon and stir/rouse as the wort fills the fermenter. Pitch at 59–60° F (15° C) and allow to free rise to 72° F (22° C) over two to three days. Rack at about 7 °P (1.028 SG). At one week, put the beer into casks. There is no mention of dry hops in this recipe.

Analytical targets:
OG: 16.5 °P (1.067 SG)
TG: 4.9 °P (1.019 SG)
ADF: 70.3%
IBU: ~70
ABV: 6.1

AMSINCK'S NO. 25 BURTON EAST INDIA PALE ALE

Brewing liquor:
Use Burton well water (hard). Boil liquor 15 minutes, then allow to cool overnight to strike temperature (for removing carbonates).

Malt bill:
New Burton white malt 100%

Mashing and lautering:
Employ a double mash system to mash the grain. Do not sparge. *First mash:* Use a strike temperature of 165° F (74° C). Hold for 2 hours. Tap (wort) temperature should be 150° F (66° C) at the end of conversion. *Second mash:* Use a strike temperature of 180° F (82° C). Hold for 1 hour. Tap temperature should be 165° F (74° C).

Kettle boil and hopping:
Use East Kent and Mid-Kent Goldings (100%). Approximately 5 pounds per barrel equals 2.5 oz./gal. (18.7 g/L), split evenly between the two boils. *First wort:* Boil 2 hours with half the hops. After straining, leave these hops in the hopback. *Second wort:* Boil 2 hours with the other half of hops. Run over the first half of hops in the hopback.

Fermentation and aging:
Combine the worts. Pitch with fresh yeast at 58° F (14° C) and allow to free rise to 72° F (22° C) over four days. Rack at about 7 °P (1.028 SG). Transfer beer to the cask in one week. Dry hop in the cask with 100% East Kent Goldings at a rate of 0.77 oz./gal. (1.5 lb./bbl., 5.8 g/L).

Analytical targets:
OG: 16.8 °P (1.067 SG)
TG: n/a
ADF: n/a
IBU: 159 (calculated)
ABV: 8.7% (this is an estimate; it's not really possible with starting gravity)*
*Amsinck listed an 8.7% abv in his book; however, the most alcohol you can get from a 16.8 °P (1.067 SG) wort will probably be about 7.0–7.5% abv.

JAMES McCRORIE'S ORIGINAL IPA

James McCrorie provided this recipe based on the Burton IPAs of the 1800s. James is a very knowledgeable English beer historian as well as a great brewer. He has been involved with the Durden Park Beer Circle and now is part of the London-based Craft Brewing Association, a home-brewing group. I had the chance to taste his version of this beer after three years of aging, and it was marvelous—still very hop forward and very little sign of oxidation. It is massively hopped at 3.67 oz./gal. (7 lb./bbl.) in the boil.

Brewing liquor:
Add brewing salts and gypsum to water.

Malt bill:
Warminster extra pale malt 100%

Mashing and lautering:
Use a water-to-grain ratio of 2.31/1 (1.11 qt./gal.). After reaching a strike temperature of 165° F (74° C), rest for 60 minutes at 152° F (67° C).

Kettle boil and hopping:
Boil in the kettle for 90 minutes and add Irish moss at 75 minutes. Use East Kent Goldings hops (100%) with a total addition rate of 3.67 oz./gal. (7 lb./bbl., 27.5 g/L). Add 55% of hops at the start of the boil and another 22.5% at 60 minutes. Use the remaining 22.5% at the end of the boil/whirlpool.

Fermentation and aging:
Oxygenate the wort prior to pitching. Pitch Fuller's 294 yeast at 66° F (18° C) and ferment at 68° F (20° C). Rack at 4.8 °P (1.019 SG) and chill to 61° F (16° C). Use East Kent Goldings for dry hopping.

Analytical targets:
OG: 17.3 °P (1.068 SG)
TG: 2 °P (1.008 SG)
ADF: 88%
IBU: Lots
ABV: 8%

WORTHINGTON'S WHITE SHIELD

Worthington's White Shield is famous for its "Heart and Dagger" trade-marked logo, which dates back to the 1860s. It is brewed in Britain's oldest microbrewery, W. H. Worthington, on the grounds of the brewing museum in Burton-on-Trent. Worthington was one of the most notable IPA brewers in Burton-on-Trent in the 1800s. (White Shield dates back to 1830, and W. H. Worthington started in the 1700s.) The brewery merged with Bass in 1927 but continued to operate independently. After the original Worthington brewery closed in the 1960s, Bass started brewing White Shield. But like many other traditional English ales, its popularity saw a serious decline in the 1980s and the 1990s. Bass gave the beer one last gasp in the early 1990s and allowed White Shield to be contract brewed at King and Barnes, in Horsham, Sussex, to the south of London. In 2000, operations moved back to the brewing museum in Burton-on-Trent, and

the beer launched again in 2002. Former head brewer Steve Wellington, who brewed White Shield from the 1960s until his retirement in late 2011, has won multiple awards for the beer and for himself since the re-launch. Beer writer Michael Jackson acknowledged Worthington's White Shield as being the last true survivor of the historical Burton-on-Trent IPA.

Until his recent retirement, Steve Wellington had been brewing Worthington's White Shield since the mid-1960s. Photo by John Trotter.

Brewing liquor:
Use Burton-on-Trent water with 0.068 oz./gal. (0.13 lb./bbl., 0.5 g/L) gypsum added.

Malt bill:
Pale ale malt 97%
Crystal malt 3%
Sugar (added to the whirlpool)

Mashing and lautering:
Use a water-to-grain ratio of 2.66/1 (1.28 qt./lb.) and an upward infusion mash profile. Mash at 154° F (68° C) and hold for 90 minutes, then raise the temperature to 162° F (72° C). Sparge with 165° F (74° C) water and do not let the final gravity drop below 1 °P (1.004 SG).

Kettle boil and hopping:
Boil in the kettle for 90 minutes and target 10% evaporation. Add No. 1 Invert Block Sugar to the whirlpool at a ratio of 1.13 oz./gal. (7.5 lb./bbl., 0.85 g/L). Add 45.5% Fuggle (4% alpha acids) and 20% Challenger (7.4% alpha acids) at the start of the boil. Five minutes before cast (knockout) add 34.5% Northdown hops.

Fermentation and aging:
Cool wort to 61° F (16° C) and pitch with Burton Union yeast at a rate of 0.5 oz./gal. (1 lb./bbl., 3.9 g/L). Allow fermentation temperature to free rise from 61° F (16° C) to 68° F (20° C) over five days. After primary fermentation is complete, cool beer to 43° F (6° C) and hold for a minimum of three days. Rack into casks at 43° F (6° C) and add priming sugar at 2 oz./gal. (4 pints [lb.]/bbl., 15.4 g/L), isinglass finings at 2 oz./gal. (4 pints [lb.]/bbl., 15.4 g/L), and auxiliary finings at 1 oz./gal. (2 pints [lb.]/bbl., 7.7 g/L). Hold casks at 61° F (16° C) for four days.

Analytical targets:
OG: 13.13 °P (1.053 SG)
TG: 2.25 °P (1.009 SG)
ADF: 82.9%
IBU: 40
ABV: 5.6%
Color: 13.2 °L (26° EBC)

REID 1839 IPA

Kristen England, homebrewer extraordinaire and grand master Beer Judge Certification Program (BJCP) judge, works with beer blogger Ron Pattinson to brew historical ales. Pattinson graciously provided the following two recipes. The first is Reid's 1839 IPA. Reid was a London-based brewery, best known in the 1800s for its stout. Reid merged with Watney in the late 1800s.

"This is a moderate-strength ale with a heavy dose of hops," says England. Each recipe varies a bit, but this one epitomizes the theme. A single malt. A single hop. This beer is decidedly different from the ones to come later in the century. The hop flavor is truly through the roof. At nearly 5 pounds per barrel at a moderate gravity, saying this is "hoppy" is an understatement.

In his tasting notes for this beer, England wrote, "Herby, hay-ey, grassy; ladyfingers crawl through the hop mist. Thoroughly, rippingly hoppy. Hops. More hops. Hop resins. Very long, dry, and crisp finish leaves a touch of malt sweetness shellacked and varnished with hops. Delicious hop burps. Hmmmm . . . hoppy."

Malt bill:
English pale malt 100%

Mashing and lautering:
Brew using an infusion mash for 60 minutes at 158° F (70° C) and a water-to-grain ratio of 3.46/1 (1.66 qt./lb.).

Kettle boil and hopping:
Boil in the kettle for 75 minutes. Add 100% Fuggle (5.5% alpha acids) in three stages with a total addition rate of 1.54 oz./gal. (3 lb./bbl., 11.5 g/L). At the start of the boil add 33.6%. Make subsequent additions of 33.6% at 30 minutes and 32.8% at 15 minutes.

Fermentation and aging:
Ferment at 67° F (19.4° C) with Nottingham Dry Ale Yeast (WLP013 London Ale or WY1028 London Ale), and dry hop with Fuggle at 0.25 oz./gal. (0.48 lb./bbl., 1.87 g/L).

Analytical targets:
OG: 14.25 °P (1.057 SG)
TG: 3.75 °P (1.015 SG)
ADF: 73.7%
IBU: 120.7 (calculated)
ABV: 5.8%
Color: 2 °L (4.0° EBC)

FULLER'S 1897 IPA

Fuller's 1897 IPA was brewed in the period when original gravities were starting their rapid decline in England. This is still a nice representation of London IPA brewed in the late 1800s. Other than the addition of cane sugar, it follows all the traditions of the standard 1800s IPA.

England and Pattinson described the beer as "a lovely IPA. This pre-1900 IPA looks very much like an IPA you could find in any pub. The hopping is pretty much right on board with something like Meantime IPA. A good malt backbone with a heavy dose of those lovely lower alpha acid traditional U.K. hops. Keep calm and carry on indeed, sir!"

Their tasting notes describe orangina, marmalade, citrus, and spice. "Wafts of bready malt and biscuits. Ripe pomme fruit with sugar pear drops. Tannicly drying, hop resins, and citrus pith. Finish leaves you with a mouthful of bitterness with gentle touches of pure malt goodness."

Malt bill:
English pale malt 84.6%
Cane sugar 15.4%

Mashing and lautering:
Using a water-to-grain ratio of 2.61/1 (1.25 qt./lb.), brew an infusion mash for 90 minutes at 154° F (67.8° C).

Kettle boil and hopping:
Boil in the kettle for 105 minutes. Use 100% East Kent Goldings hops at 4.5% alpha acids and add them at a total rate of 0.91 oz./gal. (1.76 lb./bbl., 6.8 g/L). At 90 minutes, add 67% of the hops followed by another addition of 33% 30 minutes later.

Fermentation and aging:
Ferment at 67° F (19.4° C) with Nottingham Dry Ale Yeast (WY1968 London ESB Ale Yeast or WLP002 English Ale Yeast). Dry hop with more East Kent Goldings, 4.5% alpha acids, at a rate of 0.18 oz./gal. (0.35 lb./bbl., 1.35 g/L).

Analytical targets
OG: 14 °P (1.056 SG)
TG: 4 °P (1.016 SG)
ADF: 71.43%
IBU: 73.9 (calculated)
ABV: 5.33%
Color: 2 °L (3.9° EBC)

BARCLAY PERKINS 1928 IPA

Ron Pattinson writes the amazing blog *Shut Up about Barclay Perkins*, in which he focuses on researching historical brewing records, advertisements, and textbooks to uncover the true stories of how breweries really made their beer. His is a must-read blog for anyone interested in brewing history, historical brewing techniques, and traditional beer styles.

Pattinson uncovered this recipe for a 20th-century English IPA from Barclay Perkins. Post–World War I, the gravity had increased a bit, and the beer was amply hopped to 41 IBU. Note the use of American six-row malt and the flaked maize in the recipe.

In his blog, Pattinson had the following to say about this beer ("Let's Brew Wednesday: 1928 Barclay Perkins IPA," *Shut Up about Barclay Perkins* [blog; November 18, 2010]):

> *Great little traditional IPA recipe. OG and BU are about equal. Lots of fresh hops of three different varieties. You'll notice the No. 3 Invert, which is highly unusual for an IPA. A note in the log responds to this, "No. 2 saccharin not delivered in time. No. 3 used instead." They added a bit of caramel for a fine-tuning of the color but it's not worth it here. This beer tastes very much like Fuller's London Pride. A little more bitter but very similar.*

Pattinson's tasting notes described it as being a "deep golden colour with a pillowy head. Herbal, spice, and citrus notes. Ladyfingers and biscuits. Crisp, clean, minerally, dry hoppy finish. Bloody spot on pint."

Brewing liquor:
Use London water profile. Salt treatments are unknown.

Malt bill:
British pale ale malt 57.4%
American six-row malt 17.6%
Flaked maize 13.2%
Invert No. 3 sugar* 11.8%
*The Invert No. 3 sugar is added to the boil.

Mashing and lautering:
Employ a traditional infusion mash with a 90-minute rest at 152° F (67° C). The water-to-grain ratio uses 3.5/1 (1.68 qt./lb.).

Kettle boil and hopping:
The total boil time in the kettle will be 135 minutes. Use a single addition of 16.3% of Cluster hops (7% alpha acids) at 120 minutes. The following additions are both Fuggle (5.5% alpha acids). Add 54.7% at 60 minutes, followed by 29% at 30 minutes.

Fermentation and aging:
Pitch with Nottingham Dry Ale Yeast (WY1968 London ESB Ale Yeast or WLP002 English Ale Yeast). Ferment at 63° F (17° C) and dry hop with East Kent Goldings at 0.042 oz./gal. (0.08 lb./bbl., 0.31 g/L).

Analytical targets:
OG: 11.5 °P (1.046 SG)
TG: 2.5 °P (1.010 SG)
ADF: 78.27%
IBU: 41.2
ABV: 4.8%
Color: 10 °L (19.7° EBC)

BALLANTINE IPA NO. 1

Here is a Ballantine Ale recipe brewed to the original specifications. This recipe comes from Bill Pierce's "Make Mine Ballantine" article in the May-June 2010 issue of *Brew Your Own* (Vol. 16, no. 3). It is used with the permission of the publisher. Note that the original version would have been dry hopped with Bullion hop oils and aged for one year.

Malt bill:
Pale malt 71.3%
Flaked maize 14.7%
Light Munich malt 10.9%
Crystal malt 60 °L 3.1%

Mashing and lautering:
Use an infusion mash at 150° F (66° C) for 60 minutes.

Kettle boil and hopping:
Boil in the kettle for 90 minutes. Add 48.8% Cluster hops (7% alpha acids) at the 60-minute mark. Add 25.6% Brewer's Gold (8% alpha acids) at 25 minutes and 25.6% East Kent Goldings (5.5% alpha acids) in the final three minutes.

Fermentation and aging:
Pitch with WY1056 or WLP001 yeast and ferment at 68° F (20° C). Dry hop with 0.2 oz./gal. (0.4 lb./bbl., 1.50 g/L) East Kent Goldings. (This was originally dry hopped with a distilled extract of Bullion hops.)

Analytical targets:
OG: 18.5 °P (1.074 SG)
TG: 4 °P (1.016 SG)
ADF: 78.37%
IBU: 62
ABV: ~6.5%
Color: 7.1 °L (14° SRM)

BALLANTINE IPA NO. 2

As detailed in chapter 6, the recipe for Ballantine IPA changed drastically as the company was bought and sold, and as production was moved from Newark to Rhode Island and later to Indiana. This recipe comes courtesy of legendary brewmaster Fred Scheer. He states that the recipe changed at least 100 times over the years. This is a later version of Ballantine IPA, brewed at Schreier Malt's seven-barrel pilot brewery.

Brewing liquor:
Use municipal water with 0.2 oz./gal. (0.04 lb./bbl., 0.15 g/L) gypsum added.

Malt bill:
Pale ale malt 91.95%
Caramel malt 80 °L 8.05%

Mashing and lautering:
Use a water-to-grain ratio of 2.8/1 (1.35 qt./lb.) and sparge with 186° F (86° C) water. Add 0.008 oz./gal. (0.003 lb./bbl., 0.061g/L) gypsum 10 minutes prior to whirlpool.

Kettle boil and hopping:
Boil in the kettle for 75 minutes. The three hop additions are Styrian Goldings (4.9% alpha acids). Total hops are estimated at 0.83 oz./gal. (1.6 lb./bbl., 0.006 g/L). Add 36% at 60 minutes, followed by a 46% addition after another 30 minutes. Then 18% at the end of the boil.

Fermentation and aging:
Pitch with yeast, either WLP001 or WY1056, at 68–70° F (20–21° C). Primary should take approximately four days and cool to 50° F (10° C). Hold for two days before transferring to a cask and dry hopping. Bullion would be the traditional variety.

Analytical targets:
OG: 16 °P (1.064 SG)
TG: 3–3.5 °P (1.012–1.014 SG)
ADF: 78–81%

J. W. LEES HARVEST ALE

Although they aren't strictly IPAs, this recipe and the following one, Manchester Star, from J. W. Lees, are included because of their historical significance. The J. W. Lees brewery was founded in 1828 in Manchester, England, about 100 miles northwest of Burton-on-Trent. Most of its beers are traditional ales and are sold within a 100-mile radius of Manchester, but the brewery is world famous for some of its stronger ales.

J. W. Lees Harvest Ale—made when the brewers challenged themselves to brew a beer as strong as a wine—is a wonderful, vintage-dated strong ale. Even though it has been brewed only since 1986 and is considered by most to be a barley wine, it is today's best representation of the traditional October ale, a style that shares many common ingredients and brewing procedures with the historical English IPAs. For example, it is made with 100% low-color Maris Otter malt and 100% East Kent Goldings hops, and it is brewed only once per year in October, just after the ingredients have been harvested. All the deep amber color is developed during a 3.5-hour boil, and the fermentation is roused and repitched after a few days to ensure completeness.

Brewing liquor:
Use Manchester water (soft) with calcium chloride added at the rate of 0.29 oz./gal. (2 mL/L).

Malt bill:
New season (fresh), low-color Maris Otter malt 100%

Mashing and lautering:
Mash in and hold at 150° F (66° C) for 1 hour. After conversion, sparge with 170° F (77° C) water.

Kettle boil and hopping:
Boil in the kettle for 3.5 hours. Yes, that is right—3.5 hours. This is where the color is developed. Add kettle finings (0.6 kg) prior to the whirlpool process. Whirlpool for 25 minutes, then rest for 15 minutes before cooling the wort. Add 100% of the new season's East Kent Goldings at the start of the boil, 1.9 oz./gal. (3.7 lb./bbl., 14.3 g/L). Note that these are not "wet" or "fresh" hops, but they are from the new season harvest.

Fermentation and aging:
The yeast should be a highly attenuating, alcohol-tolerant English Ale yeast strain. Rouse fermentation and repitch after three days. Lager at 30° F (-1° C) for two to three weeks.

Analytical targets:
OG: 28 °P (1.120 SG)
TG: 6 °P (1.024 SG)
ADF: 79%
IBU: 148 (calculated wort IBU)
ABV: 11.5%
Color: 9.9 °L (19.5° EBC)

J. W. LEES MANCHESTER STAR

Manchester Star is a great example of a historical East India porter—or in other words, a hoppy black beer. It is included here to illustrate the techniques used in brewing hoppy dark ales for India, as well as to point out that, like many beer styles that are becoming popular today, there were similar beers brewed before. Manchester Star was first brewed by J. W. Lees in 1875, and the company stopped brewing it in the 1920s. Now it is re-released every year as a seasonal beer.

Brewing liquor:
Use Manchester water (soft) with calcium chloride added at 0.15 oz./gal. (1 mL/L).

Malt bill:
Pale ale malt 94.3%
Thomas Fawcett chocolate malt 5.7%

Mashing and lautering:
Mash in and hold at 149° F (65° C) for 1 hour.

Kettle boil and hopping:
Boil in the kettle for 90 minutes. At the start of the boil add 40% East Kent Goldings T90 pellets, 0.23 oz./gal. (0.44 lb./bbl., 1.71 g/L). Add a late hop addition of 60% East Kent Goldings T90 pellets, 0.34 oz./gal. (0.66 lb./bbl., 2.56 g/L). Add 0.005 oz./gal. (.009 lb./bbl., .035 g/L) finings prior to whirlpool, then whirlpool for 15 minutes and rest for 25 minutes.

Fermentation and aging:
Pitch with a highly attenuating, alcohol-tolerant English Ale yeast strain and ferment until you achieve terminal gravity.

Analytical targets:
OG: 17.5 °P (1.070 SG)
TG: 2.8 °P (1.011 SG)
ADF: 84%

IBU: n/a
ABV: 8.5%
Color: n/a

EARLY CRAFT-BREWING RECIPES

THE STORY OF BOMBAY BOMBER IPA

By Teri Fahrendorf (Its Mother)

I moved to Eugene, Oregon, to become the brewmaster for Steelhead Brewing Company. On January 22, 1991, Steelhead opened with an IPA on draft as the seasonal beer and never took it off tap. I believe Bombay Bomber was the first IPA served continuously as a standard flagship beer at any brewpub in the United States. It quickly developed a cult following. Locals still ask for a pint of "Bomber." The bitterness level was 57 IBU. My calculations showed it to be at 45, but when I had the IBU tested, it was 57. That was quite high in 1991!

When Steelhead opened, I had only a homebrew hydrometer—not a professional, temperature-corrected hydrometer—so I went heavy on the malt. You get only one chance to make a good first impression, and I didn't want to open with any wimpy beers. Perhaps part of Steelhead's initial draw was that when we opened, Bombay Bomber clocked in at 8.1% abv, although my cheap hydrometer had told me it was 7% abv. After I got a proper hydrometer, I measured it again, and that is how I learned I'd been "bombing" the customers with "Bomber." I quickly lowered the alcohol level to a more reasonable 6% abv.

You thirsty types may be wondering what Bombay Bomber tastes like. I used to say, "It's like a party in your mouth." The flavors were unusual and shocking in 1991. But it was just like a lot of American IPAs you can buy today: juicy, grapefruit, pineapple aroma with a strong malt backbone that stands up to the bitterness. The menu description said, "Deep gold. Citrus-floral hop aroma with lots of malt flavors, leading to an intense hop finish."

In 1994 I called Mark Dorber, my friend and fellow GABF beer judge who was then the cellar master at the famed White Horse on Parson's Green Pub in London, to tell him I wanted to visit him. He told me an IPA conference was scheduled at the old Whitbread Brewery, and I should attend. I did, and I smuggled five gallons of Bombay Bomber through British customs. I filled two 3-gallon Cornelius kegs, packed them in bubble wrap, and put them in a fat, square rolling suitcase, in which they fit perfectly. I had to bleed out a little of the beer to keep the weight under the 70-pound maximum. I rolled right through the "nothing to declare" section of British customs. Luckily they're not big on beer-sniffing dogs at Heathrow Airport.

At the conference, I was seated next to Paul Bayley, brewmaster at Marston's in Burton-on-Trent. Two other American brewers had brought their IPAs as well. At some point we tasted three 1860s replication beers made by the Durden Park

Beer Club. Next we tasted three modern British IPAs that were nearly water in comparison. Then we taste the three American IPAs. I was very pleased that my beer showed so well. As the "mother," you just don't know how your kids are going to behave when they are away from home.

Bombay Bomber was just the way I'd made it: deep gold, bright and clear, extremely aromatic, full on the palette, and crisply bitter on the finish. The other two American IPAs were nearly amber in color and cloudy, as they were unfiltered and the yeast had kicked up. The Brits were not impressed by the cloudy American beers.

Dr. Keith Thomas from the University of Sunderland gave us a very easy scoring mechanism: Would you (1) walk across the room for this beer, (2) walk across the street for this beer, (3) walk four blocks for this beer, or (4) walk eight blocks for this beer? I peeked at Bayley's paper to see how he scored my beer. He gave it a 4. Paul Bayley would walk eight blocks for my beer! Who needs to win on *American Idol* when the brewmaster at Marston's just gave your beer the top score? In fact, Bombay Bomber won the most walkers of all the beers tasted that day.

Then each brewer was asked to stand up and speak. I had also smuggled through customs at Heathrow Airport twenty-four 35mm film containers, in which I had packed one of each of the brewing ingredients I used at Steelhead. (Luckily no hop- or malt-sniffing dogs were at the airport, either.) I had 10 different hops in pellets, and 14 different malts in those film canisters. The caps were taped securely with duct tape. Guess which hop the brewers, including the "big boys," couldn't get enough of? Chinook, Bombay Bomber's main aroma hop. They also couldn't get over the high alpha of a hop with that much aroma.

Are you thirsty yet? Here's the recipe as it was several years ago. Hops change over time. I started with Mt. Hood hops until they lost their grapefruit character, then I switched to Crystal. Use the juiciest citrus-character hops you can find. For this recipe, avoid the resinous or sulfury hops.

BOMBAY BOMBER IPA

Teri Fahrendorf is a 23-year veteran of the American craft-brewing renaissance. She is married to a fellow brewmaster and lives in "Beervana" (aka Portland, Oregon). She is paid to visit brewers and breweries by peddling malt and hops to them. Fahrendorf founded the Pink Boots Society, a nonprofit, education-oriented association of women beer professionals (www.pinkbootssociety.org). You can read her previously published beer and brewing articles at www.terifahrendorf.com. If you brew this recipe and your IPA turns out great, Fahrendorf would enjoy a royalty payment of one bottle, because she really misses Bombay Bomber. Please send a bottle to 5215 N. Lombard St., PMB 200 B, Portland, OR 97203.

Brewing liquor:
Fahrendorf uses Eugene, Oregon, mountain runoff (soft) water with added gypsum.

Malt bill:
Western (American) two-row malt 71%
American Munich malt 10 °L 22%
American Vienna malt 4 °L 7%

Mashing and lautering:
Employ a single-step conversion mash at 153° F (67° C) for 1 hour.

Kettle boil and hopping:
Boil in the kettle for 90 minutes, whirlpool for 5 minutes, and let rest for 25 minutes. At the start of the boil, the Chinook hops are added, followed by Crystal hops at 20 minutes, and then both Chinook and Crystal at kettle knockout. Fast chill and transfer to a fermenter in 10 minutes (this is what saves the aroma!).

Fermentation and aging:
Ferment at 67° F (19° C) for 18 days. On the third day, dry hop with Chinook at bunging. Beginning on day 4, make sure to keep top pressure on the beer to naturally carbonate. Pull the yeast on day 10. Chill to 32° F (0° C) for the final three days (days 19–21), and filter for a bright, crisp taste. ("An unfiltered IPA is like an unfocused photo. You just can't get a crisp, clear picture or flavor." This is a quote from John Hathaway, one of the brewers who worked for Fahrendorf at the California Steelheads in Burlingame and San Francisco.)

Analytical targets:
OG: 14.2 °P (1.057 SG)
TG: 3.2 °P (1.013 SG)
ADF: 77.5%
IBU: 57
ABV: 6%

THE STORY OF HARPOON IPA

By Charlie Storey, Harpoon, Vice President of Marketing

Harpoon IPA was first brewed as a summer seasonal in 1992. At the time, Harpoon was a small, struggling Boston "microbrewery." Not a lot of attention was paid to recording events, let alone pondering that perhaps an entry into the pages of craft-brewing history was being written. So this is our best memory of events.

In the early 1990s hoppy pale ales were being brewed in the Pacific Northwest and in California, but there weren't craft beers being brewed in the rest of the United States that featured high aroma content from Northwest hops. Harpoon had two year-round beers, Harpoon Ale and Harpoon Golden Lager, and an emerging seasonal product line. Harpoon's first seasonal beer was Winter Warmer in 1988. The popularity of Winter Warmer quickly led to the establishment of a lineup of beers for each season. Octoberfest was the obvious choice for the fall, and we brewed a dry stout in the spring, which fit nicely into Boston's strong Irish heritage and huge St. Patrick's Day celebrations. The summertime did not, however, seem to have a style that linked the season to a particular beer by way of tradition or history. The compulsion to do something different, which was what got Harpoon started in the first place, surfaced during the summer season. We decided to make a beer that was a tribute to the Pacific Northwest. But we chose a traditional English style, an IPA, and used Northwestern U.S. hops and not English hops. It was a hybrid we thought would have a few fans and many critics. It was a *very* extreme beer for 1992. Instead of turning people off, it quickly became our best-selling beer and transformed the company. By August 1992, Harpoon was profitable for the first time since its founding in 1986. IPA made Harpoon the brewery it is today.

Tod Mott was the head brewer at the time. He had a great vision for the beer and used a blend of malts that even required us to hand-bake malt to create our own toasted malt. Everyone at the brewery would take home 10-pound bags of malt to roast in our ovens in our kitchens. He originally wanted to use Kent hops, but Rich Doyle suggested using Northwest hops, sourced from Washington and Oregon, and the formula was set. At 40 IBU the bitterness was off the charts relative to other beers in the local market.

The reception for the beer was outstanding, and sales were strong right from the start. What's more, everyone at the brewery really loved the beer. After a great first summer we did stop making it. It did not go year round until the summer of 1993.

In addition to the relatively high IBUs, the alcohol content of our IPA also drew attention. At 5.9% abv, it was another unusually high number at the time. IPA sales continued to climb, but it took some time to realize what the numbers were saying: IPA would quickly overtake Harpoon Ale—the beer the brewery was founded on—as the top Harpoon product. It is not easy to imagine displacing something so central and beloved to the entire organization. But reality prevailed, and Harpoon IPA not only became the focus of the brew schedule but led our sales and marketing efforts. In many pubs around Boston, if a customer asks for a Harpoon, they expect to get an IPA, and similarly, if they ask for an IPA, they expect a Harpoon.

In the last few years Harpoon has introduced some new beers in the "100 Barrel Series" and the "Leviathan" product line. These beers are generally unusual styles that occupy a niche market. It is wonderful when the first barrel gets tapped at the brewery. We all get to drink something new and exciting. For many of us, these new beers are our temporary "favorite" beer; in other words, we'll go right to that tap to pour a pint at the end of the workday. Coming back to the IPA, however, is always a pleasure. It makes you wonder why you ever chose to drink another beer. The clean, floral aroma is unmatched. It looks so good in the glass: a snow white, foamy head on top of the bright, copper-colored beer—just like the color of a polished copper bar top in some classic European pub. The roasted barley is always there, but the hops carry the beer to a perfect finish. It has just enough bite to make you ready for the next swallow.

We plan to brew and drink IPA for many more years to come. The Harpoon IPA story continues, and we hope it will be told repeatedly while enjoying a pint or two of this great, hoppy beer.

HARPOON IPA

The first time I went to Boston in the mid-1990s, Harpoon IPA was the rage. It was everywhere and had a great following. After I moved to the Boston area in the late 1990s, Harpoon became one of my favorite breweries, and their IPA was a mainstay in my refrigerator. The recipe comes courtesy of Al Marzi, chief brewing operator. Harpoon IPA was one of the first year-round bottled craft IPAs when it was introduced as a full-time brand in 1993.

Brewing liquor:
Use soft water with calcium sulfate added.

Malt bill:
Pale malt 94%
Victory malt* 4%
Crystal malt 60 °L 2%
*The original version used pale malt toasted in an oven.

Mashing and lautering:
Harpoon IPA uses a water-to-grain ratio of 2.6/1 (1.25 qt./lb.) and an upward infusion mash with a 20-minute rest at 152° F (67° C). Raise the temperature to 168° F (76° C) for mash-off.

Kettle boil and hopping:
Use a dynamic, low-pressure boil in the kettle for 65 minutes. Using 100% pellets, add 9% Apollo (15–19% alpha acids) at 65 minutes, followed by three Cascade additions: 19% at 20 minutes, 36% at 5 minutes, and 36% at whirlpool.

Fermentation and aging:
Using a Harpoon house yeast strain or perhaps WY1968 (London ESB) or WLP002 (English Ale) yeast, ferment at 70° F (21° C) for four days, then crash

cool to 29° F (-1.7° C) for 1.5 weeks. One week later, dry hop with Cascade pellets at 0.26 oz./gal. (0.5 lb./bbl., 1.93 g/L).

Analytical targets:
OG: 15.5 °P (1.062 SG)
TG: 2.9 °P (1.012 SG)
ADF: 81.29%
IBU: 42
ABV: 5.9%
Color: 8.6 °L (17° EBC)

BLIND PIG IPA

Vinnie Cilurzo brewed Blind Pig IPA in 1994 at his first brewery, Blind Pig Brewing Company, in Temecula, California. It was 92 bittering units and had very little malt character but a very hop-forward character. In December 1996 Cilurzo left the brewery. His former business partner continued the brewery for a few years before closing. Cilurzo was able to trademark the name again and begin brewing it at Russian River Brewing. He has changed the recipe by adding a couple of new hop varieties that were not in existence when the brewery in Temecula was open.

Brewing liquor:
Blind Pig uses Santa Rosa, California, water with gypsum added.

Malt bill:
Two-row malt 93%
Crystal malt 40 °L 4%
CaraPils malt 3%

Mashing and lautering:
Brew using an infusion mash at 153–154° F (67–68° C).

Kettle boil and hopping:
Boil in the kettle for 90 minutes. Using 100% Type 90 hop pellets, add CTZ and Chinook at 90 minutes, an addition of Amarillo at 30 minutes, and at the end of the boil make the last addition of Simcoe, Amarillo, Cascade, and Centennial.

Fermentation and aging:
Ferment with California Ale yeast (WLP001 or WY1056) at 68° F (20° C). After the primary fermentation, use a blend of CTZ, Amarillo, and Cascade pellets to dry hop, and hold for 10 days.

Analytical targets:
OG: 14.25 °P (1.057 SG)
TG: 3.25 °P (1.013 SG)
ADF: 77%
IBU: 62
ABV: 6.10%

CONTEMPORARY U.S. CRAFT-BREWING RECIPES

THE STORY OF BROOKLYN EAST INDIA PALE ALE

By Garrett Oliver

Brooklyn East India Pale Ale was launched in 1995. The direct inspiration for both the beer and the name is the second edition of William L. Tizard's 1846 book, *The Theory and Practice of Brewing Illustrated,* of which I have an original copy. Chapter 18, "Exports," contains several pages titled "East India Pale Ale" and gives information about everything from recipes to hour-by-hour fermentation charts and the workings of the beer market in Calcutta. When we launched our IPA, it was the first beer I was aware of in the United States that was brewed to that sort of specification.

Over time the bottled version has stayed essentially the same, but the draft version has changed. The reason for this is that I find British hop character—especially dry-hop character—holds up better in the bottle than American hop character. So the draft version is slanted in a more American direction, and it is also slightly lighter in gravity. One of the few beers I've had that reminds me somewhat of our bottled IPA is the old version of Young's Special London Ale.

BROOKLYN EAST INDIA PALE ALE

The Brooklyn Brewery was established in 1987 in upstate New York by Steve Hindy and Tom Potter. In 1996, with brewmaster Garrett Oliver on board, they opened their own brewery in Brooklyn, the first successful commercial brewery in New York City in 20 years. Since that time, Oliver has not only brewed award-winning traditional and innovative beers but has become one of the craft-brewing industry's best spokesmen, especially when it comes to the art of pairing beer and food.

Brewing liquor:
Brooklyn uses very soft, filtered city water that is hardened with calcium sulfate.

Malt bill:
British pale ale malt 65%
British lager malt* 30%
British crystal malt 5%
*British lager malt is very pale in color and is enlisted by brewers as a reasonable substitute for the extra pale (white) malt that was used in the 1800s IPAs.

Mashing and lautering:
A temperature-programmed mash is employed with a 10-minute rest at 122° F (50° C) and a saccharification rest at 152° F (66.7° C). Use a water-to-grain ratio of 2.8/1 (1.35 qt./lb.).

Kettle boil and hopping:
The total boil time is 75 minutes. There are three hop additions using several varieties, including East Kent Goldings, Cascade, Northdown, Challenger, Amarillo, and Simcoe. Use only T90 pellets and no extracts or oils.

Fermentation and aging:
The Brooklyn house strain, which has been running in succession since 1996 without re-culture, is used for fermentation. A comparable yeast to use here would be WY1968 (London ESB) or WLP002 (English Ale). Dry hop for five days at 52–60° F (11–16° C; rising). Use only pellets, and add them through a top port or an in-line system that grinds and feeds the hop pellets into the beer stream. The dry hop consists of a blend of Glacier, Cascade, Amarillo, East Kent Goldings, Centennial, and Pilgrim hops at a total rate of 0.52 oz./gal. (1 lb./bbl., 2.86 g/L).

Analytical targets:
OG: 16.5 °P (1.066 SG)
TG: 2.7 °P (1.011 SG)
ADF: 83.6%
IBU: 48
ABV: 7.3%
Color: 10 °L (19.7° EBC)

DOGFISH HEAD'S HOPPY INNOVATIONS

Started in 1995 in the resort community of Rehoboth Beach by Sam Calagione, Dogfish Head Brewing Company is Delaware's first brewpub. Dogfish Head can be considered one of the nation's first nano-breweries, as the brewing process was started on a 12-gallon system that used beer kegs as brewing vessels. Growing steadily every year, Dogfish Head built a production brewery in nearby Milton, Delaware, in 2002.

Known as one of America's most innovative breweries, Dogfish Head brews intensely flavored ales by using creative ingredients and brewing techniques—including a continuous hopping process and a "Randall the enamel animal" hop-steeping device for draft beer. Also, in a show of respect for the ancient heritage of brewing, they use early techniques and ingredients to brew modern and "off-centered" ales. Calagione, one of the best representatives of American craft brewing, has written several books and is in high demand as a television personality.

About Dogfish beers Calagione says the following:

Like our 60-, 90-, and 120-minute IPAs, our Aprihop and Burton Baton beers are brewed using Dogfish Head's unique continual-hopping method. I got the idea for this while watching a cooking show, where the chef said if he incrementally added many little pinches of black pepper to the soup while it was simmering, instead of adding the same amount all at once, the flavors of the pepper would come through with more nuances and give the soup more complexity. Our first continually hopped IPAs were made by sending a stream of hops down an old-school vibrating football game board. It got wet and eventually busted, but it worked. By continually hopping our beers, we found that we could make pungent, intensely flavorful beer. Because we added an inordinate amount of hops continuously, it didn't make the beer as crushingly bitter as it would have been had we added the same amount of hops in two big additions. We now have a pneumatic cannon we designed, called "Sofa King Hoppy," that shoots a small volume of hops into our IPAs every minute.

DOGFISH HEAD APRIHOP

Dogfish Head first brewed Aprihop as a draft-only beer in 1998. Pub regulars and retailers in the mid-Atlantic liked Raison d'Etre, Immort Ale, and Chicory Stout, but they wanted something hoppy. Dogfish Head had already made a blueberry beer and a cherry pale ale, but found them to be too fruity and one dimensional. So they set out to make a fruit beer for people who hate fruit beers. "[Aprihop is] basically a big ol' IPA with a fruit problem," says Calagione. "The apricot accentuated and magnified the citrusy character of the Northwest hops in the recipe."

Malt bill:
Two-row Pils malt 83%
CaraPils malt 8%
Dark crystal malt 65 °L 7%
Amber malt 40 °L 2%

Mashing and lautering:

Using a water-to-grain ratio of 2.58/1 (1.24 qt./lb.), this recipe employs a single-infusion mash profile. Mash in and hold at 156° F (65° C) for 25 minutes. Begin to draw off to the kettle and start sparging with 175° F (79° C) water when the wort is within 1 inch of the exposed grain bed.

Kettle boil and hopping:

The total boil time is 60 minutes. Make a continuous addition from the beginning of the boil over 20 minutes by using 25% Warrior, 0.13 oz./gal. (0.25 lb./bbl., 0.97 g/L). Make a second continuous addition over 20 minutes with 15% Amarillo at a ratio of 0.08 oz./gal. (0.16 lb./bbl., 0.59 g/L) and 13% Simcoe at a ratio of 0.07 oz./gal. (0.14 lb./bbl., 0.52 g/L). After the boil, add 47% Amarillo at a ratio of 0.25 oz./gal. (0.48 lb./bbl., 1.9 g/L) to the whirlpool. Add 0.25 oz./gal. (0.48 lb./bbl., 1.9 g/L) apricot purée and whirlpool hops at the start of the whirlpool process.

Fermentation and aging:

Cool wort to 68–70° F (20–21° C) and pitch with English Ale yeast. Maintain fermentation at a temperature of 68–70° F (20–21° C). Rack after 8–10 days and add the apricot purée (sterile) at a ratio of 0.25 oz./gal. (0.48 lb./bbl., 1.9 g/L). Dry hop using Amarillo hops at a ratio of 0.40 oz./gal. (0.78 lb./bbl., 3 g/L).

Analytical targets:

OG: 17.0 °P (1.068 SG)
TG: 4.0 °P (1.016 SG)
ADF: 76.5%
IBU: 45–50
ABV: 7%

BURTON BATON BREW NO. 1: OLDE ALE THREAD

First brewed in 2004, Burton Baton was designed as "a shout-out to our homies at Ballantine's," says Dogfish Head's Sam Calagione. Long before the craft-brewing renaissance, back in the 1930s and 1940s Ballantine was making its Burton Ale at 10% abv and more than 80 IBU, then aging it in wood tanks for over a year. The brewery only gave it to special guests and VIPs—never offering it for sale. "Burton Baton is our way of saying we are proud to be one of the many East Coast craft brewers proudly taking that baton of hoppy IPA brewing in hand and running with it," continues Calagione. "It is a blend of one thread continually hopped imperial IPA and one thread sorta English Old Ale."

Malt bill:
Two-row Pils malt 96%
Dark crystal malt 65 °L 2.5%
Amber malt 40 °L 1.5%

Mashing and lautering:
A single-infusion mash profile is used with a water-to-grain ratio of 2.32/1 (1.11 qt./lb.). Mash in and hold at 149° F (65° C) for 60 minutes. When the wort is within 1 inch of the exposed grain bed, draw off to the kettle and start sparging with 175° F (79° C) water.

Kettle boil and hopping:
Total boil time is 60 minutes. At the start of the boil add the dextrose sugar at a ratio of 3.2 oz./gal. (6.2 lb./bbl., 24 g/L), then make an addition of 29% Warrior hops at a ratio of 0.24 oz./gal. (0.47 lb./bbl., 1.8 g/L). Additions of 22% Simcoe at a ratio of 0.18 oz./gal. (0.35 lb./bbl., 1.35 g/L) at 15 minutes, followed by 49% Amarillo hops at a ratio of 0.40 oz./gal. (0.78 lb./bbl., 3 g/L) in the whirlpool.

Fermentation and aging:
Cool wort to 68–70° F (20–21° C) and pitch with English Ale yeast. Maintain fermentation at 68–70° F (20–21° C). After six to eight days, rack and add oak chips (sterilized by boiling in water for 5–10 minutes) at a ratio of 1 oz./gal. (1.94 lb./bbl., 7.5 g/L). Dry hop with Amarillo hops at a rate of 0.4 oz./gal. (0.78 lb./bbl., 3 g/L), and hold beer as cool as possible until it is time to blend with the Imperial IPA Thread.

Analytical targets:
OG: 23 °P (1.092 SG)
TG: 2.6 °P (1.010 SG)
ADF: 88.7%
IBU: 100–110
ABV: 11%

BURTON BATON BREW NO. 2: IMPERIAL IPA THREAD

Brew two weeks after Olde Ale Thread. After secondary, blend the Olde Ale with the Imperial IPA, package, and enjoy!

Malt bill:
Two-row Pils malt 96%
Amber malt 40 °L 4%

Mashing and lautering:
Utilize a single-infusion mash with a water-to-grain ratio of 2.32/1 (1.11 qt./

lb.). Mash in and hold at 149° F (65° C) for 30 minutes. When the wort is within 1 inch of the exposed grain bed, draw off to the kettle and start sparging with 175° F (79° C) water.

Kettle boil and hopping:

Total kettle boil time is 60 minutes. Combine 26% Warrior hops at a ratio of 0.20 oz./gal. (0.39 lb./bbl., 1.5 g/L), 12% Simcoe at a ratio of 0.09 oz./gal. (0.17 lb./bbl., 0.67 g/L), and 22% Amarillo at a ratio of 0.17 oz./gal. (0.33 lb./bbl., 1.27 g/L). Add combined hops as a continuous addition over 20 minutes at the start of the boil. During the whirlpool stage, add 40% Amarillo at a ratio of 0.30 oz./gal. (0.58 lb./bbl., 2.2 g/L).

Fermentation and aging:

Cool wort to 68–70° F (20–21° C) and pitch with English Ale yeast. Maintain fermentation at 68–70° F (20–21° C). After 8–10 days, rack and add dry hops. Dry hops are a combination of Amarillo at a ratio of 0.08 oz./gal. (0.16 lb./bbl., 0.6 g/L), Simcoe at a ratio of 0.16 oz./gal. (0.32 lb./bbl., 1.2 g/L), and Palisade at a ratio of 0.32 oz./gal. (0.64 lb./bbl., 2.4 g/L). Store the beer in a cold place for 18 days.

Analytical targets:

OG: 21.5 °P (1.086 SG)
TG: 4.6 °P (1.018 SG)
ADF: 78.6%
IBU: 90
ABV: 9%

SMUTTYNOSE FINEST KIND IPA

Peter Egelston and a group of partners founded the Smuttynose Brewery in 1994. Director of brewing operations David Yarrington has been with Smutty since 2001 and has brought some West Coast sensibilities to the New England brewing scene.

Yarrington remembers that one of the first projects he undertook after starting with Smuttynose in 2001 was designing an IPA for release. Being new to the East Coast, he decided to sample every IPA being sold in New England. "The brewing staff and I were more than up for this rigorous sensory assault," he says. The intent was not necessarily to design a beer specifically for the market, but to see what was out there commercially, find characteristics that they enjoyed, and highlight them in their own offering. The one trait that they found was an increase of malt (especially crystal malts) as the hopping rates went up. They agreed that the overly malted IPAs were quite satiating. "It's a quality that is nice in a dessert beer, but not something I'd be looking for in a sessionable IPA," says Yarrington.

At the time, the underlying wisdom had been to always balance hops with malt. But there never seemed to be talk of balancing hops within themselves. Smuttynose focused on the idea that the judicious use of specific varieties at the correct time in the process would balance flavors nicely.

"With that aesthetic firmly in mind, we proceeded to release our Finest Kind IPA. This beer is brewed with a hint of crystal 60 °L—an amount that borders on not enough. The hopping is done with a low co-humulone hop for bittering and then frequent additions of high-alpha hops during the last 30 minutes of the boil," says Yarrington. "We really like how this gives a saturated flavor profile."

Brewing liquor:
Use water treated with gypsum in a ratio of 0.076 oz./gal. (2.16 g/gal.).

Malt bill:
Two-row malt 84%
Pale ale malt 13%
Crystal malt 60 °L 3%

Mashing and lautering:
Use a water-to-grain ratio of 2.74/1 (1.32 qt./gal.) and employ an infusion mash with a 40-minute rest at 155° F (68° C).

Kettle boil and hopping:
Total boil time is 75 minutes. At the start of the boil add 41.2% of the hop bill in Magnum pellets. In equal amounts, add 24% Simcoe in 5-minute increments for the last 30 minutes of the boil. During whirlpool add 19.9% Centennial and 14.9% Santiam pellets.

Fermentation and aging:
Ferment with American Ale yeast at 68° F (20° C) until the target terminal gravity is reached, then crash cool. Dry hop for 7–10 days using whole flower Amarillo at a ratio of .25 lb./bbl. (0.13 oz./gal.,1 g/L) added into the bright tank.

Analytical targets:
OG: 15 °P (1.060 SG)
TG: 2.5 °P (1.010 SG)
ADF: 83%

IBU: 70
ABV: 6.6%
Color: 10.6 °L (20.9° EBC)

DESCHUTES QUAIL SPRINGS IPA

One of the largest and most highly respected craft brewers in the Pacific Northwest, Deschutes is also notable for being one of the two larger regional craft brewers (the other being Sierra Nevada) that still use whole hops almost exclusively in their beers. Larry Sidor was brewmaster at Deschutes for seven years and saw the brewery grow to just over 200,000 barrels production in 2010.

Deschutes began life as a "traditional British brewery," which was reflected in its line of beer. One of the first beers out of the kettle was Black Butte Porter. It quickly became the flagship, but as the years went by, Mirror Pond pale ale took over as the flagship.

The first IPA Deschutes brewed was a "British IPA" developed by maintenance engineer and homebrewer Harv Hillis. Hillis lives outside of the Bend, Oregon, city limits on a patch of land he calls Quail Springs—thus the name of this IPA, Quail Springs. Inversion IPA eventually replaced it in 2006, but Quail Springs continues to be brewed at the pubs.

Brewing liquor:
Prepare extremely soft water with 150 ppm of gypsum added to the hot liquor.

Malt bill:
Maris Otter malt 92%
Munich malt 8%

Mashing and lautering:
Use a water-to-grain ratio of 2.0/1 (0.96 qt./lb.) and brew this beer utilizing a semi-infusion mash with "all in" at 156° F (69° C). Rest the mash 25 minutes prior to mashing off at 170° F (77° C). Total boil time is 60 minutes. Note that Deschutes' elevation is 3,600 feet. Boil vigorously to flash off all dimethyl sulfide (DMS).

Kettle boil and hopping:
This beer is brewed using 100% whole hops at a total addition rate of 1.25 lb./bbl. The breakdown should be 60% Styrian Goldings, 30% East Kent Goldings, and 10% American Goldings. Add 20% at the start of the boil (60 minutes), 25% at 30 minutes, 25% at 5 minutes, and 30% of the hops in the hopback.

Fermentation and aging:

Pitch using the Deschutes house ale yeast or something similar and cool to 62° F (16.7° C). Ferment 63° F (17.2° C) for three days, bung with 2% ADF remaining. Wait 24–48 hours for diacetyl reduction, then crash cool.
Dry hopping is done post-filtration by placing whole hop East Kent Goldings in a mesh bag and securing the bag to the side of the tank. Hold the beer on the hops for seven days prior to packaging. Use a ratio of 0.155 oz./gal. (0.3 lb./bbl., 1.16 g/L) to determine hop quantity.

Analytical targets:

OG: 15.2 °P (1.061 SG)
TG: 4.2 °P (1.017 SG)
ADF: 72.4%
IBU: 50
ABV: 6%
Color: 10 °L (19.1° EBC)

STONE IPA

Stone Brewing Co.'s 1st Anniversary Ale was released as Stone IPA in 1997 and has become the company's best-selling beer. It is considered by many to be a great example of the West Coast IPA.

Brewing liquor:

Municipal water (~300 ppm hardness) is carbon filtered and goes through a reverse osmosis process. Treat to reduce hardness to 100 ppm.

Malt bill:

Pale malt 93.5%
Crystal malt 15 °L 6.5%

Mashing and lautering:

Use a water-to-grain ratio of 2.96/1 (1.42 qt./lb.). Brew using an upward infusion mash with a 30-minute rest at 150° F (66° C). Raise the temperature to 165° F (74° C) for mash-off.

Kettle boil and hopping:

Total boil time is 90 minutes. This recipe uses 100% hop pellets. Combine 26% Chinook with 23% Columbus and add at the start of the boil. During the whirlpool stage, add 51% Centennial.

Fermentation and aging:

Pitch with the Stone house yeast strain (or WLP007 and WLP002 are acceptable alternatives). Ferment at 72° F (22° C) until 3.2 °P (1.013 SG). Chill to 62° F (17° C) for 24 hours, then rack off yeast. To dry hop, use Centennial at a ratio of 0.29 oz./gal. (0.563 lb./bbl., 2.18 g/L) and Chinook at 0.033 oz./gal. (0.063 lb./bbl., 0.24 g/L). Hold for 36 hours, and then chill to 34° F (1.1° C). Hold for seven days.

Analytical targets:

OG: 16 °P (1.064 SG)
TG: 2.9 °P (1.012 SG)
ADF: 81.88%
IBU: 75
ABV: 6.9%
Color: 9.5 °L (17° EBC)

PIZZA PORT CARLSBAD WIPEOUT IPA

When Jeff Bagby got to Pizza Port Carlsbad, the former head brewer, Kurt McHale, was making Wipeout IPA. Not having any records for the brewing process, Bagby had to come up with something that would be similar to McHale's recipe. But it turned out to be a completely different IPA. Further confusing things, the San Marcos crew members (at Port Brewing Company) were also making a Wipeout IPA. Although Bagby shared his Carlsbad recipe with Port brewers in San Marcos, they have since changed it. Bagby has tweaked the Carlsbad recipe, too. He also renamed it Welcome Back Wipeout to help distinguish between the two beers. "I've been trying to stop the confusion between who makes what by making the beer something different," he says. "Our new version in Carlsbad is stronger and hoppier than my original one."

Malt bill:

Two-row malt 83.6%
CaraPils malt 7%
Crystal malt 60 °L 4.9%
Crystal malt 15 °L 2.1%
Wheat malt 2.4%

Mashing and lautering:

Brew using an infusion mash. Total kettle boil time is 90 minutes.

Kettle boil and hopping:

Use Amarillo hops for the first-wort hopping. Add Centennial and Simcoe at the start of the 90-minute boil. Add a second addition of Amarillo and Cascade at 45 minutes. During the whirlpool stage, use Amarillo and Centennial. No hop ratios or amounts were provided.

Fermentation and aging:

Pitch the Pizza Port proprietary yeast, or WLP060 American Ale Yeast Blend or WLP090 San Diego Super Yeast would work well. Ferment at 67° F (19° C) until fermentation is 50% complete, then allow fermentation to free rise to 72° F (22° C). Using a blend of Amarillo and Centennial, dry hop and hold for 10 days.

Analytical targets:

OG: 19 °P (1.076 SG)
TG: 2.5 °P (1.013 SG)
ADF: 86.8%
IBU: 75
ABV: 7.4%
Color: Deep gold/light amber

FAT HEAD'S HEADHUNTER IPA

Matt Cole, brewmaster at Fat Head's, just outside of Cleveland, Ohio, has won many awards for his Headhunter IPA. His version of a classic American IPA was inspired by a trip he took to Hayward, California, where he attended The Bistro's annual IPA Festival. This was Cole's first real exposure to a plethora of West Coast IPAs, and it inspired him to brew Fat Head's Headhunter IPA, which has medaled two years running at the Great American Beer Festival.

Brewing liquor:

Target the following mineral parameters:

Ca	163.2 ppm
Mg	8.5 ppm
Na	21 ppm
SO_4	365 ppm
Cl	23.5 ppm
HCO_3	104 ppm

Malt bill:
American two-row malt 50%
Maris Otter malt 25%
CaraHell malt 6%
Crystal malt 6%
Toasted wheat flakes 6%
CaraPils malt 2%
Dextrose 5%

Mashing and lautering:
Using a water-to-grain ratio of 2.60/1 (1.25 qt./lb.), employ an infusion mash with a 60-minute rest at 151° F (66° C). With 6.7% of the kettle hop bill, mash hop with Centennial at 9.2% alpha acids.

Kettle boil and hopping:
Total boil time is 90 minutes. At the start of the boil in the kettle (90 minutes) use 17.7% alpha acids CTZ at 23.3% of the bill. Identical additions at a ratio of 6.7% each Citra (12.4% alpha acids) and Centennial (9.2% alpha acids) are added at 45 minutes and again at 30 minutes. At the end of the boil add 23.3% Simcoe (12.2% alpha acids), 16.6% Centennial (9.2% alpha acids), and 3.3% Columbus (14.2% alpha acids).

Fermentation and aging:
Use WLP001 or WY1056 for pitching. Hold at 67° F (19.4° C) for four to five days. Hold two days at fermentation temperature for a diacetyl rest before cooling to 50° F (10° C). Crop or drop the yeast. Dry hop for 10 days using equal parts Centennial, Simcoe, Citra, and Columbus at 0.21 oz./gal. (0.40 lb./bbl., 1.54 g/L) for each hop. Allow the temperature to rise to 60° F (16° C). Rouse hops with CO_2 at days 2, 5, and 8. Drop hops (remove or rack off hops) at day 9. Cool for two days at 40° F (4° C), and finally cool to 33° F (0.6° C). This beer is not filtered.

Analytical targets:
OG: 17 °P (1.068 SG)
TG: 3.4 °P (1.014 SG)
ADF: 80%
IBU: 87
ABV: 7.5%
Color: 8.5 °L (16.2° EBC)

AVERY DUGANA IPA

The real story about DuganA IPA is on the label, but the other, less-known reason DuganA came about was that Adam Avery wanted to drink Maharaja all day long. But at 10–11% abv, this was unwise. He figured that Avery Brewing Company needed an IPA—or in his own words, "a super hop bomb." He was looking for something between the regular IPA and the Maharaja but at a lower alcohol-by-volume rate. He also wanted a different aroma profile. "I wanted the dank aroma to dominate," says Avery. "Ya mon! Mission accomplished."

Brewing liquor:
Avery has access to great water in Boulder, Colorado, that is neither too hard nor too soft, but rather "just right" to serve as a base for all their beers. They do add 110 ppm of calcium carbonate. For the DuganA just a little calcium chloride is added to the mash water at a ratio of 0.03 oz./gal. (0.06 lb./bbl., 0.22 g/L) as well as calcium sulfate at a ratio of 0.02 oz./gal. (0.04 lb./bbl., 0.15 g/L).

Malt bill:
Pale two-row malt 96%
Dingemans Aroma malt 150 2%
Great Western C-75 malt 2%

Mashing and lautering:
This recipe uses a water-to-grain ratio of 2.30/1 (1.1 qt./lb.). Prepare for an infusion mash at 148° F (64° C). Mash-in occurs at 50 minutes, rest at 20 minutes, and vorlauf at 15 minutes.

Kettle boil and hopping:
Total boil time is 60 minutes. Using 100% pelletized hops, add Bravo (15.2% alpha acids) at the start of the boil as 11% of the kettle hop bill. At 15 minutes, add 13% Chinook hops (11.8% alpha acids). Use 57% Chinook hops (11.8% alpha acids) and 19% Columbus (13.7% alpha acids) at the end of the boil.

Fermentation and aging:
Pitch A-56 yeast (from Brewing Science Institute) or WLP001 or WY1056. Ferment at 68° F (20° C) until the beer reaches 50% attenuation, then allow the temperature to rise freely (it usually gets to 74° F [23° C] by the end of fermentation). Total fermentation time is around 80–90 hours. Add dry hops while the beer is still warm at the end of fermentation. Use Columbus at a ratio of 0.28 oz./gal. (0.55 lb./bbl., 2.13 g/L) and Chinook at a ratio of 0.86 oz./gal. (1.66 lb./bbl., 6.42 g/L). Rouse hops with CO_2 every other day for 15 minutes. After five days, crash cool the beer to 30° F (-1° C) over 48–72 hours. Hold another seven days, then centrifuge or rack the beer off the hops. Continue CO_2 rousing until 24 hours prior to hop separation.

Analytical targets:
OG: 18 °P (1.072 SG)
TG: 2.75 °P (1.011 SG)
ADF: 84.7%
IBU: ~90
ABV: 8.5%
Color: 8.2 °L (15.7° EBC)

ODELL IPA

Brewing liquor:
Water is untreated Fort Collins, Colorado, municipal water. Odell's adds gypsum at a level to mimic Burton-on-Trent water. $MgSO_4$ and NaCl are also added in much lesser amounts.

Malt bill:
Pale two-row malt 84%
Caramalt 8%
Vienna malt 7%
Honey malt 1%

Mashing and lautering:
Using a water-to-grain ratio of 2.80/1 (1.35 qt./lb.), employ an infusion mash for 60 minutes, including vorlauf time.

Kettle boil and hopping:
Total kettle boil is 90 minutes. Use pellet hops for bittering and whole hops in the hopback for flavor. Amounts given are 16% Chinook, 22% Amarillo, 22% mystery hop, 12% Columbus, and 28% Centennial.

Fermentation and aging:
Odell's house yeast is a strong top cropper with medium attenuation and low-medium flocculation characteristics. Ferment at 68° F (20° C) for about 60 days. Dry hopping is done with a proprietary blend of pellets.

Analytical targets:
OG: 16.4 °P (1.066 SG)
TG: 3.2 °P (1.013 SG)
ADF: 80.5%
IBU: 60
ABV: 7%
Color: 9.5 °L (18.1° EBC)

GOOSE ISLAND INDIA PALE ALE

Opened in Chicago in 1988, the Goose Island Beer Company has grown to include a production brewery and two brewpubs. One of Chicago's first microbreweries, it has a reputation for producing excellent traditional ales, vintage-dated Belgian styles, and barrel-aged beers.

Goose Island IPA is the premier example of an American craft-brewed English IPA. Made with 100% pale malt, no crystal malts at all, and hopped with a combination of English and American hops, this beer is almost 6% abv. It falls just above where many traditional English brewers are currently brewing their IPAs.

The excellence of this beer is demonstrated by the five medals it has picked up at the Great American Beer Festival in the English IPA category (gold in 2000; silver in 2004, 2007, 2008; and bronze in 2001), and by the gold medal it won at the 2010 World Beer Cup in the English IPA category.

Malt bill:
Special pale ale malt (~3.9 °L) 100%

Mashing and lautering:
The mash pH is adjusted with an acid addition; gypsum is added directly to the mash. Begin with a 25-minute rest at 159° F (71° C) and raise the mash temperature to 170° F (77° C), then hold for 10 minutes.

Kettle boil and hopping:
Total boil time is 60 minutes. The kettle pH is adjusted with an acid addition, and finings are added during the last 10 minutes of the boil. Using only 100% pellets, add 16% of the Pilgrim T90 hops at the start of the boil. During the whirlpool, add 60% Styrian (Savinjski) Goldings T90 and 24% Cascade T45 pellets.

Fermentation and aging:
Chill wort to 62° F (17° C), oxygenate, and pitch with Goose Island proprietary English Ale yeast at ~1.1 million cells/mL/°P or a similar yeast. Allow fermentation to raise the temperature to 67° F (19° C) over the course of a five-day fermentation. Beer is typically given a 36- to 48-hour diacetyl rest before cooling. Dry hop on the fifth fermentation day at a rate of ~0.5 lb./bbl. with 66% Centennial T90 pellets and 34% Cascade T90 pellets.

Analytical targets:
OG: 15.5 °P (1.062 SG)
TG: 4.6 °P (1.018 SG)

ADF: 70.3%
IBU: 55
ABV: 5.95%
Color: 10 °L (19.1° EBC)

DESCHUTES INVERSION IPA

Inversion IPA replaced Quail Springs IPA at Deschutes in 2006. Decidedly more American in flavor profile, Inversion IPA is unique for Deschutes in that hop extract is used for the bittering portion (first kettle addition). The rest of the hopping follows the brewery's tradition of using whole hops.

Brewing liquor:
Use extremely soft water with 150 ppm of lactic acid added to the hot liquor.

Malt bill:
Pale malt 82%
Caramel malt 10%
Munich malt 6%
Crystal malt 2%

Mashing and lautering:
Use a water-to-grain ratio of 3.2/1 (1.54 qt./lb.). "All in" at 140° F (60° C) and hold for 5 minutes prior to ramping up to 158° F (70° C) for a 10-minute hold. Mash off at 168° F (76° C).

Kettle boil and hopping:
Total boil time is 90 minutes. Total addition rate is at a ratio of 0.77 oz./gal. (1.5 lb./bbl., 5.8 g/L). This is an equivalent as extract is used in the first addition. Hop varieties used are Millennium, Horizon, Centennial, Northern Brewer, Cascade, and Citra. Use 15% of the hop bill at the start of the boil, 25% at 30 minutes, and 60% at 5 minutes.

Fermentation and aging:
Pitch the Deschutes house ale yeast strain or a similar yeast. Cool to 62° F (16.7° C) and ferment at 63° F (17.2° C) for three days. Bung with 2% ADF remaining, wait 24–48 hours for diacetyl reduction, then crash cool. After filtration, the beer is dry hopped with Centennial, Cascade, and Citra at a ratio of 0.155 oz./gal. (0.3 lb./bbl., 1.16 g/L). Whole hops are placed in a mesh bag that is secured to the tank, and the beer is held on the hops for seven days prior to packaging.

Analytical targets:
OG: 16.8 °P (1.067 SG)
TG: 4.4 °P (1.018 SG)
ADF: 73.8%
IBU: 80
ABV: 6.8%
Color: 24 °L (47° EBC)

DEMON'S HOPYARD IPA

As part of a team, I helped create this beer at the Anheuser-Busch Merrimack Brewery in 2005 and 2006. It was short lived, but it had the dis-
tinction of being only the second IPA ever to be released by Anheuser-
Busch, and the first one with the designation of IPA in the name (the
first IPA was American Hop Ale, released as part of the American Origi-
nals series in 1996). The original name was Devil's Hopyard IPA, named
after a popular hiking area in New Hampshire.

Malt bill:
American two-row malt 85%
Briess 40 °L crystal malt 10%
Briess CaraPils malt 5%

Mashing and lautering:
Using a water-to-grain ratio of 2.8/1 (1.35 qt./lb.), add 0.026 oz./gal. (0.05
lb./bbl., 0.19 g/L) gypsum to the mash water. An upward infusion mash
profile is employed. Mash hop with a ratio of 0.06 oz./gal. (0.11 lb./bbl., 0.43
g/L) Palisades hop pellets. Mash in at 95° F (35° C). Raise temperature to
150° F (66° C) in 15 minutes and hold for 15 minutes. Raise the temperature
again to 163° F (73° C) in 10 minutes prior to lautering.

Kettle boil and hopping:
Total boil time is 60 minutes. Note that Anheuser-Busch used shorter boil
times due to wort strippers later in the process. A 90-minute boil would be
more appropriate in a homebrew recipe. Add .026 oz./gal. (0.05 lb./bbl.,
0.19 g/L) gypsum to the wort with the first hop addition. Total kettle hopping
rate is 1.46 lb./bbl. The first addition of 15.8% Cascade and 10.5% Palisade is
added at 60 minutes. At 50 minutes add 15.8% Cascade and 31.5% Columbus.
Third addition is 8.4% Cascade and 7.4% Columbus at 40 minutes. The final
addition at 10 minutes is 5.3% each of Cascade and Columbus.

Fermentation and aging:
Cool wort to 65° F (18° C) and pitch with a ratio of 17 million cells/mL with
NCYC1044 Ale Yeast. Ferment at 72° F (22° C). After primary fermentation,

rack off yeast and cool beer to 50° F (10° C). Dry hop with Cascade at a ratio of 0.35 oz./gal. (0.675 lb./bbl., 2.61 g/L) and Columbus at a ratio of 0.12 oz./gal. (0.23 lb./bbl., 0.89 g/L).

Analytical targets:
OG: 16.2 °P (1.065 SG)
TG: 3.5 °P (1.014 SG)
ADF: 78.4%
IBU: 120 (calculated), 70 in finished beer
ABV: 7%
Color: 14 °L (26.6° EBC)

FIRESTONE WALKER UNION JACK IPA

Firestone Walker brews some of the best West Coast IPAs. Brewmaster Matt Brynildson, a Siebel grad who brewed for Goose Island in Chicago before moving to California, worked for a time with noted hop processor Kalsec. Brynildson brings a lot of technical expertise to the beers at Firestone Walker, and he uses his experience to craft some of the best hoppy ales—and blended, wood-aged ales, too. He also is the only brewer in the United States who replicates the Burton Union fermentation system by doing a modified version of the primary fermentation in oak barrels. Brynildson likes to use some Munich malt in his grain bills to get an English malt character. Sometimes he lightens the color and body with a small (up to 5%) dextrose addition, which accentuates the hop flavor.

Brewing liquor:
Reverse osmosis–filtered water is treated with calcium (in the form of calcium chloride and/or gypsum) to take total calcium above 100 ppb. Acidify by adding phosphoric or lactic acid to achieve a mash pH of 5.4.

Malt bill:
American or Canadian two-row malt 88%
Munich malt 6%
Briess CaraPils malt 3%
Simpson 30/40 °L crystal malt 3%

Mashing and lautering:
This recipe employs a two-step conversion rest. Raise the mash temperature to 145° F (63° C) for 45–60 minutes and then rest a second time at 155° F (68° C).

Kettle boil and hopping:
At the start of the boil add Magnum, Warrior, and/or CTZ, calculating to

50 IBU at 5% alpha acids. At 30 minutes, use Cascade at 6% alpha acids, calculated to 14 IBU, and the same quantity of Centennial at 15 minutes. Brynildson will occasionally use purified isolone hop extract if he is having trouble hitting the 75 IBU mark. During the whirlpool, add a 50/50 blend of Cascade and Centennial at a ratio of .41 oz./gal. (0.8 lb./bbl., 3 g/L).

Fermentation and aging:

Cool wort to 63° F (17° C). Pitch with a London Ale strain or another soft and fruity ale yeast. Ferment at 66° F (19° C). At 6 °P, allow the temperature to rise to 70° F (21° C) for diacetyl reduction and dry hopping. When the beer is 0.5–1.0 °P above terminal gravity, dry hop with Centennial, Cascade, and small amounts of Amarillo and Simcoe at a ratio of 0.5 oz./gal. (1 lb./bbl., 3.87 g/L) total. Remove hops and yeast after three days of contact time. Using the same blend, dry hop again and hold for three days maximum before crash cooling. Brynildson is a big believer in short contact time with dry hops.

Analytical targets:

OG: 16.5 °P (1.066 SG)
TG: 3.0 °P (1.012 SG)
ADF: 81.8%
IBU: 75 in finished beer
ABV: 7.5%
Color: 8 °L (15.2° EBC)

CONTEMPORARY BRITISH RECIPES

MEANTIME BREWING LONDON IPA

Alastair Hook and Peter Haydon at the Meantime Brewery in Greenwich, United Kingdom, have researched the history of IPA extensively. In fact, their website, www.india-pale-ale.com, provides a nice history of IPA from its origins in London through present day. Hook was trained at both Heriot-Watt and Weihenstephan brewing schools, and he brews excellent lagers and ales, including authentic re-creations of the London porter and the 1800s IPA.

Meantime IPA is based on what Hook and Haydon learned in their research. When introduced, it was one of the first IPAs in recent years to be brewed to the English IPA specifications from the 1800s. At 7.45% abv, it is a big beer—especially by current English brewing standards. It is brewed with pale malt and small proportions of Munich malt, light crystal malt, and sugar, which makes the grain bill similar to the London IPAs of the late 1800s and the early 1900s. Hopping is massive—described at more than 2 pounds per barrel, or "as many hops as we can get into the copper." They use only East Kent Goldings and Fuggle for the brewhouse additions and the dry hop.

Brewing liquor:
Adjust brewing liquor to the following targets:

Calcium as Ca	~72 ppm
Magnesium as Mg	~1 ppm
Carbonate as CO_3	~35 ppm
Sulfate as SO_4	~119 ppm
Chloride as Cl	~10 ppm
Alkalinity as $CaCO_3$	~58 ppm
Total hardness	~67 ppm

Malt bill:
English ale malt 84%
English Munich malt 9%
English pale crystal malt 1%
Sugar 6%

Mashing and lautering:
Use an upward infusion and a water-to-grain ratio of 3.1/1 (1.49 qt./gal.). Mash in at 144° F (62° C). Hold for 30 minutes, then ramp in 30 minutes to 162° F (72° C). Hold at 162° F (72° C) for 20 minutes, then increase the temperature in 5 minutes to 171° F (77° C). Mash off or start the lautering process.

Kettle boil and hopping:
Total boil time is 75 minutes. Add 12.6% Goldings T90 (5.1% alpha acids) and 13.8% Fuggle T90 (4.7% alpha acids) pellets to the first wort. At 5 minutes before the end of the boil, add 20.3% Goldings T90 (5.1% alpha acids) and 21.9% Fuggle T90 (4.7% alpha acids) pellets. To the hopback add 15.7% each of whole Goldings (6.8% alpha acids) and whole Fuggle hops (3.8% alpha acids).

Fermentation and aging:
Use an English heritage ale strain for fermentation. Ferment at 72° F (22° C) until at terminal gravity. Hold at terminal gravity for 48 hours, then rack off yeast and dry hop with Goldings whole leaf at a ratio of 0.097 oz./gal. (0.188 lb./bbl., 1 g/L) and Fuggle whole leaf at a ratio of 0.097 oz./gal. (0.188 lb./bbl., 1 g/L).

Analytical targets:
OG: 16.8 °P (1.067 SG)
TG: 3.0 °P (1.012 SG)
ADF: 82%
IBU: 75
ABV: 7.4%
Color: 6–8 °L (11.8–15.8° SRM)

THORNBRIDGE JAIPUR INDIA PALE ALE

Thornbridge Brewing Company is located in the Derbyshire area of England, near the town of Bakewell in the Peak District, a place well known for hiking trails and the Bakewell Tart (an almond tart similar to a pecan pie). Simon Webster and James Harrison, a former gasket maker from Sheffield, founded Thornbridge in 2005. Their first brewery, Thornbridge Hall, was located on Harrison's estate. Recently, they built the larger Riverside Brewery closer to the town of Bakewell.

Their beers have gained renown in England not only for being extremely well crafted and delicious, but also for daringly using American and New Zealand hops—and for combining the best of English brewing traditions with newer ingredients and beer styles popularized in America. Their motto is Innovation, Passion, and Knowledge, and they strive to put the science of brewing into all their beers.

Thornbridge Jaipur IPA is a wonderful version of an IPA with pronounced hop flavor and character. It starts off malty, but hops take over quickly and dominate the finish. The Thornbridge Seaforth IPA, a more traditional IPA, is no longer brewed. Made with 100% English ingredients, it was darker than many IPAs and very hoppy. It was named Seaforth by author Pete Brown, because that was the name of one of the first ships that carried Allsopp's India Ale to Calcutta in 1823. Interestingly enough, neither of the IPAs presented here are dry hopped. But don't be fooled—these are hop-forward, wonderful versions of IPA.

Brewing liquor:
Adjust brewing liquor to the following targets:
Ca_2+ 199 ppm
Mg_2+ 20 ppm
Cl-   123 ppm
Na_2+ 30 ppm

SO_4^- 412 ppm
HCO_3^- 17 ppm

Malt bill:
Maris Otter low-color pale ale malt 3.5° EBC (1.75 °L) 96.7%
Vienna malt 10° EBC (5 °L) 3.3%

Mashing and lautering:
Using a water-to-grain ratio of 2.5/1 (1.2 qt./lb.), make a thick mash with a single-temperature infusion profile. Do a conversion rest at 149° F (65° C) for 75 minutes. Sparge with 169° F (76° C) water.

Kettle boil and hopping:
Total boil time is 75 minutes. Use whole cone hops if possible. For the first addition, add 7.3% Chinook (12.7% alpha acids), 5.2% Centennial (11.7% alpha acids), and 6.2% Ahtanum (5% alpha acids). For the second addition, 30 minutes into the boil, add 7.3% Chinook (12.7% alpha acids), 5.2% Centennial (11.7% alpha acids), and 6.2% Ahtanum (5% alpha acids). At the end of the boil make the last addition after turning off the heat source. Add 21.9% Chinook (12.7% alpha acids), 15.7% Centennial (11.7% alpha acids), and 25% Ahtanum (5% alpha acids). Then stir and leave to steep for 30 minutes before starting the wort cooling.

Fermentation and aging:
Use a neutral ale yeast that attenuates well and produces little to no diacetyl. Pitching rate should be around 6–7 million cells/mL. Allow to ferment in the primary at 66° F (19° C) for four to five days. Cool to 43° F (6° C), then remove the yeast by dumping or racking the beer off. Mature for 7–10 days, racking into casks with an addition of isinglass. Note that there is no dry hopping in this recipe. Condition at 43° F (6° C) for one to two weeks, then serve at 50° F (10° C) from a hand pump after the cask has settled and the beer has vented.

Analytical targets:
OG: 13.9 °P (1.055 SG)
TG: 2.5 °P (1.010 SG)
ADF: 82%
IBU: 55–57
ABV: 6%

THORNBRIDGE SEAFORTH IPA

Brewing liquor:
Adjust brewing liquor to the following targets:

Ca   199 ppm
Mg   20 ppm
Cl   123 ppm
Na   30 ppm
SO_4 412 ppm
HCO_3 17 ppm

Malt bill:
Maris Otter pale malt 95.2%
Thomas Fawcett crystal malt 120 °L 3.2%
Thomas Fawcett amber malt 100 °L 1.2%
Thomas Fawcett chocolate malt 0.4%

Mashing and lautering:
Using a water-to-grain ratio of 2.4/1 (1.15 qt./lb.), make a thick, single-temperature infusion mash. Make a conversion rest at 148° F (65° C) for 45 minutes, then sparge with treated water at 169° F (76° C).

Kettle boil and hopping:
Total boil time is 75 minutes. Using whole cone hops if possible, make the first hop addition at the start of the boil by using 4.5% Pilgrim (10.9% alpha acids), 4.5% Centennial (11.7% alpha acids), and 9.8% Styrian Goldings (5% alpha acids). Add the second addition 30 minutes into the boil and use 4.5% Pilgrim (10.9% alpha acids), 4.5% Centennial (11.7% alpha acids), and 9.8% Styrian Goldings (5% alpha acids). Add the last addition after turning off the heat source, and use 26.7% Pilgrim (10.9% alpha acids), 13.4% Centennial (11.7% alpha acids), and 22.3% Styrian Goldings (5% alpha acids). Stir and steep for 30 minutes before starting the wort cooling. Head brewer Stefano Cossi recommends experimenting with the final hop addition. He suggests trying other hop varieties such as Target, First Gold, Perle, Northdown, and Challenger.

Fermentation and aging:
Ferment with a neutral ale yeast that attenuates well and produces little to no diacetyl. Pitch at a rate of around 6–7 million cells/mL and ferment in the primary 66° F (19° C) for four to five days. Cool to 43° F (6° C) and remove the yeast by dumping or racking the beer off. Mature for 7–10 days, and rack into casks with an addition of isinglass. Note that there is no dry hop in this recipe. Condition at 43° F (6° C) for one to two weeks, then serve at 50° F (10° C) from a hand pump after the cask has settled and the beer has vented.

Analytical targets:
OG: 14 °P (1.056 SG)
TG: 2.5 °P (1.010 SG)
ADF: 82.1%
IBU: 50–52
ABV: 6.04%

FULLER'S BENGAL LANCER IPA

Fuller, Smith & Turner (known conventionally as "Fuller's") is located in West London. The Griffin Brewery resides on the banks of the Thames in the Chiswick district. The head brewer, John Keeling, and the brewing manager, Derek Prentice, have been more than generous in sharing information. They recently began producing Past Masters beers, which are based on historical recipes that Keeling showed me when I visited in the winter of 2010.

Fuller's brewed a substantial amount of IPA in the second half of the 1800s. Established in 1845 on a site that has been home to a brewery for more than 350 years, Fuller's is one of the last remaining practitioners of parti-gyle brewing, the technique of brewing separate worts from the same mash, then blending them together in various portions after the boil to create distinctly different beers. The brewery used this procedure when it opened in 1845 and continues to employ it to this day. Although historians are not sure that Fuller's IPA actually shipped to India (Fuller's started brewing IPA when domestic demand was peaking), its procedures appear to be similar to many of its London peers.

In the 1890s Fuller's used pale malt (often sourced from California or Central Europe), flaked corn, and sugar. Two mashes were used from the same batch of malt, and the hops were a blend of new and older Goldings. The beer was fermented with a culture of yeast that originated from Burton, which was later identified as having three distinct strains; over time this culture was isolated to one pure strain. After fermentation, the IPA was aged in barrels. The tour center at present-day Fuller's was the old Hock Cellar, where barrels were aged. The brewery rolled the barrels daily until the beer was at proper maturity to ship to market.

Due to the temperance movement and the increasing popularity of lower-alcohol pale lagers and running beers, IPA gravity dropped during the late 1800s, as did the gravities of other English beers. By 1891 the original gravity was 1.060, and by 1900 it was down to 1.053.

I had the opportunity to sample this modern IPA with Keeling at the brewery, and it was wonderful, with nice bittering hops and a very pronounced tangerine-like hop aroma. When I asked Keeling about the hop schedule, he indicated that he had used Goldings, Fuggle, and Target hops. I assumed that Target hops were selected for their bittering properties, but Keeling said he used Target in the dry hop! Definitely out of the box, and an inspiration for me: I used Target in the dry hop of our Stone 14th Anniversary Emperial IPA.

Brewing liquor:
Fuller's starts with Thames water, which is high in calcium carbonate and bicarbonate. The brewery reduces carbonate by replacing it with sulfate and adding a low level of chlorides. Further salt additions of gypsum (calcium sulfate) or calcium chloride are added to both the mash and the kettle, depending on the beer being brewed. The main base parameters are less than 90 ppm of carbonate and over 180 ppm of calcium.

Malt bill:
Pale ale malt 98%
Crystal malt 2%

Mashing and lautering:
Use a water-to-grain ratio of 2.5/1 (1.20 qt./lb.) for a traditional British infusion mash. Conversion temperature is 145–150° F (63–66° C). (Derek Prentice says, "This is 2.25 bbl./qtr. [imperial] in old money!")

Kettle boil and hopping:
Total boil time is 60 minutes, plus an additional 8 minutes for a late hop addition. The first addition of 75% Goldings is added at the start of the boil. Add the second addition of 25% Fuggle at the end of 60 minutes and hold for 8 minutes before the whirlpool.

Fermentation and aging:
Ferment with Fuller's Ale strain or a similar yeast. Pitch at 63° F (17° C) and allow to rise to 68° F (20° C) to completely attenuate. Dry hop using a 50/50 blend of Goldings and Target T90 pellets added at a rate of 0.22 oz./gal. (0.43 lb./bbl., 3.22 g/L, 0.5 lb./imperial bbl.).

Analytical targets:
OG: 13.25 °P (1.053 SG)

TG: 3 °P (1.012 SG)
ADF: 77.4%
IBU: 50 (beer)
ABV: 5.3%
Color: 10.7 °L (21° EBC)

MUSEUM BREWING COMPANY CALCUTTA IPA

Brewing in the Museum Brewery of Bass (now Coors) in Burton-on-Trent starting in 1994, Steve Wellington is a veteran of British brewing. Wellington's career started at Tuborg Breweries and Canada Breweries before joining Bass in 1971. Wellington got what he calls "the opportunity of a lifetime" when he was asked to start Bass' microbrewery at the museum in Burton-on-Trent. He has brewed there until his retirement in 2011.

Wellington worked with author Pete Brown to develop and brew this recipe for Brown's re-creation of the IPA sea journey from the United Kingdom to Calcutta, which is detailed in Brown's book *Hops and Glory*. The starting point for this beer was Bass' old Continental Ale/IPA recipe, last brewed in the 1950s.

"We only did three barrels (108 U.K. gallons). Calcutta IPA is 7% abv and features a reasonable bitterness without going over the top," says Wellington. "After three months at sea, apparently the beer was superb in Calcutta." A nine-gallon cask was flown there (14 hours) and the two were compared. "There was no question that the beer on the ship was much better than the beer by plane."

Brewing liquor:
Use Burton well water and 400 ppm $CaSO_4$ and 360 ppm $MgSO_4$.

Malt bill:
Pale ale malt 97.8%
Crystal (Caramalt) malt 2.2%

Mashing and lautering:
Using a water-to-grain ratio of 2.6/1 (1.25 qt./lb.), employ a single-infusion mash profile. Mash in with 162° F (72° C) water and hold at 150° F (66° C) for 90 minutes. Start draw-off to kettle. Target a 90-minute draw-off. First-wort gravity should be 23 °P (1.092 SG). Sparge with 162° F (72° C) water. Last runnings should not be below 1.5 °P (1.006 SG).

Kettle boil and hopping:
Total boil time is 2 hours. Add invert sugar with the hops at the start of the boil at a ratio of 9 oz./gal. (17.6 lb./bbl., 68 g/L). Add 31.5% Fuggle (6.1% alpha acids) and 37% Goldings (5.2% alpha acids) at the beginning of the boil. Five minutes prior to the end of the boil add 31.5% Northdown (8.6% alpha acids).

Fermentation and aging:
Chill wort to 62° F (16° C) and pitch with Burton Union Dual Strain yeast. Allow the temperature to rise to 68° F (20° C), and maintain that temperature for primary fermentation. Allow the beer to ferment to 2.5 °P (1.010 SG), then chill to 43° F (6° C). Hold at 43° F (6° C) for one week. Rack into casks, dry hop, and hold for four weeks.

Analytical targets:
OG: 16.25 °P (1.065 SG)
TG: 2.5 °P (1.010 SG)
ADF: 84.6%
IBU: 55
ABV: 7%

DOUBLE IPA RECIPES

RUSSIAN RIVER PLINY THE ELDER

Considered by many to be the standard for the double IPA style, Russian River Brewing Company's Pliny the Elder is one of the first brews in the U.S. craft-brewing world to use dextrose powder in the brewing process (it lowers the malt intensity and allows the hops to be more forward). Pliny the Elder has won numerous awards over the years.

Brewing liquor:
Russian River uses Santa Rosa, California, city water with some gypsum added.

Malt bill:
Two-row malt 86%
Crystal malt 40 °L 4%
CaraPils malt 4%
Dextrose 6%

Mashing and lautering:
Employ an infusion mash at 152–153° F (66.7–67.2° C).

Kettle boil and hopping:

Total boil time is 90 minutes. Add the first hop addition, 40% CTZ, at the beginning of the boil. Use Simcoe, 9% of the hop bill, at 45 minutes, and 11% Centennial at 30 minutes. The final hop addition, 40% of the bill, is a blend of Cascade, Simcoe, Amarillo, and Centennial added at the end of the boil.

Fermentation and aging:

Ferment at 68° F (20° C) with California Ale yeast (WLP001 or WY1056). Dry hop at a rate of 0.5 oz./gal. (1 lb./bbl., 3.9 g/L) with equal proportions of CTZ, Centennial, and Simcoe pellets. Hold for 14 days. Note that Russian River uses a double-dry-hop method where they add about 25% of the first dry-hop rate in a second dry hop to enhance the hop character. They frequently adjust the timing and amounts of the hops used in the dry hops, depending on the hop quality, so I decided not to include any more specifics on this process.

Analytical targets:

OG: 17.25 °P (1.069 SG)
TG: 2.75 °P (1.011 SG)
ADF: 84%
IBU: 92
ABV: 8%

ONE MAN'S MISTAKE IS ANOTHER MAN'S HOPPY PLEASURE

Tim Rastetter of Thirsty Dog Brewing Company in Akron, Ohio, is a craft-brewing industry veteran. (He started his career at Great Lakes Brewery in Cleveland in 1992.) His VIP Ale, brewed in 1996, is one of the first versions of an imperial IPA. The story of this beer is another great example of a happy accident.

After brewing on systems with low brewhouse efficiency at both Great Lakes and Akron's Liberty Street Brewing Company, Rastetter was given the opportunity in 1996 to design his own brewhouse at BrewWorks at the Party Source, then in Covington, Kentucky (just across the Ohio River from Cincinnati). To better handle high-gravity beers, he redesigned the lauter tun. He brewed his first high-gravity beer (his fourth brew, an IPA) and noticed he got much better efficiency than he expected. As he lautered this IPA, Rastetter realized the gravity was going to be much higher than he planned—and that he had a bit of a monster on his hands. Since this was a first-ever brew, nobody had any expectations of this beer, so he did all he could to make the best out of it. He threw in more hops! Not having time to calculate everything, he knew he was going to have an approximately 19 °P beer, which reduces the bitterness. So he erred on the side of—what else?—hops! By the time it was done, the calculations came out to around 95 IBU.

In Tim Rastetter's Own Words

It was wonderful to see the local crowd enjoying my mistake. I knew now I had an audience with which to have fun. I wanted to balance out the future brews and told a few customers of my intentions. None of them wanted me to change a thing, but I still did.

I actually mashed subsequent brews a little warmer to leave a few more unfermentables in the beer, thus balancing out the extreme bitterness. So nobody would notice the perceived drop in bitterness, I decided to—you guessed it—add more hops. Final calculations totaled 110 IBU. I also added more grain to boost the Plato to 20.

Once I was giving a brewery tour to a number of high-profile brewers, magazine publishers, and owners, and I took samples of the VIP Ale from the fermenter and distributed them to the group. One of the individuals in the group took his sample and walked away with it. Everyone stayed around the fermenter and proceeded to taste this 110 IBU beer. While tasting we heard a laugh from the individual who had walked away. He was returning to the group with a big smile on his face and confessed that he walked away so he could dump the beer, as he had tasted so many overly hoppy, unbalanced IPAs. Having never heard of IBUs at the level I had mentioned, he had prepared himself not to like it. He congratulated me on the beer and had a refill, which of course prompted everyone else to do the same. [Author's note: I believe I was there that day, and I won't name the individual whom Tim speaks of . . . but I think his initials are Daniel Bradford.]

As a side note, I still couldn't believe my efficiencies on that IPA, and until I got it all sorted out, I made another error and created a huge porter. It was as big as the VIP Ale, and it appropriately got named R.I.P. (for Russian Imperial Porter).

VIP ALE (OR VERY INDIA PALE ALE)

Brewing liquor:
Add minerals to bring water to these specifications:

Calcium	100–150 ppm
Magnesium	20 ppm
Sodium	25 ppm
Sulfate	300–425 ppm
Carbonate	0 ppm
Chloride	16 ppm

Malt bill:
Two-row malt 89.66%
Briess CaraPils malt 3.45%
Wheat malt 3.45%

Briess Victory malt 1.72%
Caramel malt 60 °L 1.72%

Mashing and lautering:
Using a water-to-grain ratio of 3.22/1 (1.55 qt./lb.), employ an infusion mash. Mash in at 151° F (66° C) for 60 minutes.

Kettle boil and hopping:
Total boil time is 90 minutes. At the start of the boil add 20.4% Magnum (15.2% alpha acids). Then add 12.6% English Northdown (8% alpha acids) at 30 minutes and 20% Fuggle (4.9% alpha acids) at 15 minutes. Make an addition at 10 minutes of 20% Hallertau (3.8% alpha acids). During the whirlpool, add 27% Goldings (4.5% alpha acids).

Fermentation and aging:
Ferment with WY1028 at 70° F (21° C). There is no dry hop in this beer.

Analytical targets:
OG: 20 °P (1.080 SG)
TG: 4.8 °P (1.019 SG)
ADF: 76%
IBU: 110 (calculated)
ABV: 8.3%
Color: 6.7 °L (13.2° EBC)

PIZZA PORT HOP 15

Pizza Port's Hop 15, a double IPA, is famous for using 15 different hop varieties in the brewing process in an unusual 3.5-hour boil. Tomme Arthur and Jeff Bagby originally brewed Hop 15 in 2002 to celebrate the 15th anniversary of the opening of the Pizza Port Solana Beach, California, location. "We took the grist from one of our house pale ales and pumped everything up. It ended up as this giant IPA with a ton of hop character," says Bagby. The original recipe featured 15 ounces of 15 different hop varieties added every 15 minutes. The beer was draft only (brewpub) and not widely distributed until Port Brewing opened. It is a two-time GABF silver medalist (2003, 2005) and a bronze medalist (2008), all for the Imperial/Double IPA category. Hop 15 was crowned Alpha King in 2008, and finished second in 2009.

Brewing liquor:
Solana Beach city water is treated with a reverse osmosis unit to take total dissolved solids (TDS) to about 300 ppm.

Malt bill:
American two-row malt 95%
Crisp malt 15 °L 5%
Dextrose 3.5 oz./gal. (6 lb./bbl., 25.8 g/L) enough to get OG to 22 °P

Mashing and lautering:
Use an infusion mash at a low temperature, 146–148° F (63–64° C), for 60 minutes, including vorlauf time.

Kettle boil and hopping:
Boil wort for 3.5 hours and add hops every 15 minutes after the start of the boil. Hops used are Challenger, Goldings, Chinook, Tettnang, Magnum, Phoenix, Sterling, Cascade, Centennial, Simcoe, Columbus, Galena, Amarillo, Saaz, and Aurora.

Fermentation and aging:
Pitch a 50/50 blend of California Ale yeast (WLP001 or WY1056) and the Port proprietary ale strain or a similar yeast. Another yeast option is WLP090 San Diego Super Yeast. Ferment at 67° F (19.4° C) until fermentation is 50% complete, then allow fermentation to free rise to 72° F (22° C). Use Centennial at a ratio of 0.52 oz./gal. (1 lb./bbl., 3.87 g/L) and Simcoe at a ratio of 0.52 oz./gal. (1 lb./bbl., 3.87 g/L) for dry hopping. Hold beer on dry hops for 10 days.

Analytical targets:
OG: 22 °P (1.088 SG)
TG: 3 °P (1.012 SG)
ADF: 86.4%
IBU: 71 (as analyzed in finished beer)
ABV: 10%
Color: 10 °L (19.7° EBC)

SMUTTYNOSE BIG A IPA

Smuttynose Brewing Company was one of the first East Coast brewers to release a double IPA in the West Coast style. Dave Yarrington follows the lead of many Southern California brewers by avoiding the use of any specialty malts in his recipe and instead employing a complex blend of American hop varieties to make a double IPA almost 10% abv and over 100 IBU.

"With the Big A IPA we stick to a similar hopping pattern—utilizing slightly different hops—but drop the crystal malt entirely," says Yarrington. We find that a beer starting at 21 °P will have plenty of sweetness for the increased malt and alcohol content, thus allowing us to create a 120 IBU beer without it being overly cloying."

Brewing liquor:
Add gypsum at a ratio of 0.08 oz./gal. (2.3 g/gal.).

Malt bill:
Two-row malt 80%
Pale ale malt 20%

Mashing and lautering:
Using a water-to-grain ratio of 2.66/1 (1.28 qt./gal.), employ an infusion mash with a 40-minute rest at 154° F (68° C).

Kettle boil and hopping:
Total boil time is 75 minutes. Add 17.5% Magnum pellets and 14.3% Cascade pellets at the start of the boil. Use 53.4% Bravo pellets in equal amounts every 5 minutes for the last 30 minutes of the boil and 14.8% CTZ pellets during the whirlpool.

Fermentation and aging:
Ferment at 64° F (18° C) with American Ale yeast until terminal gravity is reached. Dry hop with Glacier, Nugget, and Centennial added in equal amounts for a total of 1.6 oz./gal. (3.1 lb./bbl., 12 g/L). Add these hops as pellets into the fermenter after primary fermentation and keep at 64° F (18° C) for seven days. Then crash cool for another 14 days on the hops.

Analytical targets:
OG: 21 °P (1.084 SG)
TG: 4 °P (1.016 SG)
ADF: 81%
IBU: 120 (calculated)
ABV: 9.8%
Color: 13.4 °L (26.4° EBC)

BREWDOG HARDCORE IPA

When James Watt and Martin Dickie started BrewDog in 2007, they set out to break from English brewing standards and customs and brew assertive, American-style craft beers. They embrace controversial viewpoints and present their beers with a unique sense of humor—thus earning them much notoriety. But make no mistake; they are serious brewers who brew excellent, groundbreaking beers. In addition to their original brewery in Fraserburgh, Scotland, they now own four craft-beer bars in the United Kingdom and are planning a large production brewery near Aberdeen.

Hardcore IPA, touted as an "Explicit Imperial Ale" with "more hops and bitterness than any other beer brewed in the U.K," is also described as "hopped to Hell, and then dry hopped to Hell, too." Brewed with extra pale and crystal malts, and Columbus, Centennial, and Simcoe hops, Hardcore IPA won a gold medal in the 2010 World Beer Cup Double IPA category.

Brewing liquor:
Burtonize the water with salts.

Malt bill:
Maris Otter low-color pale malt 90%
Caramalt 6.5%
Crystal malt 3.5%

Mashing and lautering:
Mash on the dry side; because it is a big grain bill, it needs to fit! Use a single-temperature infusion mash at 149° F (65° C).

Kettle boil and hopping:
Total boil is 75 minutes. Using T90 pellets for all additions, add 21% Columbus and 21% Centennial at the start of the boil. After 10 minutes, add 5.3% each of Columbus and Centennial. The final addition at the end of the boil is 15.8% of each, Columbus, Centennial, and Simcoe.

Fermentation and aging:
Ferment at 68° F (20° C) using an American Ale yeast strain and dry hop with Columbus pellets in a ratio of 0.23 oz./gal. (0.43 lb./bbl., 1.7 g/L). Hold on hops for four to five days, then chill the beer and remove the hops when they settle out.

Analytical targets:
OG: 20.75 °P (1.083 SG)
TG: 3.5 °P (1.014 SG)
ADF: 83%
IBU: 148 (calculated)
ABV: 9%
Color: 9.9 °L (19.5° EBC)

STONE RUINATION IPA

Released in June 2002, Stone Ruination IPA was the first regularly bottled imperial or double IPA in the world.

Brewing liquor:
Use municipal water (~300 ppm hardness) that has been carbon filtered and reverse osmosis treated to reduce hardness to 100 ppm.

Malt bill:
Pale malt 94.2%
Crystal malt 15 °L 5.8%

Mashing and lautering:
Using a water-to-grain ratio of 2.93/1 (1.41 qt./lb.), employ an upward infusion mash with a 30-minute rest at 152° F (67° C). Raise the temperature to 165° F (74° C) for mash-off.

Kettle boil and hopping:
Total boil time is 90 minutes. Using only pellets, add 62.5% Columbus at the start of the boil, then add 37.5% Centennial during the whirlpool.

Fermentation and aging:
Use the Stone Brewing Co. house yeast strain (or WLP007 and WLP002 are acceptable alternatives). Ferment at 72° F (22° C) until 3.1 °P (1.012 SG). Chill to 62° F (17° C) for 24 hours and rack off yeast. Dry hop with Centennial at a ratio of 0.52 oz./gal. (1 lb./bbl., 3.86 g/L). Hold for 36 hours and chill to 34° F (1° C). Hold for seven days.

Analytical targets:
OG: 17.8 °P (1.071 SG)
TG: 2.9 °P (1.012 SG)
ADF: 83.71%
IBU: 105
ABV: 7.8%
Color: 10 °L (19.7° EBC)

STONE 14th ANNIVERSARY EMPERIAL IPA

After learning so much about historical IPAs during the research phase for this book, I was inspired to brew this beer for Stone Brewing Co.'s 14th anniversary celebration. We imported one-ton Super Sack containers of British extra pale malt from two English maltsters, used East Kent Goldings hops, and taking a page from Fuller's, added some Target hops in the dry hop. We also heavily Burtonized the water and used an English Ale yeast strain to ferment the beer. It was an exciting beer to brew, and despite the "drink fresh" recommendation on the label, it still tastes great more than a year from release.

Brewing liquor:
Use municipal water (~300 ppm hardness) that is carbon filtered and reverse osmosis treated to reduce hardness to 100 ppm. Burtonize mash water with calcium sulfate at a ratio of 0.11 oz./gal. (0.21 lb./bbl., 0.81g/L) and calcium chloride at a ratio of 0.08 oz./gal. (0.15 lb./bbl., 0.57 g/L) to target 650 ppm sulfate and 400 ppm calcium.

Malt bill:
British white/extra pale malt 100%

Mashing and lautering:
With a water-to-grain ratio of 2.80/1 (1.35 qt./lb.), utilize an upward infusion mash with a 150-minute rest at 148° F (64° C), then raise the temperature to 165° F (75° C) for mash-off.

Kettle boil and hopping:
Total boil time is 90 minutes. Use 100% English hops in pellet form. At the start of the boil add 13.7% Boadicea (5.8% alpha acids) and 60% Target (91.5% alpha acids). During the whirlpool, add 26.3% East Kent Goldings (5.5% alpha acids).

Fermentation and aging:
Pitch with WY1028 or WLP 013 London Ale yeast. Ferment at 68° F (20° C) until 2.7 °P (1.011 SG). Chill to 62° F (17° C) for 24 hours, then rack off yeast. Dry hop using a ratio of 0.26 oz./gal. (0.5 lb./bbl., 1.9 g/L) for East Kent Goldings and 0.39 oz./gal. (0.75 lb./bbl., 2.9 g/L) ratio for Target hops. Hold for 36 hours, then chill to 34° F (1.1° C). Hold for 10 days.

Analytical targets:
OG: 19 °P (1.076 SG)
TG: 2.5 °P (1.010 SG)
ADF: 86.8%
IBU: 105
ABV: 8.9%
Color: 9.5 °L (18.7° EBC)

STONE 10TH ANNIVERSARY IPA

Stone 10th Anniversary IPA was the first anniversary ale that I was involved with after I joined Stone in the winter of 2006. The lead brewer,

John Egan, and the facilities manager, Bill Sherwood, both brewed pilot brews for recipe development. Both used the Summit hop—a brand-new variety that year—at 100%. We chose Egan's malt recipe, but as a group we thought the hopping needed some more complexity—and something to reduce the oniony character of the Summit hop—so we added some Simcoe, Crystal, and Chinook for flavoring and dry hop. We also bumped up the alcohol by volume to target 10%, since it was our 10th anniversary! It turned out to be one of our most popular anniversary ales and is frequently requested for re-brew, especially by members of Team Stone. But we have yet to pull the trigger on brewing it again.

Brewing liquor:
Use municipal water (~300 ppm hardness) that is carbon filtered and reverse osmosis treated to reduce hardness to 100 ppm.

Malt bill:
Pale malt 93.6%
Victory malt 6.4%

Mashing and lautering:
Using a water-to-grain ratio of 2.96/1 (1.42 qt./lb.), employ an upward infusion mash with a 60-minute rest at 150° F (65.6° C), then raise the temperature to 165° F (73.9° C) for mash-off.

Kettle boil and hopping:
Total boil time is 90 minutes. Use 100% pellets and add 26% Summit at the start of the boil. During the whirlpool, add 37% each of Chinook and Crystal.

Fermentation and aging:
Use the Stone Brewing Co. house yeast strain (or WLP007 and WLP002 are acceptable alternatives). Ferment at 72° F (22.2° C) until 4.2 °P (1.013 SG). Chill to 62° F (16.7° C) for 24 hours, then rack off yeast. Dry hop using Simcoe hops with a ratio of 0.52 oz./gal. (1.0 lb./bbl., 2.86 g/L) and Crystal with 0.26 oz./gal. (0.5 lb./bbl., 1.43 g/L). Hold for 36 hours and circulate or agitate three times at 12-hour intervals. After 36 hours, chill to 34° F (1.1° C) and hold for seven days.

Analytical targets:
OG: 24 °P (1.096 SG)
TG: 4 °P (1.016 SG)
ADF: 82.5%
ABV: 10%
IBU: 95
Color: 15 °L (30° EBC)

BLACK IPA RECIPES

VERMONT PUB AND BREWERY BLACKWATCH IPA

This is the recipe for the original craft-brewed black IPA.

Brewing liquor:
Source water for this beer at Vermont Pub and Brewery has a pH of 6.5, 46 ppm alkalinity, 65 ppm hardness, 40 ppm chloride, and 28 ppm carbonate. Treat with 2 g/gal. calcium sulfate, 0.06 g/gal. calcium chloride, and 0.21 mL/gal. 85% lactic acid. Treated water targets are 30 ppm alkalinity, 500 ppm hardness, 50 ppm chloride, and 18 ppm carbonate.

Malt bill:
Thomas Fawcett Maris Otter pale malt 72.7%
Best Malz pale wheat malt 13%
Thomas Fawcett crystal malt 7.3%
Thomas Fawcett chocolate malt 7%

Mashing and lautering:
Use a water-to-grain ratio of 2.58/1 (1.24 qt./lb.). Target a pH of 5.25 in the mash and hold a conversion rest at 149° F (65° C) for 1 hour. Finish by sparging with 172° F (78° C) water.

Kettle boil and hopping:
Total boil time is 90 minutes. Add 27% Chinook pellets (11.1% alpha acids) at the beginning of the boil. At 45 minutes, add 44% Horizon pellets (10.25% alpha acids). Fifteen minutes before the end of the boil, add 0.2 g/gal. Irish moss. At the end of the boil, add 29% whole hop Fuggle (4.5% alpha acids).

Fermentation and aging:
Pitch at 15 million cells/mL the "Conan" ale yeast (the Vermont Pub and Brewery's and The Alchemist's house strain) or a suitable alternative. Ferment at 68° F (20° C). Dry hop with Fuggle at 0.15 oz./gal. (0.28 lb./bbl., 1.13 g/L). Age for 14 days at 39° F (4° C).

Analytical targets:
OG: 14.5 °P (1.058 SG)
TG: 2.5 °P (1.010 SG)
ADF: 83%
IBU: 60
ABV: 6.2%

THE ALCHEMIST EL JEFE

"I lost my hop virginity in 1992. Her name was Bigfoot," says John Kimmich, owner of The Alchemist. He had just turned 21, and prior to that night, the hoppiest beer he had been exposed to was Bass. "What a mind-blowing experience. This was back when Bigfoot was in the 11–12% abv range. My palate, and my opinion of hops, would never be the same." Three years later Greg Noonan hired Kimmich to be head brewer at the Vermont Pub and Brewery. While working there, he resurrected Noonan's recipe for Blackwatch and modified it by changing the dark malt from chocolate to dehusked Carafa. Noonan's beer was the inspiration for El Jefe, a dark IPA he brewed before opening The Alchemist. His wife suggested naming it after their now-dead cat, El Jefe.

El Jefe was a big, fat, black cat. The original tag line, "Big, Bold, and Bitter as Hell," came about after his Christmas photo shoot. El Jefe has evolved over the seven years at The Alchemist. It came into its own about five years ago when Kimmich turned it into an all-Simcoe brew. "I wanted it to have that great piney character, reminiscent of spruce, for the Christmas holiday season." John refers to it as an India dark ale, and not a black IPA, mostly because he keeps the SRM at around 16. He found that if he took it much darker, it would have too much roast character for his taste. "I always felt that using a coloring agent like Sinamar was a bit like cheating," says Kimmich, so he used dehusked Carafa III as the coloring malt. He felt that chocolate malt and roasted barley made it just a little too roasty and actually masked some of the resinous character he was after. "The El Jefe is one of my all-time favorite beers," he says.

Brewing liquor:
Target 400 ppm hardness and 50 ppm alkalinity for your water.

Malt bill:
Thomas Fawcett Pearl malt 88–89.5%
Caramalt 8%
Carafa Special III malt dehusked 2.5–4%*
*Malt color may vary. Calculate Carafa III usage to target 16 °L (32° EBC) in beer.

Mashing and lautering:
Use a water-to-grain ratio of 2.25/1 (1.08 qt./gal.) for a single-temperature infusion mash. Target a mash pH of 5.2. Mash at 148° F (64° C) to target 3 °P

(1.012 SG) terminal gravity (old recipe) or mash at 153° F (67° C) to target 4 °P (1.016 SG) terminal gravity (newer recipe).

Kettle boil and hopping:
Total boil time is 60 minutes. Hops are 100% Simcoe pellets to target 90 IBU. Use 44% of the hops at the start of the boil and add 56% when there is 5 minutes left.

Fermentation and aging:
The Alchemist house yeast strain is "Conan." Pitch low at 6–7 million cells/mL, and start at 68° F (20° C). On day 3, let the temperature rise to 72° F (22° C). At the end of fermentation, chill to 42° F (6° C) and hold for three days. Remove the yeast and dry hop with fresh Simcoe pellets at a ratio of 0.83 oz./gal. (1.6 lb./bbl., 6.2 g/L). Rouse hops two to three times with CO_2 over a week, then separate the beer from the hops and age cold another two weeks.

Analytical targets:
OG: 17.5 °P (1.070 SG)
TG: 4 °P (1.016 SG)
ADF: 77%
IBU: 90 (calculated)
ABV: 7%
Color: 16 °L (31.5° EBC)

THE SHED'S DARKSIDE BLACK IPA

Shaun Hill is a Vermont brewing veteran who brewed his first black IPA (Darkside) in 2005 while at The Shed in Stowe, Vermont. His inspiration was John Kimmich's El Jefe (via the Vermont Pub and Brewery's Blackwatch). After leaving The Shed, Hill spent some time brewing in Denmark and is now back home in Vermont, brewing at his own brewery on his family's farm.

Malt bill:
Pale malt 61.5%
Munich I malt 24.6%
Cara 120 malt 4.5%
Wheat malt 4.5%
Carafa Special I malt dehusked 4.5%
Oats 0.35%
Chocolate malt 0.05%

Mashing and lautering:
Use a water-to-grain ratio of 2.77/1 (1.33 qt./lb.) for an infusion mash. Strike temperature is 160° F (71° C). Mash rest at 148–150° F (64–66° C) for 60 minutes.

Kettle boil and hopping:
Total boil time is 70 minutes. Use all pellets and start with 16% Simcoe and 23% Amarillo at 60 minutes. The second addition of 9% Simcoe, 10% Goldings, and 7% Cascade is added at 45 minutes. Use 11% Amarillo, 7% Cascade, and 8% Tettnang at 15 minutes for the third addition, and 9% Simcoe during the whirlpool.

Fermentation and aging:
Pitch an American Ale yeast and ferment at 68° F (20° C). Dry hop using Simcoe, Amarillo, and Cascade pellets in equal proportions at a ratio of 1 lb./bbl. total (0.52 oz./gal., 3.86 g/L). Add when beer is racked into the conditioning tank.

Analytical targets:
OG: 17.2 °P (1.069 SG)
TG: 4.2 °P (1.017 SG)
ADF: 72 %
IBU: Unknown
ABV: 7.1%
Color: Black

PIZZA PORT CARLSBAD BLACK LIE

When Jeff Bagby was at Pizza Port Carlsbad, he developed San Diego's first black IPA about the same time Stone Brewing Co. was developing Stone 11th Anniversary IPA. His beer came out a month before Stone's. Back when the Liar's Club was still around (in the Mission Beach neighborhood of San Diego), Pizza Port used to sell the club's owner, Louis Mello, quite a bit of beer for his bar. When asked by Mello if he could brew a black IPA for the club's anniversary, Bagby drew up a brand-new IPA recipe with a standard malt bill and hop schedule. Before whirlpooling the beer, he added a bunch of Sinamar (black malt extract) to the kettle. He also added a little more Sinamar into the bright tank because he didn't feel that the beer was black enough. The result was a black beer with no dark malt aroma or flavors. "It had a huge hop aroma and flavor," Bagby says. "The beer sold like crazy at the Liar's Club and here in Carlsbad." Pizza Port Carlsbad has made the beer annually since then.

Malt bill:
Two-row malt 93.6%
Crystal malt 15 °L 2.8%
Wheat malt 2.6%

Mashing and lautering:
This beer uses an infusion mash and is mash hopped with Simcoe hops.

Kettle boil and hopping:
Total boil time is 90 minutes and no hopping rates are given. At the start of the boil add Columbus hops followed by Chinook at 45 minutes. Use Cascade, Centennial, and Liberty during the whirlpool. For color, add Weyermann Sinamar black malt extract during the whirlpool.

Fermentation and aging:
Pitch Pizza Port proprietary strain or a comparable yeast. Ferment at 67° F (19° C) until fermentation is 50% complete, then allow fermentation to free rise to 72° F (22° C). Dry hop with a blend of Centennial, Simcoe, Amarillo, and Cascade and hold for 10 days.

Analytical targets:
OG: 18.5 °P (1.074 SG)
TG: 3.25 °P (1.013 SG)
ADF: 82.4%
ABV: 6.9%
IBU: 75
Color: Black

STONE 11th ANNIVERSARY ALE/ STONE SUBLIMELY SELF-RIGHTEOUS ALE

Brewing liquor:
Use municipal water (~300 ppm hardness) that is carbon filtered and reverse osmosis treated to reduce hardness to 100 ppm.

Malt bill:
Pale malt 90.6%
Crystal malt 60 °L 4.5%
Carafa Special III malt dehusked 4.9%

Mashing and lautering:
Use a water-to-grain ratio of 2.84/1 (1.36 qt./lb.) for an upward infusion mash with a 60-minute rest at 148° F (64° C). Allow the temperature to rise to 165° F (74° C) for mash-off.

Kettle boil and hopping:
Total boil time is 90 minutes. Using 100% pellets, add 66% Chinook at the start of the boil. Add 17% each of Amarillo and Simcoe during the whirlpool.

Fermentation and aging:
Use the Stone Brewing Co. house strain (or WLP007 and WLP002 yeasts are acceptable alternatives). Ferment at 72° F (22° C) until 3.1 °P (1.012 SG). Chill to 62° F (17° C) for 24 hours, then rack off yeast. Dry hop with Amarillo and Simcoe using a ratio of 0.39 oz./gal. (0.75 lb./bbl., 2.9 g/L). Hold for 36 hours, then chill to 34° F (1° C). Hold for 10 days.

Analytical targets:
OG: 20 °P (1.080 SG)
TG: 3.5 °P (1.014 SG)
ADF: 82.5%
IBU: 85
ABV: 8.7%
Color: 110 °L (197° EBC)

HILL FARMSTEAD JAMES BLACK IPA

Inspired by Greg Noonan and John Kimmich, Shaun Hill cut his teeth on brewing black IPAs when he brewed Darkside at The Shed in Stowe, Vermont. After starting his Hill Farmstead Brewery, he brewed James, a black IPA, by using both Carafa malt and Sinamar black malt extract, which he believes allows the hop character to come through. It is a classic black IPA, and one in which Hill amps up the bitterness—as do many double IPA brewers—by the addition of a hop CO_2 extract in the boil.

Malt bill:
Rahr two-row malt 86.4%
CaraHell malt 4%
CaraAroma malt 1.5%
Carafa Special III malt dehusked 5%
Sinamar 1.1%
Flaked oats 2%

Mashing and lautering:
Use a water-to-grain ratio of 2.8/1 (1.35 qt./gal.) for a single-infusion mash at 152° F (67° C). Add 4% Columbus hops at first wort.

Kettle boil and hopping:

Total boil time is 60 minutes. At the start of the boil use 20% Simcoe plus CO_2 extract, followed by 12% Centennial plus CO_2 extract at 45 minutes. The next addition calls for 15% Centennial plus CO_2 extract at 10 minutes, and finally 17% Centennial and 32% Columbus during the whirlpool.

Fermentation and aging:

Use an English Ale/house proprietary yeast. Ferment at 68° F (20° C). After primary dry hop with 0.52 oz./gal. (1 lb./bbl., 3.86 g/L) total of a 50/50 blend of Columbus and Centennial pellets.

Analytical targets:

OG: 18 °P (1.072 SG)
TG: 5 °P (1.020 SG)
ADF: 72%
IBU: 120 (calculated)
ABV: 7.2%
Color: 87.3 °L (172° EBC)

DESCHUTES HOP IN THE DARK

Hop in the Dark is an example of what former Deschutes brewmaster Larry Sidor likes to call a Cascadian dark ale. Brewing with black barley and chocolate malt—as opposed to the dehusked Carafa that is typical of black IPAs brewed in other regions—is noteworthy. This beer is unique because Deschutes mashes the dark malts cold and separately, then combines this with the wort made from a second mash of pale malt, oats, and crystal malt.

Brewing liquor:

Use extremely soft water with 25 ppm lactic acid added for pH correction.

Malt bill:

Mash No. 1
Chocolate malt 15%
Black barley malt 5%
Mash No. 2
Pale malt 67%
Oats 5%
Crystal malt 8%

Mashing and lautering:

There are two mashes and lauters per brew and the water-to-grain ratio is 2.8/1 (1.35 qt./lb.). Combine the worts in a pre-run tank prior to the kettle. The first mash is cold water of only the dark malts. The second mash is an upward step mash. It's "all in" at 122° F (50° C). Hold for 10 minutes prior to ramping up to 154° F (68° C) for a 25-minute hold and mash off at 168° F (76° C).

Kettle boil and hopping:

Total boil time is 60 minutes. (Note that Deschutes' elevation is 3,600 feet.) Boil vigorously to flash off all dimethyl sulfide and use 100% whole hops. The total addition rate for this beer is 1.9 lb./bbl. Hop varieties used are Nugget, Citra, Cascade, Centennial, and Northern Brewer. Add 10% of the hop bill at the start of the boil, 20% at 30 minutes, and 70% in the hopback.

Fermentation and aging:

Use Deschutes house ale strain or comparable yeast. Cool to 62° F (16.7° C). Ferment 63° F (17.2° C) for three days, then bung with 2% ADF remaining. Wait 24–48 hours for diacetyl reduction and then crash cool. Dry hop after filtration and hold the beer on the hops for seven days prior to packaging. Place whole hops in a mesh bag that is secured to the tank. Use Centennial and Cascade at a ratio of 0.155 oz./gal. (0.3 lb./bbl., 1.16 g/L).

Analytical targets:

OG: 16 °P (1.064 SG)
TG: 4.0 °P (1.012 SG)
ADF: 75%
IBU: 65
ABV: 6.5%
Color: 90 °L (177° EBC)

APPENDIX A: ANALYSIS OF VARIOUS IPAs FROM THE 1800s

Table A.1 Analysis of Various IPAs from the 1800s

Year	Brewer	Country	Beer	Package	OG (°P)	
1844	Unknown, Edinburgh	UK	90/- IPA Export, India	Bottled	16.53	
1844	Unknown, Edinburgh	UK	84/- IPA Export	Draught	14.86	
1844	Unknown, Edinburgh	UK	95/- IPA Export	Draught	16.95	
1844	Unknown, Edinburgh	UK	90/- IPA Export, India	Draught	16.23	
1844	Unknown, Edinburgh	UK	84/- IPA Export, India	Draught	15.23	
1844	Unknown, Edinburgh	UK	81/- IPA Home	Draught	14.60	
1844	Unknown, Edinburgh	UK	60/- IPA Export, India	Bottled	13.31	
1844	Unknown, Edinburgh	UK	60/- IPA Export, India	Bottled	13.33	
1844	Unknown, Edinburgh	UK	60/- IPA Export, India	Bottled	13.41	
1844	Unknown, Edinburgh	UK	90/- IPA Export, India	Bottled	16.06	
1844	Unknown, Edinburgh	UK	95/- IPA Export, India	Bottled	16.42	
1844	Unknown, Edinburgh	UK	90/- IPA Export	Bottled	16.84	
1844	Unknown, Edinburgh	UK	60/- IPA Home	Bottled	11.16	
1844	Unknown, Edinburgh	UK	60/- IPA Home	Bottled	12.41	
1844	Unknown, Edinburgh	UK	60/- IPA Home	Bottled	11.75	
1844	Unknown, Edinburgh	UK	81/- IPA Export	Bottled	15.07	
1844	Unknown, Edinburgh	UK	81/- IPA Export	Bottled	14.39	
1844	Unknown, Edinburgh	UK	66/- IPA Export	Bottled	13.46	
1844	Unknown, Edinburgh	UK	90/- IPA Export, India	Bottled	17.11	
1844	Unknown, Edinburgh	UK	90/- IPA Export	Bottled	16.46	
1845	Unknown, Edinburgh	UK	81/- IPA Home	Draught	13.31	
1845	Unknown, Edinburgh	UK	81/- IPA Home	Bottled	13.56	
1845	Unknown, Edinburgh	UK	81/- IPA Home	Bottled	14.44	
1845	Unknown, Edinburgh	UK	81/- IPA Home	Bottled	14.80	
1845	Unknown, Edinburgh	UK	81/- IPA Home	Bottled	14.49	
1845	Unknown, Edinburgh	UK	90/- IPA Export	Draught	15.39	
1845	Unknown, Edinburgh	UK	90/- IPA Export	Draught	15.75	
1845	Unknown, Edinburgh	UK	90/- IPA Export	Draught	15.33	
1845	Unknown, Edinburgh	UK	90/- IPA Export, India	Bottled	16.75	
1845	Unknown, Edinburgh	UK	60/- IPA Export	Bottled	12.03	
1845	Unknown, Edinburgh	UK	63/- IPA Export	Draught	12.33	
1845	Unknown, Edinburgh	UK	81/- IPA Export	Bottled	14.51	

OG (SG)	FG (°P)	FG (SG)	Attenua-tion	Real FG	ABV	ABW	Real Atten.
1067.61	2.01	1007.75	88.54%	4.63	7.6	6.30	71.97%
1060.38	1.36	1005.25	91.30%	3.80	7.0	5.80	74.40%
1069.43	2.07	1008.00	88.48%	4.76	7.8	6.46	71.91%
1066.28	2.07	1008.00	87.93%	4.63	7.4	6.12	71.46%
1061.98	2.58	1010.00	83.86%	4.87	6.6	5.44	68.02%
1059.25	3.09	1012.00	79.75%	5.17	6.0	4.93	64.55%
1053.75	1.69	1006.50	87.91%	3.79	6.0	4.95	71.54%
1053.82	1.30	1005.00	90.71%	3.47	6.2	5.12	73.94%
1054.18	3.35	1013.00	76.00%	5.17	5.2	4.29	61.46%
1065.55	3.09	1012.00	81.69%	5.44	6.8	5.60	66.13%
1067.10	1.88	1007.25	89.20%	4.51	7.6	6.30	72.54%
1068.93	1.94	1007.50	89.12%	4.64	7.8	6.47	72.47%
1044.69	1.30	1005.00	88.81%	3.08	5.0	4.15	72.39%
1049.93	1.10	1004.25	91.49%	3.15	5.8	4.79	74.62%
1047.18	1.56	1006.00	87.28%	3.40	5.2	4.30	71.07%
1061.28	0.78	1003.00	95.10%	3.36	7.4	6.14	77.67%
1058.38	0.85	1003.25	94.43%	3.30	7.0	5.80	77.11%
1054.40	1.04	1004.00	92.65%	3.29	6.4	5.29	75.59%
1070.10	2.65	1010.25	85.38%	5.26	7.6	6.29	69.24%
1067.28	2.33	1009.00	86.62%	4.88	7.4	6.12	70.33%
1053.75	1.69	1006.50	87.91%	3.79	6.0	4.95	71.54%
1054.83	1.56	1006.00	89.06%	3.73	6.2	5.12	72.52%
1058.55	1.30	1005.00	91.46%	3.67	6.8	5.63	74.55%
1060.13	1.30	1005.00	91.68%	3.74	7.0	5.80	74.73%
1058.80	1.36	1005.25	91.07%	3.74	6.8	5.63	74.21%
1062.65	3.16	1012.25	80.45%	5.37	6.4	5.27	65.11%
1064.23	3.16	1012.25	80.93%	5.44	6.6	5.44	65.50%
1062.40	3.09	1012.00	80.77%	5.31	6.4	5.27	65.38%
1068.53	2.71	1010.50	84.68%	5.25	7.4	6.09	68.65%
1048.35	1.10	1004.25	91.21%	3.08	5.6	4.62	74.40%
1049.60	1.43	1005.50	88.91%	3.40	5.6	4.62	72.43%
1058.88	0.98	1003.75	93.63%	3.42	7.0	5.80	76.41%

Table A.1 (continued)

Year	Brewer	Country	Beer	Package	OG (°P)	
1845	Unknown, Edinburgh	UK	63/- IPA Export	Bottled	13.66	
1845	Unknown, Edinburgh	UK	90/- IPA Export	Draught	16.84	
1845	Unknown, Edinburgh	UK	90/- IPA Export	Draught	16.89	
1846	Unknown, Edinburgh	UK	90/- IPA Export	Draught	13.56	
1846	Unknown, Edinburgh	UK	90/- IPA Home	Draught	13.68	
1846	Unknown, Edinburgh	UK	90/- IPA Export	Bottled	12.96	
1846	Unknown, Edinburgh	UK	65/- IPA Export	Bottled	15.23	
1870	Bass	UK	IPA			
1870	Unknown, Bremen	Germany	IPA		16.21	
1887	Fuller, Smith & Turner	UK	IPA	Draught	14.67	
1887	Fuller, Smith & Turner	UK	IPA	Draught	14.99	
1897	Copland Brewing Co., Toronto	Canada	IPA	Bottled	14.73	
1897	Copland Brewing Co., Toronto	Canada	IPA	Bottled	14.47	
1897	Dawes & Co., Lachine, PQ	Canada	IPA	Bottled	14.14	
1897	Eaton Bros., Owen Sound	Canada	IPA	Bottled	13.70	
1897	Fuller, Smith & Turner	UK	IPA	Draught	13.83	
1897	Geo Sleeman, Guelph, ON	Canada	IPA	Bottled	12.85	
1897	J. McCarthy, Sons & Co., Prescott, ON	Canada	IPA	Bottled	15.08	
1897	Labatt, London, ON	Canada	IPA	Bottled	12.38	
1897	S. Jones, St. John, NB	Canada	IPA	Bottled	13.93	
1897	W. Dow & Co., Montreal, QC	Canada	IPA	Bottled	16.26	
1898	Fuller, Smith & Turner	UK	IPA	Draught	13.96	

OG (SG)	FG (°P)	FG (SG)	Attenua-tion	Real FG	ABV	ABW	Real Atten.
1055.23	0.85	1003.25	94.11%	3.16	6.6	5.46	76.85%
1068.93	1.94	1007.50	89.12%	4.64	7.8	6.47	72.47%
1069.18	2.01	1007.75	88.80%	4.70	7.8	6.47	72.19%
1054.83	1.56	1006.00	89.06%	3.73	6.2	5.12	72.52%
1055.33	1.69	1006.50	88.25%	3.85	6.2	5.12	71.82%
1052.25	1.30	1005.00	90.43%	3.41	6.0	4.95	73.71%
1061.95	1.36	1005.25	91.53%	3.87	7.2	5.96	74.58%
1060.00							
1066.20	3.70	1014.40	78.25%	5.97	6.8	5.41	63.20%
1059.56	4.61	1018.00	69.77%	6.43	5.39	4.31	56.00%
1060.94	4.27	1016.62	72.73%	6.21	5.76	4.61	59.00%
1059.80	3.20	1012.40	79.26%	5.28	6.18	4.95	64.14%
1058.70	1.81	1007.00	88.07%	4.10	6.78	5.42	71.65%
1057.30	0.55	1002.10	96.34%	3.01	7.27	5.81	78.75%
1055.40	1.56	1006.00	89.17%	3.75	6.47	5.18	72.61%
1055.95	4.27	1016.62	70.30%	5.99	5.10	4.08	57.00%
1051.80	1.76	1006.80	86.87%	3.77	5.88	4.71	70.68%
1061.30	2.46	1009.50	84.50%	4.74	6.78	5.42	68.57%
1049.80	3.60	1014.00	71.89%	5.19	4.64	3.72	58.07%
1056.40	2.02	1007.80	86.17%	4.17	6.36	5.09	70.04%
1066.40	2.07	1008.00	87.95%	4.64	7.67	6.14	71.48%
1056.51	4.34	1016.90	70.10%	6.08	5.14	4.11	56.00%

Sources: Data from Roberts, The Scottish Ale Brewer and Practical Maltster (1847), 171 and 173; the Bass price list; August Wilhelm von Hofmann, Bericht über die Entwickelung der chemischen Industrie während des letzten Jahrzehends (1877), 382; Fuller's brewing records; Canada Department of Inland Revenue, Report, Returns, and Statistics of the Inland Revenues of the Dominion of Canada (1898), 34–49.

APPENDIX B: 1900s ENGLISH IPA ANALYTICAL PROFILES

Table B.1 Whitbread IPA: 1901–1944

Year	Style	Package	OG (°P)	OG (SG)	FG (°P)	FG (SG)
1901	IPA	Draught	12.73	1051.3	3.35	1013.0
1910	IPA	Draught	12.40	1049.9	3.73	1014.5
1923	IPA	Bottled	9.06	1036.0	2.07	1008.0
1931	IPA	Draught	9.23	1036.7	2.84	1011.0
1931	Export IPA	Bottled	11.57	1046.4	3.86	1015.0
1933	IPA	Bottled	9.48	1037.7	1.56	1006.0
1939	IPA	Draught	9.33	1037.1	2.07	1008.0
1940	PA	Bottled	9.21	1036.6	1.58	1006.1
1940	IPA	Draught	9.36	1037.2	1.81	1007.0
1940	IPA	Draught	9.14	1036.3	1.94	1007.5
1944	IPA	Bottled	7.84	1031.0	1.45	1005.6

Sources: Whitbread brewing log; *Whitbread Gravity Book.* Courtesy of Ron Pattinson.

Table B.2 Barclay Perkins IPA: 1928–1956

Year	Style	Package	OG (°P)	OG (SG)	FG (°P)	FG (SG)
1928	IPA		11.50	1046.0	2.50	1010.0
1936	IPA	Bottled	11.23	1045.0	2.58	1010.0
1939	IPA	Bottled	10.98	1043.9	3.60	1014.0
1939	IPA	Bottled	10.95	1043.8	3.35	1013.0
1940	IPA	Bottled	9.73	1038.7	2.97	1011.5
1941	IPA	Bottled	9.29	1036.9	1.94	1007.5
1942	IPA	Draught	7.92	1031.3	1.81	1007.0
1943	IPA	Draught	7.97	1031.5	1.56	1006.0
1946	IPA	Draught	7.97	1031.5	2.33	1009.0
1950	IPA	Bottled	7.50	1029.6	1.35	1005.2
1950	IPA	Bottled	8.02	1031.7	2.15	1008.3
1951	IPA	Bottled	7.38	1029.1	2.02	1007.8
1951	IPA	Bottled	7.89	1031.2	1.97	1007.6
1954	IPA	Bottled	7.89	1031.2	1.94	1007.5
1956	IPA	Bottled	7.72	1030.5	1.89	1007.3

Sources: Barclay Perkins brewing log; *Whitbread Gravity Book.* Courtesy of Ron Pattinson.

Attenuation	Real FG	ABV	ABW	Real atten.	Color (EBC)	Color (SRM)
74.66%	5.05	4.98	3.98	60.37%		
70.94%	5.30	4.59	3.67	57.28%		
77.78%	3.34	3.64	2.91	63.20%	24.0	12.18
70.03%	4.00	3.33	2.66	56.73%	23.0	11.68
67.67%	5.25	4.06	3.25	54.61%		
84.08%	2.99	4.13	3.30	68.46%	23.0	11.68
78.44%	3.38	3.78	3.02	63.73%	18.5	9.39
83.33%	2.96	3.97	3.17	67.84%	18.5	9.39
81.18%	3.18	3.93	3.14	66.03%	18.5	9.39
79.34%	3.24	3.74	2.99	64.50%	18.5	9.39
81.94%	2.61	3.30	2.64	66.74%	18.0	9.14

Attenuation	Real FG	ABV	ABW	Real atten.	Color (EBC)	Color (SRM)
78.27%		4.80	3.84		20	10.00
77.78%	4.15	4.55	3.64	63.08%	20	10.15
68.13%	4.94	3.87	3.10	55.03%	20	10.15
70.34%	4.72	3.99	3.20	56.87%	22	11.17
70.31%	4.19	3.53	2.82	56.93%	23	11.68
79.69%	3.27	3.82	3.06	64.78%	23	11.68
77.64%	2.92	3.15	2.52	63.14%	21	10.66
80.95%	2.72	3.31	2.65	65.91%	17	8.63
71.43%	3.35	2.91	2.33	57.98%	22	11.17
82.43%	2.46	3.17	2.54		19	9.64
73.82%	3.21	3.03	2.43		20	10.15
73.20%	2.99	2.76	2.21		20	10.15
75.64%	3.04	3.06	2.45		17	8.63
75.96%	3.02	3.07	2.46		19	9.64
76.07%	2.95	3.01	2.41		19	9.64

Table B.3 Worthington's IPA: 1921–1957

Year	Beer	Package	OG (°P)	OG (SG)	FG (°P)	FG (SG)	
1921	IPA	Bottled	13.58	1054.9	1.92	1007.4	
1922	IPA (Belgian sample bottled by J. Baker, Brussels)	Bottled	13.60	1055.0	1.22	1004.7	
1931	IPA (bottled by R. P. Culley)	Bottled	14.54	1059.0	3.37	1013.1	
1947	IPA	Bottled	13.18	1053.2	0.86	1003.3	
1948	IPA	Bottled	13.39	1054.1	1.32	1005.1	
1948	Export IPA	Bottled	13.18	1053.2	1.63	1006.3	
1951	IPA	Bottled	14.00	1056.7	1.87	1007.2	
1951	IPA	Bottled	13.51	1054.6	1.58	1006.1	
1953	IPA	Bottled	15.03	1061.1	3.48	1013.5	
1955	IPA (Green Shield)	Bottled	15.54	1063.3	2.43	1009.4	
1955	IPA (White Shield)	Bottled	15.63	1063.7	0.76	1002.9	
1959	IPA	Bottled	12.80	1051.6	2.97	1011.5	
1961	IPA (Green Shield)	Bottled	12.92	1052.1	2.28	1008.8	
1961	IPA (White Shield)	Bottled	13.32	1053.8	2.25	1008.7	
1967	IPA (Green Shield)	Bottled	12.07	1048.5	2.48	1009.6	
1967	IPA (White Shield)	Bottled	13.04	1052.6	3.04	1011.8	

Source: Whitbread Gravity Book. Courtesy of Ron Pattinson.

Table B.4 Other U.K. Brewers' IPAs

Year	Brewer	Beer	Package	OG (°P)	OG (SG)	FG (°P)	FG (SG)	
1936	Hammerton	IPA	Bottled	10.03	1040.0	1.07	1004.1	
1938	Hammerton	IPA	Bottled	7.94	1031.4	1.14	1004.4	
1938	Hammerton	IPA	Bottled	9.70	1038.6	1.99	1007.7	
1944	Hammerton	IPA	Bottled	7.01	1027.6	1.17	1004.5	
1946	Hammerton	IPA	Bottled	6.69	1026.3	0.52	1002.0	
1947	Hammerton	IPA	Bottled	6.91	1027.2	0.73	1002.8	
1947	Hammerton	IPA	Bottled	6.78	1026.7	0.60	1002.3	
1949	McEwan's	Export IPA	Bottled	11.66	1046.8	2.20	1008.5	

Sources: Whitbread Gravity Book; Daily Mirror (July 10, 1972), 15. Courtesy of Ron Pattinson.

Attenuation	Real FG	ABV	ABW	Real atten.	Color (EBC)	Color (SRM)
86.52%	4.03	6.22	4.97	70.35%		
91.45%	3.46	6.60	5.28	74.57%		
77.80%	5.39	5.98	4.79	62.91%		
93.80%	3.09	6.55	5.24	76.58%	20	10.15
90.57%	3.51	6.42	5.14	73.82%	20	10.15
88.16%	3.72	6.14	4.91	71.76%	19	9.64
87.30%	4.06	6.48	5.19	71.00%	18	9.14
88.83%	3.74	6.35	5.08	72.32%	19	9.64
77.91%	5.57	6.21	4.97	62.97%	27	13.71
85.15%	4.80	7.06	5.65	69.11%	18	9.14
95.45%	3.44	8.02	6.42	77.96%	18	9.14
77.71%	4.75	5.22	4.17	62.93%	18	9.14
83.11%	4.20	5.65	4.52	67.48%	20	10.15
83.83%	4.25	5.89	4.71	68.08%	20	10.15
80.21%	4.22	5.07	4.05	65.07%	18	9.14
77.57%	4.85	5.31	4.25	62.80%	20	10.15

Attenuation	Real FG	ABV	ABW	Real atten.	Color (EBC)	Color (SRM)
89.75%	2.69	4.69	3.75			
85.99%	2.37	3.51	2.81			
80.05%	3.39	4.02	3.21			
83.70%	2.22	3.00	2.40		19.0	9.64
92.40%	1.64	3.16	2.53		19.5	9.90
89.71%	1.85	3.17	2.54		19.5	9.90
91.39%	1.72	3.18	2.54		19.0	9.64
81.84%	3.91	4.99	3.99	66.47%	19.5	9.90

Table B.4 (continuted)

Year	Brewer	Beer	Package	OG (°P)	OG (SG)	FG (°P)	FG (SG)	
1950	Hammerton	IPA	Bottled	8.26	1032.7	1.20	1004.6	
1950	Charrington	IPA	Draught	10.95	1043.8	2.43	1009.4	
1950	McEwan's	Export IPA	Bottled	12.14	1048.8	3.25	1012.6	
1954	Charrington	IPA	Draught	11.47	1046.0	2.28	1008.8	
1954	Charrington	IPA	Draught	11.64	1046.7	2.07	1008.0	
1954	Mann Crossman	IPA	Draught	10.99	1044.0	2.53	1009.8	
1954	Mann Crossman	IPA	Draught	10.99	1044.0	2.99	1011.6	
1954	McEwan's	IPA	Bottled	12.09	1048.6	2.12	1008.2	
1957	Charrington	Best IPA	Draught	11.16	1044.7	2.92	1011.3	
1957	Mann Crossman	IPA	Draught	10.44	1041.7	1.58	1006.1	
1957	McEwan's	Export IPA	Can	11.57	1046.4	2.76	1010.7	
1959	Greene King	IPA	Bottled	8.41	1033.3	2.58	1010.0	
1960	Greene King	IPA	Bottled	8.33	1033.0	1.99	1007.7	
1960	Mann Crossman	IPA	Draught	10.32	1041.2	2.56	1009.9	
1961	McEwan's	Export IPA	Bottled	11.23	1045.0	2.99	1011.6	
1961	McEwan's	Export IPA	Bottled	11.97	1048.1	3.14	1012.2	
1968	Greene King	IPA Bitter	Draught	8.82	1035.0	1.43	1005.5	
1972	Greene King	IPA	Draught	8.87	1035.2	1.74	1006.7	
1972	Charrington	IPA	Draught	10.15	1040.5	2.89	1011.2	

Attenuation	Real FG	ABV	ABW	Real atten.	Color (EBC)	Color (SRM)
85.93%	2.47	3.66	2.93		25.0	12.69
78.54%	3.97	4.47	3.58	63.73%	29.0	14.72
74.18%	4.86	4.70	3.76	60.01%	25.0	12.69
80.87%	3.94	4.84	3.87	65.66%	32.0	16.24
82.87%	3.80	5.04	4.04	67.34%	27.0	13.71
77.73%	4.06	4.45	3.56	63.05%	25.0	12.69
73.64%	4.44	4.20	3.36	59.62%	26.0	13.20
83.13%	3.93	5.27	4.22	67.54%	24.0	12.18
74.72%	4.41	4.34	3.47	60.52%	27.0	13.71
85.37%	3.18	4.64	3.71	69.50%	23.0	11.68
76.94%	4.36	4.64	3.71	62.35%	22.0	11.17
69.97%	3.64	3.02	2.41	56.74%	25.0	12.69
76.67%	3.14	3.16	2.63	62.31%	25.0	12.69
75.97%	3.96	4.06	3.25	61.61%	23.0	11.68
74.22%	4.48	4.18	3.47	60.10%	20.0	10.15
74.64%	4.74	4.49	3.73	60.40%	22.0	11.17
84.29%	2.76	3.69	3.07	68.66%	18.0	9.14
80.97%	3.03	3.70	2.96	65.87%		
72.35%	4.20	3.80	3.04	58.60%		

APPENDIX C: READING HISTORICAL BREWING RECORDS

We have found several challenges in deciphering English historical brewing records. These lie in the units of measurement, brewing techniques, legibility, and brewers' codes or shorthand used in the logs.

UNITS OF MEASUREMENT

The units of measurement used in brewing records have changed significantly over the last 200 years. For example, today we use pounds or kilograms of malt, while in historical records, bushels were the unit of measurement for malt. Hops were added based on how many bushels were used instead of on how many barrels of wort are produced. Specific gravity measurements weren't available, and when they were, brewers often used "brewers pounds" to describe original gravity. Below are some conversion factors, constants, and assumptions that can be used to calculate recipes from historical ledgers by using today's units.

Brewers pound (BP) and extract calculations:
BP = the weight of 1 barrel of wort vs. 1 barrel of water
bbl. = beer barrel = 31 gal.

Conversions:
BPs = OG (expressed as the last 2 digits of SG) x 0.36
For example, 64 SG (or 1.064) = 23 BP

Therefore:
$$\frac{((BP \times 2.77) + 1000)}{1000} = SG$$
For example, 23 BP = 1.064 SG
Balling = SG/4
For example, 64 SG = 16 °Balling

Constant:

85 BP per quarter malt

Balling = (BP x 2.6 x 100) / (360 + BP)

Balling = 260 x BP / (360 + BP)

Malt Weights

Conversions:

1 bushel = ~42 pounds, volume of grain held by 8 gallons water

Current day = ~48 pounds malt

Hoop or measure = 4 bushels

Peck = .25 bushels (2 gallons)

8 bushels = 1 quarter = 336 pounds pale malt

Scottish quarter = 252 pounds

Brown malt quarter = 244 pounds

(dark malts, variable weights per quarter)

Sugar quarter = 224 pounds

2 bushels = 1 strike

4 bushels = 1 coomb, sack, or barrel

5 quarters = 1 weigh or load

10 quarters = 1 last

Constants:

1 quarter yields 3 bbl. wort at 1.074 SG

2 bushels malt = 1 bbl. beer at 1.056

2 bbl. water/quarter malt = 76–84 pounds extract

40 pounds extract/quarter/barrel

Examples

1. A brew is made with 55 quarters of malt and the SG is 1.065.
   How many barrels of wort were produced?
   a. 1.065 SG: 65 x 0.36 = 23.4 brewers pounds
   b. 85 BP/qtr x 55 qtr. x 1 bbl./23.4 BP = 200 bbl.

2. A brew is made with 30 quarters of malt and the brew length is 70 barrels. What is the theoretical OG of this brew?

    a. 30 qtr. x 85 BP/qtr. /70 bbl. = 36.4 BP/bbl.

    b. 36.4 brewers pounds/.36 = 101, or SG 1.101

Other Useful Conversions

Volumes

British beer barrel:	36 gallons (note that some literature references a British ale barrel at 32 gallons)
Ale barrel:	30 or 32 ale gallons
1688:	34 ale gallons
1803:	36 ale gallons
1824:	36 imperial gallons
Beer barrel:	36 beer gallons
1688:	34 beer gallons
1803:	36 beer gallons
1824:	36 imperial gallons
Hogshead:	54 gallons (63 gallons in Scotland; in the 17th century could be 54, 56, or 63, depending on quality)
Puncheon:	72 gallons
Butt:	108 gallons (sometimes 126), 2 hogsheads, 3 barrels
Tun:	216 gallons
Noggin:	1 pint
Pot:	1 quart

Hops

Bitterness Index:

Hopping/OG x 100, where hopping = lb./bbl. at 5% alpha acids,
and OG = last 2 digits (1.070 OG = 70).
A bitterness index of 3 or below is considered mild.

Bag:	A bale of hops weighing 2.25 cwt
Pocket:	A bale of hops weighing 1.25 cwt

BREWING TECHNIQUES

It is impossible to decipher a brewing log without having a good understanding of the brewing processes that were used at the time. I hope I have provided enough background on multiple mashing, parti-gyling, Burton Union fermentation, cask aging, and other brewing techniques that are no longer common. The same goes for ingredients—it helps to know that English brewers were using California (CA) hops and malts and European hops and malts in their beers. Often these ingredients are abbreviated in the logs.

LEGIBILITY OF BREWING LOGS

Brewing logs were the official records of the breweries and are typically contained in ornate logbooks. The handwriting is very flamboyant and can be very difficult to read. It gets easier with practice, but it is difficult to decipher individual words, let alone meanings.

BREWERS' CODES

Brewers' codes are used in many logbooks. There are some examples of brewing codes shown in Dr. John Harrison and the Durden Park Brewing Circle's book, *Old British Beers and How to Make Them.*

APPENDIX D: CONDUCTING YOUR OWN IPA HUNT

Researching the material for this book has been an intensely rewarding experience for me. Although I have always been interested in brewing history, this project has awakened a passion for all things related to beer history, the myths, and the truths of how beer was brewed and sold in the past. If you have any interest in researching brewing history, here are some places that I've found are invaluable and wonderful resources.

BLOGS/WEBSITES

Zythophile

Written by beer historian and author Martyn Cornell, this blog has amazing information on the history of many British beer styles. Cornell was the first beer historian I read who debunked the myths of the origins of both IPA and London porter. Amazing, eye-opening information.

Shut Up about Barclay Perkins

Written by beer historian and author Ron Pattinson, this blog includes research into recipes for many historical English, Scottish, and German beers. Included are snippets from textbooks, advertisements, and brewing logs that give an accurate representation of how beers were brewed over the past 200 years. Amazing recipes are included, along with homebrewing re-creations and tasting notes from noted homebrewer Kristen England.

My Beer Buzz

This blog by Bil Corcoran has posted some great historical information about pre-Prohibition American breweries such as Feigenspan and Ballantine.

Google Books

This site offers scanned pages from some of the best historical brewing textbooks, including *Country House Brewing in England, The Theory and Practice of Brewing Illustrated, The Brewing Industry: A Guide to Historical Records, The Brewing Industry in England,* and *The Curiosities of Ale and Beer.* I cannot recommend Google Books enough as a resource.

HISTORICAL BREWING BOOKS

There are many great historical brewing books in archives and libraries, and to some extent, on Google Books. Although some are rare, these books have a lot of great information and provide much insight into how brewers approached their craft. Here are the books I used:

- *The Theory and Practice of Brewing*, Michael Combrune, 1762
- *The Theory and Practice of Brewing Illustrated*, William L. Tizard, 1846
- *The Complete Practical Brewer: Or, Plain, Accurate, and Thorough Instructions in the Art of Brewing Ale, Beer, and Porter*, Marcus Lafayette Bryn, 1852
- *The Scottish Ale Brewer and Practical Maltster*, W. H. Roberts, 1847
- *The Curiosities of Ale and Beer*, John Bickerdyke, 1886
- *The Noted Breweries of Great Britain and Ireland*, Alfred Barnard, 1889 and 1891
- *Practical Brewings: A Series of Fifty Brewings*, George Amsinck, 1868
- *The Brewer: A Familiar Treatise on the Art of Brewing*, W. R. Loftus, 1856
- *The Innkeeper and Public Brewer*, Practical Man, 1860
- *The Philosophical Principles of the Science of Brewing*, John Richardson, 1805
- *Burton-on-Trent: Its History, Its Waters, and Its Breweries*, William Molyneaux, 1869
- *The Town and Country Brewery Book: Or, Every Man His Own Brewer*, W. Brande, 1830
- *100 Years of Brewing*, 1903

These books have been reprinted and are available through Raudins Publishing (www.raudins.com/BrewBooks/).

MORE RECENT BREWING BOOKS

- *A History of Brewing*, H. S. Corran, 1975
- *The History of English Ale and Beer*, H. A. Monkton, 1966
- *The Brewing Industry in England, 1700–1830*, Peter Mathias, 1959
- *Homebrew Classics: India Pale Ale*, Clive La Pensée and Roger Protz, 2003
- *Amber, Gold, and Black*, Martyn Cornell, 2008
- *Beer: The Story of the Pint*, Martyn Cornell, 2004
- *Hops and Glory*, Pete Brown, 2009

- *The British Brewing Industry, 1830–1980,* T. R. Gourvish and R. G. Wilson, 1994
- *Country House Brewing in England, 1500–1900,* Pamela Sanbrook, 1996
- *The Brewers Art,* B. Meredith Brown, 1948
- *The Brewing Industry: A Guide to Historical Records,* Lesley Richmond and Alison Turton, 1990
- *Old British Beers and How to Make Them,* Dr. John Harrison and Members of the Durden Park Beer Circle, 1976

ARCHIVES

Check the U.K. National Archives website, www.nationalarchives.gov .uk/2a2/. It catalogs all archive material in the United Kingdom. Search for "brewery" or a specific brewery name.

London Metropolitan Archives
40 Northampton Road, London EC1R 0HB
www.Cityoflondon.gov.uk/lma
Includes archives from Courage & Co.; Watney Combe & Reid; Truman Hanbury; Buxton; Fuller Smith and Turner; Allied Breweries; and Whitbread.

Brewery History Society Archive
Birmingham Central Library, Chamberlain Square, Birmingham B3 HQ
www.birmingham.gov.uk
Archive of the Brewery History Society.

National Brewing Library
Oxford Brookes University Library, Gipsy Lane, Oxford OX3 0BP
www.brookes.ac.uk/library/speccoll/brewing.html
Excellent collection of historical brewing texts, logs, and promotional books and other literature, including the late Michael Jackson's files. Located in the wonderful town of Oxford, home to some great pubs!

Scottish Brewing Archive

Archive Services, 13 Thurso St., University of Glasgow, Glasgow G11 6PE

www.archives.gla.ac.uk/sba/default.html

Major collection of records from Scottish breweries, including Youngers, one of the biggest IPA brewers in the 1800s.

Bass Archives

National Brewery Centre, Burton-on-Trent

Major resource for those researching brewing in Burton in the 1800s and 1900s. The archives contain an amazing collection that focuses on Bass, but material from Allied Breweries, Worthington, and Ind Coope is there too.

British Library

Check out the "East India Collection" for some insight on life in colonial India. Includes many newspapers and advertisements.

Portsmouth Athenaeum

This museum and archive of the Portsmouth, New Hampshire, area has great photos of the Frank Jones Brewery. Also check the Redhook Brewery and the Rusty Hammer Pub (both in Portsmouth) for more Frank Jones photos.

ORGANIZATIONS

Brewery History Society

This group of British beer historians publishes a quarterly newsletter and journal. The journal includes essays on historical breweries, brewing techniques, and book reviews. Membership to the society requires an annual fee (membership@breweryhistory.com).

MUSEUMS

National Brewery Centre and Museum, Burton-on-Trent

This museum contains many exhibits on English brewing history. Anyone with the slightest interest in the brewing history of Burton-on-Trent should pay a visit. Highlights include an entire section dedicated to the 1800s Burton IPA and an N-gauge scale model of Burton-on-Trent, circa 1920, with all the brewery buildings and railroad spurs identified. Finish your tour with some classic Worthington's ales in the museum pub!

London Museum Docklands

Great museum that focuses on the history of London as a port town and a major shipping center. Includes exhibits and artifacts from the East India Company. The museum is located in the Canary Wharf business district in East London, a short walk from the Canary Wharf tube station on the Jubilee Line.

British Museum

One of the best museums in the world.

HISTORICAL SITES AND AREAS OF INTEREST

Lea Valley Walk

The southernmost end of this area includes the former site of the East India docks at the junction of the River Thames and the River Lea. A wetlands preserve and apartment buildings are on the site now, along with remnants of the docks and plaques that tell the history. The East India docks site is located directly across the Thames from The O2 Arena. The easiest way to get there is to take the Dockland Light Railway north from the Jubilee Line at Canary Wharf station, or south from the Bow Road station and the District Line to the East India station.

Location of the Original Bow Brewery

Farther north up the River Lea are two sites that were formerly Bow Brewery sites. Both have flats on them now and are across the street from the old Bow Church. It's an easy walk east, just a few blocks, from the Bromley by Bow tube station on the District Line and Hammersmith and City Line.

Burton-on-Trent

A living brewing history museum, the entire town of Burton-on-Trent is built on British brewing history. Most of the buildings were at one time associated with the brewing industry. There are plaques intermittently placed that tell the history of some of the buildings and sites. A great town to walk around and soak up the brewing history of England.

NOTES

CHAPTER ONE

1. W. Brande, *The Town and Country Brewery Book.*

2. Martyn Cornell, "The Long Battle between Ale and Beer."

3. Lesley Richmond and Alison Turton, *The Brewing Industry.*

4. H. A. Monkton, *The History of English Ale and Beer.*

5. Brande, *The Town and Country Brewery Book.*

6. Stan Hieronymus, personal communication with author (2012).

7. Ibid.

8. Cornell, "A Short History of Hops."

9. Richmond and Turton, *The Brewing Industry.*

10. Dr. John Harrison, "London as the Birthplace of India Pale Ale."

11. Monkton, *The History of English Ale and Beer.*

12. Cornell, "The Long Battle between Ale and Beer."

13. Pamela Sanbrook, *Country House Brewing.*

14. Harrison, "London as the Birthplace of India Pale Ale."

15. Ibid.

CHAPTER TWO

1. W. H. Roberts, *The Scottish Ale Brewer and Practical Maltster.*

2. Clive La Pensée and Roger Protz, *Homebrew Classics: India Pale Ale.*

3. Martyn Cornell, "Pale Beers."

4. Dr. John Harrison and Members of the Durden Park Beer Circle, *Old British Beers and How to Make Them.*

5. La Pensée and Protz, *Homebrew Classics: India Pale Ale.*

6. Cornell, interview with author (February 2010).

7. Cornell, "The Long Battle between Ale and Beer."

8. Harrison et al., *Old British Beers and How to Make Them.*

9. Pete Brown, research files for *Hops and Glory* (supplied to author 2009).

10. Brown, "Mythbusting the IPA."

11. Ibid.

12. Michael Combrune, *The Theory and Practice of Brewing*.

13. H. A. Monkton, *The History of English Ale and Beer*, and Thom Thomlinson, "India Pale Ale: Parts 1 and 2."

14. Alan Pryor, "Indian Pale Ale: An Icon of an Empire."

15. Dr. John Harrison, "London as the Birthplace of India Pale Ale."

16. Cornell, "IPA: Much Later Than You Think."

17. Cornell, *Amber, Gold, and Black*.

18. Cornell, interview with author (February 2010).

19. Cornell, "Hodgson's Brewery, Bow, and the Birth of the IPA."

20. W. Brande, *The Town and Country Brewery Book*.

21. Roberts, *The Scottish Ale Brewer and Practical Maltster*.

22. Geoffrey Boys, *Directions for Brewing Malt Liquors*.

23. La Pensée and Protz, *Homebrew Classics: India Pale Ale*.

24. Randy Mosher, *Radical Brewing*.

25. Roger Protz, interview with author (March 2010).

26. Cornell, *Amber, Gold and Black*.

27. Messieur Fox, *The London and Country Brewer*.

28. Dr. Richard J. Wilson, "The Rise of Pale Ales and India Pale Ales in Victoria Britain."

CHAPTER THREE

1. Roger Putman, Ray Anderson, Mark Dorber, Tom Dawson, Steve Brooks, Paul Bayley, IPA roundtable discussions in Burton-on-Trent (March 2010).

2. Ibid.

3. Ibid.

4. Meantime Brewing Company, "India Pale Ale."

5. Alan Pryor, "Indian Pale Ale: An Icon of an Empire."

6. Ibid.

7. Meantime Brewery, "India Pale Ale."

8. Martyn Cornell, "The First-Ever Reference to IPA."

9. Pryor, "Indian Pale Ale: An Icon of an Empire."

10. Ibid.

11. Dr. Richard J. Wilson, "The Rise of Pale Ales and India Pale Ales in Victorian Britain."

12. Pryor, "Indian Pale Ale: An Icon of an Empire."

13. Wilson, "The Rise of Pale Ales and India Pale Ales in Victorian Britain."

14. John Bickerdyke, *The Curiosities of Ale and Beer.*

15. Pete Brown, research files for *Hops and Glory* (supplied to author 2009).

16. Wilson, "The Rise of Pale Ales and India Pale Ales in Victorian Britain."

17. Meantime Brewing Company, "India Pale Ale."

18. Bass, *A Visit to the Bass Brewery.*

19. Cornell, *Amber, Gold, and Black.*

20. Ibid.

21. Cornell, "IPA: Much Later Than You Think."

22. Ron Pattinson, personal correspondence with author (January 2012).

23. Scottish Brewing Archive Association, *Newsletter* 25 (Summer 1995).

24. *100 Years of Brewing.*

25. Clive La Pensée and Roger Protz, *Homebrew Classics: India Pale Ale.*

26. *100 Years of Brewing.*

27. Cornell, *Amber, Gold, and Black.*

28. Lesley Richmond and Alison Turton, *The Brewing Industry.*

CHAPTER FOUR

1. Roger Putman, Ray Anderson, Mark Dorber, Tom Dawson, Steve Brooks, Paul Bayley, IPA roundtable discussions in Burton-on-Trent (March 2010).

2. Martyn Cornell, "IPA: Much Later Than You Think."

3. Alan Pryor, "Indian Pale Ale: An Icon of an Empire."

4. Pete Brown, research files for *Hops and Glory* (supplied to author 2009).

5. Cornell, *Amber, Gold, and Black.*

6. H. S. Corran, *A History of Brewing.*

7. Putman et al., IPA roundtable discussions in Burton-on-Trent.

8. Bass, *A Glass of Pale Ale.*

9. Cornell, *Amber, Gold, and Black.*

10. Ibid.

11. Dr. John Harrison and Members of the Durden Park Beer Circle, *Old British Beers and How to Make Them.*

12. Putman et al., IPA roundtable discussions in Burton-on-Trent.

13. Marcus Lafayette Bryn, *The Complete Practical Brewer.*

14. Harrison et al., *Old British Beers and How to Make Them.*

15. James Steel, *Selection of the Practical Points of Malting and Brewing.*

16. H. A. Monkton, *The History of English Ale and Beer.*

17. James McCrorie, interview with author (March 2010).

18. Putman et al., IPA roundtable discussions in Burton-on-Trent.

19. Alfred Barnard, *The Noted Breweries of Great Britain and Ireland.*

20. Ibid.

21. Putman et al., IPA roundtable discussions in Burton-on-Trent.

22. John Keeling, interview with author (March 2010).

23. Dr. John Harrison, "London as the Birthplace of India Pale Ale."

24. W. R. Loftus, *The Brewer.*

25. Meantime Brewing Company, "India Pale Ale."

26. Clive La Pensée and Roger Protz, *Homebrew Classics: India Pale Ale.*

27. Putman et al., IPA roundtable discussions in Burton-on-Trent.

28. McCrorie, interview with author (March 2010).

29. Bryn, *The Complete Practical Brewer.*

30. Ron Pattinson, personal communication with author (January 2012).

31. Cornell, *Amber, Gold, and Black.*

32. Brown, research files for *Hops and Glory* (2009).

33. Bryn, *The Complete Practical Brewer.*

34. Pattinson, "Black IPA."

35. John Bickerdyke, *The Curiosities of Ale and Beer.*

36. Roger Protz, interview with author (March 2010).

37. N. H. Claussen, *On a Method for the Application of Hansen's Pure Yeast System*, 308–331.

CHAPTER FIVE

1. John Keeling, interview with author (March 2010).

2. Dr. John Harrison, "London as the Birthplace of India Pale Ale."

3. Roger Protz, interview with author (March 2010).

4. Martyn Cornell, interview with author (February 2010).

5. Dr. Richard J. Wilson, "The Rise of Pale Ales and India Pale Ales in Victorian Britain"; T. R. Gourvish and R. G. Wilson, *The British Brewing Industry, 1830–1980.*

6. Keeling, interview with author (March 2010).

7. Ibid.

8. Ron Pattinson, "Brewing IPA in the 1850s."

9. Clive La Pensée and Roger Protz, *Homebrew Classics: India Pale Ale*.

10. Ibid.

11. Wilson, "The Rise of Pale Ales and India Pale Ales in Victorian Britain."

12. Charles McMaster, "Edinburgh as a Centre of IPA."

13. Scottish Brewing Archive Association, *Newsletter* 2 (2000).

14. James McCrorie, interview with author (August 2009).

15. McMaster, "Edinburgh as a Centre of IPA."

16. McCrorie, interview with author (August 2009).

17. McMaster, "Edinburgh as a Centre of IPA."

18. Pattinson, personal communication with author (January 2012).

19. McMaster, "Edinburgh as a Centre of IPA."

20. McCrorie, interview with author (August 2009).

21. Pete Brown, research files for *Hops and Glory* (supplied to author 2009).

22. Randy Mosher, *Radical Brewing*, 133.

23. *100 Years of Brewing*.

24. Mark Benbow, "Frank Jones."

25. Bil Corcoran, "Local Brewing History."

26. Michael Jackson, "Jackson on Beer: Giving Good Beer the IPA Name."

27. *100 Years of Brewing*.

28. Philip Withers, Thunder Road Brewing Co., personal correspondence with author (2011).

29. Roger Putman, Ray Anderson, Mark Dorber, Tom Dawson, Steve Brooks, Paul Bayley, IPA roundtable discussions in Burton-on-Trent (March 2010).

30. *100 Years of Brewing*.

CHAPTER SIX

1. Meantime Brewing Company, "India Pale Ale."

2. Ron Pattinson, personal files, supplied to author.

3. John Keeling, interview with author (March 2010).

4. H. A. Monkton, *The History of English Ale and Beer*.

5. Ibid.

6. Pete Brown, research files for *Hops and Glory* (supplied to author 2009).

7. Monkton, *The History of English Ale and Beer.*

8. Paul Sunderland, "Brew No. 396: Parti-gyled Brew of India Pale Ale."

9. Ibid.

10. Roger Putman, Ray Anderson, Mark Dorber, Tom Dawson, Steve Brooks, Paul Bayley, IPA roundtable discussions in Burton-on-Trent (March 2010).

11. Scottish Brewing Archive Association, *Newsletter* 25 (Summer 1995).

12. Falstaff, "Ballantine XXX Ale."

13. Gregg Glaser, "The Late, Great Ballantine."

14. Falstaff, "Ballantine XXX Ale."

15 Glaser, "The Late, Great Ballantine."

16. Ibid.

CHAPTER EIGHT

1. Vinnie Cilurzo, personal correspondence with author (2010).

2. Ibid.

3. Faulkner, Frank, *The Theory and Practice of Modern Brewing.*

BIBLIOGRAPHY

Amsinck, George Stewart. *Practical Brewings: A Series of Fifty Brewings.* London: Author, 1868.

Ashton, John. *Social Life in the Reign of Queen Anne.* London: Chatto & Windus, 1882.

Baker, Julian. *The Brewing Industry.* London: Methuen, 1905.

Barnard, Alfred. *The Noted Breweries of Great Britain and Ireland.* Vol. 1. London: Causton, 1889.

———. *The Noted Breweries of Great Britain and Ireland.* Vol. 4. London: Causton, 1891.

Barth-Haas Group. *Barth-Haas Hops Companion: A Guide to the Varieties of Hops and Hop Products.* Washington, DC: John I. Haas, 2009.

Bass. *A Glass of Pale Ale.* Burton-on-Trent, 1884.

———. *A Glass of Pale Ale,* 2nd ed. Burton-on-Trent, 1950s.

———. *A Visit to the Bass Brewery.* Burton-on-Trent, 1902.

Bayley, Paul. "A Thousand Years of Brewing in Burton-on-Trent." *The Brewer International* 2, no. 8 (2002).

BeerHistory.com. "Shakeout in the Brewing Industry." Accessed September 27, 2011. http://www.beerhistory.com/library/holdings/shakeout.shtml.

Benow, Mark. "Frank Jones." RustyCans.com. Accessed May 2010. http://www.rustycans.com/HISTORY/jones.html.

Bickerdyke, John. *The Curiosities of Ale and Beer.* London: Field & Tuer, 1886.

Boys, Geoffrey. *Directions for Brewing Malt Liquors.* London: J. Nutt, 1700.

Brande, W. *The Town and Country Brewery Book: Or, Every Man His Own Brewer.* London: Dean and Munday, 1830.

Brockington, Dave. "American IPA." *Brewing Techniques*, September/ October 1996.

Brown, B. Meredith. *The Brewers Art*. London: Whitbread, 1948.

Brown, Pete. *Hops and Glory: One Man's Search for the Beer That Built the British Empire*. London: Pan Macmillan, 2009.

———. "Mythbusting the IPA." *All about Beer Magazine* 30, no. 5 (November 2009).

Bryn, Marcus Lafayette. *The Complete Practical Brewer: Or, Plain, Accurate, and Thorough Instructions in the Art of Brewing Ale, Beer, and Porter*. Philadelphia: H. C. Baird, 1852.

Child, Samuel. *Every Man His Own Brewer: Or, a Compendium of the English Brewery*. London, 1768.

Cilurzo, Vinnie. "Brew a Double IPA." *Zymurgy* 32, no. 4 (July/August 2009).

Cilurzo, Vinnie, and Tom Nickel. "Brewing Imperial/Double IPA." Presentation at the Craft Brewers Conference. San Diego, 2004.

Claussen, N. H. "On a Method for the Application of Hansen's Pure Yeast System in the Manufacturing of Well-Conditioned English Stock Beers." *Journal of the Institute of Brewing* 10: 308–331.

Combrune, Michael. *The Theory and Practice of Brewing*. London: [Printed by J. Haberkorn], 1762.

Corcoran, Bil. "Local Brewing History: Christian Feigenspan Pride of Newark Brewery." *My Beer Buzz* blog. May 11, 2010. http://mybeerbuzz.blogspot.com/2010/04/local-brewing-history christian.html.

Cornell, Martyn. *Amber, Gold, and Black: The History of Britain's Great Beers*. Middlesex, UK: Zythography Press, 2008.

———. *Beer: The Story of the Pint; The History of Britain's Most Popular Drink*. London: Headline, 2004.

———. "FAQ: False Ale Quotes." *Zythophile* blog. 2007. http://zythophile.wordpress.com/.

———. "The First-Ever Reference to IPA." *Zythophile* blog. March 29, 2010. http://zythophile.wordpress.com/.

———. "Hodgson's Brewery, Bow, and the Birth of the IPA." *Journal of the Brewery History Society* 111 (Spring 2003).

———. "IPA: The Executive Summary." *Zythophile* blog. March 31, 2010. http://zythophile.wordpress.com/.

———. "IPA: The Hot Maturation Experiment." *Zythophile* blog. June 17, 2010. http://zythophile.wordpress.com/.

———. "IPA: Much Later Than You Think; Parts 1 and 2." *Zythophile* blog. November 19, 2008. http://zythophile.wordpress.com/.

———. "The Long Battle between Ale and Beer." *Zythophile* blog. December 14, 2009. http://zythophile.wordpress.com/.

———. "Pale Beers." *Zythophile* blog. November 26, 2009. http://zythophile.wordpress.com/.

———. "A Short History of Hops." *Zythophile* blog. November 20, 2009. http://zythophile.wordpress.com/.

Corran, H. S. *A History of Brewing.* London: David and Charles, 1975.

Curtin, Jack. "Black and Bitter: True Origins of Black IPA." *Ale Street News* 19, no. 4 (August–September 2010).

Daily Mirror. July 10, 1972.

Falstaff Brewing. "Ballantine XXX Ale." Last modified February 20, 2012. http://falstaffbrewing.com/ballantine_ale.htm.

Faulkner, Frank. *The Theory and Practice of Modern Brewing,* 2nd ed. London: F. W. Lyon, 1888.

Foster, Terry. "Historical Porter." *Brewing Techniques* 16, no. 4 (2010).

Fox, Messieur. *The London and Country Brewer.* London, 1736.

Glaser, Gregg. "The Late, Great Ballantine." *Modern Brewery Age,* March 2000.

Glover, Brian. *Cardiff Pubs and Breweries.* Stroud, UK: History Press, 2005.

Gourvish, T. R., and R. G. Wilson. *The British Brewing Industry, 1830–1980*. Cambridge, UK: Cambridge University Press, 1994.

Grant, Bert. *The Ale Master: How I Pioneered America's Craft Brewing Industry, Opened the First Brewpub, Bucked Trends, and Enjoyed Every Minute of It*. Seattle: Sasquatch Books, 1998.

Great American Beer Festival. "GABF Winners." Accessed December 2010. www.greatamericanbeerfestival.com/the-competition /winners/.

Harrison, Dr. John. "London as the Birthplace of India Pale Ale." Paper presented at the Guild of Beer Writers IPA Conference. London, 1994.

Harrison, Dr. John, and Members of the Durden Park Beer Circle. *Old British Beers and How to Make Them*. London, 1976.

Hayes, Antony. "The Evolution of English IPA." *Zymurgy* 32, no. 4 (July/August 2009).

Hough, J. S., D. E. Briggs, R. Stevens, and T. W. Young. *Malting and Brewing Science*. 2 vols. New York: Chapman and Hall, 1982.

Jackson, Michael. "Jackson on Beer: Giving Good Beer the IPA Name." *Zymurgy*, Spring 1996.

Jurado, Jaime. "A Pale Reflection on Ale Perfection." *The Brewer International* 2, no. 12 (2002).

Koch, Greg, and Steve Wagner. *The Craft of Stone Brewing Co.: Liquid Lore, Epic Recipes, and Unabashed Arrogance*. With Randy Clemens. Berkeley, CA: Ten Speed Press, 2010.

La Pensée, Clive, and Roger Protz. *Homebrew Classics: India Pale Ale*. St. Albans, UK: CAMRA, 2003.

Lewis, Michael J., and Tom W. Young. *Brewing*, 2nd ed. New York: Kluwer Academic/Plenum Publishers, 2001.

Loftus, W. R. *The Brewer: A Familiar Treatise on the Art of Brewing*. London: W. R. Loftus, 1856.

Mathias, Peter. *The Brewing Industry in England, 1700–1830*. Cambridge, UK: Cambridge University Press, 1959.

McCabe, John T., Harold M. Broderick, and Master Brewers Association of the Americas. *The Practical Brewer*. Wauwatosa, WI: Master Brewers Association of the Americas, 1999.

McMaster, Charles. "Edinburgh as a Centre of IPA." Paper presented at the Guild of Beer Writers Conference on IPA. London, 1994.

Meantime Brewing Company. "India Pale Ale." Accessed January 2010. http://www.india-pale-ale.com/.

Molyneaux, William. *Burton-on-Trent: Its History, Its Waters, and Its Breweries*. London: Trübner, 1869.

Monkton, H. A. *The History of English Ale and Beer*. London: Bodley Head, 1966.

Mosher, Randy. *Radical Brewing*. Boulder, CO: Brewers Publications, 2004.

Ockert, Karl. *MBAA Practical Handbook for the Specialty Brewer*. Vol. 1, *Raw Materials and Brewhouse Operations*. Pilot Knob, MN: Master Brewers Association of the Americas, 2006.

One Hundred Years of Brewing: A Supplement to the Western Brewer. Chicago: H. S. Rich, 1903. Reprint, New York: Arno Press, 1974.

Palmer, John. "Reading a Water Report." In *How to Brew*. Boulder, CO: Brewers Publications, 1999.

Papazian, Charlie. *The Complete Joy of Homebrewing*. New York: Avon Books, 1984.

Pattinson, Ron. "Allsopp Reassures the Public." *Shut Up about Barclay Perkins* blog. January 7, 2011. http://barclayperkins.blogspot.com/.

———. "Black IPA." *Shut Up about Barclay Perkins* blog. March 12, 2010. http://barclayperkins.blogspot.com/.

———. "*Brettanomyces* and Pale Ale." *Shut Up about Barclay Perkins* blog. April 5, 2011. http://barclayperkins.blogspot.com/.

———. "Brewing IPA in the 1850s." *Shut Up about Barclay Perkins* blog. December 28, 2010. http://barclayperkins.blogspot.com/.

———. "Burton Ale in the 1820s." *Shut Up about Barclay Perkins* blog. May 20, 2011. http://barclayperkins.blogspot.com/.

———. "Burton Water: Parts 1 and 2." *Shut Up about Barclay Perkins* blog. January 16 and January 17, 2011. http://barclayperkins.blogspot.com/.

———. "The Characteristics of IPA." *Shut Up about Barclay Perkins* blog. January 14, 2011. http://barclayperkins.blogspot.com/.

———. "The India Beer Market in the 1830s and 1840s." *Shut Up about Barclay Perkins* blog. December 10, 2010. http://barclayperkins.blogspot.com/.

———. "Logs: Lesson 1." *Shut Up about Barclay Perkins* blog. June 17, 2009. http://barclayperkins.blogspot.com/.

———. "Mr. Bass Chips In." *Shut Up about Barclay Perkins* blog. January 15, 2011. http://barclayperkins.blogspot.com/.

———. "Party-gyles." *Shut Up about Barclay Perkins* blog. April 26, 2010. http://barclayperkins.blogspot.com/.

———. "Stock Ale in the 19th Century." *Shut Up about Barclay Perkins* blog. April 10, 2011. http://barclayperkins.blogspot.com/.

Pereira, Jonathan. *A Treatise on Food and Diet.* New York: Fowlers & Wells, 1843.

Practical Man. *The Innkeeper and Public Brewer.* London: G. Biggs, 1860.

Protz, Roger, ed. *Good Beer Guide 2002.* London: CAMRA, 2001.

———. *Good Beer Guide 2005.* London: CAMRA, 2004.

Prout, Dr. William. *On the Nature and Treatment of Stomach and Urinary Diseases.* London: Oxford University, 1840.

Pryor, Alan. "Indian Pale Ale: An Icon of an Empire." Commodities of Empire, Working Paper No. 13, University of Essex, 2009.

Richardson, John. *The Philosophical Principles of the Science of Brewing.* York, UK: [Printed by G. Peacock], 1805.

Richmond, Lesley, and Alison Turton. *The Brewing Industry: A Guide to Historical Records.* Manchester, UK: Manchester University Press, 1990.

Roberts, W. H. *The Scottish Ale Brewer and Practical Maltster.* Edinburgh, 1847.

Sanbrook, Pamela. *Country House Brewing in England, 1500–1900.* London: Hambledon Press, 1996.

Scottish Brewing Archive Association. *Newsletter* 2 (2000).

———. *Newsletter* 25 (Summer 1995).

———. *Newsletter* 28 (Spring 1997).

Southby, E. R. *A Systematic Handbook of Practical Brewing.* London, 1885.

Steel, James. *Selection of the Practical Points of Malting and Brewing, and Strictures Thereon, for the Use of Brewery Proprietors.* Glasgow, 1878.

Sunderland, Paul. "Brew No. 396: Parti-gyled Brew of India Pale Ale Brewed in the Allsopp Brewhouse and Fermented in the Ind Coope Brewery, Burton-on-Trent, Wednesday, May 15th, 1935." Paper presented at the Guild of British Beer Writers IPA Conference. London, 1994.

Thomlinson, Thom. "India Pale Ale: Parts 1 and 2." *Brewing Techniques,* March/April and May/June 1994.

Tizard, William L. *The Theory and Practice of Brewing Illustrated.* London, 1846.

University of Michigan. *Contributions from the Chemical Laboratory.* Vol. 1, Part 1. Ann Arbor, MI: University of Michigan, 1882.

Wahl, Robert, and Max Henius. *American Handy-book of the Brewing, Malting and Auxiliary Trades.* Chicago: Wahl & Henius, 1902.

Wilson, Dr. Richard J. "The Rise of Pale Ales and India Pale Ales in Victorian Britain." Paper presented at the Guild of Beer Writers Conference on IPA. London, 1994.

Worthington, Roger. "Cascade: How Adolph Coors Helped Launch the Most Popular U.S. Aroma Hop and the Craft Beer Revolution." *Indie Hops "In Hop Pursuit"* blog. January 25, 2010. http://inhoppursuit.blogspot.com/.

RECIPE INDEX

HISTORICAL RECIPES

Amsinck's India Pale Ale, 231

Amsinck's No. 25 Burton East India Pale Ale, 232

James Mccrorie's Original IPA, 233

Worthington's White Shield, 234

Reid 1839 IPA, 235

Fuller's 1897 IPA, 237

Barclay Perkins 1928 IPA, 238

Ballantine IPA No. 1, 239

Ballantine IPA No. 2, 240

J. W. Lees Harvest Ale, 241

J. W. Lees Manchester Star, 242

EARLY CRAFT-BREWING RECIPES

Bombay Bomber IPA, 244

Harpoon IPA, 247

Blind Pig IPA, 248

CONTEMPORARY U.S. CRAFT-BREWING RECIPES

Brooklyn East India Pale Ale, 249

Dogfish Head Aprihop, 251

Burton Baton Brew No. 1: Olde Ale Thread, 252

Burton Baton Brew No. 2: Imperial IPA Thread, 253

Smuttynose Finest Kind IPA, 254

Deschutes Quail Springs IPA, 256

Stone IPA, 257

Pizza Port Carlsbad Wipeout IPA, 258

Fat Head's Headhunter IPA, 259

Avery Dugana IPA, 260

Odell IPA, 262

Goose Island India Pale Ale, 263

Deschutes Inversion IPA, 264
Demon's Hopyard IPA, 265
Firestone Walker Union Jack IPA, 266

CONTEMPORARY BRITISH RECIPES

Meantime Brewing London IPA, 267
Thornbridge Jaipur India Pale Ale, 269
Thornbridge Seaforth IPA, 271
Fuller's Bengal Lancer IPA, 272
Museum Brewing Company Calcutta IPA, 274

DOUBLE IPA RECIPES

Russian River Pliny The Elder, 275
Vip Ale (Or Very India Pale Ale, 277
Pizza Port Hop 15, 278
Smuttynose Big A IPA, 279
Brewdog Hardcore IPA, 280
Stone Ruination IPA, 282
Stone 14th Anniversary Emperial IPA, 282
Stone 10th Anniversary IPA, 283

BLACK IPA RECIPES

Vermont Pub And Brewery Blackwatch IPA, 285
The Alchemist El Jefe, 286
The Shed's Darkside Black IPA, 287
Pizza Port Carlsbad Black Lie, 288
Stone 11th Anniversary Ale/ Stone Sublimely Self-Righteous Ale, 289
Hill Farmstead James Black IPA, 290
Deschutes Hop In The Dark, 291

INDEX

Abbott, Edwin, 47, 50

Abbott's Bow Brewery, 50

Abbott's Pale Ale, 49

Abroad cooper, 34

Acetaldehyde, 211, 215, 216-217

Achouffe Brewery's Houblon Chouffe
Dobbelen IPA Tripel, 179

Act of 1698: 19

Adjuncts, 100, 139

Adulteration, accusations of, 55-56

Advertisements, 26, 27 (fig.), 28, 45 (fig.), 46,
47, 48, 48 (fig.), 49, 65, 66, 134 (fig.)

Aeration, 217, 218

Aging, 29, 37, 66, 67, 112, 123, 126, 140, 157,
208, 220

    Brettanomyces and, 94

    Burton Union system and, 87

    cask, 85, 99, 308

    clarity and, 102

    dry hops and, 219

    fermenting, 33-34

    flavor and, 102, 115

    process, 11, 12, 14, 21, 87, 96, 99, 219,
       230

    shipping and, 91-93

Alchemist, The, 173, 286

Alchemist El Jefe, 173

    recipe for, 286-287

Alcohol, 4, 96-97, 110, 176, 183, 210

    calculating, 75

    content of, 17, 18, 72, 122, 180, 191, 226

    fusel, 217, 218

    levels of, 18, 152

    reduced, 137, 180

    sugars and, 74

    tolerance, 30, 214

Ale breweries, 25, 133

    expansion/proliferation of, 15

Ales, 22, 66, 118, 120, 122, 139, 143, 158, 212

    advertising for, 45 (fig.)

    amber, 115, 186

    beers and, 18

    Belgian, 178, 179

    bitter, 126

    brewing, 9, 117

    brown, 20, 28, 96, 175, 177

    dark, 28

    described, 10

    draft, 140

    English, 101, 115, 144, 234

    imperial pale, 110, 115

    keeping, 17, 18, 28, 36, 96

    low-hopped, 18

    March, 35

    mild, 18, 25, 54, 96, 97, 125-126

    October, 16, 32, 34, 35, 37, 80

    old, 96

    per capita income for, 11

    real, 59, 123

    running, 59, 97, 101, 123

    Scotch, 102, 104, 108, 109, 146, 175

    small, 26, 97

    sparkling, 57

    stock, 17, 18, 30, 32, 40, 59, 60, 64, 65,
       96, 110

    strong, 25, 26, 35, 36, 98, 102

    table, 65

Alesmith, 167

Alewives, 10

Alexander Keith Brewery, IPA by, 120

Allagash's Hugh Malone, 179

Allied Breweries, 311, 312

Allsopp, Henry, 55

Allsopp, Samuel, 35, 42

Allsopp brewery, 46, 51, 67, 80, 95, 125

    adulteration and, 56

advertisement by, 49, 66

ales, 42, 43

Bass and, 52, 59

beers, 76-77 (table)

exporting by, 40

hop pressing by, 83

lager beers and, 59

maltsters, 71

Allsopp's IPA, 43, 50, 59, 75, 124-125
(table), 269

Alpha acids, 29, 74, 192, 195, 200, 204

content of, 193, 202

described, 193-194

hop, 194, 194 (table)

isomerized, 203, 208

un-isomerized, 194

Alpine Brewing Company's Exponential
Hoppiness, 181

Amarillo hops, 160, 169, 174, 176, 179,
180, 207

popularity of, 156

American beers, ABWs/ABVs of, 119 (table)

American black ales, 177

style guidelines for, 226-227

American brewers, 109

IPAs by, 118

top 10/by year, 140-141 (table)

American Hop Ale, 265

American hops, 73, 110, 149, 249, 279

character of, 226

varieties of, x

American India Black Ale, 177

American IPAs, ix, x, 74, 109-115, 117-118,
132-135, 137, 144, 160, 171, 175, 177,
178, 179, 180, 194, 212, 244, 259

article about, 151-153

brewing tips for, 224

hops for, 165, 181

ingredients for, 153

popularity of, 156

style guidelines for, 225-226

American Society of Brewing Chemists, vii

Amino acids, 185, 212, 214, 215, 216

Amsinck, George, 78-79, 231

Amsinck's India Pale Ale, recipe for, 231-232

Amsinck's No. 25 Burton East India Pale
Ale, recipe for, 232-233

"Analysis of Various IPAs from the 1800s"
(Roberts), 109

Analytical targets, described, 230-231

Anchor Brewing Company, 137, 142-143,
144, 148, 150

Anchor Christmas Ale, 144

Anchor Liberty Ale, 1, 144, 145, 151, 158

hops for, 148

original bottle of, 143 (fig.)

Anchor Porter, 143

Anchor Pub, 5

Anchor Steam Beer, 142, 143

Anderson, Ray, 6, 6 (fig.)

Anheuser-Busch (A-B), vii, xi, 2, 132, 135,
139, 207, 265

Anheuser-Busch (A-B) Merrimack Brewery,
2, 3, 265

Anti-Beer Law, 115

Apollo hops, 193, 207

Apparent degree of fermentation (ADF),
230, 231

April 1908 Licensing Bill, 126

Aromas, 178, 183, 193, 201, 202, 205, 206,
208

hop, vii, 149, 153, 177, 192, 195, 204,
207, 225, 226

malt, 177

Arthur, Tomme, 169, 278

Ashton, John, 27

Ashworth, Judy, 165

Australian brewers, 120-121

Avery, Adam, 260-261

Avery Brewing Company, 261

Avery Brewing Company Dugana IPA,
recipe for, 260-262

Bacteria, 11, 21, 30, 67, 69, 83, 94, 96

Badenhausen, Carl, 132

Badenhausen, Otto, 132

Bagby, Jeff, 176, 177, 258, 278, 288

Ballantine, Peter, 117, 132

Ballantine Ales, 137, 212

Ballantine beers, analysis of, 137 (table)

Ballantine Brewery, 110, 115, 133 (fig.), 143, 252, 309

    advertisement for, 134 (fig.)

    decline of, 135

    delivery truck, 136 (fig.)

    dry hopping by, 134

    sale of, 137

    symbol of, 132

    yeast strain of, 135, 145

Ballantine IPA No. 1, recipe for, 239-240

Ballantine IPA No. 2, recipe for, 240

Ballantine IPAs, 132, 133, 137, 139-140, 141, 144, 145, 146, 152

    label of, 135 (fig.), 136 (fig.)

    post-Prohibition, 134

Ballantine XXX Ale, 132

Ballast Point, 167

Ballast Point Even Keel, 180

Baltic porters, 168

Balton, J.: on Allsopp's Ale, 43

Barclay Perkins, 53, 95, 129, 238

    black IPA by, 170

    export market and, 41

    hops usage by, 98

    lager beers and, 59

    pale lagers and, 97

    price list from, 130 (fig.)

Barclay Perkins Anchor Brewery, 100 (fig.)

Barclay Perkins IPA

    analytical profile of, 298-299 (table)

    label for, 130 (fig.)

Barclay Perkins 1928 IPA, recipe for, 238-239

Barley, 71, 98, 113, 121, 183, 184

Barley malt, 12, 71, 110, 183

Barnard, Alfred, 80

Barrel yard, 90 (fig.)

Barrels, 87-91, 90 (fig.), 92, 93

    cleaning, 34

    exploding, 94, 106

    transporting, 88 (fig.)

Barry, Dave: quote of, 139

Bass, 5, 6, 42, 51, 64, 67, 80, 91, 95, 118, 121, 125, 152, 234, 274, 286

    adulteration and, 56

    advertisement by, 48 (fig.), 49, 65, 66

    Allsopp and, 52, 59

    barrel yard of, 90 (fig.)

    brewing log from, 74 (fig.)

    exporting by, 40

    fermentation and, 85

    hop pressing by, 83

    IPA and, 43, 50, 66, 75, 88, 128, 141, 170, 171

    price list of, 79 (table)

    size of, 52-53

    steam engine, 62 (fig.)

    water tower, 68 (fig.)

Bass, Michael Thomas, 55

Bass Ale, 42, 52, 141

    serving, 44 (fig.)

Bass Archives, 7, 312

Bass Red Triangle, label of, 66

Bay State Brewery, 113, 114 (fig.)

Bayley, Paul, 6, 6 (fig.), 243, 244

Becks, 58

Beer data, early 1700s, 17 (table)

Beer rations, 19, 57

Beer styles, 8, 143, 208

    British, 110, 124 (table), 186

    historical, 7, 16

    seasonal, 30

Beerhouse Act (1830), 57

Beers

    Belgian, 178

    bitter, 96, 97, 193

    black, 174, 177

    British/gravity of, 126 (table), 129 (table)

    brown, 16

    canned, 142

    cask, 59, 62

    classification of, 56

craft, 19, 147, 156, 160, 206
dark, 115, 174, 175
English, 15, 58, 59, 64, 67, 111, 120
flat, 106
freezing, 2
heartier, 20
high-gravity, 58, 213
history of/1700s, 15-19
hopped, 10, 169
Indian imports of, 50 (table)
keeping, 18, 34
lower-alcohol, 122, 124
March, 82
medicinal, 115
October, 14, 16, 17 (table), 22, 34,
     81-82
pale, 14, 16, 19, 22, 25, 28, 29, 30, 35,
     36, 37, 55, 96, 97
per capita income for, 11
running, 59, 60, 64
seasonal, 153
small, 17, 20
special-release, 153
sparkling, 96
stock, 18, 20, 21, 24, 93
strong, 20
table, 17, 20, 36, 57
young, 97
Belgian IPAs, 156, 160, 212
    brewing, 178-180
Belgian Wit style, 181
Bell's, 156
Bell's Hopslam, 167
Bengal Hukaru, advertisement in, 47
Bengal Wine, 46
Bere malt, 104
Beta acids, 192, 205
Betz, John, 118
Bigfoot, 286
Bigg malt, 104
Birmingham and Derby Junction Railway, 49
Bistro, The, 167, 181
Bistro IPA Festival, 259
Bittering, vii, 144, 180, 201, 207

compounds, 199
    hops and, 153, 193-194, 198, 208
Bitterness, 33, 35, 46, 73, 142, 147, 172, 174,
     192, 210
    alpha acids and, 193
    calculating, 202-205
    extracting, 194, 203, 204, 205
    hop, 26, 35, 68, 135, 142, 156, 188, 192,
         195, 204, 208, 225, 226
    increasing, 43, 46, 170, 200, 202, 204,
         206, 208
    index, 308
    IPA, 55
    levels of, 202, 203, 204
    reducing, 137, 152
Bitters, 96, 142, 180
Black Butte Porter, 256
Black IPAs, 156, 160, 170-175, 176-178
    analysis of, 178-179 (table)
    brewing tips for, 225
Blind Pig Brewing Company, 156, 165, 167,
     248
Blind Pig Inaugural Ale, 165
Blind Pig IPA, 2
    recipe for, 248-249
Blue Brewery, 52
Boils, 32-33, 82, 83, 105, 195, 200, 203, 204,
     206, 230
Bombay Bomber IPA, 153, 243-244
    recipe for, 244-245
Booth, Oliver, 117
Bottles, 66
    shipping, 92-93
Bottling, 54, 65, 67, 87, 92, 112, 119, 140,
     142, 143
    fermentation and, 78
    glass taxes and, 57-58
Boulevard Brewing Company, 181
Boulevard Brewing Company Collaboration
     #2, 181
Bow Brewery Company Ltd., 50
Bowen, Christopher, 8
Bowie, John, 56
Bradford, Daniel, 277

Bravo hops, 181

Brettanomyces clausseneii yeast, 18, 30, 75, 181
    case for, 93-94

Brew Free or Die homebrew club, 2-3

Brew Your Own, 239

BrewDog, 156, 280

BrewDog Hardcore IPA, recipe for, 280-281

Brewer and Distiller International, 5-6

Brewer, The (Loftus), 63

Breweries, 139, 150
    ale, 15, 25, 133
    commercial, 10, 15, 16, 31, 54, 97, 117,
        195
    construction of, 63
    high-altitude, 122
    porter, 15, 25, 30
    steam, 142

Brewers Association, 177

Brewer's Gold hops, 137, 145

Brewers Reserve, 96

Brewery History Society, 6, 311, 312

Brewhouse process, 183, 205-209
    described, 82-83

Brewing, 9, 12, 153, 157
    historical, 8, 309
    procedures for, 16
    seasonal, 13, 80-82, 105

Brewing books, 310-311
    historical, 28, 229

Brewing industry, 15, 139, 146
    conglomeration of, 100
    growth of, 19, 62
    homogenization of, 142
    taxes on, 40
    transition in, 54

Brewing Industry in England, 1700-1830, The
    (Mathias), 63, 66

Brewing logs, 8 (fig.), 28, 31, 74 (fig.), 98,
    103, 172 (fig.)
    legibility of, 305, 308

Brewing process, 117, 122, 185, 195, 202
    Burton IPA, 79-85, 87-89, 91-94
    consistency/control over, 15
    modernization of, 61

    parameters in, 189

Brewing tips, by style, 224-225

BrewWorks at the Party Source, 276

Bridgeport Brewing Company, 156

British Brewing Industry, 1830-1980, The
    (Gourvish and Wilson), 67

British IPAs, 244, 256

British Library, 7, 312

British Museum, 313

Brooklyn Brewery, 156, 171, 172, 249

Brooklyn East India Pale Ale, recipe for,
    249-250

Brooks, Stan, x, 148

Brooks, Steve, 6, 6 (fig.)

Brouwerij De Leyerth, 179

Browerij Van Steenberge N.V., 178

Brown, Pete, 7, 92, 269, 274

Brown IPAs, 156

Brynildson, Matt, 266

"Buffalo" Bill Owen's Alimony Ale, 171

Bull Dog, label of, 66

Bullion hops, 134, 145, 147, 239

Burch, Byron, 152

Burton ales, 16, 31, 40, 63, 65, 96, 110, 111,
    117, 132, 171
    analysis of, 75 (table)
    exporting, 19
    pale beers and, 19

Burton and Its Bitter Beer (Bushnan), 42

Burton Baton Brew No. 1: Olde Ale Thread,
    recipe for, 252-253

Burton Baton Brew No. 2: Imperial IPA
    Thread, recipe for, 253-254

Burton beers, 85, 251
    exporting, 39, 68
    water for, 67

Burton brewers, 4, 40, 49-50, 56, 71, 79, 89,
    97, 100, 121, 128
    employment with, 53
    exports by, 19, 37
    Hodgson's and, 46
    Indian market and, 42-43, 46
    IPAs by, 98, 110
    libel suit by, 70

market for, 95
number of, 52 (table)
output of, 51
recipes by, 46
reduction in, 60
relocation by, 53 (table)
Burton Bridge Brewery, 68, 156
Burton Cooper (statue), plaque for, 88
Burton IPAs, 5, 52, 55, 65, 66, 97, 98, 133,
    156, 233, 312
    brewing process for, 79-85, 87-89, 91-
        94, 110
    growth of, 51
    hopping rates for, 80-81 (table), 105
    hops for, 73-74
    ingredients for, 67-75
    and London IPAs compared, 99-100
    malt for, 71-72, 185
    popularity of, 58
    quality/flavor of, 46
    transporting, 40, 49
    water for, 67-70
    yeast for, 74-75
Burton-on-Trent, 6, 7, 19, 38, 48 (fig.), 51
    (fig.), 68-69, 68 (fig.)
    growth of, 51
    IPA output in, 52, 95
    N-gauge model of, 131 (fig.)
    visiting, x-xi, 313
Burton-on-Trent Abbey, 39
Burton-on-Trent: Its Histories, Its Waters, and Its
    Breweries (Molyneaux), 26, 48
Burton Union system, 75, 83-85, 98-99, 121
    fermentation and, x, 6, 84, 85, 87, 106,
        266, 308
    Marston's and, 85, 86 (fig.)
    swan necks of, 86 (fig.)
Burton water, ix, 85, 87, 98, 123, 283
    analysis of, 70, 70 (table)
    minerals in, 69, 69 (table)
Burtonization, 70, 100
Bushnan, John Stevenson, 42
Butler, James, 88

C. H. Evans Brewing Company, 40, 110, 111,
    113
    malt house of, 111 (fig.)
C. H. Evans Brewing Company IPA, 112,
    112 (fig.), 113
Calagione, Sam, 250, 251, 252
Calcium, 28, 32, 39, 69, 187-188
    yeast and, 37, 68, 128
Calcutta Gazette, advertisements in, 26
Caledonian Deuchars IPA, 157
Calverley, C. V., 61
Calypso hops, 160
Campaign for Real Ale (CAMRA), 142, 156
Campbell, 102
Camusi, Paul, 145
Canada Breweries, 146, 274
Canadian brewers, 119-120
Canterbury Brown hops, 29
Carafa malt, 172, 173, 174, 178, 286, 290, 291
Carawheat MFB, 174
Carbon dioxide, 20, 74, 183, 221
Carbon dioxide extract, 200-201, 201 (fig.),
    202
Carling, 142
Carlsberg, 129, 142
Carlton United Brewers, 121
Carpenter, Mark, 143, 144
Carpenter, S., 15
Carter, Jimmy, 151
Cascade hops, ix, 2, 144, 145, 146, 153, 157,
    169, 177-178, 181, 207
    story of, 147-150
Casks, 19, 20, 21, 30, 34, 38, 56, 59, 62, 78,
    80, 81, 84, 96, 98
    cleaning, 68
    coopers and, 88
    exploding, 94, 106
    fermentation, 33
    reusing, 91
    shipping, 87, 92
    storing, 88
    transporting, 49 (fig.)
Castle Spring's Lucknow IPA, 3
Catherine the Great, 40

Centennial hops, ix, 149, 153, 160, 169, 181, 207, 281

Challenger hops, 156, 157

Chapman, Captain, 43

Character, 65, 93, 98, 148, 149
    aroma, 202, 207
    balanced, 191
    bitter, 188
    hop, 67, 178, 201, 202, 208, 212, 216, 217, 221, 225, 226
    malt, 169, 178
    oak, 135

Charrington, 52, 70, 97, 100

Chemistry, 64, 68-69, 95, 187, 195

Chevalier malt, 71, 104

Chicory Stout, 251

Chinook hops, ix, 149, 153, 160, 169, 205, 244, 284

Chlorine, removing, 187

Christian Feigenspan Brewery, 115, 116 (fig.), 132, 309

Ciders, exporting, 20

Cilurzo, Natalie, 167, 169

Cilurzo, Vinnie, 2, 165, 166-167, 169, 248

Citra hops, 160, 169, 181

Clarification, 28, 67, 87, 106, 128

Clarity, 34, 46, 102, 106, 187

Claussen, N. Hjelte, 93

Cluster hops, 73, 111, 128, 145, 147, 148

Coke, 12-13, 15, 16, 29, 31

Cole, Matt, 259

Color, 13, 71, 104, 143, 180, 183, 186

Columbus hops, ix, 2, 153, 160, 169, 180, 281

Combrune, Michael, 27, 31

Complete Joy of Homebrewing, The (Papazian), 151

Consolidation, viii, 118, 121, 125, 142

Consumers Brewing Company, 118

Consumption, 78, 127
    domestic, 74, 87, 91, 97
    per capita annual, 54, 55 (table), 60

Continental Ale, 128, 274

Continental IPA, 141, 274

Conversions, 307

Cooling
    pans, 33
    vessels, 8, 106
    wort, 83, 84

Coolships, 33, 62, 83, 84, 106

Coopers, 34, 72 (fig.), 92
    image of, 88-89
    shop of, 89 (fig.)

Coors, 6, 7, 139, 274

Corcoran, Bil, 115, 116, 134, 134, 135, 136, 309

Cornell, Martyn, 4, 7, 35, 36, 309

Craft Brewers Conference, xi, 2

Craft brewing, vii, 3, 122, 147, 149, 151, 153, 157, 160, 187, 198, 200, 202, 203, 208
    growth of, 150
    movement, 156
    raw materials of, ix-x

Craft Brewing Association, 233

Craft of Stone Brewing, The, 7

Crichton, A. B., 121

Crown Brewing Company, 121

Crystal hops, 244, 284

Crystal malt, 4, 28, 72, 97, 101, 123, 128, 156, 176, 185
    limiting/eliminating, 169
    using, 186

Daniels, Ray, 231

Dark IPAs, 173

Dark Star, 156

Dawson, Tom, 6, 6 (fig.)

De Clerk, Jean, x

De Koven, Reginald, 9

De Ranke XX Bitter, 179

Defense of the Realm Act (DORA), 127

Demon's Hopyard IPA, 3
    recipe for, 265-266

Deschutes Brewing Company, 174-175, 181

Deschutes Brewing Company Chainbreaker White IPA, 181

Deschutes Brewing Company Conflux No. 2: 181

Deschutes Brewing Company Hop in the

Dark, 174
    recipe for, 291-292
Deschutes Brewing Company Inversion IPA, 256
    recipe for, 264-265
Deschutes Brewing Company Quail Springs IPA, 264
    recipe for, 256-257
Devil's Hopyard IPA, 3, 265
Diabetics, IPAs and, 54, 65
Diacetyl, 94, 170, 211, 212, 215, 219, 225, 226
    rest, 216, 218
Dickie, Martin, 280
Directions for Brewing Malt Liquors, 30
Disher, Robert, 102
Dobler Brewery, 115
Dogfish Head Aprihop, recipe for, 251-252
Dogfish Head Brewing Company, 3, 156, 250-251, 252
    IPAs by, 167, 175, 209
Dogfish Head Brewing Company Indian Brown IPA, 175
Dogfish Head Brewing Company 90 Minute IPA, 167
Dorber, Mark, 5, 6, 6 (fig.), 24, 243
Double IPA Festival, 167
Double IPAs, 2, xi, 160, 175, 178, 180, 194, 201, 206, 209, 212, 215, 278
    analysis of, 170-171 (table)
    brewing, 169-170, 191, 216, 224
    history of, 165-169
    style guidelines for, 226
    sugars and, 187
Doyle, Rich, 246
Dry hopping, ix, 30, 34, 35, 36, 67, 74, 128, 134, 137, 145, 153, 157, 165, 169, 170, 176, 181, 188, 192, 198, 201, 208, 210
    aging and, 219
    critical steps of, 221
    eliminating, 140
    hop pellets and, 199-200
    multi-stage, 209
    procedures for, 144, 219-220
Durden Park Beer Circle, 5, 35, 233, 308

Durden Park Beer Club, 152, 243-244
Duvel Moortgat, 179
Duvel Tripel Hop, 179

E. coli, 69
East India Company, 7, 78, 313
    Allsopp and, 35, 43
    business model of, 21-22
    docks site, 313
    headquarters of, 23 (fig.)
    Hodgson's and, 21-28, 36, 41-43
    seal of, 22 (fig.)
East India porter, 170, 171, 242
East Indiamen, 22, 47 (fig.)
East Kent Golding hops, 29, 46, 47, 65, 73, 74, 128, 152, 241, 268, 282
Eccles, Samuel, 119
Eckhardt, Fred, 152
Edinburgh, brewing in, 102, 103, 104
Edinburgh Ale, 108
Edinburgh and Leith Brewery, 102
Edinburgh Brewing Heritage Society, 104
Egan, John, 284
Egelston, Peter, 254
Eldridge Brewing Company, 114
Electricity, 63, 103
Elinore Rummin, wood carving of, 11 (fig.)
Empire Pale Ale, 156
Endosperms, 183, 184, 185, 188, 189, 191
England, Kristen, 8, 235, 236, 237, 309
English beers, 58, 64, 111, 120
    growth of, 15
    hopping rates in, 59
    water for, 67
English brewers, 142, 186
    IPAs by, 123-129, 131
English IPAs, 58, 109, 156, 160, 263, 267
    brewing, 98, 224
    profile of, 129
    style guidelines for, 225
Enzymes, 183, 184, 186, 188, 191
    malt, 187, 190
    sugars and, 185
Essential oils, 192, 204, 207, 209

described, 195

Essentials of Beer Styles, The (Eckhardt), 152

Estate brewing, 12 (fig.), 15, 57, 97

Esters, 59, 170, 181, 215

formation of, 211, 212, 217-218

Evans, Cornelius, 111

Evans, Neil, 112, 113

Evans, Robert, 111

Export porter, recipe log for, 172 (fig.)

Exports, 15, 20 (table), 22-24, 23 (table), 37, 41, 65, 92, 102, 108, 109

Baltics and, 41 (table)

development of, 19-21

to India, 19, 23 (table), 44 (table), 46 (table)

total, 20 (table)

Extract recovery, 13, 71, 104, 189

Extracts, viii, 173-174, 177, 207, 288, 290

carbon dioxide, 200-201, 201 (fig.), 202

Extreme Beer Fest, 175

Fahrendorf, Teri: article by, 151-153, 243-244

Falstaff Brewing Company, 137

Farmhouse brewing, 57

Farnham Golding hops, 29

Farnham hops, 29, 73, 98, 104

Fat Head, 259

Fat Head Headhunter IPA, recipe for, 259-260

Faulkins, Benjamin, 111

Faulkner, Frank, 171

Feigenspan, Christian, 110, 115, 115 (fig.)

Felinfoel Double Diamond, 129, 141

Fermentation, 13, 35, 39, 63, 75, 81, 82, 83-85, 100, 110, 134, 170, 175, 176, 177, 187, 191

acetaldehyde and, 216-217

aging and, 33-34

bottling and, 78

Burton Union system and, 6, 84, 85, 87, 266, 308

degree of, 124

described, 214-215, 230

improving, 61, 104, 106

primary, ix, 14, 33, 84, 93, 113, 208, 214, 217, 218-219

racking and, 98-99

secondary, 34, 37, 91, 92, 93, 94

slow, 93, 211

techniques, 210-214

temperature for, 30, 85, 105, 139, 142, 215, 217

vessels, 30, 74, 218, 220

wort, 190

yeast, 74, 85, 104, 181, 185, 195, 205, 208, 213

Fermenters, vii, 85, 115, 205, 208, 212, 218, 219, 220, 221

Filtration, 85, 209, 221

Finings, 34, 37, 87

described, 30

Firestone Walker, 85, 266

Firestone Walker Union Jack IPA, recipe for, 266-267

First Gold hops, 157

56103 hops, 148

Flaked maize, 100, 128

Flavor, 9, 13, 29, 62, 65, 67, 68, 73, 87, 92, 93, 94, 96, 104, 120, 122, 142, 144, 145, 181, 183, 187, 189, 205, 225, 226

adding, 169, 206

aging and, 102, 115

blending, 35, 175

buttery/butterscotch, 216

clove, 180

degradation of, 198

delicacy of, 66

development of, 211, 214-219

differences in, 213

extracting, 209, 219, 220

harsh, 33

hop, 105, 128, 135, 156, 170, 178, 180, 191, 192, 193, 195, 198, 199, 200, 201, 202, 204, 206, 207, 208, 210, 219, 220, 221, 226

malt, 177, 189

removing, 91

smoky, 11, 15, 18

sour/tart, 110

vegetative, 209, 210

yeast and, 85, 215, 217

Flocculation, 12, 39, 214

Flying Dog Raging Bitch, 179

Foaming, 194, 206, 220

Folkingham, Cyril, 183

Ford, William, 56-57

Foster's, 120, 127, 142

Founder's Devil Dancer, 181

Fountain Brewhouse, 27

Frank Jones Brewery, 113, 113 (fig.), 114, 312

Frank Jones Brewery Song, 95

Frank Jones Restaurant, 114

Free Mash Tun Act, 58

Freeminer Trafalgar IPA, 157

Fuggle hops, 73, 111, 128, 148, 156, 157, 268, 273

Fuller, Smith & Turner, 272

Fuller's Brewery, 35, 75, 282

IPAs by, 98, 100

Fuller's Brewery Bengal Lancer IPA, recipe for, 272-274

Fuller's Brewery 1845: 41

Fuller's Brewery 1897 IPA, recipe for, 237

GABF. See Great American Beer Festival

Gainesboro Captains, 87

Galaxy hops, 181

Galena hops, 146

Gandhi's Grog IPA, 153

Gaul Brewery, 118

Genesee 12 Horse Ale, 113

George, David Lloyd, 125

George's Brewery, 35, 97

Germination, 186

described, 184-185

Gin, 59, 78

Gladstone, William: beer tax and, 58, 101

Glass of Pale Ale, A (Bass), 64

Glucose, 187, 213, 215

Golding hops, 4, 29, 46, 47, 65, 73, 74, 98, 104, 111, 128, 137, 152, 156, 157, 179, 193, 241, 268, 272, 273, 282

Goldthorpe malt, 71

Goodhead, Job, 35, 42

Google Books, 309, 310

Goose Island Beer Company, ix, 263, 266

Goose Island Beer Company India Pale Ale, ix

recipe for, 263-264

Gora Gully Brewery, 121

Gourvish, T. R., 67

Graham, Tyler, 184, 192, 201

Grain, 9, 17, 176, 191, 230

milling, 188-189

Grant, Bert, 146, 147

Grant's IPA, 146, 147

logo for, 146 (fig.)

Grants Yakima Brewing and Malting Company, 150

Gravity, 13, 14, 30, 32, 35, 72, 74, 79, 94, 102, 109, 110, 122, 125, 128, 166, 176, 179, 213

British beer/by style, 129 (table)

drop in, 17, 99, 129, 133, 137

specific, 75, 82, 123, 305

standard, 58, 126 (table)

taxation and, 58

terminal, 75, 105

wort, 33, 83, 204, 216, 218

Great American Beer Festival (GABF), xi, 2, 139, 152, 176, 259, 263, 278

American IPA winners at, 158-160 (table)

described, 157-158

double IPAs and, 166, 167-168

English IPA winners at, 161 (table)

imperial IPA winners at, 168 (table)

IPA style guidelines from, 225-227

Great Lakes Brewery, 276

Great Western Railway, 119

Green Flash Le Freak, 179

Greene King IPA, 129, 141, 157

Griffin Brewery, 272

Grossman, Ken, 137, 144, 145

Hall, Greg, ix

Hallertau hops, 144, 148, 193, 194

Hare, Robert, 118

Harp, 142

Harpoon, 158

Harpoon Ale, 246

Harpoon Golden Lager, 246

Harpoon IPA, 3, 156, 245, 246
    recipe for, 247-248

Harpoon Winter Warmer, 246

Harrison, James, 269

Harrison, John, 5, 24, 35, 308

Haunold, Al, x, 148, 149

Haydon, Peter, 267

Hayes, Willard, 148

Helles lager, 13, 58

Hemocytometers, 213, 214

Henry Southern & Company Brewery, 113

Henry's IPA, 129

Hereford hops, 73

Heriot-Watt brewing school, 267

Hermitage, 27

Hieronymous, Stan, 8

Hill Farmstead Brewery, 173, 174, 175, 290
    tasting room, 137 (fig.)

Hill Farmstead Brewery James Black IPA, 173
    recipe for, 290-291

Hill, Shaun, 173, 287, 290

Hillis, Harv, 256

Hindy, Steve, 249

Hodgson, Frederick, 27, 41

Hodgson, George, 4-5, 22, 35, 36
    exporting by, 37
    IPA and, 27, 46
    marketing by, 49
    price gouging by, 23, 38

Hodgson, Mark, 25, 27, 41

Hodgson and Co., pale ale by, 55

Hodgson's ale, 97
    advertisement for, 65

Hodgson's beer, Allsopp's Ale IPA and, 43

Hodgson's Bow Brewery, 37, 38, 75, 95, 96, 97
    advertisement by, 26, 46, 49
    Allsopp and, 43
    Burton brewers and, 46

capacity issues for, 50

East India Company and, 21-28, 36,
    41-42, 42-43

export market and, 41

flats on site of, 25 (fig.)

map of, 24 (fig.)

original/location of, 313

production by, 28 (table)

Hodgson's East India Pale Ale, 49

Hodgson's Export Stout, 47

Hodgson's IPA, 5, 23, 25, 26, 27, 35, 36, 67
    advertisement for, 47, 48

Hodgson's Pale Ale, 29, 31, 42
    advertisement for, 27 (fig.)
    pricing tables of, 36
    recipe for, 35-36, 38
    summary of, 36-38

Hodgson's Pale Beer, 34

Hodgson's Stout, 49

Hogsheads, 87, 110, 112, 120

Holden, Oliver, 117

Holding, described, 31-32

Homebrewers, 151, 187, 195, 198, 203, 208

Hook, Alistair, 8, 156, 267

Hooper, Egbert, 70

Hop cones, 192, 192 (fig.), 199, 201 (fig.),
    202
    compressed, 193, 198
    described, 195, 198

Hop Growers of America, x

Hop oils, viii, 147, 170, 195, 201

Hop pellets, 201 (fig.), 201, 202, 205, 206,
    208, 220-221
    described, 198-200, 220-221
    dry hopping and, 199-200

Hop products, 170, 192
    described, 195, 198-202

Hop recipe, viii
    developing, 202-205, 209-210

Hop Research Group (USDA), 148

Hop resins, 192, 200

Hop substitutes, ban on, 18

Hopbacks, 33, 74, 83, 105, 145, 151, 198,
    207, 208

Hope Brewery, 55

Hopjack, 207

Hopping, ix, 4, 67, 102, 139, 140, 146, 176,
213
described, 230
first-wort, 206
kettle, 206
mash, 205-206
post-fermentation, 208-209
schedules, 170
techniques, 192, 205-209

Hopping data, London IPA, 99 (table)

Hopping rates, 13, 18, 19, 29, 35, 36, 59, 73-
74, 83, 110, 125, 128, 166, 176, 225
drop in, 129
early 1700s, 17 (table)
Scottish IPA, 105 (table)
Younger's, 106 (table)

Hops, ix, x, 14, 18, 31, 37, 67, 73-74, 78, 109,
121, 135, 144, 192-195
adding, 20, 32-33, 106, 195, 202, 203,
204, 205, 206, 207, 208, 221
alternatives, 10, 114
American, x, 73, 110, 149, 226, 249,
279
bales/bags of, 73, 198, 221
bittering and, 153, 193-194, 198, 208,
308
blending, 209-210
California, 308
chemical composition of, 193 (table)
described, 29-30
English, 98
European, 308
experimental, 148
flavor, 176, 201, 210
Flemish, 29
fresh, 29, 82, 202, 208
high-alpha, 74, 193-194, 206, 207
imported, 128
intensity of, 192
kettle, 202, 204

New York, 98
noble, 148, 179, 194
popular, 30-31, 156
pressing, 73, 83
quality, 104, 208
using, 10, 79, 105, 169, 199, 200, 202,
203, 203 (table), 204, 206, 207,
226
varieties of, 29, 128, 160, 180, 181, 192,
194, 195, 196-197 (table), 202,
207, 209, 210
whole, 195, 198, 199, 201, 205, 206,
208, 209, 219-220
wild, 117
yeast and, 212

Hops and Glory (Brown), 7, 92, 274

Horse Brass Pub, 174

Housman, A. E.: quote of, 39

Hull Packet, advertisements in, 65

Humulus lupulus, 167

Hunter, William, 56

Hydrometers, 15, 61

IBUs, viii, 110, 202, 203, 204, 205, 230, 231

IIPA, 165

Imperial IPAs
analysis of, 170-171 (table)
history of, 165-169
popularity of, 167-168
style guidelines for, 226
sugars and, 187

Imperial Oktoberfests, 168

Imperial Pilsners, 168

Imperial porters, 168

Ind Coope, 52, 59, 70, 100, 125, 129, 156,
312

India, shipping route to, 21 (fig.)

India pale ales (IPAs)
in 1800s, 65-66, 294-297
analysis of/various, 154-155 (table),
294-297, 300-303 (table)
brewing, 3, 4, 7, 51, 52, 95, 186, 187

craft-brewed, 5, 149, 162-163 (table)

decline of, 122, 127

development of, ix, 16, 40, 46-48

domestic, 50, 58, 78-79, 97, 99, 102

health-enhancing qualities of, 97, 112

historical, 157, 178

history of, xi, 1-2, 5, 110, 115

hunting for, 309-313

low-alcohol, 141, 157

popularity of, 53-55, 95, 97, 110, 123, 127

production of, 49, 101, 186

recipe guidelines for, 222-223 (table)

style guidelines for, 225-227

variations of, 160, 224

Indian brewers, IPAs by, 121-122

Indie Hops, 174

Industrial Revolution, viii, 10, 15, 61, 62, 64, 96, 100

Ingredients, 10, 67-75, 133, 153

in 1700s, 18-31

techniques and, 67

IPA Hunters, 6 (fig.)

Iso-alpha acids, viii, 194, 202, 203, 204, 205, 208, 210

J. W. Lees Brewery, 101, 171, 172, 241

black IPA by, 170

J. W. Lees Brewery Harvest Ale, recipe for, 241-242

J. W. Lees Brewery Manchester Star, 171, 172 (fig.), 241

recipe for, 242-243

Jackson, Michael, 145, 147, 151, 234

James McCrorie's Original IPA, recipe for, 233-234

Jeffery, Ian, x

John Betz Brewery, 118

Johnston, Grant, 151, 152

Jones, Don, 114

Jones, Frank, 110, 113, 114

Jones, Peter, 114

Jones, Johnson & Co., 114 (fig.)

Joseph Clay & Co., 40, 42

Joyce, Jack, 174

Kalamazoo Spice Extraction Company (Kalsec Inc.), vii, 266

Keeling, John, 8, 35, 272, 273

Kehoe, Tom, 8

Keith, Alexander, 120

Kent hops, 29, 46, 47, 65, 66, 73, 74, 104, 128, 152, 241, 268, 282

Kentish Gazette, advertisement in, 47

Kernels, 183-184, 185, 188

Kettle boil, 206, 230

hop utilization in, 203 (table)

Kilning, 11, 13, 15, 29, 71, 117, 184, 186

coke-fired, 16

described, 185

Kimmich, John, 172, 173, 286, 287, 290

King and Barnes, 234

Knee Deep, 181

Kornhauser, Alan, 137

Kralj, Cynthia, 167, 181

Kralj, Vic, 167, 181

Labatt, John Kinder, 120

Labatt, John Kinder, II: 120

Labatt Brewing Company, 119, 120, 146

Lagers, vi, vii, 13, 18, 133, 158, 178

development of, 60, 97

pale, 58-59, 97, 101, 122, 123

Lagunita's Maximus, 167

Laughing Dog's Dogzilla, 174

Lauter tuns, vii, 151, 189

Lautering, 188, 189, 190, 205, 206

described, 230

Lea Valley Walk, 313

Leeson, exporting by, 40

"Leviathan" product line, 246

Liar's Club, 176, 177, 288

Liberty Street Brewing Company, 276

Liverpool Mercury, advertisement in, 47, 65

Loftus, 63, 78

London and County Brewer, The, 34

London brewers, 19, 128

aging and, 99

hops for, 98

IPAs by, 95-101

London City Letterbooks, 10

London IPAs, 95-101, 187, 237, 268

    and Burton IPAs compared, 99-100

    OG/hopping data for, 99 (table)

London Metropolitan Archives, 311

London Museum Docklands, 313

London porters, 16, 18, 26, 37, 100

London Times, 47, 49, 55, 65

Long While hops, 29

Lucknow, 156

Lupulin glands, 148, 192, 198, 199

Lupulin Threshold Shift, 169

MacKechnie, Archibald, 132

MacKinnon, 121

Magnum hops, 207

Maharaja, 261

Maier, John, 165, 174, 177

Maillard reactions, 82

"Make Mine Ballantine" (Pierce), 239

Malt liquors, 65

Malt weights, 306-307

Malthouses, 52, 71, 112, 113, 127

Malting, 13, 71, 110, 111, 117

    operations, 63, 79

    process, 79, 183, 184

Maltose, 190, 191, 215

Malts, 10, 13, 17, 37, 63, 71-72, 78, 117, 128,

    135, 144, 167, 177, 183-185, 189, 230

    amber, 15, 16, 28, 72

    American, 110

    base, 104

    black, 28, 174, 175, 178, 185

    brown, 15, 16, 28, 72

    California, 308

    chocolate, 174, 175, 178

    colored, 72, 169

    complexity of, 186, 206

    dark, 186

    described, 28-29

    drying, 29

    English, 98

    European, 308

    foreign, 71

    four-row, 29

    growing, 110, 185

    high-colored, 185

    kilning, 11, 185

    measuring, 305

    milled, 31, 32, 190

    Pilsner, 71, 179, 181

    quality of, 71

    roasted, 72

    six-row, 127

    Scottish, 104

    sources of, 80

    specialty, 185-186

    taxes on, 18, 56, 57

    wheat, 181

    white, 4, 42, 71

    yellow, 71

Maltsters Association, 56

Manual of Brewing, The (Hooper), 70

March brewings, price list for, 107 (fig.)

Maris Otter malt, 127, 156, 165, 241

Marjoribanks, Campbell, 42

Marston's Beer Company, 6, 48 (fig.), 72

    (fig.), 152, 243, 244

    Burton Union system and, 85, 86 (fig.)

    IPAs and, x

Marston's IPA, 157 (fig.)

Marston's Old Empire, 157

Marston's Owd Rodger, 41

Marston's pub, 6 (fig.)

Marzi, Al, 247

Mash tuns, 32, 82, 105, 151, 185

Mashes, 187

    first, 32

    infusion, 79, 144, 151, 189-190

    mixing, 62, 82, 189

    multiple, 13

    successive, 31

Mashing, 13, 82, 105, 188, 189-191, 308

    bottom, 32

    described, 31-32, 230

    multiple, 17, 31, 32

    temperature for, 105, 190

top, 32

vessels, 190

Master Brewers Association of the Americas (MBAA), vii, xi

Mathias, 63, 66

Maytag, Fritz, 137, 144, 145, 148

Anchor Brewing and, 142-143

McCrorie, James, 5, 107, 108, 233

McDermott, Jack, 144

McEwan's, 103

McEwan's Scottish IPA, analysis of, 132-133 (table)

McHale, Kurt, 258

McMaster, Charles, 104

Meantime Brewing Company, 156, 267

Meantime Brewing Company London IPA, recipe for, 267-269

Measurements, 305-308

Medical Times and Gazette, 55

Melanoidin malt, 174

Mello, Louis, 176, 288

Mersey Canal, 40, 48 (fig.)

Microbiological stability, 21, 39, 87

Microbreweries, problems for, 150

Mild ales, 18, 25, 96, 97, 125-126

popularity of, 54

Millar, Bill, 1

Miller, 135, 139

Miller-Coors, 7

Milling, 188-189, 199

Minerals, 69, 69 (table), 187, 211

Mirror Pond, 256

Mission Bottoms Farms, hops from, 148

Mixing, 62, 82, 105, 189, 221

Moeller, Phil, 151, 158

Mohan Meakin Brewery, 121

Molson, John, 119

Molson Brewery, 119

Molson Export, 119

Molyneaux, William, 26, 48

Monks Cellar, 116 (fig.)

More Beer pilot system, 174

Moss, Alec, 151

Mott, Tod, 173, 246

Motueka hops, 160

Moving cooper, 34

Moylan's Hopsickle, 167

Mum, 12

Mumford, Geoff, 156

Munich malt, 152, 169, 174, 185, 186, 266, 267

Murree Brewery Company, 121

Museum Brewing Company Calcutta IPA, 7

recipe for, 274-275

Museum of London Docklands, 47 (fig.)

Museums, 312-313

Musgrave, exporting by, 40

My Beer Buzz (blog), 309

Narrangansett Brewery, 137

National Brewery Centre, 8 (fig.), 131 (fig.)

National Brewery Centre and Museum, 6, 7, 62 (fig.), 312

National Brewing Library, 311

National Railway, 51

National Standard Gravity, 58

Nelson Sauvin hops, 160, 169

New Brewery, 52

New Monthly Magazine, 43

Nickel, Tom, 2, 169

1977 World Guide to Beer (Jackson), 151

Nips, 143

Noonan, Greg, 171, 172, 173, 286, 290

Northclay hops, 73

Northern Brewer hops, 147

Noted Breweries of Great Britain and Ireland, The (Barnard), 80

Nottingham hops, 73, 104

Nugget hops, 207

October ales, 16, 32, 34, 35, 80

exporting, 37

October beers, 34, 81-82

brewing, 14, 16, 22

recipes for, 17 (table)

Octoberfest, 246

Odell IPA, recipe for, 262

OG. *See* Original gravity

Oggi's Brewing Company, 2, 167, 169
Oils, 134-135
Old British Beers and How to Make Them
     (Harrison and Durden Park Brewing
     Circle), 5, 308
Old Foghorn Barleywine Style Ale, 143
Olde Ale Thread, 253
Oliver, Garrett, 171, 172, 249
On the Nature and Treatment of Stomach and
     Urinary Diseases (Prout), 65
"100 Barrel Series," 246
"One Man's Mistake is Another Man's
     Hoppy Pleasure," 276-277
Original gravity (OG), 35, 36, 78, 82, 101,
     122, 124, 125, 231, 305
     drop in, 128
     London IPA, 99 (table)
     standard, 58
     Younger's, 106 (table)
"Origins of American IPA: A Craft-Brewing
     Pioneer's Perspective, The"
     (Fahrendorf), 151-153
Overhopping, described, 210
Owen, "Buffalo" Bill, 171
Oxidation, 29, 85, 195, 198, 199, 205, 215,
     226, 233

Pabst, 135, 137, 139
Pale ales, 13, 26, 27, 29, 30, 35, 96, 110, 120,
     129, 171, 178, 179
     advertisement for, 47
     aging, 37
     brewing, xi, 16, 31-34
     clarification process in, 28
     exporting, 36
     IPAs and, 64
     light, 59, 60
     as medicinal restorative, 46
     original, 123
     popularity of, 18
     stock, 4, 24
     strong, 16, 177
Pale beers, 22, 25, 29, 30, 35, 37, 55
     brewing, 14, 16, 96

Burton ales and, 19
     domestic, 97
     exporting, 19, 36
     malt for, 28
     strong, 14
Pale lagers, 122, 123
     brewing, 97
     popularity of, 58-59, 101
Pale malts, ix, 15, 28, 29, 42, 71, 98, 104, 110,
     146, 184 (fig.), 185
     British, 157
     English, 169
     using, 13-14, 16, 18, 37
Papazian, Charlie, 151, 152
Paquette, Dan, 8
Parti-glying, 82, 308
Party Source, 166, 276
Past Masters beers, 272
Pasteur, Louis, 63
Pattinson, Ron, 4, 100, 103, 108, 130, 172,
     235, 237, 238
     blog by, 309
     research by, 7
Pauwels, Steven, 181
Payen, Professor Monsieur, 55
Pepper, George, 118
Pepper, Henry, 118
Perle hops, 207
Peter Barmann Brewing Company, 112
Peter the Great, 40
Phillips Brewing's Skookum Cascadian Dark,
     174, 176-177, 291
Phipps, James, 111
Pierce, Bill, 239
Pilsner Urquell, 71
Pilsners, viii, 13, 58, 64
Pink Boots Society, 244
Piraat Tripel IPA, 178
Pitching, 30, 83, 84
     rate, 212-213, 218
Pizza Port Breweries, 156, 166, 167, 288
Pizza Port Carlsbad, 176, 258, 288
Pizza Port Carlsbad Black Lie, 176-177
     recipe for, 288-289

Pizza Port Carlsbad Welcome Back Wipeout, 258

Pizza Port Carlsbad Wipeout IPA, recipe for, 258-259

Pizza Port Hop 15: 166, 209, 210
  recipe for, 278-279

Pizza Port Solana Beach, 278

Plumage Archer malt, 71, 127

Poor Man's IPA, 166

Poperings Hommel Ale, 179

Port Brewing Company, 156, 166, 169, 258, 278

Port Brewing Company Big Wednesday, 179

Port Brewing Company IPA, 2

Porter breweries, 15, 25, 30

Porters, 6, 18-19, 26, 30, 54, 78, 96, 97, 98, 109, 110, 115, 118, 120, 122, 126
  advertising for, 45 (fig.)
  brewing, 22
  character of, 65
  decline of, 125
  exporting, 20, 36, 170
  hoppy, 174, 175
  Indian imports of, 50 (table)
  IPAs and, 64

Portland Brewing Company, 137

Portsmouth Chronicle, 113

Potter, Tom, 249

Potts, Joseph, 118

Practical Brewings (Amsinck), 31

Prentice, Derek, 8, 272

Pretty Things, 171

Pricing, 11, 36, 38, 107 (fig.), 108 (fig.)

Pride of Newark brewery, 115

Primary fermentation, ix, 14, 33, 84, 93, 113, 208, 214, 217
  process of, 218-219

Proctor malt, 127

Prohibition, vii, 113, 114, 115, 117, 118, 120, 122, 123, 127, 132, 133, 142, 147

Proteins, 185, 190, 198, 212

Protz, Roger, 7, 35

Prout, William, 65, 66

Putnam, Roger, 5-6, 6 (fig.)

Quality, 11, 20, 28, 34, 46, 67, 71, 91, 104, 110

Racking, 98-99, 208, 221

Railroads, 49, 51, 62, 119

Rainier Ale, 143

Raison d'Etre, 251

Rastetter, Tim, 166, 276, 277

Ratcliff & Gretton's Ale Stores, 53

Read Brothers, 53, 66

Recipe log, export porter, 172 (fig.)

Recipes, xi, 28, 31, 117, 177, 186
  black IPA, 285-292
  contemporary British, 267-275
  contemporary U.S., 249-267
  craft-beer, 8, 249-267
  double IPA, 275-284
  early craft-brewing, 243-249
  historical, 152, 229, 231-243
  reformulations, 42

Redhook Brewery, 312

Refrigeration, 33, 63, 73, 81, 83, 84, 100, 103, 106, 119, 120

Reid 1839 IPA, recipe for, 235-236

Repitching, 30, 84

Rests, 31-32
  conversion, 189, 190
  diacetyl, 216, 218
  mash, 191
  temperature, 79, 189

Revere, Paul, 144

Ridge Street Brewery, 98

Riverside Brewery, 269

Robert Smith India Pale Ale Brewery, 118

Roberts, W. H., 36, 83, 109

Rogue Brewery Black Brutal Bitter, 174

Rogue Brewery Brutal Bitter, 174

Rogue Brewery Brutal IPA, 174

Rogue Brewery Brutal Pils, 174

Rogue Brewing Company, 165

Rubicon IPA, 1, 156, 158

Running ales, 97, 123
  IPAs and, 59
  OG of, 101

taxation of, 101
Russian Imperial Porter, 277
Russian River Brewing Company, 3, 156, 167, 220, 248, 275
Russian River Pliny the Elder, 166-167
  logo for, 167 (fig.)
  recipe for, 275-276
Russian River Pliny the Younger, 181
Rusty Hammer Pub, 312
Ryan, Thomas, 118
Rye, malted, 110

Saaz hops, 179, 193, 194
Saccharometers, 109
Saccharomyces, 93
Salt, 42, 63, 128, 188
Salt Brewery, 51, 51 (fig.), 52, 67, 80, 125
  IPA and, 50, 75, 88
  receivership for, 59
Samuel Smith's India Ale, 157
San Andreas Malts, 151
San Diego Pale Ale, 167
Saranac's White IPA, 181
Scheer, Fred, 240
Schlitz, 132, 135, 139
Schmidt's, 118
Schreier Malt, 240
Scotch ales, 102, 108, 109, 146, 175
  hops for, 104
Scotch Burgundy, 102
Scotch Common malt, 104
Scottish Ale Brewer and Practical Maltster, The (Roberts), 63, 83, 103, 109
Scottish brewers, 102-106, 109
  exporting by, 102
  extract recovery by, 104
  technology and, 103
  water for, 104
  yeast for, 104
Scottish Brewing Archive, 312
Scottish IPAs, 97, 102-106, 109
  hopping rates for, 105, 105 (table)
Segal, George, 147
Segal, John, 147, 148

Session IPAs, brewing, 180
Shed, The, 175, 290
Shed Darkside Black IPA, 173, 175, 290
  recipe for, 287-288
Shepherd Neame Brewery, 7
Sherwood, Bill, 284
Shipping, 41, 45 (fig.), 53, 91-93, 127
Shove, George, 47
Shut Up about Barclay Perkins (blog), 4, 238, 309
Sidor, Larry, 174, 175, 181, 256, 291
Siebel Institute, 152
Sierra Nevada Brewing Company, 135, 137, 144, 150, 256
  hopping by, 220
  yeast strain of, 145
Sierra Nevada Brewing Company Celebration Ale, 1, 144, 145, 151
Sierra Nevada Brewing Company Pale Ale, 145
Sierra Nevada Brewing Company Torpedo IPA, 220
Simcoe hops, 160, 169, 173, 174, 176, 180, 207, 281, 284
  popularity of, 156
Sinamar black malt extract, 173-174, 177, 288, 290
Smith, Robert, 118
Smith, Garrett & Company, 50
Smuttynose Brewing Company, 114, 254, 279
Smuttynose Brewing Company Big A IPA, recipe for, 279-280
Smuttynose Brewing Company Finest Kind IPA, recipe for, 254-256
Social Life in the Reign of Queen Anne (Ashton), 27
Society for Diffusing Useful Knowledge, 56, 70
Sonoma County Cluster Growers Cooperative, 147
Sorachi Ace hops, 160
Sparging, 13, 17, 82, 105
Spectrophotometers, 203
Spices, 9, 12, 181

Spoilage, 68, 83, 202

Spratt Archer malt, 71, 127

Starches, 183, 185, 189, 190

Starters, described, 213

Steam, 15, 61, 62, 103

 pumping, 101 (fig.)

Steamships, 92, 106

Steele, Mitch, ix, 6 (fig.)

Steelhead Brewing Company, 153, 156, 158, 243

Steel's Masher, 62, 82, 105

Steeping, described, 184

Steiner, S. S.: Grant and, 146

Sterling hops, 174

Stock ales, 17, 30, 32, 60, 110

 character of, 65

 English, 40

 hops and, 18

 IPAs and, 59, 64

 souring of, 96

Stock beers, 18, 20, 93

 flavor of, 21

 pale, 24

Stone Brewing Company, xi, 3, 5, 156, 167, 176, 209, 282, 283, 288

 Anniversary IPAs by, 166, 175

Stone Brewing Company 1st Anniversary Ale, 166, 257

Stone Brewing Company 2nd Anniversary Ale, 166

Stone Brewing Company 3rd Anniversary Ale, 166

Stone Brewing Company 4th Anniversary Ale, 166

Stone Brewing Company 5th Anniversary Ale, 166

Stone Brewing Company 10th Anniversary IPA, 3, 8, 176

 recipe for, 283-284

Stone Brewing Company 11th Anniversary IPA, 3, 176, 288

 recipe for, 289-290

Stone Brewing Company 14th Anniversary Emperial IPA, 3, 8, 273

 recipe for, 282-283

Stone Brewing Company 15th Anniversary Escondidian Imperial Black IPA, 3

Stone Brewing Company Ruination IPA, 166, 209

 recipe for, 282

Stone Brewing Company Sublimely Self-Righteous Ale, 8, 175-176

 recipe for, 289-290

Stone IPA, 8, 166, 209

 recipe for, 257-258

Storey, Charlie: article by, 245-247

"Story of Bombay Bomber IPA, The" (Fahrendorf), 243-244

"Story of Brooklyn East India Pale Ale, The" (Oliver), 249

"Story of Harpoon IPA, The" (Storey), 245-247

Stouts, viii, 36, 47, 49, 65, 96, 111, 186, 251

 benefits of, 112

 double, 126

 brown, 115

 imperial, 173

Straining, described, 31-32

Strengths, 18, 35, 96, 109, 142, 152, 213

Stroh, 139

Strong ales, 25, 26, 35, 98

 brewing, 102

 exporting, 36

Styrian Golding hops, 152, 156, 157, 179

Sugars, 72, 74, 189, 191, 215

 adding, 110, 127

 breakdown into, 185, 190

 brewing, 59, 71, 72, 128, 144, 186-187

 dextrose, 167

 fermentable, 183, 214, 217

Sulfates, 39, 68, 188

Sulfur, 188, 211, 212, 215

Sulz, Charles Herman, 56

Summit hops, 174, 193, 207, 284

Super-Cascade hops, 153

Super Sack, 282

Surrey hops, 66, 73

Sweetness, viii, 169, 183, 186, 191

Swindell, John, 113

Tabberer, Horace, 63
    lab of, 64 (fig.)
Table beers, 17, 57
    exporting, 20, 36
Target hops, 160, 273, 282-283
Tartan IPA, 171
Taxes, 4, 10, 40, 123, 125, 133, 152
    beer, 56, 58, 101
    glass, 57-58, 92
    gravity and, 58
    influence of, 56, 79
    malt, 18
Techniques, xi, 8, 67, 81, 101, 110, 144, 180,
    192, 205-209, 210-214
    1700s, 17
    English, 100, 119
Technology, ix, xi, 12, 15, 61, 63, 64, 85,
    109, 120
    brewing, vii, 62, 123
    industrial, 61
    Scottish brewers and, 103
Temperance movements, 4, 56, 59-60, 79,
    123, 157
Temperature, 21, 212, 230
    control, 13, 190, 218
    conversion, 189, 190, 191
    fermentation, 30, 85, 105, 139, 142,
        215, 217
    kiln, 71
    mash, 32, 105, 190
    pelletizing process and, 208
    pitching, 84
Tetford's, 171
Tetley's, 53, 98, 129
Tettnang hops, 148
Textbook of Brewing, A (De Clerk), x
Theakston's Old Peculier, 41
Theory and Practice of Brewing Illustrated, The
    (Tizard), 63, 91, 249
Theory and Practice of Brewing, The (Com-
    brune), 27, 31
Theory and Practice of Modern Brewing, The

(Faulkner), 171
Thermometers, 15, 61
Thirsty Dog Brewing Company, 276
Thomas, Keith, 244
Thornbridge Brewing Company, 156, 269
Thornbridge Hall, 269
Thornbridge Jaipur India Pale Ale, recipe
    for, 269-270
Thornbridge Seaforth IPA, 269
    recipe for, 271-272
Three Floyds, 156
Three Floyds Dreadnaught, 167
Tizard, William L., 63, 83, 91, 249
    on Allsopp's beer, 46
    domestic IPAs and, 78
Tom and Jerry houses, 57
Torula yeast, 75
Transportation, 49, 54, 61
Treatise of Food and Diet, A (Pereira), 65
Treatise on Beverages: Or the Complete Practical
    Bottler, A (Sulz), 56
Trent Canal Act, 39, 40
Tringali, Ed, 151
Tripels, 13, 178, 179, 180
Triple IPA, brewing, 181
Triple Rock Brewing Company, 152
    IPA by, 1, 153
Triple Voodoo, 181
Trotter, John, 25, 47, 48, 62, 72, 74, 131, 157
Trub, 198, 207, 208
Truck Amendment Act (1831), 57
Truman, Hanbury & Buxton, 52, 70, 100
    hopping rates for, 80-81 (table)
Tuborg Breweries, 274

Urthel Hop-It, 179
U.S. Brewers Association Subcommittee of
    Hop Research, 148
U.S. Department of Agriculture (USDA),
    147, 148

Van Ostaden, Hildegarde, 179
Vassar, James, 117
Vassar, John Guy, 117

Vassar, Matthew, Jr., 117

Vassar, Matthew, Sr., 110, 117, 118

Vassar Brewery, 117

Vassar College, 117

Vats, viii, 33, 96, 116 (fig.), 117

Vermont Pub and Brewery, 171, 172, 173, 286

Vermont Pub and Brewery Blackwatch IPA,
  172, 173, 286, 287
  recipe for, 285

Very India Pale Ale (VIP Ale), 166

Vessels, 8, 30, 62, 74, 100, 106, 190, 218, 220

Victory's Hop Wallop, 165

Victory's Wild Devil, 179

Vincent, Charles, 70

VIP Ale (Very India Pale Ale), 276
  recipe for, 277-278

W. A. Brown Imperial Brewery, 41, 47

Wadsworth's, 129

Wagner, Steve, 5, 6, 6 (fig.), 7, 166

Walker, Peter, 84

Walker, Taylor, 50

Walter, Glenn, 171, 172

Warrior hops, 174, 193, 207

Washington, George, 118

Washington State Hop Growers Association,
  148

Water, 9, 63, 67-70, 187-188
  analysis of, 70 (table), 188-189 (table)
  Burtonizing, 10
  chemistry of, 68-69, 95
  described, 28
  distilled, 214
  gypsum in, 70
  hard, 100, 103, 104, 187
  soft, 28, 31, 37, 104
  treatment of, 31, 104
  well, 52

Water-to-grain ratios, 191, 230

Watney, 235

Watt, James, 280

Weathers, Carl, 148

Weathers, Don, 148

Websites, 309

Webster, Simon, 269

Weihenstephan brewing school, 267

Wellington, Steve, 6, 7, 234, 234 (fig.), 274

West Coast IPAs, 257, 259

Wetherspoon pub chain, 7

Weyerbacher's Simcoe Double IPA, 167, 209

Weyermann Carafa Special III Malt, 176

Weyermann Dehusked Carafa Special III
  Malt, 175

Weyermann Pils malt, 174

Wheat, 110, 181

Whirlpool hopping, described, 207-208

Whirlpools, 33, 200, 207-208

Whitbread Brewery, 95, 97, 129, 152, 243
  export market and, 41

Whitbread Brewery IPA, 124, 170
  analytical profile of, 298-299 (table)

White Horse on Parson's Green Pub, 5, 243

White IPA, brewing, 181

White Labs, yeast from, 135

Wilkinson, Bruce, 67-68, 156

Willamette hops, 157

Wilson, exporting by, 40

Wilson, Benjamin, 42

Wilson, R. G., 67

Woodstock IPA, 137

Worcestershire hops, 73

World Beer Cup, 2, 263

Worthington, W. H., 234, 312

Worthington's IPA, analytical profile of, 300-
  301 (table)

Worthington's Museum Brewery, 6, 40, 63,
  64 (fig.), 125, 129

Worthington's White Shield, 7, 129, 141, 157
  recipe for, 234-235

Worts, 13, 75, 82, 145, 183, 188, 207, 213
  all-malt, 211
  boiling, 32-33, 83, 105, 195, 200, 203
  calculating, 205
  cooling, 83, 84, 105, 106
  diluting, 191
  extra-strong, 32
  fermentation, 190, 214
  gravity, 33, 83, 204, 216, 218

heating, 101 (fig.)
pH of, 68
producing, 83
sugary, 214
Wyeast, 135

Yakima Golding hops, 137
Yarrington, David, 254, 255, 279
Yeast, vii, viii, ix, 9, 33, 63, 74-75, 96, 180, 190, 230
active, 214
ale, 18, 144, 212, 213, 283
Belgian, 156
Burton, 85
calcium and, 37, 68, 128
California Ale, 212
cells, 211, 215, 217
choosing, 170
collecting, 85
cultures, 30, 75, 93, 104, 146
discovery of, 30
fermentation of, 74, 85, 104, 181, 185, 195, 205, 208
flavors and, 85, 215, 217
fusel alcohol and, 217
growth of, 210-212, 217, 218
health, 214
hops and, 212
iso-alpha acids and, 205
lager, 18
liquid, 213
management of, 20, 74, 101
metabolization of, 183, 214, 216
nutrients, 215-216
performance of, 214-219
removing, 84, 219
rotating, 104
settling, 74-75
slurry, 230
strains, 63, 180, 212, 213, 216
top-cropping, 85
top-fermenting, 74, 84
wild, 94
Younger, Don, 174

Younger Brewery, 53, 88, 102, 103, 103 (fig.), 106, 109, 312
malt for, 104
price list by, 107 (fig.), 108 (fig.)
Younger Brewery IPA, 127
analysis of, 132-133 (table)
hopping rates for, 106 (table)
OG for, 106 (table)
Young's Special London Ale, 249
Young's Winter Warmer, 41

Zimmermann, Charles, x, 148, 149
Zythophile (blog), 4, 238, 309